The Myth of Shangri-La

To my Mother and Father

The Myth of Shangri-La

Tibet, Travel Writing and the Western Creation of Sacred Landscape

PETER BISHOP

UNIVERSITY OF CALIFORNIA PRESS
Berkeley and Los Angeles

University of California Press
Berkeley and Los Angeles, California

©1989 by Peter Bishop

Library of Congress Cataloging-in-Publication Data
Available on request

ISBN 0–520–06686–3

Printed in Great Britain
1   2   3   4   5   6   7   8   9

Contents

Introduction

The concept of sacred place has been important in religious studies but has usually been applied to sites that are either traditional, such as in Australian Aboriginal culture, or well established, as for example in Classical Greece. Such sacred sites are therefore presented as somewhat static, as fixed and complete. By tracing the images evoked in the encounter between Tibet and travellers from Europe, Russia and America, but especially from Britain, this study aims to examine the phenomenology of a sacred place in the process of its creation, fulfilment and subsequent decline. It explores the differences between a geographical location, a sacred place and a utopia. The study is especially concerned with the relationship between the interior phenomenology of a sacred place and the wider context outside its boundaries. It is therefore less of a historical narrative than an in-depth analysis of the inner meanings that Tibet came to hold directly for a considerable number of Westerners and also indirectly for their cultures as a whole.

A way of reading the texts of travel and exploration is developed. It sees them as psychological documents, as statements of a psychology of extraversion, which reveal significant aspects both of the fantasy-making processes of a culture and of its unconscious. In addition it explores the complex relationship between geography, imagination and spirituality.

While the study is methodologically based in archetypal psychology, it also draws widely from such disciplines as humanistic geography and French deconstructionism in an attempt to situate the travel texts within a series of broad psychological and social contexts. It is therefore an attempt to develop an imaginal approach to cultural analysis, one that traces the movement and transformation of images whilst simultaneously leading them back to their root-metaphors. The study is unique in that it presents one complete tradition of travel writing. As such it throws light on the development of the wider genre of travel writing itself, and its place in the complexities of Western spirituality.

The primary texts are those written by explorers and travellers both in Tibet and also around its borders – in the Himalayas and in Central Asia – between 1773 and 1959. These years have been selected because they mark the boundary between the first British visitor to Tibet in modern times and the final exile of Tibet's spiritual and secular ruler, the Dalai Lama. Whilst travellers from many Western nations journeyed to Tibet during this period, relations between Tibet and the Western world were dominated by the British. This was primarily due to their presence as imperialists in India and the Himalayan region. It is therefore this relationship which serves as a focus for the study. All the primary texts have been published in English. This is less of a restriction than it would first appear to be, for travellers and explorers to Tibet formed a fairly cohesive international community, one which shared interest and familiarity, if not friendship. They were certainly familiar with each other's work. This fact, together with the British government's vested interest in the region, ensured that most accounts were soon translated into English.

Tibet is revealed in these texts as an imaginal complexity rather than a unity – a conclusion that is perhaps widely applicable to sacred sites. There were many 'Tibets': historically, as the wider social and psychological contexts altered, and as the place itself acquired its own imaginative momentum; and synchronically, as through each traveller was expressed a very particular archetypal style of fantasy. At certain, limited moments, such imaginal diversity assumed a common coherence – usually under pressure from institutions such as the Royal Geographical Society, or from the more diffuse promptings of a collective need, or from the coherence of Tibet itself, its *genius loci*; but the place was always a site of contending fantasies. This study shows that the interior phenomenology of Tibet as a sacred place was never sharply delineated and isolated from the demands of the outside world – indeed that the two spaces continually interpenetrated each other – and that the threshold of a sacred place is a significant region in its own right, one that expresses imaginal depth and tension. A sacred place is in a continual state of process.

The creation of Tibet is located within the wider struggle by Europeans to redefine both global geography and their own place within it. The emergence of a geopolitical imagination and a mythology of imperialism are seen as crucial to Western fantasies of Tibet. By tracing the recent history of Western perceptions of Himalayan, Central Asian and Tibetan landscape, this study reveals the late-nineteenth-century development of a radically new aesthetic appreciation of wilderness regions. The crucial struggle between empirical observation and imaginative interpretation is identified and documented. The development of a wilderness aesthetic is traced to a series of separate imaginative moves: for example, a shift of emphasis away from landscape *forms* and an increased awareness of light and colour; Darwin's theory, which drew all the landscapes of the world into a common schema: then Ruskin's achievement in laying the basis for a kind of natural morality of landscape; and finally, the sense that many Westerners had of belonging to such distant places.

A close imagistic reading of the texts makes it clear that Tibet has provided many in the West with a sense of historical continuity – whether through associations with archaic ancestors, or with Ancient Egypt, or with some primal occult wisdom. Tibetan religion, culture and geography were intertwined and virtually inseparable in Western fantasies until the first half of the twentieth century. Then, under the increasing sense of threat to the perceived isolation and purity of Tibet, there was a separation between fantasy and geographical place. 'Shangri-La' marks the final movement of Tibet from a geographically grounded sacred place to a placeless utopia.

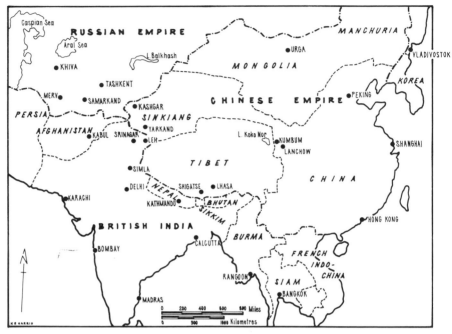

Greater Tibet and Surrounding Countries in 1900

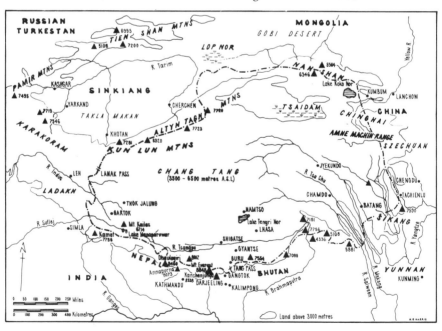

The Physical Features of Greater Tibet in 1900

1

An Imaginative Geography

New myths spring up beneath each step we take.

(*L. Aragon* [1980])

A Global Mosaic

In one sense, natural landscape does not exist. We inescapably shape the world, even if only with our minds and not our hands. When we shape the world, we create *places*. 'To be human', writes Relph, 'is to live in a world that is filled with significant places: to be human is to have and to know *your* place.' It has been said that to be without a relationship to a place is to be in spiritual exile.[1] Humans seem to need such special, even sacred, places. The space under the stairs, or in the corner of a room, so essential in childhood, is echoed again and again in sacred groves, caves, churches and temples.[2] Here, it is hoped, it is possible to form a closer connection with some unseen power: lofty and divine, or hidden in the depths of individual memory or of collective *memoria*.[3] Often these special places are purely personal, idiosyncratic and random, but most cultures also have their officially sanctioned sacred sites. Europe, for example, was once covered with such places, each linked by ancient routes of pilgrimage.[4]

In addition to both the informal respect bestowed by individuals upon their own special places and the collective worship of sites recognized by an entire culture is the grander, but more elusive, fascination with *faraway* places. With these places the fabulous and the empirical merge indiscriminately; sometimes embracing vast regions – Cathay, Tartary, the Orient, the Indies – sometimes much more specific – the mountains of the Moon, the source of the Nile, Arcadia.[5] As the old European pilgrim routes fell into disuse and an age of exploration was initiated, these faraway places became increasingly mobilized by a Europe that was seeking a new *global* orientation and identity. A succession of empirically surveyed geographical places, although still fabulously imagined, evoked the hopes and fears of generations from the seventeenth century onwards.[6] At the same time, in Europe itself, pilgrimage was superseded by *travel* as a leisure activity for aristocrats and the rising middle classes. Then, in the mid-nineteenth century, the era of mass travel began, although long-range journeys for leisure, sport or science still remained the prerogative of Europe's upper classes.[7]

1

Some authors have insisted that there was a decline in the sense of sacred place as European culture moved into the industrial era of the nineteenth century,[8] but such a conclusion ignores the changes occurring both in the *experience* of the sacred and in the notion of *place*. From the Alpine peaks to the Arctic, from Tahiti to Tangier, European imagination spanned the globe. Europeans were constantly taking bearings from these remote places. This global involvement revolutionized European conceptions of the world: as a physical, social, political, spiritual and aesthetic reality.

These 'faraway' places frequently came to exert a mysterious fascination. I would argue that they were truly sacred places, but in modern guise.[9] Whereas sacred places in traditional cultures seem to have been created *ex nihilo*, to have existed always, these new places can be seen in a process of creation, fulfilment and decline. In them we can trace how a geographical location becomes transformed into a sacred place. They offer a unique opportunity to follow the relationship between cultural imagination, physical landscape and the sense of the sacred. They are windows into the changing spiritual aspirations, the soul, of modern Europe.[10] Tibet was one such place. It began almost as a mere rumour in the mid eighteenth century, but a hundred years later it had evolved into one of the last great sacred places of Victorian Romanticism. Its significance still reverberates strongly through European fantasies to this day. This is therefore a study of the encounter between Tibet and Western fantasy-making as revealed in the stories told by travellers and explorers: a study in the *creation* of a sacred place.

Travel Writing and the Exploration of Tibet

There have been several excellent studies of Tibetan exploration, but without exception they are straightforward narrative histories.[11] In addition, some reference to the story of exploration is frequently included in more general studies of Tibetan culture, as well as in historical accounts of Western political intervention in Central Asia.[12] Whilst performing the invaluable role of documenting Western involvement in the region, these accounts are singularly lacking in a number of crucial areas. The context within which these journeys were made is either ignored or limited to that of imperial politics, and even then only to the most strategic levels. The full psychosocial *context* of Tibetan travel has not received its due attention. This has resulted in a failure to situate travel accounts against the background of Western culture, and hence to assess the *inner meaning* that Tibet has held for the West. Also, in these studies, the travel accounts have usually been analysed on a simplistically literal basis, valued only in terms of their apparent factual truth, their contribution to a supposedly evolving empirical knowledge about Tibet. No attempt has been made to understand the genre of travel writing and how it can be interpreted.

This is, upon reflection, an astonishing omission. It assumes that travel writing is unequivocal in its meaning. All too often it is conceived to be either a poor cousin of scientific observation, or else to fall short of the creativeness of 'pure' fiction. Travel writing has its own history, its own stylistic schisms and struggles.[13] As a genre it is something of a complex hybrid and has been connected with autobiographies, eye-witness accounts and travelogues. It has been called a sub-species of memoir, a form of romance (quest, picaresque or pastoral), a vehicle for essays (ethical or scientific) or a variant of the comic novel.[14]

Travel writing can be seen as the art of the collage: newspaper clippings, public notices, letters, official documents, diary extracts, essays on current affairs, on art, on architecture, comic dialogues and homilies, are somehow clustered together to form a coherent and satisfying whole. The *internal coherence* of these assorted collages of essays, sermons, and so on, relies extensively on the image of geography and landscape, but this coherence can encourage too literal a reading of travel accounts.

The gross physicality, the geographical locatability, of travel books should not blind us to their fictional nature. Travel writing is not concerned only with the discovery of places but also with their creation. This is the case no matter how much effort is devoted to being as true as possible to the 'empirical' material. Frequently the travel account masks a totally fictional and imagined journey. Norman Douglas, for example, actually admitted inventing characters. Whole passages of Robert Byron's accounts bear scant correlation to what actually took place, and it has been said that Evelyn Waugh seemed to behave as if 'descriptive passages do justice rather to potentialities than to facts'.[15]

Robert Byron, the well-known travel writer of the 1920s and thirties, attempted to justify travel as a way of gaining knowledge, and it is this concern which is central to any debate about travel literature in its cultural context. Knowledge produced by this form of activity is akin to the *bricolage*.[16] The travel writer then becomes the *bricoleur*, the odd-job person, who creates a body of knowledge from the materials at hand – a process that is primarily orientated around the senses. Byron, in fact, wrote that 'the travelling species' is involved in a quest for 'an organic harmony between all matter and all activity ...'.[17] Above all, travel accounts are involved in the production of imaginative knowledges. They are an important aspect of a culture's myth-making, yet this perspective is frequently overlooked.

The density of the text, and hence its claim to empirical truth, arises from a number of elements, each of which contributes towards the coherence of a travel account. Geography, locatable places and map co-ordinates can be verified, their empirical reality bestows authenticity on other aspects of the discourse.[18] But such a concrete actuality can obscure a poetic, or psychological, role in the creation of the text.[19] The use of photographs also encourages a literal reading. Certainly, the place of photographs in travel accounts is highly problematic, it is difficult to understand how they are selected and why they are included. Frequently they appear incidental and seem to be chosen at random or merely on the basis of personal whim. Defying any obvious logical connection, all too often they are merely 'postcards' which say: 'I have actually been here, at such and such place. This proves it'. Like the random use of foreign words, photographs impart a certain density and authenticity. Dates, in particular, give an apparent rigour and factuality to travel texts. Fussell writes that 'travel is thus an adventure in time as well as distance'.[20]

Maps, with routes carefully marked, combine both landscape *and* time. Routes are the temporal and spatial threads around which the *bricolage* is organized. No matter how wide the digression, no matter how disparate the topics, the route provides a datum to which we can, and *must* return. Once the route is left, we could say that the travel account is over. A travel account, unlike purely geographical descriptions or guidebooks, is organized as a narrative. Narrative, it has been observed, 'mystifies our understanding by providing a false sense of coherence'.[21] In fact, travel accounts pose some interesting questions for any theory of narrative: they present a constant interplay between two levels. The objective, tangible world of physical geography and chronological time consistently slides over, and breaks into, subjective personal experiences and digressions. Most travel accounts consist of small islands of personal narrative afloat on an ocean of dates and geography. These well-structured stories are often threaded together into a sequence which is entirely dependent on the idea of *route*. The image of the *route* emerges as the key to their apparent coherence and authenticity. Even the personal experiences of the traveller are secondary to the coherence and logic of the route; the route gives the traveller the authority to narrate.

The logic of the route must be established by the author if the text is to work *as* a travel discourse. The route is basically a trace left in geographical space and chronological time, but the imaginative continuity and quality of this trace can vary. The route can be socially structured and sanctioned, as in pilgrimages, or Aboriginal visits to sacred sites along sacred routes, or carnivals and street processions. When pilgrims begin their journey, they know precisely where they are going. So too, the individual traveller who follows the path of a Marco Polo, or an Alexander the Great, also follows, like the Aboriginal, well-mapped routes and socially recognizable sites. In all these cases the route is known beforehand. It is already mythic, already a narrative *before* the journey is undertaken. The journey merely activates and actualizes the route and the map. However, there are times when the physical geography *becomes* symbolic as the actual journey unfolds. The landscape and the route are mythologized as a result of the journey. There is no set route; it is rarely repeatable. For example, Matthiesson's journey into the Himalayas in search of the rare snow leopard became a soulful walk only as it progressed. The further he moved from Western civilization, the deeper he journeyed into the uncharted regions of his psyche and imagination.[22]

The route must be shown to possess a structure, an order of meaning, over and above mere chronological sequence or geographical position. Often this is achieved by means which are quite transparent. As we have seen, either the route is the trace of a collective idea such as a path for trading, or pilgrimage, or it is based on the traveller's subjective desire – for example, to climb a particular peak, see a specific view. However, the most sublime art of all is to make the elements of the route – the physical geography and chronological sequence – appear to tell their own story. We then find that the authenticity of geography and dates is reinforced by the authenticity of narrative, and by the privileged access to truth accorded to it in our contemporary culture.

Finally, the use of the first-person account of experience gives the strength of testimony to the discourse. Autobiographies and diaries also carry this authenticity. Hillman forcefully argues that such a confessional mode supports the idea of a 'unified experiencing subject' confronting a chaotic and fragmented world. He emphasizes that in a literal, personalistic confession there is a loss of connection to the *anima mundi*, to the aesthetics of soul *in* the world. Foucault, moving along a parallel trajectory, has pointed to the way the confessional mode in literature, derived substantially from the church confessional, has reinforced the ideology of an autonomously creative author. He writes: 'Since the Middle Ages at least, Western societies have established the confession as one of the main rituals we rely on for the production of truth.'[23] Travel accounts are often a form of secularized pilgrimage. Travel *and* experiential narrative are a powerful combination. The claims to truth of such a narrative depend, however, upon the authority of the narrator. Hayden White argues that the 'very *right* to narrate' hinges upon this.[24] In travel accounts it is the *physical* act of journeying along a specific *route* which bestows such authority.

In Laurence Sterne's important eighteenth-century work, *A Sentimental Journey*, travel was combined with a radical sensitivity towards subjective states. This combination of outer physical geography and the inner world of private subjective experience seems at first to be an anomaly, but they have an ancient association. Victor Turner has commented that in the ritual of pilgrimage, personal experience becomes public.[25] For travel the reverse is also true: physical geography and public space become personalized.[26]

To a certain extent every travel account presents the image of several planes of discourse, sliding across one another, conflicting, contradicting, reinforcing and interrupting one another. Historical, geographical and personal experience all have their own modes of coherence and authenticity. Frequently personal narrative may appear to be eliminated whilst, for example, certain social, archaeological or botanical observations are made, but I would suggest that in the travel account such narrative is never nullified, only temporarily subdued.

Travel can function as a metaphor for inner experiences. Similarly, geography can provide maps for the description of consciousness. Each place, frontier or natural feature then becomes filled with symbolic resonance.[27] This seems to be the crucial aspect of travel accounts as a form of knowledge: not that geography (and so on) authenticate personal experience, but quite the reverse. The travel account creates a symbolic landscape filled with subjective meanings: even the descriptions of the weather can provide precise impressions of mood. It would also be wrong to assume that the creation of landscape is solely the work of an isolated individual. As Lowenthal comments, 'Every image and idea about the world is compounded...of personal experience, learning, imagination, and memory.'[28]

Any study that refers to travel writing as a primary source needs to separate out these various levels of discourse and to note how they influence each other. For example, one must distinguish between the various nationalities and their specific imaginal relationship to Tibet. Britain, France, Italy, Russia, the USA, Germany and Austria all have a long tradition of Tibetan, Himalayan and Central Asian exploration, but whereas the British and Russians were involved in aggressive imperial expansion, the other countries were not. Political concerns were not, therefore, an explicit part of their accounts. For the British in the Himalayas, the room available for imaginative play was structured by the realities of administration, territorial defence, and executive power. But for explorers from other countries, without any explicit colonial presence in the region, a different set of constraints operated and revealed themselves at work in their accounts of travel and exploration.

Nevertheless, there was also a certain consensus among European and American travellers to Tibet, the Himalayas and Central Asia, despite national and personal differences. As we shall see, travellers were frequently familiar with each other's accounts, many of which were soon translated into English. In a very real sense, then, any travel account that had been translated into English immediately became part of the general stock of experiences and aspirations upon which British travellers drew and which therefore became their own. This internationalism was assisted by the similarities in class and gender among explorers and travellers, no matter what their nationality. They were invariably from upper-middle-class or aristocratic backgrounds, and they perhaps had more attitudes and values in common than their diverse national backgrounds would at first suggest. This international communality was particularly strong during the golden age of Tibetan exploration in the last quarter of the nineteenth century.

Reading Travel Accounts

It is frequently through extreme geographical differences that a culture reflects upon, and tells stories about, itself. The gradual emergence of the image of *Christian* Europe, for example, depended extensively on the development of fantasies about an *Islamic* Orient. Fantasies of *Tartary*, of the *East*, of the *West*, and of *Asia* acquired a coherent shape only quite recently. They were formed within the context of Europe's struggle for self-definition and image. Tibet was part of the oppositional fantasy between East and West, between Occident and Orient.

This study is therefore not a narrative history of the exploration of Tibet; it is primarily concerned with how Tibet was directly experienced and imagined by Westerners, particularly the British, over a period of nearly 200 years. Travel texts are of particular value to such a study for they lie at the intersection of individual fantasy-making and social constraint. More regulated than, say, dreams, but one of the most personal documents, they are a unique record of a culture's imaginative life. I will argue that Tibet's fringe of its everyday concerns has been directly responsible for the consistently rich fantasies evoked by that country. In a sense, Tibet's peripheral place gave permission for many Europeans and Americans to use it as an imaginative escape, as a sort of time out, a relaxation from rigid rational censorship. Time and again Tibet was endowed with all the qualities of a dream, a collective hallucination. As with dreams, issues that are central to everyday life emerge symbolically in a striking, unashamed naivety.

Travel writing is often more candid than conscious autobiography, often less defensive than observations made closer to home. As life at the centre of Europe's empires became more organized, their values more protected, accounts of life at the distant periphery seemed to become more revealing. Here European fascination with geographical Otherness could be readily indulged. As Yi-Fu Tuan notes, 'Peripheral location is a geographical emblem of anti-structure.'[29] For example, many nineteenth-century travel writers presented the Orient as a certain type of experience.[30] It was a place of pilgrimage, a spectacle, a totally homogeneous and coherent world of exotic customs, of distrubing yet alluring sensuality, combined with horrific bestiality and perverse morality. As Said wryly notes, 'In the Orient one suddenly confronted unimaginable antiquity, inhuman beauty, boundless distance.'[31] For many, the Orient was a place of loss, of self discovery, of transcendence, of ennui. For Flaubert, for example, it provided a landscape of the macabre, of sadomasochism, of the *femme fatale*. 'Sexual promise (and threat), untiring sensuality, unlimited desire, deep generative energies' were attributed to the 'Orient' by such writers.[32]

As James Hillman points out, there was a close relationship between nineteenth-century European and American images of geographical places, and their conceptual images of the unconscious. For many of the Romantics, for example, the unconscious was 'the inner Africa'. Hillman writes: 'the topological language used by Freud for "the unconscious" as a place below, different, timeless, primordial, libidianal and separated from consciousness recapitulates what white reporters centuries earlier said about West Africa.'[33] Also, seminal figures in the West's so-called 'discovery' of the unconscious, from Goethe to Carus to Jung, undertook long journeys that were formative for their ideas. there can also be little doubt in the services of natural science, or merely anecdotal – played in the formation of ideas about the unconscious. In some ways too, as Hillman astutely observes, the myth of the 'discovery' of the unconscious paralleled the myth of the 'discovery' of the world. One cannot presume that one preceded the other or was somehow primary: 'Psychology conveniently imagines white men projected their unconscious onto Africa but projection works two ways; geography's Africa appears as psychology's unconscious.'[34]

The respective images of Otherness, both geographical and psychological, seemed to resonate in step with each other, from the naive worship by early Romantics to a later, more circumspect awareness of its shadows, contradictions and paradoxes. but although so-called inner and outer 'exploration' moved in step, they by no means followed identical trajectories. It would surely be a mistake simplistically to reduce one into the other. Nevertheless, we shall see that as the geographers, explorers and imperial surveyors charted the geographical regions of Tibet, they were at the same time establishing the contours of an imaginal landscape. Similarly, they were plotting not just the physical routes into Tibet, but also the psychological routes between Europe and aspects of its unconscious.

I am proposing, then, that we entirely *reverse* the usual reading of travel texts. Rather than being solely concerned with where the travellers and explorers were *going*, I want to examine from where they were *coming*. Two centuries of travel writing on Tibet tell as much, if not more, about Western fantasies than they do about a literal Tibet. Travel accounts can be read as extroverted dreams, and it is to studies in the language of dreams that we can turn for methodological guidance: from Freud's work come ideas of condensation and displacement in symbol formation; from Jung's psychology we find the method of amplification, of reflecting individual imagery against the wider background of cultural symbolism; Hillman and archetypal psychology insist that the utmost respect and attention be given to the fullness and depth of images, with due regard for their aesthetics, paradoxes and ambivalences.[35]

Whilst psychological studies of exploration and travel have been made before, these have almost invariably been with the aim of understanding the mentality of the *individuals* concerned.[36] Such accounts generally follow one of two directions: they are concerned either with the explorer-traveller's *motivation*, or with the *experience* of a particular place.[37] However, another kind of approach attempts to understand the cultural significance of landscapes, in terms of both their creation and their appreciation.[38] This study is closer to the latter approach than to any concern about individual psychology.

The Contours of Sacred Place

Places are produced by a dialogue between cultural fantasy-making and geographical landscape. The 'mountains seemed . . . surprised to see us', exclaimed the nineteenth-century French explorer Grenard, as he made his torturous way across the bleak vastness of northern Tibet.[39] For many of these travellers, the landscape was alive: It *evoked* the depth-imagination. Places can be considered to have a *genius loci* that expresses something beyond the needs and aspirations of individuals, or even of an entire culture.[40] Particularly close attention is therefore given to the *images* evoked in the encounter between the imagination of travellers from Europe and America and the geographical places of Tibet.

Approaches to the idea of sacred landscape have emphasized a number of concerns:

1. The mythic, or archetypal dimension has been stressed by Eliade, Jung, Hillman, Casey and Layard.[41]
2. The phenomenology, perception and experience of landscape and place have been investigated by Relph, Bachelard, Yi-Fu Tuan, Lowenthal and Heidegger, amongst others.[42]
3. The social context of sacred landscape and of the perceptions of landscape have been studied by many of the authors cited above. In addition, many valuable theoretical conclusions have been drawn from extensive studies of Australian Aboriginal sacred sites and sacred journeys.[43]

Yi-Fu Tuan has coined terms such as 'geopiety' and 'topophilia' to describe the intense relationship between humans and such specific geographical entities as woods, streams, hills, or more general places such as home, Motherland or Fatherland – even the whole earth itself.[44] Heidegger conceived a *place* to be where mortals, gods, earth and sky are gathered and where we mortals could 'dwell poetically on earth'.[45] Aristotle connected place with the image of a vessel. This should not be thought of as a mere passive container, but rather in terms of places providing their own boundaries, because they evoke a fascination – they are always affairs of the heart.[46] Tibet became a landscape to which the soulful imaginings of many Westerners were drawn; one which has sustained a deep fascination over the centuries.

Sacred space has been defined in terms of its separation from the profane world, by the limited access accorded to it, by a sense of dread or fascination, by intimations of order and power combined with ambiguity and paradox. Sacred places also seem to be located at the periphery of the social world. As we shall see, so far as the West is concerned, Tibet easily fits such a description.

A sacred place, or *temenos*, always has a defined boundary and a centre. At its perimeter lies the threshold. This, writes Eliade, 'is the limit, the boundary, the frontier that distinguishes and opposes two worlds – and at the same time the paradoxical place where those worlds communicate, where passage from the profane to the sacred world becomes possible'.[47] Rituals accompany the crossing of the threshold, guardians protect the passageway.[48] At the centre of the sacred place is the *axis mundi*, the world axis, the link between heaven, earth and the Underworld. Such places give orientation and establish order. They allow access to imaginal depth and meaningfulness whilst holding chaos at bay. Sacred places provide an essential continuity with the past, with the Ancients of one's cultural tradition.[49] Whilst grounding the present in memory, they also provide an orientation for the future, give it meaning.

Sacred places are sites of paradoxical power – of destruction, and also of renewal. They can induce a sense of both serenity and terror. Such places are terrible, yet also fascinating. Contemporary use of the term 'sacred place', frequently lacks such paradox, too often sacred places are imagined merely as benign places for healing and contemplation.[50] But as we shall see in the case of Tibet, once paradox has been too easily resolved, contradiction replaced by harmony, ambiguity by certainty; once fear and darkness have yielded to unequivocal hope, then the sacred place has become a utopia. A whole new set of fantasies is then mobilized.[51]

Notions of sacred space and travel come together in the phenomenon of pilgrimage. Like travel accounts, pilgrimage has its landscapes, its sacred places, its sacred routes and its literature of guidebooks and individual accounts, often written in a confessional style.[52] Victor Turner has emphasized the peripheral yet important nature of pilgrimage: geographically, culturally and imaginatively.[53] I want to argue for a wider definition of pilgrimage, or of sacred journey, which will encompass exploration and travel. As with the more conventional pilgrimage, travel and exploration can also convey a public sense of the sacred. Through the ceremony of travel the individual can be involved in a collective celebration, production and maintenance of the sacred and of the mythic. It is from such a perspective that Tibet can be seen as one of the modern sacred sites of western pilgrimage.

This study argues that *places*, such as the one Tibet became, provide a society's imaginings with a vital *coherence*. It seeks to show how such a landscape is produced, established and reproduced both within a historical period and also over a long span of time. In the case of Tibet and the British imagination, for example, three imaginative contexts were of primary importance, although they were not always harmoniously related:

1. The imagination of imperialism, particularly in India, exerted its influence throughout the formative years of Britain's involvement with Tibet. Imperial rivalry, global geopolitics, a sense of imperial destiny, the consolidation of the empire through exploring, mapping and surveying, in addition to concerns of trade, were uppermost in the imperial imagination.

2. The geographical imagination found one of its fullest developments in the nineteenth century and dominated Britain's relationship with Tibet. Especially important were the changing attitudes towards wilderness landscapes, as well as to exploration and travel. Under the heading of exploration can be included adventurers and mountaineers, as well as scholars in geography, archaeology, ethnology, and the physical and natural sciences. This period saw the birth and consolidation of many intellectual disciplines in their modern form – geography, archaeology, anthropology, and comparative religion. But in the nineteenth century many explorers, by inclination or necessity were active in a variety of overlapping concerns rather than being narrow specialists.

3. Ideas about personal experience were also undergoing profound changes. Especially important were the decline of Christianity's spiritual hegemony in Europe, the rise of interest in Eastern and traditional religions, and the development of theosophy, existentialism and psychoanalysis. In particular, the mystical imagination has formed a continuous thread in Britain's relationship with Tibet. Indeed, it seems that missionary activity in Tibet assumed a low profile in the popular imagination, perhaps because of the consistent respect shown for Buddhism.

Each of these imaginative paradigms had its own specific tradition and history, but each was also part of a larger social-historical milieu. Hence the various landscapes of Tibet were sketched not in isolation by the individual travellers but, for example, against a background of British Victorian attitudes towards religion, 'primitive' cultures, the 'East', social class, sexuality, aesthetics, and even travel itself.

This is therefore a unique study of a complete tradition of travel writing in its psychosocial context. But as we shall see, so compelling was this *place*, with its strange yet profound religion, its harsh yet benign theocracy, its splendid and archaic civilization, its impossible landscapes of mountains and deserts, its rugged yet amiable people, its frustrating and tormenting isolation, its position atop the highest mountains on the globe, that it touched and questioned virtually every area of Western endeavour.

Power and the Production of Places

Foucault argues that power and knowledge are inseparable. We are, he writes, 'subjected to the production of truth through power, and we cannot exercise power except through the production of truth'.[54] The 'truth' about a place such as Tibet, therefore, was not discovered, but produced as a result of specific social and imaginative relationships. Tibet was always in the process of being created, always adjusting its contours in step with the changing requirements of the European fantasies. But *places* are not only the result of such complex social processes; they also help to organize them and give them coherence.

Edward Said's seminal study, *Orientalism*, is directly concerned with the creation, maintenance and reproduction of such a *place*, in this case the 'Orient'. He argues that the Orient was, and is, a fundamental place in the landscape of Western imagination. Said sees imaginative geography as crucial to the organization of knowledge: 'Geography was essentially the material underpinning for knowledge about the Orient. All the latent and unchanging characteristics of the Orient stood upon, were rooted in, its geography.'[55] These places – the Mediterranean, the Arctic, or the Orient – are like islands which provide a coherence for the Western fantasy of itself.[56] As Said remarks, 'these geographical entities thus support and to an extent reflect each other.'[57] In the case of the 'Orient', this mythological reality became so closed, so dense and literal, that a whole scholarly discipline arose around it – Orientalism. Said astutely comments that such learned pursuits promote more of a 'refinement' of 'Western ignorance' than 'some body of positive Western knowledge which increases in size and accuracy.'[58] Following Foucault, we could say that these discourses are concerned with the expression and organization of *doubt* as much as anything else.[59]

Some insight into the relationship between knowledge and imaginative geography can be also gained from Gladwin's study of navigation among Pacific islanders. He was puzzled by their mapping of *imaginary* islands.[60]

The navigators were highly pragmatic people, and these precisely co-ordinated and meticulously plotted imaginary islands at first seemed an anomaly to Gladwin, yet he discovered that these islands were essential for the *coherence* of the navigational maps and techniques. The Orient, the Mediterranean, Tibet, the source of the Nile, Greece, and so on, were similarly both factual and yet also imaginary. They could be located precisely, geographically, on a map, yet at the same time were imbued with additional symbolic meaning. They provided an internal coherence for the structure of Europe's mythological foundation and sensibility.[61] They were impossible but necessary.

Through the practical repetition of discourses, including those of travel, a surface is produced on which an imaginary place appears, replete with people, customs, landscape, weather, food, clothing, history, and so on.[62] Said has extensively detailed this production process for the 'Orient'. Traders, explorers, adventurers and missionaries were among the first to travel and to return laden with stories. These laid the foundations and began to shape the contours of these distant places. They also established the routes – both imaginary and geographical – by which such places could be approached. It will be seen, in the case of Tibet, that the travellers' fantasies varied according to whether they approached by way of Afghanistan (adventure, mountain climbing), India (British Raj, colonial rivalry with Russia), China (Tibeto-Chinese rivalry), or Mongolia (Silk Route, archaeology). Subsequently, anthropologists and other specialist 'travellers' also came to tell their stories. James Boon, for example, writing about the practice of anthropology, points to the 'ritually repetitive confrontations with the Other which we call field work'. He documents the way Bali, as a place, emerged from out of this 'ritual repetition'.[63] Each era reconstructs the contours of these imaginary worlds, but on surfaces already laid down.

The nineteenth-century and twentieth-century travel accounts already had a stage replete with 'the Sphinx, Cleopatra, Eden, Troy, Sodom and Gomorrah, Astarte, Isis and Osiris, Sheba, Babylon, the Genii, the Magi, Nineveh, Prester John, Mahomet, and dozens of other characters, scenes and plots.'[64] In addition, any subsequent discourse about the 'Orient' had to 'pass through the learned grids and codes provided by the Orientalists'.[65] Said argues that the contours and culture of this vast imaginary landscape became self-validating. Orientalists referred to other Orientalists for verification. In much the same way, we shall see travellers in Tibet refer to each other's accounts for confirmation.

The British discovery and exploration of Tibet occurred in the shadow of the Royal Geographical Society's hegemony. This institution established early in the nineteenth century, exerted its control by means of funding, co-ordinating, training and publishing; its extensive network of connections among the leaders of British imperialism; its pioneering role in geography and its leadership in geographical education. Above all, the Royal Geographical Society's aims and practices dovetailed with the needs of nineteenth-century imperialism: they both conformed with, and confirmed, prevailing geopolitical values.[66] Yet the society's control was never absolute. The struggle against its hegemony was to be a fundamental characteristic of Tibetan travel literature, although rarely was such a challenge direct or overt. Also, the constraints imposed by the Royal Geographical Society's hegemony were more often *conducive* to the production of knowledge than to its restriction. One could argue that control is most often effective when it encourages investiagation in a certain direction rather than preventing it altogether.[67] Through these various constraints – theoretical, ideological, empirical, imaginative and political – vessels are created which actually assist and support specific imaginative production. Said, for example, points to a 'linguistic Orient, a Freudian Orient, a Spenglerian Orient, a Darwinian Orient, a racist Orient – and so on'.[68]

European and American fantasies about Tibet were never a vague abstraction, never just a set of images carried around in the heads of individual travellers. they were always tangible, always embodied in distinct practices, ranging from accepted styles of prose and landscape description to how expeditions were organized and equipped. The imagination was embodied in the relationship between explorer-travellers and their non-European guides, companions, escorts, servants. Institutions such as the Royal Geographical Society, the Royal society, the Alpine Club and the Survey of India simultaneously encoded, concentrated and legitimized fantasies. Above all, they had the power to establish these imaginative practices as *truth* and to impose this upon what Said has dramatically called the 'silent Other'.[69]

The Psychosocial Context

Quite clearly, the evolution of Tibet as a sacred landscape ocurred within a complex psychosocial context. Numerous discourses intersected in Tibet, or wove themselves around its creation. This study must therefore follow the trails left by botanists, geologists, linguists, missionaries, students of comparative religion, Buddhists, Buddhologists and Tibetologists, anthropologists and archaeologists, aesthetes of both landscape and art, mountaineers, journalists, surveyors, soldiers, diplomats, photographers, mystics, traders, professional travellers, adventurers and poets, as they made their way into Tibet or around its formidable perimeter. These individuals lived and worked during a period of unprecedented global expansion by the Western powers, of unrestrained urbanization and industrialization; at a time when revolutions were ocurring throughout the full range of social and physical sciences, as well as in the political and social life of Western societies.

The creation of Tibet, between 1773 and 1959, coincided almost exactly with the rise and fall of European, and particularly British, imperial aspirations. Tibet was witness to a massive reorganization of global time, space and identity. Old empires collapsed as the modern era was ushered in. The new geopolitical order was legitimized by a complete realignment both of memory and of expectations. In their role of story-tellers, travellers and explorers played a crucial role in this process. By studying these accounts we are allowed privileged access to the imagination, both unconscious and conscious, of the ruling and upper-middle classes of Britain and other Western nations.

We shall see that during most of this long period travel accounts were usually conservative protests against modernism, the masses, and the changing world order. But they also played a crucial part in the creation of a thoroughly new *Weltanschauung* – with respect to traditional cultures, the peoples and geography of the world, nature and science and, above all, personal meaning. New myths emerged, old ones became revitalized – the Wise Men of the East, an Arcadia hidden in a remote secluded valley, the mastery of death, the search for the Self, the vitality of the frontier.

Five eras in the unfolding of the West's imaginative relationship with Tibet have been selected. Although these are not completely arbitrary, there could just as easily been six or seven. Nevertheless, each of these eras offers a view of a particular Tibet, complete within itself yet also in process, replete with tensions and contradictions. This is therefore a study not of one, but of five 'Tibets': of their individual genesis, development and decline. Each 'Tibet' was very much an integral part of its era – hence the necessity of as full an understanding as possible of the psychosocial context. But as we shall see, the transformation from one imaginative 'Tibet' to the next was not solely dependent upon the vicissitudes of its cultural context. This movement had its own internal logic, its own relative independence. Also, despite the satisfying coherence of each of these individual imaginative 'Tibets' we shall see that there was also an *overall* shape to the fantasies about Tibet which spanned nearly two hundred years.

The boundaries of each era have been selected, first, in terms of some significant event in the history of Western involvement with Tibet; and secondly in terms of some core, or root-metaphor that gave the era its apparent cohesion. Sometimes the beginning and end of such an era are quite definite and are dictated by unquestionable events – this was true of the first 'Tibet' to be imaginatively created in modern times. In 1773 British troops clashed with the Bhutanese, thus evoking a direct response from Tibet. In 1774 George Bogle became the first modern non-ecclesiastic Westerner to enter Tibet and leave a written account. The close of that optimistic era is similarly beyond dispute. In 1792 Tibet barred its frontiers to Westerners in the aftermath of a series of Gurkha invasions from Nepal for which Britain was held partly responsible. Most of Tibet then remained sealed off from Western curiosity for over a hundred years. It was this single fact alone that initiated the 'next' era.

Excluded from Tibet itself, Westerners, particularly the British, began a systematic exploration of the surrounding Himalayas. Hence Tibet began to acquire a shape. Its boundary began to be mapped. A few intrepid individuals made solitary journeys into the country even reaching Lhasa itself, so reminding the West of that hidden, unknown land beyond the mountains; but most of all, Westerners were fascinated with the Himalayas. This era was also dominated by a revolution in landscape aesthetics in Europe and America: mountain Romanticism was in its first full flowering. Yet this era did not lack pertinent historical events concerning Tibet, and it came to a definite conclusion in around 1842. The British attempt to establish hegemony in the Himalayas, and thus to ensure a stable, well-controlled northern frontier for India, received a series of major setbacks between 1841 and 1842. The Sikhs had already conquered Ladakh in 1834, and in 1841 they invaded Western Tibet. Britain had recently had an army annihilated in Afghanistan, and its somewhat *laissez-faire* approach to imperialism seemed inadequate to cope with the situation.

The next period, between 1842 and 1875, was marked less by external events than by a single-mindedness of purpose. Systematic and scientific exploration was the ideal of the day, with Darwin's famous work hovering inescapably over the whole era. The Himalayas were mapped and their place in the British imagination was assured. A new landscape aesthetic was emerging under the careful tutelage of Ruskin. Behind its well-protected and well-defined frontiers, Tibet came to symbolize something very special. Both its religion and its position, 'on top of the World', began to exert a fascination with Western travellers. As an ancestral source of the Aryan race, these lofty regions were quietly beginning to evoke deep longings.

1875, the beginning of the next era, bears no relation to any significant historical event – it is merely the gateway to the closing quarter of the nineteenth century. During this time the tradition of Tibetan exploration finally acquired its own internal dynamic and entered its golden age, which culminated in the British armed expedition to Lhasa in 1904. Then it seemed that a decisive breakthrough had occurred: that the 'Forbidden City' had finally been reached, and Tibet now lay open at last to Western curiosity. But this *fin de siècle* Tibet was merely one of a series and not, as was hoped, the final resolution of an enigma. A travel restriction once more descended, and in some ways the country became even more isolated than before.

The final period of this study begins with an event far from Tibet yet so monumental for the West as to overshadow all else: the First World War. It ends, however, with an event that was intensely specific to Tibet: the final exile of the Dalai Lama in 1959, and the apparent destruction of traditional Tibetan religious culture in its homeland.

Any contextual study that attempts to do justice to the complexities of an era can quite easily become lost among the historical details of politics, social analysis, aesthetics, geographical understanding, military strategy, missionary work, botanical investigations, and so on. Clearly we must remember our primary objective and stay as close as possible to the phenomenology of the imagination, to the Western sense of the sacred with regard to Tibet. In addition, this is a study of the imagination *in process*, and careful attention has to be directed at the subtle transformations of fantasy.

An Imaginative Analysis

James Hillman has clearly articulated the concerns of such an imaginatve analysis. 'Depth psychology', he writes, ' has applied its method to the study of alchemy, myth, religious dogma and ritual, scientific theory, primitive behaviour, cosmologies, psychiatric ideas – all in terms of the archetypal fantasy therein expressed.'[70] An archetypal reading of these Tibetan travel texts therefore seeks to uncover the deep structure of the imagination and to plot its transformations.[71] Hillman writes:

> We can extend depth psychology from persons to things, places and ideas as manifestations of imagination. The same imagination, the same soul, that presented itself in fifteenth and sixteenth century alchemy showed itself in the extraverted psychology of the explorers seeking gold, the journey across the perilous seas, the seven cities, the impossible passage, the fountain of youth, the black man and the lost Atlantis – the world as metaphor.[72]

From such a perspective the imaginative relationship to the world is clearly primary and not, as it is from another viewpoint, a subjective confusion and contamination of empirical understanding.[73] An imaginal reading also emancipates us from a progressive and evolutionary evaluation of the European and American understanding of Tibet. Again Hillman writes: 'No first and last, better and worse, progression and regression. Instead, soul history as a series of images, superimposed'.[74] Transformation should not be reduced solely to development.

The use of a wide range of theoretical perspectives in a study such as this raises important methodological questions. Some critical reflection on the relationship between them is certainly necessary as regards the main theorists, but I believe we must distinguish clearly between an archetypal-psychological analysis and, say a philosophical one. The former is less concerned with logical or epistemological differences between, for example, Jung's ideas and Eliade's, or Hillman's and Foucault's, than with their archetypal and metaphorical relationships. A theoretical consistency becomes less important than an imaginal one. Also, in an imaginal analysis the relationship between theory and text is crucial: how shall we place the theories in relation to the *prima materia*, to the other, primary, texts?

Jung himself inspired such an attitude by insisting that the crucial differences between his own ideas and those of Freud and Adler were differences of personal metaphor or imaginal orientation. He saw theories as tools, to be used *according to the demands of the material*.[75] Similarly, when Hillman criticizes Foucault's ideas, for example, it is not because of their logical incompatibility with his own, nor due to some internal inconsistency in Foucault's arguments, but in terms of their overall relationship to the image. In this regard he accuses Foucault of 'anarchic nihilism' – of reducing psychopathology, and hence image-making, to mere linguistic and social convention. Foucault's insights and radical deconstructionalism, whilst paralleling some of the de-literalizing ideas of archetypal psychology, must therefore be used cautiously when it comes to making moves in image-work. Finally, as Holt insists in his study 'Jung and Marx', the aim is not to achieve a theoretical reconciliation but to open up a field of ideas that has both the width and the capacity to endure contradictions.[76]

I would suggest that an imaginal analysis must bear in mind the dominant root-metaphors of any theory that it uses to craft the imaginal material. A polytheistic approach does not exclude any perspective on the grounds of theoretical incompatibility, but instead tries to relate theories through their common grounding in imaginal reality. Eliade's ideas, for instance, are clearly based on oppositional thinking, insisting upon an almost unequivocal polarization between the sacred and the profane. His distinctions are fixed and sharply defined rather than fluid and in process. Also, Eliade presents the struggle to attain otherworldliness as *the* most valued orientation of *Homo religiosus*. Perhaps we can see the archetype of the hero at work in these striking oppositions and bold, almost desperate, struggles to attain some sacred Other; or that of the senex in his insistence upon clearly defined boundaries and rigid demarcations between classes of experience.[77] Similar archetypal perspectives appear in his portrayal of sacred Otherness as a timeless *unity*. As we shall see, Western fantasies of Tibet reveal images of the sacred in the process of creation: images that have a complex and contradictory multiplicity even with an occasional, overall, imaginal coherence. Tibet was an imaginal place whose boundaries – both in space and time – and defining internal characteristics were continually in flux, ever changing. These images reveal a sacred domain that was *never* sharply delineated from the profane world – one where the sacred and profane interpenetrated, confirmed and contested each other.

The archetypal dominants in Foucault's work move between an almost Dionysian dismantling of concretized and totalizing images and Apollonian distancing from the material, with a corresponding attention to rational clarity. Foucault's work also reveals, at times, a delight in a Hermetic or trickster-like word-play. However, Said's analysis of 'Orientalism', whilst owing much to Foucault's theoretical ideas and perspective, fails to echo his root-metaphors on an imaginal level. Instead Said's work is marked by puer-earnestness, an attempt to gather up history in the services of a political cause in the present. Any anima-inspired lingering delight in the mysterious intimacy of the past is speedily bypassed as he hurries to reach the present in order to construct his grand theory.[78]

Listening in such a way to the root-metaphors of these theories relieves them of their literalness and allows space for the material, the textural images, to speak pluralistically. Our analysis itself then becomes a matter of image-work, a crafting of images. The theories do not then, as it were, stand *above* the primary material, claiming a privileged position; instead they too take their place as imaginal texts alongside the travel accounts and other historical documents. There is a mutual reciprocity between these various classes of text as they reveal, contextualize, marshal and organize the disparate wealth of imagery evoked in the encounter between the West and Tibet.

An Archaeology of Shangri-La

This study therefore presents an archetypal reading of an imaginal 'Tibet': not as an abstraction, but as a sensual reality: not as a series of disembodied ideas, but as a complex world of images – shapes, colours, textures. An archaeology of the imagination is concerned with uncovering the past foundations of present fantasies. In it, memory is not just a precondition for the present but a part of its essential structure. The past is not absent but is ever-present beneath the apparent surfaces of daily life. One of the final and most complete embodiments of Tibet as a sacred place in the Western imagination was the utopia of Shangri-La described in Hilton's famous 1933 novel *Lost Horizon*.[79] In a very real sense, then, this study is an archaeology of Shangri-La.

An imaginative archaeology uncovers personalities and characters of earlier eras – the Dalai Lama, the Potala, Lhasa, the unceasing wind, the vast Tibetan plateau, the colours and the light, the yeti, the lamas and of course, the explorers, both known and unknown. The creation of these successive Tibets was not a process of remorseless continuity. Embellishments, or streams of fantasy which did not pass into the next era but instead came to a dead end, are as vital to the understanding of imaginative processes as those dominant themes which spanned the entire period of nearly two hundred years. British troops firing at giant rhubarb plants in the mistaken belief that they were Tibetan soldiers, or the inexplicable fascination Western travellers had for the variety of hats worn at Lhasa, cannot be simply left out of the study just because they seem tangential to the main story.

The Ceremony of Travel

The individual intentions of travellers and explorers, or governments and institutions, are often less interesting than the *way* they went about things, or how things eventually went about their own way. So, for example, each era had its own *ceremony* of travel. The travel atmosphere of each was replete with its own fantasies – tropical landscapes, love and romance, nervous frontiers, horrible places.[80] These fantasies spoke through hotels, rest-houses, mountainside bivouacs, travel guides, postcards, photographs and, above all, what was actually *taken* on the journey. The renowned Russian Prejevalsky, for example, set out across Siberia in 1879 with twenty three camels laden with two and a half hundredweight of sugar, forty pounds of dried fruit, a crate of brandy and a crate of sherry. His party was armed with a formidable arsenal of rifles, revolvers, a hundredweight of powder, 9,000 rounds of ammunition and four hundredweight of lead shot. His 'gifts for the natives' included tinted pictures of Russian actresses. An additional gift was some wild strawberry jam which Prejavalsky had bottled personally for the Dalai Lama. He boasted that if necessary he would bribe or shoot his way to Lhasa.[81]

The most notable non-Europeans to enter Tibet were the 'pundits'. These were Indians trained in survey work, who carried compasses fixed to the top of their walking staves, notes hidden inside their prayer wheels, and used beads on the rosary to count their paces and hence to measure the vast distances.[82] In 1935 Peter Fleming and Tina Maillart travelled 3,500 miles from Peking to Kashmir, brushing around the back of Tibet. The journey took seven months. Their supplies speak eloquently. Apart from old clothes, a few books (including Macaulay's *History of England*), two compasses and two portable typewriters, they carried: two pounds of marmalade, four tins of cocoa, six bottles of brandy, one bottle of Worcester sauce, one pound of coffee, three small packets of chocolate, some soap, a good deal of tobacco, a small store of knives, beads, toys, etc., by way of presents, and a random assortment of medicines.[83] Their only weapon was a second-hand ·22 rook rifle to shoot food *en route*. Such lists are endless, yet each in its own way is a vignette of fantasies, hopes, fears and expectations. This study will listen carefully to such things as well as to ideas.

The Selection of Texts

We can locate with some precision those moments, when as an indication of a changing sensibility, a new and fundamental image appears. Sometimes it may only flicker briefly and then soon fade. Other images are more fertile: we can trace their establishment and the subtle contours of their evolution. Sometimes a long-ignored image will reappear many years after apparently hibernating, out of sight, underground. A changing imaginative context will have given it a new meaning and a restored relevance. We can also distinguish between *seed-images* and *contextual-images.* The former are characterized by a unique specificity, whereas the latter attempt to embrace and encompass. Seed-images, for example would include those that refer to a specific mountain, such as Everest. Contextual-images, on the other hand, would embrace the social attitude towards mountains in general.

It is often possible to identify key, or primary, texts in relation to these images. For example, Volume 4 of Ruskin's *Modern Painters* or Darwin's *Origin of Species* generated images that created whole imaginative contexts. The *Himalayan Journals* of botanist-explorer Joseph Hooker, the future director of Kew Gardens (1855), on the other hand, were formative in creating the imaginative contours of the eastern Himalayas: they fulfilled a more limited but no less important function than, say, Darwin's work. Other texts neither shaped a whole context nor seeded the region with definitive and fertile imagery. They were nevertheless crucial in echoing many of the major concerns, as well as embellishing more minor issues. Between them these more secondary texts created the overall 'tone' of the *place,* its atmosphere and its density.

Each chapter therefore draws upon a limited number of primary texts, some of which are contextual, whilst others are specific to Himalayan and Tibetan exploration. In the first chapters, selection of travel texts is not a real problem, but as Tibetan travel became more established, a bewildering range of accounts became available. Some, like Hooker's *Himalayan Journals*, Freshfield's mountaineering epic *Around Kanchenjunga*, or the French priest M. Huc's *Travels in Tartary, Tibet and China*, were acknowledged classics in their day, and so select themselves. These apart, I have chosen a range of texts that is representative of the remarkable spectrum of perspectives held by Western travellers, yet also faithful to the *balance* of the era's fantasies. Accounts of travel and exploration tend to be clustered in distinct, but overlapping groups. All these textual groups have their own very unique traditions. They share both style and purpose. These clusterings of texts were sometimes indicative of established and powerful interest groups such as the Royal Geographical Society, or the Royal Society.

We are therefore caught in a dilemma. If texts are selected merely to be as representative as possible of the *range* of travellers, then the relative value of each text in terms of the era's fantasy-making could be grossly distorted. Landon's monumental, and official, study of the British 'invasion' of 1904, *Lhasa*, was clearly far more formative for the British imagination than Millington's witty volume *To Lhassa at Last*, produced as a result of the same expedition. Yet precisely because it *was* humorous, a rarity in early Tibetan travel accounts, Millington's slim work is of inestimable value. If we give weight only to texts that were deemed important at the time, we are in danger of merely reproducing the *official* story. This may or may not represent the actual state of the era's Tibetan fantasies. For example, Bogle's diary, the first secular account of Tibet in modern times, was not published until about a hundred years after it was written. Clearly it played little or no part in *forming* the fantasies of Bogle's time, but it has a great claim to acknowledgement as a crucial *expression* of its era. In many ways it is of more value than Turner's famous account, written and published only a few years after Bogle's journey, for it is less polished, less 'prepared' for publication.[84]

Publication, distribution and recognition of travel accounts are profoundly affected by vested interests, be they a matter of institutional values or of simple economics – will they be popular and sell? The less well-known texts therefore have a value in helping us to glance behind the official story. Often they show revealing views from the edge of the dominant paradigm: sometimes contradicting it, sometimes reinforcing it. Also, even within a single travel text there may be a variety of viewings: some mainstream, others idiosyncratic.

Before travellers even arrived at the Tibetan border, their imaginations had been prepared. The actual encounter with the empirical place then merely activated their fantasies, either confirming or contesting them. As Bachelard writes: 'Before becoming a conscious sight, every landscape is an oneiric experience.'[85]

Showing or Telling?

A distinction has frequently been made between those accounts which show and those which tell.[86] It would be relatively straightforward to *tell* the story of the Western encounter with Tibet, the experiences of the explorers, their discoveries, the meaning of their fantasies. But this is not intended to be just a study *of* the imagination, but *in* the imagination. I therefore want to show as well as to tell. As much as possible I want the images to 'speak for themselves' and not be reduced to abstractions. For instance, a study of landscape painting could scarcely be feasible without profuse illustrative examples, and central to this account is the study of landscape imagery – word-paintings, as they were called in the nineteenth century. But I prefer to use these descriptive passages not just as illustrations for a conceptual argument but as part of the construction of the argument itself, woven into the text, integral to it.

Whilst an imaginative, or archetypal, study has to let the images speak for themselves, at the same time it must interpret, deepen and work them. This is an especially pressing concern in a complex, multicontextual study such as this. We can begin by recognizing the polymorphous nature of any image. Every image has many forms and faces: personal, political, historical and, of course, sacred. By bringing these diverse contextual levels into close alignment with each other, the multifaceted nature of any image is amplified. By using analogy, or by allowing resonances to occur between each group of images and metaphors, we can both deepen and shape the material without being seduced into assigning any single meaning to an image or event.

This is a work of patience; one which often moves indirectly; one that gathers images; circular rather than linear. Such a procedure therefore continually lays down one level of imaginative context after another: historical narrative; landscape aesthetics; personal experience; the genre of travel writing; imperial politics and fantasies, and so on. As this account moves slowly around an image, care has been taken that sufficient imaginal space is left for the image to reflect itself. The complexities, richness and subtleties of image-work are as much to do with tone, rhythm, tempo, texture and shape as they are with content.

From what position can we read these travel texts and images? For example, each era has looked back at preceding landscape aesthetics from a position of assumed superiority. To the earliest Romantics, Classical aesthetics seemed soulless, impersonal, over-formalized. They felt that they alone had discovered the essential truth of nature. But to the nature-lovers of the mid-nineteenth century these early Romantics seemed over-indulgent, vague about specific details, too subjective. To many people in the second half of the twentieth century both these earlier views appear too narrow, too fragmented, over-concerned with superficial aesthetics: they ignore wilderness regions, they are pre-ecological, pre-the age of conservation. To place the reflections and imaginings of early-nineteenth-century Himalayan travellers within a late-twentieth-century ecological context will therefore expose them to ridicule or irrelevance. At best it neatly locates them within a historical account of the so-called evolution of landscape appreciation towards some fantasy of 'truth'. On an artistic parallel this is equivalent to reducing Constable to a mere precursor of, say, Turner. The delicacy, force, subtlety and wit of the original image becomes lost beneath the weight of a literalized evolutionary fantasy. Passages of landscape description in these two centuries of travel texts have to be considered aesthetically in addition to historically, or politically, and so on. The framing, contextualization and amplification of these textual images is hence a vital, albeit indirect, procedure in imaginative analysis.

2

Tibet Discovered
(1773–92)

The love of mountains came in with the rights of man ... It seems as if the philosophers fancied they had found a fragment of the genuine Arcadia still preserved by the Alpine barrier against the encroachments of a corrupt civilization and mountains came in for some of the admiration lavished upon the social forms which they protected.

(L. Stephen [1871])

Images of Travel

1773 was a momentous year for the British East India Company: it found itself reluctantly at the centre of two wars. The dumping of a shipment of its tea into the waters of Boston harbour by protesting colonists, on 16 December 1773, precipitated the American Revolution. Whilst this famous war of independence was being fought by troops of the British Crown, the company's own soldiers were engaged in the little-known first Anglo-Bhutanese War. If this date marked the beginning of modern America, it also saw the birth of Tibet as a landscape in modern Western fantasies. As a result of this border war, the East India Company despatched George Bogle to Tibet in May 1774. Bogle, the offspring of a well-to-do Scottish commercial family, had been in India for four years when at the early age of twenty-eight he was selected to go on this journey by his friend and mentor Warren Hastings, Governor of Bengal. His journey to Tibet was followed in 1783, by that of Captain Samuel Turner, who also represented the East India Company. The accounts written by these two men are classics of eighteenth-century travel.

Other Europeans had previously visited Tibet. The legendary medieval journeys of Marco Polo, Friar Odoric, and other idiosyncratic individuals were followed in the seventeenth and eighteenth centuries by the systematic missionary activity of Jesuit and Capuchin monks.[1] But the encounter between Britain and Tibet in the last quarter of the eighteenth century marked the beginning of something new: the sustained creation of Tibet as an important imaginal landscape for Western cultures. Echoes of an older, almost medieval, geographical imagining continued to be heard throughout the creation of this 'new' Tibet, but the journeys of Bogle and

Turner coincided with a revolution in British geopolitical awareness.

Only two years before Bogle's entry into Tibet, Cook had returned from his epic voyage into the South Pacific. A new age of scientific exploration had begun.[2] At exactly the same time, the European – and in particular the British-relationship to mountain landscape was reaching a new pitch of intensity. In the Alps, de Saussure was spearheading the final break-through from 'mountain gloom to mountain glory', from the old distrust of mountains to a new aesthetic of Romanticism and sensual realism.[3] The eighteenth- and nineteenth-century British imagination constantly reflected Tibet and the Himalayas in the mirror of the Alps. Alpine travel was assumed to be the exemplary form of mountain experience through-out the nineteenth century. As we shall see, only in the early twentieth century were the Himalayas to come into their own and shrug off con-tinual Alpine comparison.

In the final quarter of the eighteenth century, landscape aesthetics was also poised between an allegiance to Classical formalism and a desire for Romantic realism. Such a tension existed between the spontaniety and enthusiasm of Bogle's account and the restraint exercised by Turner. The sense of an individual quest is constantly present in Bogle's diary; in this way it points forward to the early nineteenth century. But for Turner this unusual journey seemed to be nothing but an extremely interesting and curious duty. A flavour of the 'Grand Tour' lingered over both accounts and seemed to turn Tibet into a mere extension of it.

This attitude towards their journeys to Tibet is only to be expected. The 'Grand Tour' gave secular Europe the first sustained alternative to the almost abandoned medieval fantasy of pilgrimage. It provided a complex, precise, systematic, coherent, prestigious and exemplary model for the imagination of travel.[4] Its influence was extensive and profound. Ancient cultural locations became sacred sites, geographical features became views, tracks and roads became routes. But thrown out with the medieval passion for pilgrimage went popular, lower-class travel. Unless in the role of servants, soldiers, artisans, and so on, representatives of the peasant masses in Britain did not generally go on extensive journeys in the eighteenth and early nineteenth centuries – in other words, they travelled for employment and not as the aristocrats and bourgeoisie were fashion-ably doing, in search of significant places and landscapes.

Alpine landscape initially belonged to the 'Grand Tour' only as an unpleasant, unfortunate section of the route, best accomplished as fast as possible and preferably with the blinds down. However, by the late eighteenth century the Alps had radically changed the British imagina-tion of travel. All the evocative power of 'the sublime', which had been gathering strength for a century, was suddenly focused upon, and con-centrated into, these mountains. Although initially they were to be admired leisurely and at a distance, by the late eighteenth century the

Alps had many explorers climbing to their summits.

The 'Grand Tour' had long been considered routine and stale by the late eighteenth century, and Alpine travel was well advanced in providing Britain with an exciting and alternative imaginative map. At one stage on his journey Turner commented playfully, upon a Tibetan woman singing, 'I am not ashamed to own that the song she sang, was more pleasing to my ear, than an Italian air.'[5] Both Bogle and Turner would have grown up in the atmosphere of the 'Grand Tour', but would also have been aware of the 'Alpine Experience'. In some way, too, they would have realized that they were participating in the radically new domain of scientific global exploration.

The obsessive fervour towards exploration that gripped the Victorian era's imagination would have seemed remote and alien to these two eighteenth-century gentlemen travellers. Bogle, for example, was instructed by Hastings to plant some potatoes at every halting place on his journey through Bhutan and into Tibet.[6] At least three deductions can be made about this unusual task. The narrowness of the commercial imagination is matched by the thoroughness of Hasting's curiosity. In addition it tells of the insignificance of Bogle's actual *journey* to Tibet compared with those of later travellers, who would have been content just *to go there* without any specific reason. But both journey and destination were secondary objectives for Bogle and Turner. Tibet was only one place among many possible goals. Afghanistan, Assam or Burma would all have been similarly curious places to visit in the course of one's employment and duty. Also, the *going* was not as valued as much as the *arriving*. Travel for its own sake was still relatively uncommon. Such an attitude is revealed when at one point on his journey Turner writes: 'Being indolently disposed and prompted merely by curiosity, I strolled among the houses.'[7] Bogle comments in a similarly offhand manner: 'I may as well describe this temple while I am here.' Later nineteenth-century travellers would, by contrast, be furiously observing, noting, measuring and collecting images of the place and the route.

There also seemed to be no urgency about publishing the two journals. Turner was unsure about public interest in his journey, and the journal was published only in 1800, seventeen years after his return. Bogle's was not published until 1876, almost a century after he left Tibet. Another journal, written by Kirkpatrick outlining his journey to Nepal in 1793, was not published until 1811, and it was only with extreme reticence that the author sought publication.[8] Indeed, in Kirkpatrick's case the services of 'a literary gentleman' were sought, eventually to no avail, in order to prepare the manuscript 'properly' to meet the 'public eye'. In other words, travel accounts had to be 'literary'; there was still doubt about interest in the journey itself.

British contact with Tibet also coincided with the spread of European power over the globe; this brought the West face to face with extensive

unknown races and customs. Eighteenth-century ethnographic speculations by Rousseau, Voltaire and others were based upon the increasing
number of accounts by global travellers.[9] Questions about race, species,
the geographical influence on culture, geological history, the nature of
civilization and individual freedom, dominated the closing years of the
century.[10] The accounts by Bogle and Turner take their place firmly within
these debates and concerns.

The British involvement with Tibet witnessed a struggle over the
imaginative relationship to natural and cultural landscapes that was to
continue right up until the present day. The incident and circumstances
that led to the first British–Tibetan contact struck up a rich and complex
theme upon which variations were to be played over the next hundred
and fifty years.

A border incident between the Bhutanese and the British East India
Company led to the first of a series of small wars that Britain was to wage
for over a century in the mountainous northern frontier of India. Eventually these were to culminate, in 1904, with the 'invasion' of Tibet. The first
contact with the small Himalayan country of Bhutan had been made in
1766 by James Rennell whilst pioneering the great survey of India.[11] The
East India Company's help had been requested by the Newars of Nepal,
who were struggling against the aggressive expansion of the Gurkhas.
Trans-Himalayan trade had been disrupted by Gurkha expansion and 'the
Company' sent a small expedition into Nepal to intervene. It was a failure,
and from that moment the Gurkhas became a permanent feature of British
Himalayan involvement. Subsequently, in 1773, Cooch Behar appealed to
'the Company' for help against the invading Bhutanese. A small force was
despatched to the malarial swamp and jungle region that provided Bengal
with its north-east fronter. Despite extensive losses through sickness, the
Company's forces were successful in defeating the Bhutanese. The ruling
Gurkhas in neighbouring Nepal, alarmed at the expansion of British
power, asked the Panchen Lama, the second most influential figure in
Tibet, to intervene.[12] He sent a letter and gifts to Warren Hastings; these
were received in Calcutta on 29 March 1774. Hastings was quick to seize
upon this opening into the unknown and enticing northern land, and
within two months sent a mission to Tibet headed by George Bogle. Bogle
spent five months at the Panchen Lama's residence in Tashilhumpo, and
the contours of Tibet as a place in the British imagination began to take
shape. From that moment, frontier concerns were to become a defining
characteristic of Tibet's image in the West.

Warren Hastings's Tibet: Lists and Diaries

The Panchen Lama's letter was impressive, and Turner referred to it as 'an authentic and curious specimen of the Lama's good sense, humility, simplicity of heart, and, above all, of that delicacy of sentiment and expression which could convey a threat in terms of meekness and supplication'.[13] This letter and the accompanying gifts were studied assiduously by Warren Hastings for any clues about their land of origin. From his meditations Tibet emerged as a place of conciliation, diplomacy, and cultural sophistication. Obviously this was not a land of rude, illiterate primitives. Tibet clearly considered itself an authority in the Himalayas, but the British still had to determine the exact nature of its power. A complex web of allegiances spun its threads over the region between Nepal, Bhutan, China and Tibet. The elegance and calm self-assurance of the Panchen Lama's letter heightened Warren Hastings's curiosity.

The gifts, too, were revealing:

> gilded Russian leather stamped with the Czar's double-headed eagle, and Chinese silk, which suggested external commerce; small ingots of gold and silver, purses of gold dust, and bags of musk, which seemed evidence of internal wealth; and Tibetan wool cloth, which together with the well-made chests in which the gifts had come, indicated a knowledge of arts and industries.[14]

Hastings concluded that the country and government of Tibet

> are represented as a simple, well-disposed people, numerous and industrious, living under a well-regulated government, having considerable intercourse with other nations, particularly with the Chinese and northern Tartars, and possessing at home the principal means of commerce, gold and silver in great abundance.[15]

Whilst it was not the Arcadian utopia of the newly discovered South Pacific Islands, Tibet promised to become an important place in the confident, youthful and adventurous – yet well-regulated – imagination of commercial capitalism. In another letter Hastings wrote of the 'length of the journey and the natural difficulties ... the severity of the climate and the rudeness of the country'.[16] Right from the start, the landscape and the culture of Tibet seemed to be at opposite polarities: the one as barren and harsh as the other was rich and sophisticated.

The letter and gifts from the Panchen Lama did not fall into an imaginative vacuum: indeed, they activated ancient rumours and vague fragments of knowledge that had been steadily accumulating over the centuries. Hastings's primary concern was with trade, but he also instructed Bogle to determine 'the nature of the road between the borders of Bengal and Lhasa, and of the countries lying in between; the communications between Lhasa and the neighbouring countries, their government, revenue and manners'.[17] Whilst Tibet had an approximate *location*, it was still almost without any coherent *shape* in the British imagination.

Hastings also gave Bogle a list of ten items, as a private commission. A pair of shawl goats was his first request, followed by a pair of yaks. The third request was for 'fresh ripe walnuts for seed ... and any other curious or valuable seeds or plants, the rhubarb and ginseng'. His next demand was for 'any curiosities, ... or what else may be acceptable to persons of taste in England. Animals only that may be useful, unless any that may be remarkably curious'. The fifth item concerned Tibetan government, especially revenue collection. Then Bogle was instructed to keep a diary, a running commentary on whatever seemed to be significant. Next Hastings wanted Bogle to ascertain 'what countries lie between Lhasa and Siberia, and what communication there is between them'. The same instruction was also directed towards Tibet's position with regard to China and Kashmir. Trade between Tibet and Bengal came next, followed by a delightful request: 'Every nation excells others in some particular art or science. To find out this excellence of the Bhutanese.' Then, almost as an afterthought, Bogle was instructed to ascertain the course of the Brahmaputra.[18]

What do we make of this remarkable document, the instructions given to the first British visitor to Tibet in modern times? First of all, it is a list, and draws our attention to the important place that lists occupy in travel discourse. They are sometimes written, sometimes memorized and frequently a source of worry: what to see; what to take; what to do; what not to do; where to stay; where to go; where not to go; what to buy and bring back; how much things cost. The *linear* nature of travel discourse (route, chronological sequence) evokes this list mentality. In addition, those items that do not appear on the list are as important as those that do. In Hastings's instructions we find that Bogle's attention is not drawn to religion, to military matters, to Tibetan history, to details of the Tibetan landscape. Things rather than landscapes or mysteries are uppermost in Hastings's mind: things for trading, things that are productive or unusual such as animals, plants, manufactures, paintings, food, buildings, coins. The blend of enthusiastic commercialism and restrained 'scientific' curiosity in these lists contrasts with the intense geographical and religious focus that was to characterize subsequent Tibetan travel discourses. In Hastings's private commission to Bogle, ethnographic concerns (manners, customs, and so on) are really included only in item number six: in the injunction to keep a very general, spontaneous and unstructured diary.

This era believed itself to be at the beginning of a new 'scientific' exploration. Explorers such as Cook, Humboldt and Banks took pride in this radical departure from mere gentlemen travellers, traders, pilgrims or soldiers. Strict observation and empirical data were foremost in their aims. Yet the casual diary was to gain importance in travel accounts throughout the nineteenth century. The generalized, personal diary format contrasted with the attempt to regulate, specialize and isolate scientific observations. In Hastings's injunctions and in the subsequent accounts by Bogle and Turner, the diary sections, whilst only item number six on the agenda, nevertheless expressed the growing presence of the subjective and Romantic imagination. These diaries follow a different fantasy in relation to the natural world than that taken by the concern for objectivity and scientificity which simultaneously was also making its presence felt.[19] As we shall see, the diary format gradually became increasingly central in travel accounts.

Diaries express a different kind of knowledge about a place from that found in reports for specialized intellectual disciplines. Whereas the latter seek abstraction and distance, the former desire immersion and involvement. The tension between these two forms of knowledge, these two types of imaginative processes, was to become intense by the mid-nineteenth century. Subsequently they were to become alienated from each other, and two kinds of travel writing emerged: specialized, single-purpose, scientific accounts: and generalized travel diaries. The former became identified with professionals, the latter with amateurs and littérateurs.[20] The former quickly lost their connection with travel or even scientific expeditions and came to be regarded as 'objective' accounts. Their role in a creative and imaginative process became submerged beneath an urgent desire for facts, literal truths and explanatory theories. Ethnographic accounts, for example, are rarely situated within the genre of travel texts; instead they have come to be read as a form of objective reporting. The presence of the reporter remains hidden beneath a theoretical certainty and a compulsive thirst for hard data. However, as Fabian points out,

> when modern anthropology began to construct its Other in terms of topoi implying distance, difference and opposition, its interest was above all … to construct ordered Space and Time – a cosmos – for Western society to inhabit, rather than 'understanding other cultures', its ostensible vocation'.[21]

The diary perspective, by contrast, came to be known as *the* travel text, in which the presence of the traveller is well to the fore – indeed, is the narrative's *raison d'être*. But in Hastings's injunctions to Bogle such an absolute split between these differing orders of knowledge had not yet occurred.

Hastings's instructions were accompanied by a document equally as interesting as the private commission: a memorandum on Tibet. Hastings, perhaps the first example of a modern Tibetophile, compiled a brief summary of all extant knowledge on the country[22.] It is a distillation of medieval rumours, seventeenth – and eighteenth-century accounts by Catholic missionaries, and the information supplied by two lama surveyors trained by French geographers in Peking in 1717 and incorporated into the 1736 atlas of Jean Baptiste Bourgignon d'Anville.[23] Hastings's memorandum gathered the strands of the past, and led them into the context of modern imaginings on Tibet. It was an attempt to give a coherent *shape* to the place of Tibet, to define its contours.

The memorandum is only four pages long: the opening half page deals with Tibetan history. The power of the lamas and their relation to China takes up the next full page. Another page on Tibetan religion is followed by one-third of a page each on China and Tartary, on polyandry and on geography. Hastings writes: 'The history, government and religion of Tibet are no doubt more interesting objects of inquiry that its climate or topographical and physical characters; yet these, too, are highly curious.'[24] He draws comparison with the Incas, that other ancient, high-altitude civilization in the Andes – indeed, in these early accounts, comparisons between the Himalayas and the Andes were common.[25] But despite the low priority given to Tibetan geography (especially surprising in view of the obsession it was to become in barely fifty years' time), Hastings began the memorandum with the observation: 'Tibet is a cold, high, mountainous country'. Half a page later he comments: 'The Caucasus formed a barrier at the south that protected reciprocally both Hindustan and Tibet from any dangerous hostilities in that quarter[26].'

Tibet, from the very beginning was imagined geographically: cold, high, mountainous, isolated, enclosed. Similarly, right from the start, Tibet as a place meant religion and religious power. Despite Hastings's failure to focus Bogle's specific attention on religious and geographical questions in his direct instructions, they make up nearly two-thirds of his memorandum. He writes, without comment, that the Dalai Lama's 'excrements are sold as charms at a great price among all the Tartar tribes of this region'.[27] We can detect here the beginning of that fascination which was to play such a powerful role in subsequent Tibetan exploration. This fascination is enhanced by Hastings's thoughts on polyandry, which take up a further third of a page – a surprisingly large amount in such a short paper.

Europe and Asia: an Archaeology of Imaginative Landscapes

Hastings's memorandum makes continual reference to the 'Chinese', 'Tartars' and 'Moghuls', and reminds us that this creation of Tibet was taking place within a much wider context of global imaginings and global imperialism. By the eighteenth century, the world had already been divided and imagined many times before. It was already an archaeological mosaic of imaginative places and landscapes. The reference to the Tartars in Hastings's memorandum, as well as in Bogle's and Turner's accounts, was a late residue of medieval European fantasies of Asia and the East. It connected this late-eighteenth-century, Classical creation of Tibet back to a totally different conception of European identity.

For most of its history, Britain had been one of the European countries most removed from the Orient, or the East. Historically and geographically it was remote from direct contact with Islam, and from the eastern border struggles experienced by the Hungarians, Russians, Poles, Austrians, Italians and Spanish. For example, whilst the Tartars were remote from Britain both in time and space, for Russia they were intensely immediate. The history of Russia had been dominated by the Mongols and Tartars;[28] imperial Russian expansion into Central Asia throughout the eighteenth century had made them anything but a remote and archaic memory. Turner's journey to Tibet, for example, coincided with the Russian annexation of the Crimean Tartars. The expansionist Russian struggles may have reversed the ancient domination, but for them no discontinuity lay between the Tartars as old oppressors and as newly subjugated peoples.

For Britain, on the other hand, the Tartars lay on the other side, not just of the Himalayas but of a historical discontinuity. The fact that they had never been a real threat meant that they were to become an ideal bearer of Romantic projections in the nineteenth and twentieth centuries. This historical and geographical discontinuity heightened the sense of the Tibetans' Otherness in the British imagination. In the eighteenth century, however, the Tartars still evoked, even for the British, the medieval European fear of unstoppable warriors streaming out from Central Asia under leaders such as Genghis Khan. So we find Turner exclaiming with surprise after an act of kindness towards him by a Tibetan: 'I take pleasure in recording this striking instance of tenderness and attention, so different from the ferocity commonly annexed to our ideas of a Tartar.'[29]

The references by Hastings, Bogle and Turner to the presence of precious metals in Tibet are also echoes of ancient fantasies. The Greek historian Herodotus wrote of large ants in the desert to the north of India that created sandhills rich with gold.[30] For many Europeans Tibet had the reputation of being something of an Asian El Dorado. Tibet was also caught up, however slightly, in the medieval fantasy of the lost Christian kingdom of Prester John. Turner, in a passage rich with imaginative resonances, also related Tibet to Ancient Egypt because of their shared ritual use of lion imagery:

> Between [Egypt] ... and Tibet, there seemed at some time or other,
> to have existed a frequent communication; and Egypt appeared even

now to merit respectful mention, whenever they named it. From hence perhaps they have derived their veneration for the sovereign of brutes ... [31]

He then goes on to connect Tibet with an even earlier milieu:

> If the lion ever existed in a state of nature here, it must have been at the same time with those vast monsters, whose bones are found in huge heaps in various parts of Tartary and Siberia at this day, and clearly point to some great convulsion and change, in the order of our globe. [32]

Such ruminations on global catastrophes, when combined with Egyptian speculations, were attempts to locate Tibet precisely within a new imaginal landscape that was emerging among the British. The close of the eighteenth century was marked by a rise of enthusiasm for both geology and Egyptology. In both cases Europe was *reconstructing* the history of the world and at the same time *redefining* itself. Such a process would reach its full development only much later, in the next century.

In these texts by Hastings, Bogle and Turner, we are confronted by an archaeology of imaginative landscapes. Sometimes their presence is revealed only by a single clue, such as a word or a phrase, but these details are doorways into ancient landscapes.

The most recent past, out of which modern Europe was struggling to reimagine itself, was dominated by the great medieval Moghul and Ottoman Empires. Whilst these were still forces to be reckoned with, their decay was obvious and the waning of their power inevitable in the face of aggressive Western expansion in Asia. [33]

In the late eighteenth century, future global politics seemed likely to be dominated by Russian imperial aggrandizement, by British colonial and commercial expansion, but above all, especially in the case of Tibet, by the largest, the most remarkable and enduring empire of all, the Chinese. The Celestial Empire was still unknown, revered and a force in Eastern politics. Its internal stagnation and decay lay hidden behind its closed frontiers. One cannot appreciate the Tibetan landscape that was forming in the imagination of eighteenth-century Britain without simultaneously understanding the era's fantasy of China.

In 1730, only fifty years before Bogle's journey, the Capuchin monk Francesco Orazio Della Penna, in his report on Tibet, had commented upon the Tibetans: 'They are also dirty and nasty, and without refinement; but from their intercourse with the Chinese in 1720 they have begun to be a little more cleanly and civilized.' [34] By comparison, when Bogle left Tibet in 1775 he exclaimed in a letter to his sister:

Farewell, ye honest and simple people! May ye long enjoy that happiness which is denied to more polished nations; and while they are engaged in the endless pursuits of avarice and ambition, defended by your barren mountains, may ye continue to live in peace and contentment, and know no wants but those of nature.[35]

A fundamental tension in eighteenth-century Western fantasies about non-European peoples is expressed here. On the one hand Europe was fascinated by the Chinese culture – ancient, orderly, refined, sophisticated, restrained. China seemed a vast land of harmony, peace, aesthetics and tranquillity, the very apogee of civilization. For example, whilst Bogle remarked that 'The manners of the Tibetans are in general very engaging', he also commented that a Tibetan friend, 'by a long residence at the Court of Peking, has improved upon them'.[36]

Della Penna, in his enthusiasm for China, was merely expressing a sentiment about Chinese civilization that had been forged into common currency by earlier Catholic missionaries to the East. Chinese aesthetics – especially interior decorating, gardening, decoration, fashion, and so on – became immensely popular for a while in eighteenth-century Europe.[37]

On the other hand, this was also the time of Rousseau and the fantasy of the 'Noble Savage'. Baudet comments: 'The eighteenth century was one of those centuries that wished to escape from itself and from the heavy burden imposed by a thousand years of culture.'[38] Hence, he continues, it 'experiences a perpetual longing for the uncivilized'. Cook's return from his epic voyage in 1771, with tales of a Pacific island paradise, Tahiti, seemed to confirm the ideas of those who felt that European culture was burdened by guilt, hypocrisy, ambition and other diseases of civilization. In Tibet these two worlds, the natural and the cultured, seemed to meet. In these early travel texts, Tibet's relation to China was used to express this tension between simplicity and sophistication, between two conflicting images of Utopia.

Locating Tibet

Turner commented that it would be advantageous to discover 'the contiguity of Tibet to the western frontier of China (for though we knew not where they were joined, yet we knew that they did actually join) ... '.[39] The rapidity of European global expansion in the eighteenth century outstripped available geographical knowledge and made old global contours redundant. It demanded an entirely new division of the world, one that was far more precise, systematic, rational and ordered. It is no coincidence that this was the period of the great map-makers: Cook set out to map the vast unknown South Pacific in 1767; Rennell initiated the immense Survey of India in 1765.[40] The ostensible reason for this rush of cartographic activity was the demand by the new global commercialism for accurate and reliable charts, routes and communications, but the next two centuries of scientific mapping were to create an entirely new sense of global inclusiveness. It was an imagination of frontiers, routes, wealth, power. Above all, by remapping (classifying, defining, measuring) the globe, Europe sought to redefine itself and its position in the world. By locating Tibet in relation to China, Britain was attempting to locate *itself*, not just geographically but imaginatively.

The old global landmarks of Tartary, Muscovy, Byzantium, the Celestial and Ottoman empires, were becoming imaginative residues, and were clearly inadequate for eighteenth-century commercial navigation. Nevertheless they gave the emerging global vision an imaginative history: they located it within time. History, ethnography and mapping became global in the eighteenth century and fortified European identity, culture and sense of place.[41] Tibet, along with other distant landscapes, helped the eighteenth-century Europeans to get their bearings, to know themselves better. It provided them with a mirror for reflection and self-criticism. Bogle, for example, wittily observed that 'the Tibetans have great faith in fortune-telling, which indeed seems to be common to all mankind, except our European philosophers, who are too wise to believe in anything.'[42] Later he exclaimed: 'Let no one who has been at a public school in Europe cry out against the Tibetans for cruelty.'[43] Unlike Turner, Bogle was always prepared to use Tibet as a springboard for criticism of Europe. In particular he was bitter about European self-satisfaction. Whilst observing monks debating he wrote, with measured irony:

> They were carried on with much vociferation and feigned warmth, and embellished with great powers of action, such as clapping hands, shaking the hand etc. These gestures are no doubt very improper and ridiculous, because they are quite different from those used by European orators, who are the true standards of what is just and what is graceful.[44]

For Bogle the Tibetan way of life had to be encountered on its own terms. Hence when confronted by some strange food he wrote: 'It is far from unsavoury, when one can get the better of European prejudices.'[45] For both Bogle and Turner, every culture had its own customs, ceremonies, manners and values. They did not travel to evaluate the Tibetans, except as a commercial proposition, and nearly all critical reflection was directed back at European self-righteous insularity.

The empirical precision of eighteenth-century mapping did not preclude its imaginative dimension. Turner proclaimed, with commendable exactitude,

Teshoo Loomboo, or Lubrong, the seat of Teshoo Lama, and the capital of that part of Tibet immediately subject to his authority, is situated in 29° 4′ 20″ north latitude, and 89° 7′ east longitude, from Greenwich.[46]

However, he was locating Greenwich just as much as Tibet – indeed, he was gathering the landscapes of the world around it. Remoteness became a measurable and empirical fact as Greenwich moved to the centre of the global map. Tibet became remote from, yet also connected to, Britain.

Within this eighteenth-century global redistribution of imaginative and material power, Chinese hegemony was unquestioned. In a sense it was the *only* extant established world empire. Russian expansion was still only a distant concern. For instance, Turner discovered that commercial overtures had been made by the Russians towards Tibet, but only with a limited degree of success because China jealously guarded its imperial rights.[47] As yet, British expansionist aspirations were too unformed for the Russian presence in Tibet to be a threat. The main concern was China. Following the spectacular Chinese defeat of the Gurkhas in Tibet and then in Nepal, a British observer nervously exclaimed: 'This government now beheld for the first time, the extraordinary spectacle of a numerous Chinese force occupying a position which probably afforded it a distant view of the valley of the Ganges, and of the riches of the East India Company's possessions.'[48] A regular commercial interchange with the mysterious and powerful Chinese Empire was one thing, but having the Chinese camped on the frontier of British Bengal was quite another. For the time being, an Asiatic power still had hegemony in Asia, but Europe was steadily moving towards its own unique form of geopolitics.

Geographically and imaginatively for Britain, Tibet lay 'somewhere' between China, India, Siberia and the expanse of Central Asia.[49] Baudet writes of the eighteenth century: 'East and West still had no separate identity.'[50] The various images of the Other – the exotic, the primitive, and so on – were all jumbled up geographically, all available for any indiscriminate use. The 'Orient' had scarcely arrived, but by the close of the eighteenth century the imaginative landscapes of the globe were beginning to acquire that systematization, orderliness and categorization so characteristic of the late nineteenth and twentieth centuries.[51] British exploration of Tibet coincided exactly with this new revisioning of the globe. It drew extensively upon the linguistic discoveries in Sanskrit and Arabic, the beginnings of 'scientific' ethnography – by the French in Egypt, by the British in India.[52] But Tibet, unlike most of the 'Orient', was studied less as a 'textual universe' and more as a *visual* display, as an integral *place*.[53]

The Frontier as a Place

1. Setting Out

Whilst Tibet was a place of curiosity and interest for a few Europeans in the late eighteenth century, it was not yet the object of all-consuming fascination it was to become in less than a hundred years. So Bogle, on receiving his instructions to travel to Tibet, remarked:

> I was glad of the opportunity which this journey through a country hitherto unfrequented by Europeans would give me of showing my zeal for the Governor's service, at the same time that it gratified a fondness I always had for travelling, and would afford me some respite from that close and sedentary business in which I had for some years been engaged.[54]

Tibet was not yet a *place*, it was still only an unfamiliar geographical location. Exploration, too, was not yet a heroic venture necessitating arduous preparations. Bogle's response was merely one of pleasure, but even the cause of his delight was not specifically Tibet itself, rather the prospect of visiting a place unknown to Europeans and of excelling in his duty to the Company. His hopes lay not with any athletic mountain mysticism, so common among later aspirations to reach Tibet, but simply with getting away from his desk job and into the outside world. His expectation was not of mountain adventures but of convivial travel.

2. Approaching the Frontier

Nevertheless, the *entry* into Tibet was still an event of significance. It is an occasion that we will encounter throughout Tibetan travel literature. Even at this early stage, Tibet lay on the other side of a frontier, and to enter it one had to cross a threshold. Turner wrote of the 'enormous height, and vast extent of the mountains' – the 'Mons Imaus', the 'Himaloya', the 'Bod-la'.[55] When he first saw this mountain range directly, he exclaimed:

> The vastness and obscurity of this enormous boundary, remote and indistinct as it appeared when it first burst upon the sight in ill-defined and fantastic shapes, could not but excite very powerful emotions in the mind; and I looked upon the formidable barrier I had to pass with mingled awe and admiration.[56]

It was these unbelievable mountains, not Tibet, that initially evoked the awe of the British and other Europeans. Bogle commented, in a similarly dramatic way, 'The chain of mountains which stretches along the northern frontier of Bengal, 18 miles distant, seemed over our heads.'[57] Tibet did not simply lie over the other side of these vast unexplored mountains but somehow partook of them, of their Otherness, of their mystery and power.

These mountains did not just *separate* Tibet and India, but created a qualitative difference in the way each place was imagined. Turner, for example, wrote that the 'strangeness, prevailing between Bengal and Bootan' was almost equal to that of the mountains that lay in between.[58] The mountains were a zone of transformation, of transition between one mode of imagining and another. Whilst sacred space must have a clearly defined boundary, this boundary or frontier is a place in its own right.[59] The Himalayan range was such a place of fascination, of awe, of mystery, for these eighteenth-century travellers and for others who followed. In their accounts the apparently simple action of crossing from one imaginative space to another became far more complex. The frontier was first approached and then entered. Within the boundary-place travellers were suspended between two imaginings. Leaving it, they then crossed the final threshold and entered the land on-the-other-side. Each of these three movements has an imaginative quality all its own. In the case of these early British travellers it was the direct experience of this boundary-place that coloured their perception of the unknown place on-the-other-side. For later travellers, however, Tibet had itself become a place of fascination, and this sacred landscape then affected in its turn the experience of the mountain frontier. Fantasies about the one reinforced fantasies about the other.

3. Entering the Frontier

Upon entering the Himalayan range, Bogle paused at a vantage point for a last view of Bengal: 'It is impossible to conceive any change of country more abrupt or any contrast more striking.'[60] After gazing at the extensive plains of Bengal, he exclaimed:

> Whether it be that I am partial to hills or not, I beheld the opposite part of the prospect with much greater pleasure. The rapid descent, the deep glens, the hills covered with trees the most lofty and luxuriant, the town of Buxa-Duar immediately below at a great distance, and behind nothing but mountains with their tops hid in the clouds.[61]

The mountains, whose immense height was to be greeted with disbelief when it was estimated a few years later, marked an abrupt break, a discontinuity that was geographical, cultural and imaginative.

4. *The Passage across the Threshold*

Whilst Tibet was by no means the sacred landscape it was later to become in Western fantasies, nevertheless the moment of entry for Bogle and Turner was replete with pregnant symbolism. As they stepped out from the frontier, and crossed over the last summit before Tibet, both were confronted by the plain of Phari. There was a certain irony in this first glimpse of Tibet. The expectation was of mountainous country, yet by comparison with what they had just come through, Tibet seemed quite *flat*. Bogle complained that this plain, whilst surrounded by hills and mountains, was 'on every account abundantly bleak, and bare and uncomfortable'.[62] Even the Tibetans seemed less robust and well-built than the people of the mountain frontier.[63]

Also, by one of those quirks of fate that seem to occur in history, the route by which Britain first gained access to Tibet entered that country at a place set aside for funerals. Bogle commented: 'The first object that strikes you as you go down the hill into Tibet, is a mount in the middle of the plain. It is where the people of Pari-jong expose their dead.'[64] Turner, nine years later made exactly the same observation. Bogle also happened to arrive just as a body was being carried to the hill: 'Eagles, hawks, ravens, and other carnivorous birds were soaring about in expectation of their prey.'[65]

When considering these kinds of phenomena it is tempting to endow them with deep symbolic significance, with a presentiment far beyond that of mere chance. So, Tibetans are Tartars; the word 'Tartar' comes from Tartarus, the river of the Netherworld; and here guarding the threshold of that landscape is a scene of desolation and death, etc., etc. Obviously such an approach could be facile, yet we must tread carefully. Bogle's and Turner's attention was *drawn* to this phenomenon. At that precise moment of entry they selected *that* specific feature to focus upon. Both men quickly seized the opportunity to deliver a short résumé on Tibetan burial practices. Bogles was well informed and discussed the general variations in this custom, whereas Turner was obviously quite struck solely by the one immediately in front of him. Is it significant that the first paragraphs written directly about Tibet by British travellers should be devoted to the unusual funeral rites of that country?

Travel journals create places rather than discover them. They construct these places from selective perceptions, from unequal weight given to various themes and from the manner in which all these are then placed in relationship to each other. From such a perspective, these first moments, these first glimpses, are crucial. We can often look back at the initial moments in a new place – a country, a town, or a work situation – and smile at our first impressions. They may have an intuitive truth about them, a crisp freshness, yet they subsequently seem to belong to a different world once we become familiar with the new environment. Such initial impressions and observations clearly tell us as much about our own fantasies as about the place itself. The question, then, is not what Bogle and Turner saw, but what they selected to be of significance; not what was presented to them, but what they chose to comment upon, and in what order. As we have seen right from the start, even before British travellers had reached Tibet, it was imagined as a place of difference. If it was not yet a place of mystery and fascination (qualities which became dominant only in a later cultural milieu), then at least Tibet represented an extreme of Otherness. It was a truly *unknown* place. The bizarre funeral – which, as Turner remarked, 'is in direct opposition to the practice of almost all other nations' – was an ideal signifier for eighteenth-century British fantasies about Tibetan Otherness.[66]

For the next two weeks, Bogle made his way towards his planned rendezvous with the Panchen Lama. Such was the subsequent intensity of this encounter that it overshadowed this first part of his journey, yet these two weeks marked his *entry* into Tibet. Unlike the long period of close personal contact with Tibetans and his almost uneventful and settled life, these intitial weeks were full of constant travel and of hasty but perceptive glimpses along the route. In rapid succession we are introduced to most of the themes that were to fascinate Europeans for the next hundred and fifty years – funerals, dogs, diplomacy, bureaucracy, religion, polyandry, national character, dirt, landscape views and lamaistic power.[67]

The Imagination of Mountains

From the inception of British involvement, Tibet and its religion were imagined geographically. Landscape, culture and place were inextricably enmeshed. Whilst Tibetan religion was given a geographical basis, mountain landscape was given a spiritual basis.

In these travel texts, the passages of landscape description are critical for understanding the prevailing attitude towards nature. In the days before photography, such word-images were the main resource of explorer-travellers, but it would be a mistake to read these descriptive passages (sketches and photographs too) as if they were merely objective accounts of the landscape. They express an imaginative relation to the environment and reveal the fantasies of the author as much as they depict the object of description. We are used to discussing landscape paintings in terms of artistic style – Rococo, Romantic, Expressionist, Impressionist, Cubist, Surrealist, and so on. Passages of word-painting (as it later became known) must also be read stylistically in terms of their root-metaphors. In the early eighteenth century, for example, it was generally believed that natural landscape could not improve the mind and hence was not so worthy of artistic portrayal as mythological and biblical themes.[68] Such a devaluation continued to exert its presence right through the century. Landscape painting continued to be placed low on the scale of artistic values until the success of the Romantic revolution; hence we find an ambivalence in Bogle's and Turner's accounts. The actual passages of evocative landscape description are surprisingly few as compared with later travel texts. Also, most of them are restrained attempts at an objective realism. Bogle wrote:

> On the former part of the journey there were nothing but glens, now there are valleys. But the sides of the mountains are more bare; there are few large trees, mostly fir; the road is more level, except at two or three places ... [69]

Alternatively, the budding sciences of botany and geology were used for landscape description: 'pine-apples, mango tree and saul timber are frequently to be met with in the forests or jungles. Find many orange trees towards the foot of the hills, ... '.[70] Or again, 'The mountain is composed in some places of clay; but for the most part it consists of a flinty stone, striated with talc, and intermixed with marble.'[71] Such descriptive passages highlight the eclectic 'scientific' curiosity towards nature so characteristic of these early travellers. However, they are generally only lists of things. Only vague attempts are made to compose them into a coherent story. (The discovery of the concept of 'environment', for example, as an organizing schema lay some years in the future.)

But here, amidst these sober, restrained and studied appraisals, we come across glimpses of other landscape aesthetics. Turner exclaimed:

> The prospects, between abrupt and lofty prominences, were inconceivably grand: hills, clothed to their very summits with trees, dark and deep glens, and the tops of the highest mountains, lost in the clouds, constituted a scene of extraordinary magnificence and sublimity.[72]

He was invoking the sublime, the Romantic imagination of landscape. The essence of such a perspective depended upon four factors: an immense scale; a sense of natural power; contrasting extremes; and a dynamic verticality. Only nine years earlier, Bogle had been slightly hesitant about revealing his feelings about the landscape. Almost apologetically, he commented:

> Whether it be that I am partial to hills or not, I beheld the opposite part of the prospect [the mountains rather than the plains] with

much greater pleasure. The rapid descent, the deep glens, the hills covered with trees the most lofty and luxuriant ... and behind nothing but mountains with their tops hidden in the clouds.[73]

Similar themes echo through both Bogle's and Turner's accounts. Both travellers, whilst passing through the mountain frontier, experienced something entirely new, something largely outside European sensibility. Even in Europe, the Alps were only just beginning to attract travellers and explorers rather than mere mountain-viewers and sightseers. It has been said that in 1755 the fashion of climbing mountains and reviewing glaciers had not yet been introduced into Switzerland, but by 1783 the first rush of travellers and sightseers had occurred.[74] The European imagination was just beginning to accommodate itself fully to the Alps. The Himalayas, like the Carpathians, the Rockies and the Andes, were to demand another, future revolution in landscape aesthetics.

In another passage Turner writes:

The weather was serene, the atmosphere clear, and the sun shone full upon the distant mountains. In the rear of all, swelling high above the rest, the mountains of Ghassa were distinctly visible, clothed in perpetual snow, whose smooth unsullied surface was nobly contrasted by the deeply shaded rocky eminences in the foreground. A few luminous and fleecy clouds hung on the border of the horizon, which as they verged towards the snow assumed a darker and thicker appearance, adding much to the effect of this beautiful view.[75]

Here is delight in variety and contrast – high/low, light/dark. This contrast reveals a certain ambivalence towards the landscape mountains. These high summits had traditionally been imagined as the dwelling-places of both malevolent and benevolent supernatural beings. In Bogle's and Turner's accounts, the dark glens, the deep shadows, were integral to their mountain aesthetics.[76] The image had not yet been irrevocably split into pure peaks and unwholesome valleys, but the beginnings of such a one-sided attitude can be detected in the passage from Turner quoted above, where the 'unsullied' snow increases in nobility when contrasted with the darker regions of the landscape.

Each of these three descriptions of mountain views provides evidence of the new Romanticism, with its emphasis on expansiveness and an uplifting emotional response to landscape. There was still a human scale to such a mountain appreciation: one was *filled* with the sense of the sublime.[77] But the barren immensity and the a-human Otherness of the Himalayas still eluded even this radically new aesthetic. Bogle continually complained about the incessant 'bleak bare hills' and their failure to inspire a fine prospect.[78] Turner similarly wrote: 'The country now opened and improved ... and the view of the trees and houses, afforded a very grateful change from the dreariness of our late prospects.'[79] Later, he commented: 'I took an opportunity to ascend the rock, but my expectations were by no means realized by the view I had from it. Bare narrow valleys, naked hills, and a biting frosty air, impressed my senses with a picture inhospitable, bleak, sterile in the extreme.'[80] Such awful barrenness had clearly not yet acquired its connotations of majesty, nor of revealing God's power and human insignificance.[81]

The picturesque is still encountered in these passages, and frequently Bogle and Turner retreated to its safe familiarity:

> The banks of the river are lined with willows and the surrounding mountains have some timbered trees, inter-mixed with the fir and pine; whilst a number of single houses and some monasteries, having orchards and hanging fields of corn about them, ornament the finely romantic views, with which we were delighted from every part of this valley.[82]

Such an evaluation of landscape was well established and was familiar territory to the late-eighteenth-century traveller.

The illustrations in Turner's account, drawn by his companion, Samuel Davis, reveal a mixture of naturalism and Rococo artificiality.[83] An illustration showing the Palace of Punukka in Bhutan, for example, has two small figures in the foreground – one lying relaxed under a tree, the other walking unhurriedly by the side of a lake. Such a view is an embodiment of the Rococo pastoral dream: warm, romantic landscapes, and tranquillity. In Kirkpatrick's book, an illustration of Kathmandu is similarly elegaic and Arcadian. Small figures are sitting in groups; travellers leisurely cross a bridge or stand in conversation by the river's edge. These illustrations followed established formulae: the clouds are obviously decorative, the mountains are clearly hovering between a realism derived from close observation and a certain vague boldness of outline used purely for effect.[84]

In these sketches there is also the unmistakable orderliness and geometric regularity so dear to the eighteenth century. Irregularity was abhorred. Turner wrote: 'Bootan presents to the view nothing but the most misshapen irregularities.' He then continued:

> Tibet ... strikes a traveller, at first sight, as one of the least favoured countries under heaven ... It exhibits only low rocky hills, without any visible vegetation, or extensive arid plains, both of the most stern and stubborn aspect.[85]

44

Such aesthetics were also applied to Tibetan architecture: 'the windows, regular, flat-roofed and of good appearance from without; within, irregular and smoked'.[86] At one point Turner was refreshed by a welcome display of 'regularity and softness of feature, that is seldom seen in the wild but sublime scenery of Bootan'.[87]

There are therefore four contending landscape aesthetics in these journals: the Classic (formal, regular); the Picturesque (intimacy, delight, variety); the Romantic (uplifting, emotional, sublime); and the Naturalistic (close attention to detail, objective, representative). Any land form which could not be encompassed by one of these four perspectives was either depreciated or simply ignored, but these were early days in Europe's involvement with mountains. Significantly, in these eighteenth-century texts, no direct comparisons were made with the Alps. Only with increasing Alpine familiarity in the nineteenth century do we find them constantly invoked as Europeans attempted to come to terms with the aesthetic challenge posed by the more immense Himalayas.

The late eighteenth century was a time of transition and evolved its own synthesis of restrained Romantic-Picturesque. Turner wrote:

> We were presented with many beautiful and highly romantic views. The sides of the montains thinly clothed with unthrifty pines, rapid flow and hollow roar of the river, partly concealed by clustering trees, enclosed in high verdant banks, which rose, as they receded, into bold rocks, with here and there a fir stirring from a crevice, whilst other ridges appeared completely covered with them, served to combine the most striking features of wild nature in her barren, as well as her most luxuriant dress.[88]

At this point we can see the basis being laid for a genuine, if somewhat restrained, mountain mysticism. Critical developments in this process included the emancipation of landscape from the evaluations of a dogmatic theology, the increasing attention given to detailed observation (encouraged by the popularity of geology, geography and botany, as well as by the close encounter between mountaineer and landscape), and the sudden availability of a variety of mountain ranges for the purposes of comparison (Alps, Carpathians, Himalayas, Rockies, Andes).[89] The earlier love of the picturesque and of geometric formality began to be supplemented by a desire for direct attention to details – either outwardly, towards the objective sensual landscape, or inwardly, towards the experiential response.

The Mythology of Mountain Air and Peoples

Whilst the Romantic vision of splendid mountains and sublime experiences seems to be of most obvious relevance to notions of *sacred* landscape, it would be an error to leave the apparently more restrained fantasies of the eighteenth century with too much haste. The Romantic imagination, in one form or another, will dominate the story of Tibetan travel for the remainder of its duration, so this 'eighteenth-century Tibet' offers a singular opportunity to examine a different and earlier aesthetic. In addition to the passages of landscape description discussed above, two other themes provide clues to the mythological nature of this pre-Romantic sensibility: the quality of mountain air, and the character of the indigenous people.

When de Saussure, that pioneer of Alpine exploration, climbed Mont Blanc just a few years after Turner's return from Tibet, he took with him a large number of scientific instruments. He wished to determine the effect of rarefied air on breathing. On his visit to Monte Rosa in 1789 he used mules to carry, among other instruments, 'a glass sphere, a foot in diameter, for measuring the density of the air, a weighing machine, [and] a tent to use it in … '.[90] As James Hillman points out, the eighteenth century was the age when air was the prime focus of scientific fascination. Beginning with Boyle's studies in the late seventeenth century, the attention given to airs and gases reached its peak by the close of the eighteenth.[91]

Turner's account is more restrained and formal than Bogle's. It harks back to the closing phases of the Enlightenment, whereas Bogle's anticipates the dawn of the Romantic era. Throughout his account Turner makes repeated observations about various airs. At one point on his journey he comments: 'The most luxuriant trees … clothe the skirts only of the loftiest mountains: these before us … carry their heads into an atmosphere, too rare to afford nourishment to the great and flourishing productions of the vegetable kingdom.' He notices that recluses seem to prefer 'these pure regions and … judiciously abandon the low hollows, with their putrid and humid exhalations … '.[92]

The ancient ambivalence towards mountain peaks had shifted from a belief in various demons into a concern about the different qualities of air. At high altitude the 'air' cannot provide nourishment: it is almost *too* pure. At low altitude the air is malevolent. Later, as he crosses the last pass into Tibet, Turner comments on the superstitions of the Tibetans. They believe in *genii loci* or spirits:

> No mountain is thought to be wholly exempt from their influence;
> but they are particularly given to range in the most elevated regions;
> where, drenched with dews, and worried by tempestuous weather,

they are supposed to deal around them, in ill-humour, their baneful spells, to harass and annoy the traveller.[93]

Turner quite clearly believed he was from a culture that had left such superstitions behind, yet the evidence clearly shows that the same metaphor, the same ambivalence, remains, albeit in a scientific guise. For example, later he writes distastefully about a flat, swampy region: 'The exhalation', from such a surface of vegetable matter and swamps, increased by an additional degree of heat from the reflection of the hills, affect the air to a considerable extent, and render it highly injurious to strangers ... '.[94] In Turner's imagination it was the *air* which was harmful, not spirits or bacteria; it was the air which failed to sustain rich vegetation, not the soil or the climate, nor the *genius loci*.

Mountain air was unexplored territory. At one point Turner was anxious not to linger upon a lofty summit overlooking the low humid plains of Bengal. He reasoned that such a peak, 'from its superior eleva-tion, stands in the way, to intercept much of the vapour exhaled from the extensive waste, that lies spread far and wide beneath its base'.[95] He was particularly fascinated by the prevalence among mountain-dwellers of goitre, the disease which causes a massive glandular swelling at the throat. The usual theory traced its cause to snow water, but Turner thought otherwise, and suggested that the disease proceeded 'from a peculiarity in the air of situations in the vicinity of mountains ...'.[96] The lower classes, he argued, are most open to risk because they are the 'most exposed to the unguarded influence of the weather, the various changes that take place in the air of such situations'. Quite clearly the air served Turner as a vessel for something unresolved in his imagination.

The Enlightenment stands between the older use of demons as an objective explanatory principle and the Romantic's proto-psychological celebration of subjective experience. An earlier traveller would have at-tributed uncomfortable or exalted feelings totally to the influence of nature spirits residing at that particular place. The later Romantics would attribute such experiences to a subtle yet profound interaction between the imagination of the traveller and the landscape. Turner never resorted to spirits and only occasionally to personalistic psychology. Instead he used the explanations of a materialistic science: he blamed the air. But within such a seemingly objective process we can detect the imagination at work.[97]

Even though Turner assigned ambivalent properties to the 'air' at both high and low altitudes, he seemed consistently to favour the pure air of the mountain heights. He was quite surprised that the Tibetans, living at a higher altitude than the Bhutanese, were less robust. He argued that they were exposed to more pure and rarefied air; also, they were at a remove from 'stagnant waters' which 'charge the air with noxious vapours'.[98] He consistently mentioned the low lands in terms of 'noxious exhalations'.[99] He was almost surprised that such regions and such air could support any life at all', and commented: 'its influence hath wholly debased in them the form, the size, and the strength of human creatures.'[100] We can sense here the beginnings of that theme which was to dominate future Tibetan travel literature: the relation between altitude and cultural personality. So Turner contrasted 'the feeble bodied and meek spirited native of Bengal and their active and Herculean neighbours, the mountaineers of Bootan'.[101] In later texts we shall find an almost unequivocal division between the positive qualities of those who live at the highest altitudes and the negative attributes of those who live down in the valleys or on the plains. Tibetans living at the highest altitudes are considered to be naturally favourably endowed. The complex concept of 'environment' is evoked in the nineteenth century to help provide a scientific explanation for this phenomenon, but Turner did not have this concept at his disposal.

Turner did not irrevocably separate the pure heights from the noxious depths. There is a slight tension in his account. Nevertheless, 'up there' live the spiritual recluses, 'up there' one expects to find the most perfectly formed race of individuals; down in the forests and jungles one finds 'debased' humans. Also in Turner's imagination, such characteristics, whether wholesome or not, were confined to *physical* qualities and did not, as in subsequent accounts, include mental and spiritual ones. The bias favouring the people of the mountains in both Bogle's and Turner's accounts was fundamentally related to the imagination of landscape. The local people were figures in a landscape; from the landscape they derived their qualities.

For Bogle, it was not so much the *air* as the isolation and protection they afforded from the *cultural* contamination of civilization that gave mountains their special significance, but such an attitude emerged from precisely the same Enlightenment milieu that gave rise to Turner's fascination with air. Bogle pictured common sense, security, comfort and simple life as existing in the remote mountains. In the nineteenth and twentieth centuries the high mountains gradually supplemented, if not replaced, remote islands as the imagined location of idealized communities. This process culminated in the twentieth-century fantasy of Shangri-La.

Fascination with air, images of unsullied mountain peaks, uncontaminated simplicity of mountain life: all share a common thread. They are all images of aspiration – of a desire to transcend, or just to escape from, a materialistic world. Whilst Turner's repetitive brooding over the various kinds of air may seem far removed from religious questions, we have seen its continuity with traditional landscape mythologizing. Indeed, his fantasies provide an important link between an older nature worship and Romantic nature mysticism. Both his studied ruminations and Bogle's

Arcadian enthusiasms are two sides of the same coin. They express, at its fullest tension, the eighteenth-century spiritual dilemma concerning nature, a tension that was to be resolved only with the Romantic solution.

Tibetan Religion and the Geopolitical Imagination

Even in the eighteenth century Tibetan religion and landscape followed parallel trajectories in Western imaginings. Subsequently we find fantasies about the one influencing and reinforcing fantasies about the other. However, at this early stage the religion did not even have a name. Hastings, in his memorandum on Tibet, stated: 'Any information with regard to the antiquity and to the creed of this religion, as well as to the authority, civil and ecclesiastical, of the lamas, could not fail to be extremely interesting.'[102] In this passage he was posing a series of questions that would preoccupy the West for most of the next two centuries. The issue of power was pivotal. In addition, there was the question of where to locate this religion within the broad spectrum of known faiths. Finally, Hastings was curious about its antiquity and its origins. Tibetan religion, like that of Ancient Egypt, was increasingly to become a vital link in the West's imaginative connection with *memoria*, with the past, with the Ancients. However, in the eighteenth century Tibetan religion had a low priority in the minds of the British, and despite the curiosity Hastings showed in his memorandum no mention was made about it in either of the two official directives issued to Bogle.

At this stage in the century, Eastern religion was still predominantly the object of either scorn by Christian fundamentalists or superficial curiosity by social dilettantes. Hastings was one of a select few who valued its spiritual insights. He had encouraged a translation of the *Bhagavad-Gita*, the first direct translation from Sanskrit into English. He used to quote passages from it in letters to his wife.[103] The great founder of Western Sanskrit scholarship, William Jones, received much assistance and support from Hastings. Both would have been familiar with the detailed accounts of Tibetan religion given by the earlier Jesuit and Capuchin missionaries to Tibet. But it was to be Turner's journal which was to provide the West with its only direct observation of Tibetan religion by a non-ordained traveller for many years.

Hastings wrote: 'We are told that the Dalai Lama is held to be an incarnation of the legislator prophet, or god Buddha or Fo, who over all Hindustan gives his name (like Thauth or Mercury, the prophet legislator and god of the Egyptians) to the planet Mercury, and to the fourth day of the week.'[104] Buddhism as a distinct religion was as yet unknown; instead, Hastings attempted to relate the Buddha to known archaic, Classical and Hindu mythology. Here he was prefiguring later work by Jones, who in many ways founded comparative mythology. He compared the Indian gods and philosophers with those of Classical Greece: Maru was Saturn and Indra was Jupiter, whilst Vilimic, Vyasa and Kalidasa were the Hindu equivalents of Homer, Plato and Pindar.[105] Jones identified the Buddha with Odin, whilst Chambers, in the first mention of Buddhism in the 1780s, correlated the Buddha with Mercury, thus agreeing with Hastings. In addition to inaugurating comparative mythology and Indo-European studies, Jones, perhaps inadvertently, realised that any East–West dialogue had to strike a note which resonated on a deep symbolic level. On such a level, it is unimportant whether Indra can be truly substituted for Jupiter. Greek culture was held in almost uncritical and reverent esteem in England: it was viewed as the exemplary model of philosophy, art and culture.[106] Jones's comparison touched upon a root-metaphor of eighteenth-and nineteenth-century European belief. It struck a chord in the mythological foundations of European ideals, and helped to raise the status of Indian culture in the West.

Surprisingly, Turner's otherwise detailed account contains only a single reference to the Buddha and Buddhism. When he mentions the Buddha and Tibetan religion, he does so in the context of world religion: 'It seems then, to be the schismatical offspring of the religion of the Hindoos, deriving its origin from one of the followers of that faith, a disciple of Budh, who first broached the doctrine which now prevails over the wide extent of Tartary.'[107] Turner observed that the name of the founder varies in different countries: 'he is styled Godama or Gowtama, in Assam and Ava; Samana, in Siam; Amida Buth, in Japan; Fohi, in China; Budha and Shakamuna, in Bengal and Hindostan; Dherma Raja and Mahamoonie in Bootan and Tibet.' Twenty years after Hastings's memorandum, Kirkpatrick, in his account of Nepal, referred to 'the Boudhite system of theology, at present so little understood'.[108] Clearly the closing two decades of the eighteenth century were critical in the formation of Western ideas about Buddhism as a world religious system, and in particular about the Tibetan version of it.

The notion of Buddhism as a distinct world religion emerged in the context of four other such faiths: Christianity, Islam, Hinduism and Confucianism. The last, seen purely as a system of ethics and morals, and as clearly unique to China, was seldom invoked in a direct comparison with Tibetan religion. References to the other three occur continually throughout these early travel texts. Christianity, of course, was the 'known' religion and was subjected to a wide range of attitudes: from scorn and indifference by sceptical philosophers, to a fervent belief in its sole claim to spiritual truth. Hastings, Bogle and Turner lay somewhere in between these positions, but Bogle, in particular, overlooked no opportunity to use Tibetan values as a way of critically reflecting back upon European culture. All three men showed a remarkable tolerance and open-mindedness towards Tibetan religion. Hastings went so far as to encourage the building of a Tibetan temple in Bengal, albeit primarily for commercial reasons. Travel accounts from the seventeenth century to the nineteenth constantly compared Tibetan religion with Roman Catholicism. Bogle, for example, suggested a parallel between the Dalai Lama and

> the ancient Roman Pontiffs. The situation of the former, with respect to the monarchs of China, might well be compared with the protection and authority, which the successors of St Peter derived from the German emperors. Their pretensions to infallibility, the veneration in which they are held by the people, the wide extent of their spiritual dominion ... are perfectly similar.

Turner, too, was struck by a similarity between Tibetan ritual and the Catholic Mass.[109]

Hinduism was, of course, the religion of the people over which the British ruled, and whilst Tibetan religion was clearly related to Hinduism, the travellers were also quick to point out how they differed. Despite Hastings's and Jones's respect for Hindu *scriptures*, the general attitude towards the Hindus themselves, in both Bogle's and Turner's accounts, was somewhat derogatory. Bogle wrote: 'The Gentoo [Hindu] Fakirs, as far as I can judge, are in general a very worthless set of people, devoid of principle ...'.[110] They were contrasted unfavourably with the high ideals of Hindu religion. Bogle also contrasted 'the plain, honest manners of the Tibetans' with 'the fulsome compliments and cringing humility' of some Hindu visitors.[111] In addition, Turner observed with relief the Tibetans' relative freedom from prejudices and complexities of caste. In contrast to the apparent confusion in Hinduism between worldly and spiritual authority, he praised the 'system and order' of the Tibetans, and their 'sober and reflecting character'.[112] In eighteenth-century comparisons with Hinduism, Tibetan religion always came out best on the level of daily practice, despite the respect shown to Hindu texts. It was as if the orderly religion of the mountains, like its lofty air, was preferable to that of the plains, with its attendant murky and debilitating vapours.

Islam was the old enemy of Christian culture against which Europe had struggled to define itself for nearly a thousand years. As Europe expanded its geographical horizons in the eighteenth century, far beyond Islamic countries, it still used the old relationship to orientate itself. Whilst Islamic literature had begun to occupy a respected place in eighteenth-century European intellectual thought, in these accounts of Tibet Islam is presented in a less auspicious light.[113] For Turner Islam meant 'fanatical zeal' and a 'hostility ... against all who are not its professors'.[114] Compared with Tibetan religion, Islam was one of militant intolerance. Observing the Panchen Lama's compassion towards some 'Mussulman fakirs', despite Islamic hostility towards Tibetan religion, Bogle exclaimed: 'he is possessed of much Christian charity'.[115] Clearly Islam was being invoked in order to highlight the gentle and tolerant qualities of Tibetan religion.

The wide influence of Tibetan religion throughout Central Asia, and its kinship with Asian religions generally, was consistently remarked upon.[116] Turner commented that the Panchen Lama was 'respected and obeyed through all the region of Tartary; nor was his influence bounded, but by the limits of the extensive empire of China'.[117] China's prestigious place in the Western imagination also gave added lustre to the authority of this strange, unknown Tibetan religion, to which even the Celestial Emperor bowed his head. Tibetan religion therefore became firmly integrated into Britain's new global geopolitical awareness.

Religious System and Secular Power

Turner was initially struck by how conspicuous and extensive religious practices were in Tibet: obviously religion was central to the daily coherence of Tibetan life.[118] At the heart of this social coherence, he observed a symbiotic relationship between two entirely different cultural orders:

> The Nation is divided into two distinct and separate classes, those who carry on the business of the world, and those who hold intercourse with heaven. No interference of the laity ever interrupts the regulated duties of the clergy. The latter ... take charge of all their spiritual concerns; and the former by their labours, enrich and populate the 'state'.[119]

He made it quite clear that he respected such a clearly regulated social system: 'Both, united in one common bond of union, the one part to labour, the other to pray, enjoy peace and harmony, the fruits of their industry.'[120] Turner, that late representative of the Enlightenment, was clearly drawn to this union between two discrete, mutually non-interfering, complementary divisions of society. He claimed that because of such a harmonious system, the Tibetans 'find it unnecessary to support a single man in arms'. Throughout their accounts both Bogle and Turner make it abundantly clear that they felt religion and commerce should refrain from any interference in each other's sphere of influence. At one point, for example, Bogle was obliged to discuss Christianity with the Panchen Lama: 'I had no mind to attempt an explanation of the mysteries of the Trinity. I felt myself unequal to it ... The answer I gave him was in the same tolerant spirit [as he had shown]: for I am not sent as a missionary ... '.[121] Turner wrote in a similar vein: 'with the errors of their opinions or their practice,

I had no concern'.[122] Both men reassured the Tibetans that the British clergy stay in Britain and have no inclination towards missionary activity.

Both travellers belonged to the vanguard of an elite bureaucracy that was to figure so prominently and proudly in British fantasies of Victorian India. The gentleman bureaucracy of the East India Company had not yet become the formidable imperial Indian Civil Service, but even at this early stage interest was being shown in other traditions of orderly and well-regulated administration. China, with its Confucian ideals of government, was considered exemplary. Its vast bureaucracy, apparently based solely upon examination and merit, drew the admiration of many, including Voltaire.[123] The diplomatic nuances and cultured manners of Tibetan officials had already been noticed and seemed to complement the smooth-running system of mutual exchange between secular and spiritual life. In addition, the system of election by reincarnation drew Bogle's admiration:

> The apparent wisdom of this system is evident. In other governments, to qualify a person for the supreme administration requires a course of study and observation too long for human life; and after all, the waywardness of subjects will dispute his comments; but in Bhutan the Chief Magistrate is instructed by the experience of ages and his orders carry with them all the weight which on this account they deserve.[124]

Bogle seemed to be entranced by a vision of well-regulated government administered by divine elites. Turner, too, was drawn to the order and authority so characteristic of this religious system, which seemed to embody a synthesis between Platonic elite inspiration and the Classical era's love of system, order and regulation.[125] But Turner was less sure than Bogle about the reincarnation lineage, with its absolute authority. He reflected that 'the mind readily obeys the superiority it has been accustomed to acknowledge'. He raised questions about the absoluteness of the Lama's power, and whilst not overtly passing judgement seemed reticent about giving it unqualified approval:

> A sovereign-Lama, immaculate, immortal, omnipresent, and omniscient is placed at the summit of their fabric. He is esteemed the vice-regent of the only God, the mediator between mortals and the Supreme ... He is also the centre of all civil government, which derives from his authority all its influence and power.[126]

This Tibetan blend of an absolute power legitimated by mystical doctrines, combined with a well-regulated and orderly administration, was to fascinate Westerners for the next two hundred years. As we shall see, attitudes towards it would fluctuate between the extremes of approval and repugnance. If geography and religion were inseparable from the start of British imaginings on Tibet, so too were the unlikely partners of bureaucratic power and religion.[127]

Lhasa: the City of Power

Perhaps the single most important discovery that Bogle made – and Turner subsequently confirmed – was the critical importance of Lhasa. In this city seemed to be concentrated all the supreme authority of Tibet: both spiritual and secular, both actual and symbolic. In these eighteenth-century accounts, Lhasa as the unreachable quintessence of Tibet was born. Whilst neither man reached this remote and aloof city, its presence brooded continually over their journeys. The extraordinary centralization of power in Tibet – not just in the Dalai Lama but also in the city of Lhasa – had not previously been emphasized,[128] but it was to become an obsession with both the British and the Tibetans. The former increasingly saw Lhasa as the key to meaningful and influential communication with supreme Tibetan authority; the latter regarded the protection, sanctity and isolation of this city as essential for the maintenance of national and religious integrity. From this moment on, Lhasa emerged as a central character in the story of Tibetan exploration. It was to take its place alongside Mecca and the source of the Nile as one of the fabled places, one of the supreme goals, of nineteenth-century European exploration. The extreme reverence shown by the Chinese Emperor towards Tibetan religion also helped to create the fantasy of Lhasa as the Rome of Central Asia,[129] but for these early travellers, who perhaps could have easily reached Lhasa with more persistence, Peking was more of a prized goal.

At the centre of Rome is of course the Pope, and whilst neither Bogle nor Turner had an audience with the Dalai Lama, they both made an intense connection with the Panchen Lama, the second most powerful figure in Tibet. Both men were familiar with working and interacting with aristocracy and easily attuned themselves to the Tibetan variant. The ritual life of Tibetan court ceremonial was a drama for which Bogle and Turner quickly learnt their (not so unfamiliar) parts. The way to acceptance was therefore already prepared for the Panchen Lama, who sat at the centre of an impressive and conspicuous display of reverence, power and authority. This theatre of ritual was the dominant landscape of Tibet experienced by Bogle and Turner. They entered that world far more than the world of mountain landscape or peasant life. Whilst no traveller in Tibet was completely to elude this tightly orchestrated symbolic drama, Bogle and Turner were the first – and the last for over a century – to be welcomed into

54

it and interact deeply with it. Appropriately enough, they came from that era in British cultural life when the commercial bourgeoisie had not yet seriously challenged aristocratic hegemony. The revolutionary events in France five years after Turner's return were to mark the watershed between the old and new regimes in the European imagination.

The Panchen Lama

The principal character in this ceremonial theatre, as presented in the narratives of Bogle and Turner, was the Panchen (Teshoo) Lama. Whilst Bogle struck up a close friendship with him as a young man, Turner was the participant in an extraordinary encounter with his reincarnated infant successor. Both Bogle and his Panchen Lama friend died suddenly only a few years after their meeting. Turner was later introduced to the eighteen-month-old child who was considered to be the reincarnation of the Lama.[130]

Here was a strange re-enactment as the successor to Bogle, a pragmatic and mature military man chosen in typical Western style, supposedly on proven ability, met the 3rd Tashi Lama's successor, a child chosen in typical Tibetan fashion by oracles and a mystical system of reincarnation. So, whilst British hopes were never to be fulfilled in trade from Tibet, Turner brought back something else which was to prove far more durable than material goods: an idea, a fantasy, a tale of the marvellous. In his strangely formal and unemotional report Turner presented Britain and Europe with one of the first detailed and first-hand experiences of the Tibetans' living system of reincarnate lamas.

Turner was assured that the eighteen-month-old child could understand what was said even though he could not speak. In a scenario that was both moving and bizarre, this soldier, diplomat and trade agent delivered a formal address to the infant whilst unsure how much credence to give to the stories of this child's unspoken wisdom and ancient lineage. Certainly Turner was impressed by his calm presence, and had nothing to gain by disputing the Tibetans' claims. His was a position of respectful curiosity and suspended judgement. In an extraordinary speech to the child Turner said:

> The Governor-General, on receiving the news of his decease in China, was overwhelmed with grief and sorrow, and continued to lament his absence from the world, until the cloud that had overcast the happiness of this nation was dispelled by his reappearing ... The Governor ... was hopeful that the friendship which had formerly subsisted between them, would not be diminished ...

He reported that 'The little creature turned, looking steadfastly towards me, with the appearance of much attention while I spoke, and nodded with repeated but slow movements of the head as though he understood and approved every word.'[131] During the course of the following century the system of reincarnate lamas – the living gods, as they were so often called – was the subject of wide-ranging assessments from Western observers. Initially, the attitudes towards these all-powerful reincarnate lineages varied from quizzical curiosity to sceptical indifference.

Bogle gave the Panchen Lama nothing but praise, and could find no defect whatsoever in his character. He even found himself caught up in the general veneration and joy evoked in his followers by the Lama's presence.[132] In a comparison with the Pope's position in Roman Catholicism, Bogle adjudicated in favour of the Tibetans: 'this influence over the minds of the people, possessed by both, has been exercised by the Lamas, perhaps, in a manner more conducive to the happiness of mankind.'[133] Even Turner, whilst not as effusive, passed favourable judgement upon the results of lamaistic authority.[134]

Amidst Gods and Whirligigs: Religion in Practice

Whilst monasticism was regarded favourably as a general system of authority and government, it was viewed less kindly in its internal details. Bogle commented on the monks: 'They seem to lead a joyless, and, I think, an idle life.'[135] He used the term 'monkish' in a playful but critical way and at one point exclaimed: 'of a truth, an ounce of mother-wit is worth a pound of clergy.'[136] He became increasingly frustrated living in a quasi-monastic situation, and moaned:

> What can I do to break the thread of these tiresome ceremonies? And how can I render the account of the tedious and uniform life I spent at Teshu Lumbo agreeable? It was monastic to the greatest degree. Nothing but priests: nothing from morning to night but the chanting of prayers, and the sound of cymbols and tabors.[137]

Whilst the idea of order and regularity appealed to Bogle's idealized fantasies, the experience of its tedious routines was insufferable. Even the halting conversations he looked forward to whilst learning the language 'yielded an entertainment listless and insipid when compared with the pleasures of society'.[138]

Both travellers were curious about the extensive use of ritual, but were hardly excited by it. At one point, for example, Turner exclaimed:

> On every third day, the morning was devoted to proclaiming aloud

the attributes and praises of the supreme Being, a service which was performed with a vehemence of vociferation perfectly astonishing, and, as I thought, altogether inconsistent with the decorum of a well-regulated assembly.[139]

For him the close-up actualities of monastic life seemed at odds with the monks' wider role in sustaining a regulated social harmony. For Bogle its boring routinization contrasted with the inspiration evoked by the lamas, the system's elite. For both men there was a split between the idealized fantasy and the unpleasant details. But neither seemed disturbed by this kind of contradiction; contradictions were integral to Tibet as a special place in the British imagination.

In addition to high lamas and ordinary monks, both travellers also commented upon two other groups of religious practitioners – hermits and ordinary folk. Each of these four sections of the Tibetan population would suffer mixed fortunes in the estimations of future British travellers. As we shall see, by the beginning of the twentieth century the high lamas would be out of favour – as also, indeed, would the religious system itself. Religious recluses also drew a varied response over the years. Only the ordinary folk consistently commanded respect for their religious sincerity throughout the nineteenth century. In these eighteenth-century accounts, however, the ordinary Tibetans, whilst liked for their basic personal qualities, were not treated seriously in terms of their religiosity. They were portrayed as devoted but superstitious: collecting the Dalai Lama's excrement to be sold as charms: rushing to kiss the Panchen Lama's cushion immediately he vacated it.[140] Turner commented on their 'absurd' and 'ridiculous' ceremonies to placate nature spirits. The prevalence of demonology and a blind adherence to ritual prompted him to exclaim: 'religion, especially among a people so bigoted to its forms, was a subject to which I adverted, with ... scrupulous caution.'[141] The idealized simple mountain peasant, whilst enviable at the level of physical and emotional naivety, had not yet become the focus of European spiritual admiration.

Religious recluses fared somewhat better than either monks or ordinary folk in these travel accounts. A possible reason for this was their aloofness and isolation from the tedious regimentation of monastic life, from the noisy excesses of devotion and its myriad forms and rituals, and from the mass of popular superstition. More than any other religious group, the recluses seemed to echo the emerging Romantic vision of the landscape. Bogle observed that high up on a particular mountain, 'some solitary cottages, the retreat of dervises, are here and there dropped as from clouds. In these airy abodes they pass their days in counting their beads, and look down with indifference on all the business and bustle of the world from which they are entirely excluded.'[142] He affectionately and playfully referred to them as 'these self-denying sons of abstinence'; and clearly they partook of the Romantic sense of the sublime, of the contemplative solitar-iness of mountain peaks. Even the more restrained Turner, using his characteristic language of air, seemed favourably disposed towards them: 'Many of the sons of piety plant their dwellings in these pure regions, and in general, judiciously abandon the low hollows with their putrid and humid exhalations.'[143]

Whilst these comments are examples of an old anti-monk and pro-friar tradition in British religiosity, they also show the convergence of spiritual purity and mountain peaks in the imagination of these two eighteenth-century travellers. Recluses embodied the quintessence of both Bogle's and Turner's tentative landscape mysticism. As we have seen, Bogle regarded the mountains as special because they afforded isolation and protection, whilst enhancing a life of noble simplicity; it is therefore not surprising to notice that his recluses were 'aloof' and 'indifferent' to the 'bustle of the world'. On the other hand, Turner's mountaintop recluses breathed only the purest air, hence exactly expressing his vaporous land-scape ideals.

But Tibetan religion, in all its forms, drew unqualified respect from Bogle and Turner for the high level of morality that it inspired. Bogle viewed even the frequent lapses from its high ideals as mere human weak-ness, not hypocrisy. Turner made special mention of the strict sexual restrictions of monastic communities. In his mind there was no doubt about their enforcement. Morality and the preservation of order and regu-larity were the two most admired characteristics of Tibetan religion. Was this religious system civilized or primitive? Where did sophistication end and tedium begin? When did natural simplicity become mere supersti-tion? What was the difference between spiritual and political power?

The Absence of the Marvellous: Science and the Occult

When the Panchen Lama showed Bogle a knife that he claimed 'had fallen from the clouds', Bogle remarked: 'It was almost the only part of his con-versations that was marvellous.'[144] The category of 'the marvellous' was common in travel accounts both before and after Bogle's and Turner's but their texts lay poised between the earlier delight in strange forms (ani-mals, plants, people, customs, uncanny phenomena and religious mir-acles) and the later nineteenth-century thirst for occult and mystical mar-vels. Bogle made his comment with relief, because the *absence* of the marvellous enhanced the authenticity of the Tibetan Arcadia. It seems as if he was almost expecting to be inundated with the marvellous in Tibet. This absence is one of the most striking features of both accounts. One wonders what either earlier or later travellers would have made of the encounter with the reincarnate infant Lama? Even the restrained and aloof Turner could scarcely contain his enthusiasm at such a meeting. Neither traveller was particularly interested in looking for marvels in Tibet – indeed, it would almost seem that they went out of their way *not* to see them: Bogle was excited by Tibetan simplicity, whilst Turner was enthusiastic about Tibetan organization.

In fact it was the scientific gadgetry carried by Bogle and Turner that excited the sense of the marvellous in the Tibetans. Turner remarked: 'A variety of mechanical, mathematical and optical instruments which I had with me, attracted the attention of my visitors, by their novelty, or their use.'[145] Hamilton, Bogle's travelling companion, aroused considerable interest with his microscope. Turner also recounts how he provoked amusement with his electrical apparatus. 'The quick and incomprehensible action of the electric fluid', he wrote, 'produced frequently a very laughable spectacle, among crowds of Booteeas, who were attracted by curiosity to our apartments. It was extremely entertaining to communicate the shock to a large circle.'[146] One can sense Turner's delight in playing with scientific gadgets in a way that was so popular in the salons back home. He later drew astonishment from the Tibetans with his ice-skates, as he challenged and outpaced a man on horseback.[147]

In one incident, whilst Turner was 'astonishing' the Tibetans with his telescope, a young lama seized him by the hand and proceeded to read his fortune. Turner was nonchalant about this and remarked: 'I submitted to his examination with no very serious apprehension from his profound knowledge of the occult science of palmistry.'[148] Turner belonged to an age that still delighted in its own scientific and rational achievements. An occult resurgence lay some time in the future, when *delight* in science had become transformed into a far more serious technological *confidence*.

Neither History nor Tradition: Geography and the Coherence of Knowledge

Geography held this *bricolage* of ideas and impressions together: it gave it coherence. Geographical and geological speculations were immensely popular at the close of the eighteenth century.[149] At the summit of one peak, Bogle was forced to exclaim: 'What fine baseless fabrics might not a cosmographer build on this situation, who, from a peat or an oyster-shell can determine the different changes which volcanoes, inundations and earthquakes have produced on the face of this globe.'[150] Such 'antediluvian reveries', he continued, 'make the head giddy'. The rapid proliferation of long-range journeys from Europe, and the sudden global expansion of British commercial interests, fed this revolution in geographical imagining. On being asked why the English leave their homeland so extensively, Turner rejected Tibetans suggestions that it was due to a great internal defect in their own country. Instead he replied to the Tibetan Regent that the English, 'prompted by curiosity, not less than by a desire of wealth, spread themselves over every region of the Universe'.[151] With some pride, he continued:

> In these voyages, lands had been discovered, and nations explored, of which neither history, nor tradition, supplied the slightest information: and navigators, by publishing to the world their observations, and their accounts of these newly-discovered countries, had communicated much curious and important knowledge.

Turner was correct in his reply, for travel provided the basis of the next century's revolution in physical and social sciences.[152]

In eighteenth-century Britain a consistent, and increasingly coherent, global imagining began to emerge. Geopolitics was in its infancy, as was a kind of geosociology. Whilst the modern concept of 'environment' had not yet been formulated (in the sense of a defining milieu with which, and within which, an organism interacts), nevertheless a simplistic geographical context was consistently invoked as an explanatory principle.[153] Time and again, race, character, temperament, physical stature and civilizational status were attributed to geographical circumstance. As the nineteenth century progressed, Tibetan religion in particular was to be constantly explained in terms of geography; but in these late-eighteenth-century travel narratives, most speculation was confined to racial character and physique.

Bogle suggested that the widely differing geographical milieu between Bhutan and Bengal produced 'robust and hearty' inhabitants in the former, but 'weak and thin-skinned' natives in the latter.[154] Turner constantly used similar reasoning, but he also extended his reflections from physique to philosophical and mechanical advancement. In pursuit of such enquiry, he conjured up some fine imaginative landscapes. For example, he reasoned that perfection could not be expected 'in an inland region, remote from intercourse with strangers, and shut out from the rest of the world by inaccessible mountains, by Imaus [Himalayas], on the one hand, and by the inhospitable deserts of Gobi, on the other'.[155] Clearly he did not share Bogle's celebration of isolation but instead subscribed to cultural cosmopolitanism as an explanation of civilizational progress. Among the nomads to the far north of Tibet even less could be hoped for, Turner reflected:

> ... in more northerly regions, where one half of the year is a season of profound darkness, and the wretched inhabitants are compelled to seek refuge from the severity of the seasons, in deep and gloomy

caverns: where, possibly, the powers and faculties of the mind, are in some degree benumbed by the same powerful operation of intense cold.

Such reasoning dovetailed with the prevailing landscape aesthetic and its failure to embrace wilderness. Once the idea of *barren majesty* entered British landscape imagining, precisely the same geographical conditions would be used to explain the *attributes* of Tibetan culture and mysticism: the evaluation would be entirely reversed.[156]

Such geographical reflections brought order to the influx of impressions that threatened to overwhelm the old classification systems and the encyclopaedic approach to knowledge,[157] but the new geographical imagination also helped to define Britain as a nation. For whilst a cultural universalism, a global humanism, pervaded eighteenth-century philosophical reflections, this was soon to be replaced by nationalism as the basis of ethnographic explanation.[158] In the nineteenth century history became defined as the progress of European nations, not as the story of world culture. For Bogle and Turner, however, progress in the attributes of civilization (philosophy, arts, sciences, manners) was due primarily to the accident of geographical circumstance and not to some inherent racial or cultural superiority.

Said suggests that four eighteenth-century elements were crucial in helping to lay the basis for modern Orientalism as a Western fantasy: 'Global expansion, historical confrontation, sympathy and classification'.[159] Tibetan exploration clearly takes its place within such an emerging structure. These four elements in their turn were supported upon the new global geographical imagination. Said writes:

> these elements had the effect of releasing the orient generally ... from the narrow religious scrutiny by which it had hitherto been examined (and judged) by the Christian West ... Reference points were no longer Christianity and Judaism, with their fairly modest calendars and maps, but India, China, Japan, and Sumer, Buddhism, Sanskrit, Zoroastrianism, and Manu.[160]

Travel and geography emancipated non-Western cultures, and hence European self-identity, from the confines of textual religious authority. Global definition was increasingly displaced from tradition and text to broadly geographical observations and historical research. As we shall see, these became the basis for a new, uniquely European, creation of sacred landscape.

Conclusions: the Closure of the Vessel

Tibetan landscape focused and concentrated several imaginative discourses: those of ethnography, geography, government and personal experience. In particular the religion, unlike Buddhism elsewhere, was enmeshed in its cultural, geographical and political origins. It was inseparably part of the *place* of Tibet, a place that had to a significant extent been shaped by the engaged imagination of these eighteenth-century travellers. This place did not provoke any sudden challenge to entrenched British values at the time; nor, initially, did it inspire the intense excitement that China or Tahiti evoked. But Tibet promised to be a place of sufficient imaginative complexity to satisfy the radical demands of the next century. In a very real sense, Britain needed such a place. Whilst these eighteenth-century travellers may have been unsuccessful in opening Tibet to commerce, instead they brought back something of equal value: a *place* of crucial importance for the British imagination. As the highest country in the world, bounded by the highest mountains on the globe, Tibet was ideally situated to play a leading part in the extraordinary nineteenth-century upsurge of British and European mountain Romanticism. The *Himalayas* were a region of novelty and fascination for these early travellers, for whom Tibet was little more than a curious rumour. Initially it was this mountain frontier that bestowed its imaginative power on Tibet. Only subsequently did the reverse occur and the fantasy of Tibet intensify Western fascination with the Himalayas.

Tibet adjoined the sensitive frontiers of what was to become Britains's most prestigious overseas possession, India. Even in the eighteenth century the East India Company felt itself vulnerable from this northern direction, yet Tibet constantly lay just beyond the reach of British power and influence. It was kept firmly in the British imagination by its geographical location at a time of intense geopolitical rivalry between imperial powers. It would not go away; it could not be ignored. It sat there, a vast unknown land at the very limits of British expansion. Geographically it lay at the meeting point of British, Russian and Chinese imperial aspirations. Each of these three powers had its own unique relationship to Tibet, and to each other. For the next two hundred years Tibet would play a small but significant role in the restructuring of geopolitical fantasies. It was like a vacuum that simultaneously demanded, yet refused, to be filled.

As we have seen, the timing of the 'discovery' of Tibet, late in the eighteenth century, was also critical for its subsequent place in the British imagination. Historically and mythologically, Tibet connected nineteenth-century global imagining with more ancient world mappings. Old empires and imaginative landscapes were disintegrating, whilst new ones had yet to emerge. Tibet provided an archaic continuity for the modern world.

Tibet seemed to contain a strange mixture of opposites: the religion appeared rational yet thoroughly superstitious: to combine a high level of morality with rampant demonology and occultism. As a system it seemed exemplary in terms of its organization and its attainments in diplomacy and manners; yet dirt, idleness and mindless uniformity were conspicuous on a daily level; the leadership of the high lamas was, on every account, singularly inspiring yet carried with it dark overtones of spiritual and political absolutism; on the surface the country seemed naively content, but radiating out from Lhasa was a web of political and religious intrigue.

Whilst apparently closed off and isolated from the mainstream of the world, Tibet seemed to exert an extraordinarily far-reaching spiritual influence. Even the landscape was at one and the same time exhilarating and boring. There always seemed to be *more* of Tibet – more of it geographically, and more of it in terms of its contradictions. Rationalists, Utopians, Romantics, primitivists, Humanists, Moralists and Mystics would each be irresistibly drawn to something exemplary in Tibet, yet at the same time puzzled or repelled by something else that just could not be ignored. It presented the West with a true *complexio oppositorum*, a rich complexity of contradictions and oppositions.[161] This *complexio oppositorum* was to provide the basis of Tibet as a sacred place in the Western imagination.

Upon his return from Tibet, Turner wrote: 'I am sorry to add too, that events ... have concurred to throw almost insuperable difficulties in the way of re-establishing our intercourse with Tibet, at least for some considerable time to come.'[162] It is doubtful whether even Turner would have realized that over a century would elapse before official intercourse would be re-established. The circumstances of the break in relations – a series of Gurkha invasions of Tibet, repulsed by a huge Chinese army; British indecision about aiding Tibet and seeming to support the Nepalese – are not so important as the break itself. Britain and Europe became exiled from the first coherent Tibetan landscape in Western fantasies. The subsequent history of Tibetan exploration is, to a significant degree, the story of this exile. Turner's account was to be the main reference for over half a century. These eighteenth-century journeys themselves became located within the fantasy landscape of Tibet: they came to be viewed as part of a lost golden age in Tibetan exploration. Hastings, recalled and humiliated in London, became the misunderstood and persecuted visionary.

This deep gap in sustained, direct communication with Tibet sealed Western fantasies into an almost closed vessel. All the imaginative ingredients were contained within it. The mountainous walls of this sealed vessel increasingly became the focus of exploration: their majestic presence and the mysteries that lay hidden behind them mutually enhanced each other. Whilst the closure of Tibet was essentially political, it came to symbolize its cultural, geographical and spiritual Otherness.

3
Inventing The Threshold
(1792–1842)

The threshold is the limit, the boundary, the frontier that distinguishes and opposes two worlds – and at the same time the paradoxical place where those worlds communicate, where passage from the profane to the sacred world becomes possible.

(Mircea Eliade[1959, p.25])

In 1825 a certain Lieutenant George White took advantage of the easier access to the Himalayas that followed the Gurkha Wars of 1815 by going on a short journey to contemplate the views. His travels took him to 'the provinces of Sirmour, Gurwhal and Kumaon',all of which had recently been 'annexed' by Britain following the conclusion of the difficult and costly, but otherwise successful, war in Nepal. This war marked the beginning of Britain's long struggle to contain the rival expansion of the vigorous, militant Gurkha people. At one point, whilst travelling through these new additions to the burgeoning Indian Empire, White was moved to comment: 'The view of the Himalaya from a spot in the vicinity of Saharunpore, is of that dreamy, poetical description, which, though full of beauty, presents little that is definite …'.[1] He then went on to rhapsodize about

> … the pyramidal snow-capped heights, which seem to lift themselves into another world, crowning the whole with almost awful majesty. From this site, the mountain ranges have all the indistinctness which belongs to the land of faerie, and which, leaving the imagination to luxuriate in its most fanciful creations, lends enchantment to the scene. The pure dazzling whiteness of the regions of eternal snow, give occasionally so cloud-like an appearance to the towering summits, as to induce the belief that they form a part of the heaven to which they aspire.

Clearly we have entered a different world to that imagined by Bogle and Turner. Here, in White's account, is landscape Romanticism in its first full flowering. Bogle's descriptions of Himalayan landscape, written only fifty years earlier, seem restrained and hesitant alongside White's endless flourishes, his obsession both with views and with a kind of detached, rather gratuitous sense of the sublime. The district of Saharunpore gave White his first glimpse of the mountains, and in addition to inspiring an enthusiastic but dreamy Romanticism, it set him speculating on the value of the region for 'scientific travel': extensive fossil remains have been found in the hills; the cultivation of the tea plant looks favourable. [2]

These comments in White's journal underline the shift that was occurring in the British relationship with the Himalayas during the first half of the nineteenth century. The years between 1792 and 1842 were highly significant politically for this immense mountain region. 1792 had seen the audacious Gurkha invasion decisively defeated by the remote Chinese overlords, whose presence and authority in Tibet and the Himalayas was thereby enhanced and subsequently reached an unprecedented intensity. Relations between Britain and China over this war were severely strained; the Chinese ever suspicious, the British vacillatory. Suddenly the border with Tibet was firmly closed. As Lamb comments: 'a decisive change had taken place in the political alignments of the Himalayas'. [3] The following years saw Britain nervously but steadily consolidating its control of the Indian subcontinent, whilst simultaneously the Himalayas increasingly became imagined as its northern bastion.

The difficult war with the Gurkhas (1814 – 16) was merely the most dramatic event in a series by which Britain extended its power and influence into the Himalayan region of northern India. Kumaon, Garwhal, the Sutlej valley, Spiti and Lahul were those districts most effectively subsumed by this policy of expansion, containment and stabilization, but Kashmir, Ladakh, Sikkim, Nepal, Bhutan and Assam were also similarly drawn deeply into British imperial policy-making. The war brought British territorial influence into direct contact with Tibet for the first time. White's journey in search of sublime views shows just how quickly the military and political appropriation of these regions was followed by an *aesthetic* one. This early Romantic engagement with the Himalayas was also accompanied by an amateurish scientific curiosity that scanned the landscape for both knowledge and profits.

The Himalayan Tour

As early as 1822, seasoned travellers and explorers were taking the first tourist groups up into 'the snowy range', in the vicinity of what would soon become the hill-station of Simla. [4] Lieutenant White, too, clearly saw himself as charting out a kind of 'Grand Tour' of the Himalayas, as simply transposing the well-established appreciation of picturesque and sublime mountain views, forged in the European Alps, on to the newly acquired Himalayan regions of the British Empire. At the front of his book, for example, he placed a quotation from Captain Skinner's earlier dash through the same landscape:

I have beheld nearly all the celebrated scenery of Europe, which poets and painters have immortalized, and of which all the tourists in the world are enamoured; but I have seen it surpassed in these infrequented and almost unknown regions.

There are numerous such references to early European landscape painters in contemporary Himalayan journals. In 1805, for example, one traveller exclaimed:

These two mornings exhibited a spectacle which in sublimity and beauty surpassed all power of description and to which even the pencil of Claude would have been incapable of doing justice.[5]

The passage refers to Claude Lorrain (1600 – 84), a seminal figure in the history of landscape painting, with his 'nostalgic dreams of lands of enchantment'.[6] In his landscapes Claude concentrated upon capturing an almost mythic and religious sense of ideal Nature: 'the pure and trembling light seemed to dissolve all structure and form'.[7] Along with Salvator Rosa (1615 – 73), who specialized in wild and dramatic landscapes, Claude played an essential role in shaping eighteenth-century mountain aesthetics. Certainly the names of both Claude and Salvator Rosa had become adjectives for describing landscape in the vocabulary of eighteenth-century travellers on the 'Grand Tour' of Europe.[8]

Such references also draw attention to a problem when reading travel texts. Before the age of photography, the traveller had recourse to four ways of capturing landscapes: by sketching and painting; by descriptive prose passages (later known as word-painting): by comparison with well-known European landscapes, especially the Alps; or by referring to previous landscape portrayals, either in poetry or painting. Any single travel text usually encompassed most of these methods. As Michel Le Bris points out, landscape painters in general tended to lag behind other forms of dramatic painting in the portrayal of the natural sublime. They were, he writes, 'still too subject to the temptation of the picturesque'.[9] The Picturesque-Romantic appreciation of mountain landscapes and of the people who inhabit such places still exerts its dominance today. In the early nineteenth century it seemed to mesmerize the imagination of travellers and cast its floating sense of beauty over most attempts to describe the Himalayas. References either to familiar European landscapes or to famous illustrations were generally conservative. Avant-garde landscape painters such as Caspar Friedrich (1774 – 1840) or Joseph Turner (1775 – 1851) were seldom evoked. Even seminal landscape poets such as Wordsworth were rarely mentioned. Sketching and painting of the Himalayas, too, never freed themselves from the demands of representation and illustration. They never played a leading role in the development of landscape painting as did, for example, the Alps, North Africa or, much later, the American West. Only in passages of descriptive prose did the Himalayas gradually force a radical re-evaluation of European landscape aesthetics in the nineteenth century.

The Savage and the Sublime

The geopolitical and Romantic imaginations converged in the Himalayas during this period. White is equally comfortable in both. He is as thoroughly at home in the Romantic imagination as he is out of place in the unknown mountains. Whilst the Himalayas pressed their unfamiliar presence upon him he was on totally familiar ground within his own sentiments. Imperial identity and mountain appreciation were clearly commonplace to him. He knew what he was looking for in the mountains. His evaluation of 'views' was unquestioned and in no need of justification. The Himalayas did not challenge White's imaginative map of landscape aesthetics, they confirmed it. Such a challenge – and with it a new, deeper, and richer phase of Romantic landscape appreciation – would have to wait until late into the century. But even though such a challenge lay some decades away with the rise of true mountain-explorers, White still experienced occasional moments of unease, moments when his mountain aesthetics seemed inadequate for his experiences:

> From this point we might be said to traverse a land whose savage aspect was seldom redeemed by scenes of gentle beauty, the ranges of hills crossing, and apparently jostling each other in unparalleled confusion, being all rugged, steep and difficult to tread ... [10]

He draws a clear distinction between the picturesque, the sublime, the savage and the dismal,[11] and he was not alone with such categorizations. The British surveyor Herbert, whilst attempting to cross a pass in 1819, commented:

> Those who have travelled through such desolate and unfrequented parts will alone understand ... the sight of even the first straggling sheep ... was hailed almost as that of a friend. An animal, even a bird, any living thing in fact, serves to take from such a scene the almost ... death-like character of solitude ... .[12]

Desolation and solitude combine with an overwhelming immensity of landscape confusion to produce a sense of *dismal savagery*. Lieutenant Alexander Gerard, another British soldier-explorer of the Himalayan passes, wrote in 1818: 'Here the rocks are more rugged than any we had yet seen, they are rent in every direction, piled upon one another in wild disorder ... '.[13] Later he comments:

> The country ... has a most desolate and dreary aspect, not a single tree or blade of green grass was distinguishable for near 30 miles, the ground being covered with a very prickly plant ... this shrub was almost black, seeming as if burnt, and the leaves were so much parched from the arid wind of Tartary, that they might be ground to powder by rubbing them between the hands.

The landscape was also deceptive in terms of distance. It produced frequent headaches; nausea was common: ravines and precipices abounded:

> A single false step might have been attended with fatal consequences, and we had such severe headaches, and were so much exhausted, that we had hardly strength sufficient to make the effort, and it required no inconsiderable one to clear the deep chasms which we could scarcely view without shuddering. I never saw such a horrid looking place, it seemed the wreck of some towering peak burst asunder by severe frost.[14]

'Confused jumble[s] of gigantic masses of rock':[15] endless barren vistas: these lay outside the embrace of the new Romantic aesthetic forged over the turn of the century in the European Alps and in the English Lake District. As late as 1871 the well-known Victorian mountaineer Leslie Stephen argued for the superiority of the Alps over the Caucasus, the Carpathians, the Rockies and the Himalayas. 'All beautiful scenery ... ', he writes, 'should be dashed with melancholy, but the melancholy should not be too real.'[16] For Stephen, mountains could be a little too wild, too bleak and stern, really needing some sign of human habitation or labour to enhance their beauty. The English scholar-eccentric Thomas Manning, on his 1811 journey to Tibet, shared this sentiment:

> We continued along the barren valley, seeing no diversity, but the ever-varying shapes of the still more barren mountains, whose colour, where it was not actually sand, slate or granite, was a melancholy pale mouldy green.[17]

There was, however, a tradition for appreciating certain *details* of wild landscape, a kind of *savage splendour*. One of White's fellow-travellers, overlooking a mountain torrent, exclaimed:

> Those who have brains and nerves to bear the frightful whirl, which may assail the steadiest head, plant themselves on the bridge that

spans the torrent, and from this point survey the wild and awful grandeur of the scene, struck with admiration at its terrific beauty, yet, even while visions of horror float before them, unable to withdraw their gaze.[18]

This safe – albeit seemingly precarious – experience masks the outermost limit of early-nineteenth-century landscape aesthetics. As early as the mid-eighteenth century, Rousseau had exclaimed: 'I must have torrents, rocks, pines, dead forests, mountains, rugged paths to go up and down, precipices beside me to frighten me.'[19] As Michel Le Bris points out, here was a fundamental shift in Western imagining: 'a whole age that was coming to an end shunned mountains because they were horrible, while the … [next] sought out their ravines and waterfalls precisely in order to be carried away by their thrilling horror.'[20]

'Natural sublimity' differed from both the Baroque sublime and the classical sublime: it expressed the ability of nature to unleash the deepest passion, to transcend reasoning, to transport the soul.[21] Terror in the face of some overpowering aspect of nature was integral to this natural sublimity. However, this sense of the sublime had more to do with the subjective experience of the observer than with the particularities of the geographical place. The *precise forms* of the place were incidental, only a platform for the intensification of individual experiences. It was these *experiences* that were being acclaimed in early Romanticism, rather than natural wilderness landscape. In these early Himalayan accounts we have not yet reached that decisive point when the imaginal balance shifts: that point where the immensity of nature, rather than exalting or filling the human soul, dwarfs and crushes it.

If we step back just a little from gazing with exquisite horror at the wild splendour of nature, the early-nineteenth-century aesthetic is once again on firm ground, with a kind of *noble sublimity*:

> On the right, the snowy ranges shoot up their hoary peaks to a tremendous height … shewing an endless variety of forms … Imagination, however vivid, can scarcely figure to the mind a prospect so grand and thrilling …[22]

Distance brings order to the irregular chaos; a variety of forms redeems barren sameness.[23] The early accounts of Himalayan travel are full of 'grand prospects', 'solemn majestic' views, picturesque scenes and, of course, 'glorious landscape':

> There is no possibility of conveying to the mind of the reader the gratification which we have experienced in some new burst of scenery, when, emerging from the sombre labyrinths of a thick

forest, we come suddenly upon one of those glorious landscapes which fill the whole soul with ecstasy![24]

These early travellers were not only engaging with an unfamiliar and over-whelming outer landscape, they were also struggling to chart a corresponding set of inner experiences. Wherever possible, individual experience and landscape scenes were constantly being brought into alignment, and when the effect was undesirable the result was summarily abandoned. Nevertheless, as we have seen in these few examples, the Himalayas inevitably drew European travellers to the boundary of their known aesthetic paradigm, constantly demanding new modes of appreciation. Unlike those who journeyed in Europe, Himalayan travellers could not judiciously avoid dismal, chaotic and disturbing places: these were inevitable. Slowly a second generation of landscape Romanticism was emerging, one that combined sweeping experiences with close attention to particularities and details. A new way of looking, observing, experiencing – of *engaging* with the landscape – was slowly gathering strength: one that was disgusted with the rampantly indulgent subjectivity of earlier mountain appreciation.[25] But the *extremes* of barren, dismal and endless wildernesses would have to wait even longer, until eventually redeemed by a subtle appreciation of light and space that appeared only towards the very end of the nineteenth century.[26]

In 1841 – 2, early British confidence in the 'naturalness', of their imperial presence in Asia received a series of major setbacks. Wars in Afghanistan and China, with a crushing defeat in the former, were only the most visible of manifestations. The Sikh nation under its vigorous leader Gulab Singh, rivalled the Gurkhas in both military ability and expansionist desires. Both powers threatened to reconcile their differences and unite, a possibility that sent shudders through British Himalayan aspirations. The Sikhs had already successfully invaded Ladakh in 1834, thus coming into direct contact with China; then, in 1841, they invaded western Tibet. With an army recently annihilated in neighbouring Afghanistan, British moves towards Himalayan hegemony had reached a critical stage.

One Tibet or Many

Lieutenant White's journal stands exactly midway through this highly formative period in the British relationship with the Himalayas and Tibet, but the self-assurance of his text is deceptive. In some ways White's *confidence* points forward to the mid-century, mid-Victorian synthesis, to the popular excursions from the hill-stations of Simla and Darjeeling. On the other hand, in its *naivety* it harks back to a simpler time when the Himalayas seemed to lie outside complex political intrigue: to a time before their full integration into Western history, into the new global, geopolitical map. White's journal is not typical, but in fact the period produced no *typical* Himalayan travel accounts. We have not yet reached the stage in Himalayan exploration when the selection of texts for interpretation becomes a problem. Travel texts during these years are both extremely limited in number and highly idiosyncratic. Nevertheless they do fall into certain patterns and each helped, in some essential way, to lay the foundations for the Western creation of a Tibet that was imaginatively rich, complex and substantial.

Although there were comparatively few of them, the travellers among the Himalayas during the first half of the nineteenth century formed a highly diverse group. Manning, the only Englishman actually to reach Lhasa during the whole of the century, was an eccentric devotee of Chinese culture who had little interest in Tibet and was instead totally preoccupied with reaching the 'forbidden' city of Peking from India.[27] The French Lazarist priests Huc and Gabet, the only other Europeans to reach the capital of Tibet, were also unorthodox. Journeying from northern China and through Mongolia, they were the final representatives of a line of intrepid Catholic missionaries to Lhasa extending back into the seventeenth century.[28]

But what constituted an *orthodox* Himalayan traveller? Moorcroft was one of the most famous, yet he was spurned by the British administration in India. A mixture of adventurer, meticulous observer and trader, with his warnings about the Russians he was also one of the first British travellers with a global, imperialist perspective on the politics of the region.[29] The wandering Transylvanian hermit-scholar Csoma de Koros had his British, scholarly counterpart in Brian Hodgson.[30] Compared with the enigmatic brilliance of the Hungarian, who died in poverty in 1842, Hodgson steadily exerted his powerful presence as a Himalayan scholar, administrator and innovator throughout most of the century.

Each individual represented a new kind of Himalayan traveller: the British officers Lieutenant Webb, Captains Raper and Hearsey; the Austrian botanist Baron Carl von Hugel: the renegade Scotsman Dr John Henderson and the Harrow-educated English sportsman Godfrey Vigne; the three Gerard brothers from Aberdeen; the French botanist, dilettante and socialite Victor Jacquemont; the enigmatic, cosmopolitan adventurer Colonel Alexander Gardiner, half Scottish, quarter English and quarter Spanish; the religious eccentric Joseph Wolff, son of a Bohemian rabbi.[31] Caught up in the beginnings of the 'Great Game', the imperial rivalry between Britain and Russia, they combined adventure and trading with a mixture of surveying, mapping and spying. Among the other travellers, James Fraser and George White were like adventurous tourists. On the other hand, Francis Hamilton and Captain Pemberton were engaged on straightforward diplomatic missions to the independent Himalayan kingdoms of Nepal and Bhutan.[32] Henry and Shipp were soldiers, whereas Herbert was a surveyor.[33]

Whilst they were highly individualistic, these early travellers nevertheless shared a common sense of kinship of which Moorcroft and Gardiner were the acknowledged founding fathers.[34] In 1835 von Hugel and Henderson met in Kashmir; earlier Jacquemont and von Hugel had crossed paths in Poona;[35] Moorcroft and Trebeck had, by chance, encountered the solitary Csoma de Koros whilst traversing Ladakh in 1820;[36] the Hungarian subsequently died in the company of Hodgson in Darjeeling. These encounters and the familiarity with each other's work helped to lay the foundations for a coherent tradition of Himalayan travel writing.[37]

During this period Tibet was closed off, sealed in. It was becoming a hermetic vessel for Western projections. The frontier, the boundary, of this potentially sacred place began to be invented. At the same time a new and crucial element was introduced into Himalayan travel: concern about the *validity* both of the travellers and of their texts. Evaluations began to be made about the relative value of different travellers and their reports.

Any fantasy about a particular place always rests upon ideas about the particular route followed and the travelling style adopted, but above all on the type of people who travel and the kind of observations they make. Almost ritual notions came to exist as to the status and validity of any journey to Tibet. Indeed, as we shall see, women, non-Europeans, lower classes, amateurs, eccentrics and young people all, at some stage, had their jouneys discounted. By selecting and encouraging one style of travel and reporting, whilst discouraging others, the British exerted the power of their fantasies over 'the Himalayas' and 'Tibet', creating a very specific type of place. At the same time they legitimized an equally specific way of looking at the landscapes of the world, an aesthetic of *geopolitical Romanticism*.

In the creation of a *place*, a critical point is always reached with a struggle over the selection and evaluation of texts. Assessment is made about their relative usefulness in the creation of a particular, desired landscape. Struggle over texts is always a struggle between contending landscape fantasies. In the case of the Himalayas and Tibet, this issue was never to be completely resolved: there would always be *many* Tibets. But imperialism and nineteenth-century scientificity demanded systematic, cultural, commercial, political and geographical surveys, and these quickly gained the ascendancy. Britain needed and created a coherent, rational and well-mapped Tibet as the century progressed. The geopolitical rivalry with Russia provided the impetus for the hegemony of this kind of travel text, whilst the establishment of the Royal Geographical Society in 1830 furnished this landscape perception with a powerful and efficient headquarters. The only exception to these systematic, scientific, political and commercial perspectives that was looked upon with some favour was the aesthetic, but even this would not receive dedicated attention until much later.,

By the middle of the nineteenth century, Tibet and the Himalayas were 'known' territory, not in terms of geographical and cultural details but by virtue of their absorption into the established rhetoric of travel and exploration. Blank spot or not, early in the century Tibet had been *located*, at least within the grid and co-ordinates of Britain's global map. When that most ungeographically aware traveller Thomas Manning wrote, whilst in Tibet in 1811; 'the latitude and longitude of Lhasa ... are pretty well ascertained', he was implying a symbolic, as well as a geographical, location.[38]

Whilst its full impact would not be felt until the second half of the nineteenth century the Royal Geographical Society (RGS), after its founding in 1830, soon began to shape the contours of British exploration. India and the Himalayas received considerable attention as a region where 'British interests were most intensely concentrated'.[39] Between 1830 and the end of the century, explorers of the Western Himalayas received twelve of the Society's Gold Medals; a number unmatched anywhere else in the world,[40] but the RGS's intense interest in the Himalayas was still only a part of its more global geographical concern. It has been said that 'to know the world and to map it were clear responsibilities of the RGS'.[41] The Society's preference for 'scientific' and useful travel was also made fairly clear as early as 1835, when its journal contained an article that was bitingly critical of what it called the 'travellers' tales' type of geography.[42]

Moorcroft: A Traveller without a Place

Towards the middle of the century, the British, anxious about the security of their Indian possessions, were desperately attempting to collect and collate extant information about Tibet and the Himalayas. The authorities began to search the earlier accounts for 'useful' facts. In most cases they were to be sorely disappointed: Manning's diaries were full of 'gossip and complaints';[43] Huc and Gabet clearly used poetic licence quite freely to improve their story;[44] Gardiner reached for geography only when he thought he was lost and in need of directions.[45] None of these travellers was desperately concerned about geographical accuracy. Moorcroft's massive journals, whilst packed with cultural details, were not of the kind British imperialism felt it needed. In 1873 Wilson, their patient editor, lamented: 'To say the truth, Mr Moorcroft's writings were so voluminous, so unmethodical, and so discursive, that the chance of meeting with any person willing to ... [collect and edit] them was remote'.[46]

Wilson, a member of the Royal Asiatic Society (founded in 1823), also exclaimed:

The whole of the intervening country between India and China is a blank; and of that which separates India from Russia, the knowledge which we possess is but in a very slight degree the result of modern European research, and is for the most part either unauthentic or obsolete.

Under the pressure of imperial demands, travel journals began to be arranged chronologically; older accounts were considered unreliable, out-dated, relegated to the realms of the 'amusing' and the 'curious'. Earlier in the century the British had been conspicuously indifferent towards seminal accounts such as Moorcroft's (1819 – 25) or Manning's (1811), yet in 1837 Wilson was seriously complaining that the journeys of the Catholic missionaries during the seventeenth and eighteenth centuries gathered 'very little useful information'.[48]

Towards the middle of the century, Tibet and the Himalayas became increasingly drawn into the grid of Western history and its attendant global geography. As Baudet comments in his perceptive study of Euro-pean ideas about non-Europeans, eighteenth-century social and human universalism was replaced in the nineteenth century by the myth of the nation. Fundamental to this change was the notion of national history: 'History ... was first and foremost the history, the growth of their own nation ... there was no place here for the non-European world unless it served the interests of the national idea.'[49] A decisive shift was taking place in British identity throughout the first half of the century. Travel in the Himalayas, Tibet and Central Asia played a small but critical role in this transformation.

By 1837, along with the founding of the RGS, the concept of 'modern travel' was already becoming established. Moorcroft's journals did not easily fit into this mould and, as we have seen, took a long time to be pub-lished. They were not entertaining, nor were they full of the sublime uplifting quality that had come to be expected from descriptions of wild mountain landscapes. Again the weary Wilson groans: 'Much that recom-mends travels in the present day – liveliness of general description, mov-ing incidents by flood or field, and good-humoured garrulous self-sufficiency – are not to be looked for.'[50] It was to individuals such as Lieutenant Alexander Burns of the Bombay army that fame would be extended in this period. His *Travels into Bokhara* (1833) combined extens-ive, carefully checked observations with an inspired narrative and assess-ments that were 'portentous but modest and discreet'.[51] It impressed the general public as well as political and scientific circles. Burns was intro-duced to the king at court in London, elected a member of both the pres-tigious Royal Asiatic Society and the Royal Geographical Society, and awarded the latter's Gold Medal. He was acclaimed in Europe and his book, in three volumes, sold 900 copies on the day of publication. Clearly the contrasting fate of these two explorers, Moorcroft and Burns, and of their journals, reveals much about the British expectations of travel in the first half of the nineteenth century.

As Keay points out, when Moorcroft was in the field 'there was no Royal Geographical Society to acknowledge ... [his journey]; even the concept of the explorer was not current.'[52] It was argued, too, that Moorcroft was not scientifically trained in geography, 'neither was he an oriental scholar or an antiquarian'.[53] Between Moorcroft's mysterious disappearance in 1825 and Burn's journey to Bokhara in 1832 much had changed. Burns was an exemplary figure of the new era: a scholar, a diplomat and adventurer with a good sense of what the time and place wanted. As the mid-century approached, there was a demand for accounts that contained precise and scientifically accurate observations on politics, geography and culture – facts that would be useful, for British imperial aspirations. At the same time such accounts should, ideally, reinforce the unquestioned exuberance and self-confidence of the new British global presence and identity.

Thomas Manning in Tibet

It is somewhat ironic that even by the idiosyncratic standards of early Himalayan travellers, the only Englishman to reach Lhasa during the whole of the nineteenth century was an eccentric among eccentrics. Thomas Manning seems to defy any categorization as a traveller. Indeed, so at variance was he with the demands of nineteenth-century British geopolitics that his journal becomes a valuable social document almost by default: it is the exception that proves the rule. By virtue of its position *outside* the 'common-sense' ideas about travel, it serves as a critical vantage point from which to observe the logic behind the nineteenth-century British creation of 'Tibet'. Manning was like the fool to the subsequently established 'court' of the Royal Geographical Society. His journal always seemed to be greeted with a sense of frustration, as if it represented an opportunity wasted. As Markham, who edited it for the first time in 1871, wrote: 'good or bad it stands alone'.[54] He suggested that Manning had the ability to 'have written a good account of his remarkable journey but never did'. Markham grudgingly conceded that Manning's journal does contain *some* insights into the social habits of the local people, but overall it was clearly unsatisfactory: 'His narrative is to a great extent filled with accounts of personal troubles and difficulties.'[55]

Whilst Markham was writing in 1871 and is most representative of that time, his sentiments, as we have seen, are not alien from those expressed earlier, around the middle of the century. It would be difficult to find two individuals so diametrically at odds in their understanding of what constituted useful information about Tibet. Factual details – whether about geography, politics, religion, trade or landscape – all succumb to Manning's delightful eccentricity. No wonder Markham, the exemplary Victorian systematizer on Tibet, continually felt thwarted by Manning's odd text.

One night, having finally reached Lhasa, Manning lay ill with rheumatism. He felt an obligation to go on to the roof of his 'miserable' little house so as to take bearings from the stars, but quickly persuaded himself against any exposure to the night air: 'there was nothing I could do for geography that would compensate the risk I must run.'[56] Manning was no hero, nor a martyr for science; he was ill, and went into an extended discussion about his illness. Despite repeatedly calling for help, he had been left alone all night in his bed. Finally his Chinese travelling companion came into his room and told him to be quiet. Manning wanted to beat their servant for his neglect, but his Chinese companion objected. Manning faithfully recorded their argument:

You can't strike anyone here in Lhasa.
Can't? Oh, we will see.
You can't.
But I will beat him.
You can't.[57]

One can imagine Markham's frustration with page after page of these apparently domestic trivia. Manning's endless disputes and complaints, whilst obviously vital to Manning himself, hardly seemed the stuff of Tibetan exploration to Markham. Indeed, so obscurely tangential is Manning's mind that he actually footnotes this argument: 'In Latin', (Manning and his Chinese companion always spoke to each other in Latin) 'he used the words "non Potes". He ought to have said, "non licet". My response was, "at verberabo".'[58]

Meanwhile Markham desperately scanned these endless anecdotes for a hard, geographical fact. He attempted to deal with Manning's whimsy by employing his own 'rigorous' style of footnotes. So in contrast to Manning's pedantic footnote about Latin grammar, Markham, seemingly desperate to put some backbone into the narrative, inserts one of his own:

The pundit of 1866 reached Lhasa on January 12, and remained until April 21. He says that city is two and a half miles in circumference, in a plain, surrounded by mountains. It is in 29° 39′ 17″ N and 11,700 feet above the sea according to the Pundit[59]

This particular 'scientific' footnote is prompted by the bizarre opening of Manning's chapter on Lhasa. Here is the first eye-witness account of this fabled city by an Englishman – and indeed, the only one for well over a hundred years. How does Manning open the chapter? With exclamations about the architecture, or the colourful people? Comments about the dirt or perhaps a date, or just a titbit of geographical detail? No. He writes: 'Our first care was to provide ourselves with proper hats.'[60] Are proper hats really that important in Lhasa, or are we confronting another strange twist in Manning's mind? Whatever the answer, he provides us with details about what was considered to be a 'proper' hat among the Chinese community in Lhasa in the winter of 1811. Clearly these were not the kind of details that Markham considered useful.

Manning was like a Laurence Sterne , an Irish raconteur, let loose in Tibet.[61] In fact, not only did the geographers and scientists have grounds for complaint with his journal, so too did the lovers of mountain scenery. When he climbed to the top of a prominent hill, instead of describing the view he wrote: 'When I got to the top, my servant had palpitation, sweated profusely, eruption broke out, and the next day he said his skin peeled away. I told him it would do him good and prevent fever. Next day I bargained for people to carry us in our chairs.'[62] We are left none the wiser about the scenery.

Even the highly conspicuous religion of Tibet becomes almost invisible behind Manning's delightful preoccupation with his own experiences. He delayed visiting a temple until he could find someone to explain it. He was under pressure to make such a journey, for he was disguised as a lama from Bengal. People began to wonder why this strange foreign lama, who had been in Lhasa for several months, had not yet visited a temple. After much characteristic vacillation he finally arrived at one, but immediately became involved in a loud argument with his servant who, exclaimed Manning, 'was ignorant as a beast'.[63] Frustrated by his servant's lack of religious knowledge, Manning became angry and made a scene in front of numerous Tibetan devotees. In the end we learn absolutely nothing about the religion except for a totally vague footnote: he cannot recall the name of a Tibetan deity and, leaving a blank space in the body of his narrative, writes: 'This is the name of their great saint or religious lawgiver. I never could rightly make out his story.'[64] Of the religion we are still ignorant, but of Manning's complex relationship to it we have a rich store of anecdotes.

It would be easy to isolate Manning and consider his travel diary as an oddity, an aberration; but in reality his text belongs firmly within a tradition of Himalayan travellers and travel writing which presents the 'inside story' of Tibet. This tradition is concerned less with big views, or with scientific and geographical exactitude, than with the journey itself as an experience, a series of daily events. As we have already seen, such a development can already be found in the intimate corners of Bogle's account, but with Manning it reached an unequivocal intensity. A twentieth-century representative of this tradition, Fosco Maraini, called his book *Secret Tibet*.[65] In this he was referring not to occult rituals but to the small, everydayness of Tibetan life which so frequently eluded Western travellers and hence remained secret.

This tradition also includes that officer-comedian in Britain's eventual invasion of Tibet in 1904, Powell Millington. With a measured irony, given the desperate attempts to reach the capital of Tibet, he called his account *To Lhassa at Last*.[66] No military record of Powell Millington exists, and his true identity has never been discovered. Robert Byron's account, *First Russia: Then Tibet*, is similarly full of humour and extensive sidetracks.[67] Peter Matthiesson's *The Snow Leopard* (1980) is another of these almost inside-out accounts.[68] Here geographical details merely provide the springboard for introspection, or are reduced to a suitable location for the intriguing details of everyday life. However, under the early hegemony of the Royal Geographical Society and pressing imperial demands, this other way of imagining Tibet was to be ridiculed and trivialized: its authors were constantly criticized for being unscientific, even selfish and narcissistic.[69] Yet these few texts were an important antidote to the overwhelming number that were preoccupied with the 'Great Game', with the grandiose creation of global geopolitical fantasies, with Tibet as a heroic or occult proving-ground.

Manning clearly offered no mapping of Tibet, but did he offer anything other than the mapping of his own idiosyncracies? Even Markham suggested that 'for those who know how to find it, there is much wheat to be gathered from amongst Mr Manning's chaff.'[70] As well as Markham's wheat, what does Manning's chaff offer?

As we have noted, Manning presents an inside view of Tibet, a perspective from the early-nineteenth-century Chinese community in Lhasa. His account takes its place with other ethnographic portraits such as Bogle's intimate glimpse of late-eighteenth-century Tibetan court life, or the Japanese monk Kawaguchi's detailed experience of Tibetan monasticism at the end of the nineteenth century.[71] Like these other travellers, Manning felt at home in his small corner of Tibetan society, sympathetic to the mundane details that made up its everyday life. He had an acute ear for the gossip, slander and other tales that abounded in such an isolated, semi-exiled community as the Chinese in Lhasa. We hear, for example, a story about the animosity between a 'Tartar dog' and a 'crack-brained mandarin': another about the execution of 'a good mandarin', told from both the Chinese point of view and the Tibetan; about the Chinese spies and informers that kept close watch on the community in Lhasa: 'my bile used to rise when the hounds looked into my room', exclaimed Manning.[72] He operated as a doctor, both to the Chinese and to the Tibetans. At one stage he even treated the Dalai Lama's own physician. The Tibetan doctor refused to take Manning's medicine: 'He was childish, they said; he did not like the taste or the smell.'[73] A short while later, to Manning's genuine sorrow, he died.

Manning's account also contains numerous short essays – on clothing, food, beards, translations, horses.[74] At first glance these too may seem to be as trivial as his poignant glimpses into the small Chinese subculture in Lhasa, but many of his observations are acute and pertinent. We must not be misled by his gentle humour and his outrageous irritations: for example, two pages devoted to the problems with his horse and saddle were quite relevant in an age before motor vehicles.[75] His reflections about clothing were not just whimsy but sensitive and astute. He praised the local costume and ridiculed European stubbornness in continuing to wear inappropriate clothing.[76] He also reflected, whilst wearing the local Chinese gown, how such a dress – similar in many respects to that worn by a Western woman – restricted movement, engendered caution and took away boldness. It would be some years before women explorers arrived at similar conclusions.

Manning's view is from the back streets of Lhasa and is not overly concerned with the scientific, political or geographical needs of British imperialism, nor with its landscape aesthetics. Recovered and reviewed late in the nineteenth century when such attitudes were assumed to be self-justifying, when heroism and self-sacrifice for the good of the nation – or at least for science – were expected, Manning's account was treated as a weird curiosity. Yet he upheld the tradition of the 'little' traveller, one who does not presume to be the mouthpiece and representative of an entire nation. In Lhasa he was desperately poor, often ill, generally afraid and virtually friendless. In his diary he constantly gives rein to his anxieties, yet his story has a poignant dignity. Forced to sell nearly all his meagre possessions, he reassures himself: 'I managed so as to keep up a certain respectability; and though I was not invited anywhere to dinner … wherever I went I was treated as a gentleman.'[77]

Inventing the Frontier

In 1818, some seven years after Manning's journey to Lhasa, Lieutenant Alexander Gerard of the Bengal Native Infantry set out to explore the Himalayan passes in the vicinity of the Sutlej river, hoping eventually to enter Tibet itself. His narrative begins:

From Soobathoo, in latitude 30° 58′ and longitude 77° 2′ situated about twenty miles from the plains, and 4,260 feet above the level of the sea, I marched to Mumleeg nine miles, three and a half miles from Soobathoo, crossed the Gumbur, an inconsiderable stream, but it had swollen so much from late rain, that its passage was effected with great difficulty.[78]

Gerard, with his crisp precision and concern for geographical exactitude, was clearly a different traveller to Manning. At the end of his narrative he assures the reader; 'Throughout the ... tour, the road was surveyed with some care, and a number of points were fixed trigonometrically ... '.[79] Gerard belonged to a tradition of scientific exploration that, whilst not new, was to assume increasing importance as the century progressed. His journey to discover, explore and map the Himalayan passes was a model of its kind, and in following its progress we can gain access to some basic landscape fantasies of that period. Like the equally seminal account of the journey to Lake Manasarovar in Tibet by Moorcroft and Hearsey in 1812, Gerard's is highly eclectic in its concerns. He presents a continual series of vignettes: about the villages, crops, temples, dogs, plants, religion, people, administration and languages. Both scope and detail are breathtaking. In quick succession we move from the pleasure of grapes –

In the summer season, from the reverberation of the solar rays, the heat in the bed of the Sutlej, and other large streams is oppressive, and quite sufficient to bring to maturity grapes of a delicious flavour.[80]

– to the study of languages:

The Koonawur language, of which we made a collection of nearly 1,000 words, differs much from the Hindee, most of the substantives ending in -ing and ung, and the verbs in -mig and nig.[81]

Unlike the scientific specialists who were to dominate the second half of the century, these earlier travellers were eclectic amateurs. Their capacity for observing, noting and collecting was relentless. At one state in his journey, Moorcroft had reached utter exhaustion: 'though I climbed as slowly as possible, I was obliged to stop every five or six paces to take breath'. Nevertheless he still had energy to discover 'two kinds of rhubarb – one I took for the Rheum palmatum, the other was much smaller'.[82] He went into extensive details about these plants. Then, the next day, he again embarked upon 'a toilsome ascent of five hours'. After a brief but appreciative comment on the view, Moorcroft immediately set about collecting plant specimens from 'a dark green carpet formed by a short narrow leaved grass of a springy nature, and enamelled with small blue polyanthuses in tufts, with anemones and ranunculuses ... '.[83] The most striking thing about this exercise is its totally random character. Moorcroft simply gathered 'all the varieties within ... reach'. Here was a veritable plenitude – wherever one happened to glance, discoveries could not help but be made. Indeed, in the face of this over-abundance, how does one go about 'scientific' exploration? What actually *is* important; what should one look for and collect? In the early nineteenth century such questions were still wide open, despite the underlying pressure generated by the growing needs of British imperialism.

Both Moorcroft's and Gerard's journeys were ostensibly undertaken to satisfy very specific questions. Moorcroft's was concerned with trade, particularly the lucrative wool from the shawl goat. Geography, let alone botany, was clearly secondary. Even finding the exact location of the fabled and sacred Lake Manasarovar assumed importance only later. Gerard, too, was primarily concerned with mapping precisely some of the major Himalayan passes:

> This pass [The Brooang] is situated in latitude 31° 23; and longitude 78° 12:, it separates Choara from Koonawur, another of the grand divisions of Busahir, which lies on both banks of the Sutlej, extending from latitude 31° 30: to 32°, and from longitude 77° 53′ to 78° 46′ It is a secluded, rugged and barren country ... It is terminated on the north and NW by a lofty chain of mountains covered with perpetual snow, upwards of 20,000 feet high ...[84]

As the Himalayas became increasingly imagined as a protective frontier, the British avidly set about locating and evaluating all the major and minor passes through them. The early-nineteenth-century enthusiasm about possible trade routes was replaced by the late-nineteenth-century concern about potential invasion routes. Confidence in the expansion of trans-Himalayan communication was replaced by a paranoiac need to be in complete control of the passes. Gerard's journey was merely the forerunner of many that would be made throughout the century with the purpose of locating and evaluating any possible weak points in the mountain frontier-wall.

We get only glimpses of the 'romance' of travel in these early accounts. Gerard, for example, writes:

> We should have afforded an amusing spectacle, seated upon blankets near a fire in the open air, surrounded by our servants, dissecting the partridges with the *kookree*, or short sword worn by the Goorkhalees, and smoking plain tobacco out of a pipe little better that what is used by the lowest classes.[85]

Not only does such a comment remind us of the aristocratic and bourgeois domination of Himalayan travel throughout the nineteenth century and well into the twentieth, it also presents us with an early example of an exploration anecdote. Exploration, as it would be understood and celebrated in the second half of the century, had scarcely been formulated in 1818, and there is still a certain pleasing naivety about Gerard's self-conscious reflections on his novel experiences. Such anecdotes would become increasingly familiar as the century progressed, finally ending their days in the twentieth century as tourist clichés.

Eventually Gerard found his path blocked by Chinese officials. Such an experience would become commonplace to Westerners throughout the century, as Tibet became a hermetically sealed-in landscape. In the history of Tibet as a sacred place, such moments of attempted entry assume crucial proportions.[86] The era of the unopposed, let alone welcomed, entrance experienced by Bogle and Turner would be a long time returning. For over a hundred years Western travellers resorted to disguise, bluff and other such subterfuge, in an attempt to enter Tibet. Moorcroft and Hearsey for example, also found the way denied them, but with a mixture of disguise (as Hindu pilgrims), stubbornness, diplomacy and, above all, the liberal use of Western medical skills, they overcame the opposition to their journey.[87] As we have seen, Manning also resorted to disguise and to the supreme bargaining power of Western medicine. Gerard used neither and was forced to turn back.

But it would be a mistake to imagine the mountain passes blocked by desperate and ferocious anti-European warriors. Whilst this image had some substance further West, on the borders with Afghanistan and Dardistan, it was almost the opposite in the Buddhist Himalayas. Gerard writes: 'The Tartars pleased us much, they have none of that ferocity of character so commonly ascribed to them.'[88] Even the incidents which finally led him to abandon his goal of entering Tibet were full of humour and good feeling. The Chinese official admitted that he did not have the means physically to prevent Gerard and his party from continuing, but in such an eventuality he, as the official in charge, would probably lose his head. All he could do was withhold provisions. This firm, but non-violent, closure of the Tibetan passes added its own qualities to the mysterious and unknown land that lay beyond.

One result of this closure was that Gerard was forced to turn back into the Himalayan frontier and to direct all his astute observational powers on to this mountain region. The Himalayas became increasingly seen as a region in their own right. Through the travels of Gerard, Moorcroft, Hearsey and others, they were shown as imaginatively alive and inhabited, as culturally and geographically rich.

The Liminal Zone

Heidegger has written that 'a boundary is not that at which something stops but ... is that from which something *begins*.'[89] Boundaries have two edges, and in between they have depth. Between the edge at which things stop and the edge at which things begin is a place of transition, of suspension: a liminal zone.[90] In such a space one is neither here nor there: one has left but not yet arrived. In the ensuing years the Himalayas gradually became imagined as such a boundary-place. At first such a fantasy was somewhat subdued, revealing itself only in isolated references or as a kind of fragmented background echo, but late in the nineteenth century, when imperial politics *demanded* a coherent boundary, the Himalayas would emerge, as if from nowhere, as a fully evolved 'frontier'. In 1774 such an image of the 'frontier of Empire' was almost meaningless, but a century later it had become fully established and integral to British identity.

In understanding the creation and maintenance of a sacred landscape, the genesis of the boundary deserves the closest possible attention. Its unique qualities are enhanced by the tension between its two edges: the known and the unknown. These complement, contradict and refract each other, causing some features of the boundary to be enhanced and others diminished. Fantasies about it are affected by the land on either side – in this case the familiar, conquered, administered and controlled territory of British India, as compared with the evasive and aloof Tibet.

The most immediately striking quality about the Himalayan region is, of course, the immensity of its mountains. As we have seen, the first estimates of their height provoked disbelief. Only gradually, by around 1821, was it accepted that they were the highest in the world, higher even than the Andes.[91] Yet the Himalayas were more than just mountain peaks. The valleys and their inhabitants, the rich flora and fauna, the complex cultural and political networks, all played their part in the creation of the Himalayan 'frontier'. Scientific curiosity, political expediency, aesthetic delight, adventure and individual self-improvement, colonization and commerce, mystic aspiration and self-fulfilment have all fed, in one way or another, upon the contents of this region, and helped to shape its imaginative contours.

Three imaginative movements were apparent in the emerging fantasy of an Himalayan frontier: a concern with crossing it; a concern with establishing it as a known, controlled, well-defined boundary; and a fascination with it as a place in its own right.

Crossing the Threshold: Going Out

Before being imagined as the northern bastion of imperial India, the Himalayas merely lay at the crossroads of British aspirations for Central Asian trade and Far Eastern communications – a place of crossings, of routes, both real and imagined. Most of the earlier travellers were more concerned with discovering ways through and across the mountains than with exploring them for their own sake.

In addition to a general curiosity about what lands lay on the other side, early-nineteenth-century British interest in the pathways across the 'snowy range' was especially motivated by an intense desire to find a channel of communication with Peking. As one diplomatic mission after another failed to be admitted at the front door of China, Tibet came to be imagined as a possible back door.[92] Using the route through Tibet to reach Peking had been vaguely considered as early as 1792, but twenty years later such a thought had more urgency about it. Compared with the firm and somewhat haughty closure of China, Tibet's exclusion of Westerners seemed easier to overcome. As we have seen, Manning nearly succeeded in taking the high road to Peking, through the back door of Lhasa.

Tibet and the Himalayas lay in the penumbra of the fascination evoked by the Celestial Empire in the West. The British gaze passed through Tibet on its way to Peking, firmly imprinting its trace across the landscape. In the first half of the nineteenth century the British were constantly reticent about their involvement in Himalayan politics, for fear of alienating China. British policy-making always had only one eye on the Himalayas whilst keeping the other on Peking.[93]

During this period, the British image of the Himalayas began to be differentiated into discrete *regions*. Attention shifted from one end of the mountain range to the other, depending on the imagined suitability of each region as a point of access to Lhasa, and hence ultimately to Peking. The early use of Bhutan was denied after 1792. Nepal then seemed to offer the best possibility, despite the violent unrest in that country. As the hopes held for Nepal slowly dimmed, attention became directed on Sikkim.[94]

This regionalization of the threshold marks a critical phase in its overall creation. The particular route taken, and the region traversed when crossing over the boundary, profoundly modify the final image of the sacred land. With a traditional *temenos*, whether holy city, sacred grove or temple precinct, it was always a matter of importance by which gate one entered or left: east, west, north or south.[95] In Tibet, such a formal orientation around the cardinal points was not so important as geographical and cultural directions. Images of Tibet were profoundly modified depending on whether the traveller approached from India in the south, with its abrupt change in landscape, culture and climate; or from China in the east, where the changes were more gradual. Alternatively, travellers entering from Ladakh would already have experienced an abrupt transition much further west when journeying from Kashmir, and would notice no change when entering Tibet. Similarly, explorers venturing from the north, from Russian territory, would have a completely different set of expectations and experiences. In addition to these objective geographical and cultural factors, there were also overriding elements of fantasy. Routes connect: they bring dissimilar places into alignment. To enter Tibet from the fabled Silk-Route to the north was quite different to approaching it from the south, from India, from the 'jewel in the crown'. But early in the last century, such well-defined regional differentiations did not exist. They were merely beginning to announce their presence.

In 1815 Sikkim's ruler was 'persuaded' to act as a link between Calcutta and Lhasa. The British viewed the relationship between Sikkim and Tibet primarily in terms of their shared religion. As the British government became more aware of the extended influence of Tibetan religion through-out the Himalayan region, its interest changed from one of detached fas-cination to one of intense concern. An understanding of this strange reli-gion, so embedded in Tibetan cultural life, in aristocratic allegiances and intrigues of state power, steadily came to be viewed as essential to any suc-cessful political or economic involvement in the Himalayas. Gradually the lines of rival imperial policy shifted away from Peking and began to inter-sect at Lhasa. By the middle of the century Britain was attempting to com-municate with Lhasa less in order to reach Peking than to improve its own Himalayan trade and to stabilize Himalayan politics.

But Sikkim, at once so rugged and so lush, was not to be fully exploited as a route to Lhasa until late in the century. In the meantime British interest shifted once again – this time to the far western Himalayas, espe-cially the barren, high-altitude deserts of Ladakh. This western region provided access to the lucrative shawl-wool trade which, as we have seen, was the explicit object of Moorcroft's journey to Lake Manasarovar. In addition, following the conclusion of the Gurkha War, Britain had a com-mon frontier with Tibet in this region. Given its remoteness from Peking, and from Lhasa, the British also hoped that their involvement in the west-ern Himalayas would not be subject to rigorous scrutiny from China. But perhaps the most important reason for their close attention to the Western Himalayas was the establishment of a hill-station at Simla. By 1827 the benefits Simla offered to European health had already been attested to by such personage as the Governor-General and his family. Suddenly, a vital centre of British imperial administration and cultural life became estab-lished in the foothills of the western Himalayas. At the same time, the acquisition of Kumaon and Garwhal brought the British into intimate con-tact with the complex and ancient ties that bound these regions with Tibet, Nepal, Ladakh, Sikkim and Bhutan.

Crossing the Threshold: Coming In

Increased British interest in the western end of the Himalayas was also the result of a quiet but critical shift in Britain's imperial political concerns. Early in the century Moorcroft had warned that the Himalayas around Kashmir were as much Russia's back door to India as they were Britain's back door to China.[96] With the conclusion of the wars against Napoleon, British anxiety about possible threats to their Indian possessions shifted towards the Russians, who were single-mindedly and vigorously expanding eastwards. It was the beginning of the 'Great Game', that nineteenth-century cloak-and-dagger precursor to the twentieth-century Cold War which was to affect every aspect of Himalayan imagining.

Both Moorcroft and Gerard were caught up in the earliest days of the 'Great Game', and mapping the passes of the western Himalayas was viewed as an increasingly urgent task.[97] The Russian victory over Persia in 1828 drew British attention to the unknown regions that formed the northern and north-western frontier of their Indian possessions. As Russia moved its Asian frontier eastwards through the course of the nineteenth century, British fantasies about the Himalayas shifted accordingly. By the middle of the century only the western end of this mountain chain was unduly affected by these insecure fantasies, but the second half of the century saw such fears extended to the central region and to Tibet itself, the eastern region of the Himalayas, on the other hand, always remained comparatively unaffected by the 'Great Game'.

Here is the beginning of a fundamental tension that would extend, with varying intensity, from one end of the Himalayas to the other. Were the numerous passes the gateways to China, to the fabled gold mines, to a lucrative trade with the vast, untapped markets of Central Asia, or were they the almost undefendable back doors into the always vulnerable British Indian Empire, its Achilles heel? Such contradiction and paradox was basic to the imaginative creation of the Himalayan frontier. As Britain became increasingly established in India and as the 'Raj' became a critical landmark of British identity, the fantasy of the Himalayan passes as the gateways to 'the Beyond' would be replaced almost entirely by a fortress mentality.

Such a nervous ambivalence is hinted at in the 1818 report by the surveyor Herbert. Whilst exploring one of these passes, he mused:

> Neither this one or any of the others had been yet examined by Europeans; indeed, previous to the commencement of the present survey, *the existence of such passes had not even been suspected ...* the Himmaleh having been always supposed to form an impenetrable barrier between Hindoostan and Chinese Tartary.[98]

Similarly, when Francis Buchanan Hamilton compiled his classic account of Nepal in 1819 for the East India Company, he wrote:

> The ridge of snowy alps ... has few interruptions, and, in most places, is said to be totally insuperable. Several rivers that arise in Thibet pass through among its peaks, but amidst such tremendous

precipices, and by such narrow gaps, that these openings are in general totally impracticable.[99]

As the century progressed closer attention to these mountains revealed a veritable honeycomb of passes. It must be remembered that mountaineering was in its infancy, and that apart from traversing well-worn trade and pilgrim routes, the inhabitants of the Himalayas were not mountaineers. The closer the British engaged with the mountains, the more passes appeared. What was considered impractical to the early-nineteenth-century traveller often came to be viewed as almost a highway by later, more experienced mountaineers. The very nebulousness of the Russian threat also encouraged a variety of fears. A pass that was too difficult for an army could still be of use to a small and determined band of saboteurs.

The Imaginative Gradient

Attention must be given to the two edges of the liminal zone that protects and defines a sacred space: the edge that leads from the known, and the edge that leads into the unknown. These two extremes create a steep imaginative gradient between them, a tension of opposites which intensifies the contradictions, ambivalences and paradoxes of the landscape that separates them. This *coincidenta oppositorum*, or meeting of opposites, expresses the mystery of passage, of passing over and of returning. The Himalayas increasingly became a place where a radical and abrupt change in consciousness was both expected and desired.

Throughout the whole of the nineteenth century a struggle ensued between European Romanticism, its enthusiasm reinforced by imperial confidence, and the Himalayas themselves, which continually refused to be constrained within such fantasies. The immense *verticality* of the mountains, with their steep contrast between perpetually silent, snow-clad peaks and dark, densely vegetated valleys, echoed the intense *horizontal* mystery of the frontier. Moving from one side of the boundary to the other was increasingly likened to entering a new world, a world outside time and space. So too, the ascent of these soaring mountains, whether physically or merely in the eye of the imagination, was likened to a passage between the realm of impermanence and that of immortality. Standing back on the plains and just gazing at the Indian edge of this threshold was sufficient to turn the mind to an intimation of higher things. As Robert Colebrook, the Surveyor-General, wrote in 1807: 'The weather was clear, and the whole range of snowy mountains was visible, and presented a scene which for grandeur can scarcely be rivalled.'[100] The Tibetans came to be viewed as the gentle guardians of the threshold, past whom only the most deserving could venture – but this is to look ahead.

As yet, in the first half of the nineteenth century, the 'frontier' lacked imaginative coherence. Even as late as 1849 that tireless explorer-scholar Brian Hodgson bemoaned that the Himalayas were 'quite without a plan'.[101]

We have seen that as the century progressed, British interests increasingly demanded a rational and systematic mapping of the Himalayas. The name of Hodgson was associated with two notable early attempts at achieving such a goal, but it belonged to two very different men and two very different enterprises. Between 1815 and 1818 John Hodgson began the first systematic survey along the length of the Himalayas, until illness obliged him to hand over the task to others. This mammoth undertaking, completed in 1822, produced an important map: *The Mountain Provinces between the Rivers Sutlej and Ganges, and bounded on the North by Chinese Tartary and Ladak.*[102] The Himalayas were now effectively connected to the grid which the Great Trigonometric Survey had thrown across India, and hence were now 'rationally' and tangibly joined to Britain and to its scientific and imperial aspirations.

The other mapping of the Himalayas associated with the name Hodgson was one which embraced the study of geology, languages, customs, religions, fauna, flora and politics. This project was begun by Brian Hodgson in the first half of the century and continued by him almost until its conclusion. Brian Hodgson's work was of seminal importance, not just for the Himalayas but also in the formulation of the new sciences – from ethnography to linguistics.[103]

But once again we have moved ahead just a little too quickly: the early nineteenth century was not yet obsessed with exhaustive and systematic scientific surveys. The collection of geological and ethnographic details, of landscape views and botanical specimens, was made only from what lay within immediate reach. Rather like Moorcroft hastily gathering plant specimens whilst lying exhausted on the ground, it was all a matter of chance encounters. Items tumbled over one another in a gloriously random profusion. Wherever one looked, whenever one stopped to gather, fresh discoveries were to be found. In most cases, only the route and chronology of the journey gave any semblance of order to the collection.

The attitude of many British early in the century was perhaps expressed best by Lord Moira, the Governor-General, on an official tour up-country in 1814: 'The sight was truly grand. The snow, illuminated by the beams, looked exquisitely brilliant … Yet at this moment I am speculating on the trade which may be carried on beyond it …'.[104] Views and trade, trade and views– these were the dominant sentiments of the age, both dovetailing delightfully in the Himalayan landscape.

The Dalai Lama, Lhasa, and the Creation of Tibet

And what of Tibet, the unknown land that lay on the other side of the newly emerging frontier? In fact, for most of the early nineteenth century the British were not unduly concerned with Tibet, except in so far as it was caught up in Anglo – Chinese communications. Of course, Tibet was still the place of rumours – the sacred Lake Manasarovar mentioned by Pliny and Marco Polo, the source of the Ganges and of the Brahmaputra, the place of gold and silver mines. It was also viewed optimistically in terms of possible trading links with India. But by 1816 the Tibetan policy initiated by Warren Hastings had all but been abandoned. Nevertheless, scholarly research was still being supported, if not enthusiastically, as in Csoma de Koros's Tibetan dictionary and Brian Hodgson's collection of religious manuscripts.

In many ways, the British attitude towards the Dalai Lama mirrored all the ambiguities in their wider relationship to the whole of Tibet. While the Dalai Lama would have to wait until much later in the nineteenth century before assuming a central role in Britain's Tibetan drama, innumerable lines of influence were already beginning to converge on his Potala palace at Lhasa. The Dalai Lama was waiting in the wings, his script being prepared, until on cue he would step fully evolved into centre-stage. His physical elusiveness throughout the century was a crucial aspect of the evolving myth, forming a sharp contrast with the absolute centrality of his position within Tibetan culture and politics.

Only one British traveller actually met the Dalai Lama in well over a hundred years. Thomas Manning, like Bogle and Turner before him with the Tashi or Panchen Lama, underwent a profound experience upon his rare encounter.

> The Lama's beautiful and interesting face and manner engrossed almost all my attention. He was at that time about seven years old: had the simple and unaffected manners of well-educated princely child. His face was, I thought, poetically and affectingly beautiful.[105]

Manning left the interview deeply moved: 'I could have wept through strangeness of sensation.' Later he wrote, 'I strove to draw the Lama.' One of his characteristically eccentric yet most intimate footnotes reads:

> 1st Dec., 17th of tenth Moon. This day I saluted the Grand Lama! Beautiful youth. Face poetically affecting; could have wept. Very happy to have seen him and his blessed smile. Hope often to see him again.[106]

Manning, that exemplar of late Classical Europe, had made contact with an image of divine perfection. His adoring salutation to the Dalai Lama belongs, along with Bogle's to the Panchen Lama, to a past era of reason, order and spiritual ecstasy. Western adoration of the Dalai Lama then went into quiescence and reappeared only eighty years later, in the theosophical imagination.[107] In both Manning's diary and the writings of the founder of theosophy, Madam Blavatsky, the Grand Lama transcends any political, social and religious connections but never loses his unique Tibetan-ness. But Manning's image of the Lama comes as if from nowhere, whereas Blavatsky's, as we shall see, had been gathering the fragments of its form throughout the nineteenth century. Just as Manning's image of the Tibetan Lama's divinity simultaneously ended one era and initiated another, so too would Blavatsky's. Her Lama arose from the carefully gathered images that had been brought back from Tibet over nearly a hundred years. Images that had found increasingly fertile ground in the Western imagination.

After Manning's late, unpublished but ecstatic salutation, the Dalai Lama became a distant, elusive and enigmatic figure of power and authority in the journals of Western travellers. But for all his physical absence, he gradually came to exert a formidable *imaginative presence*. Travellers were constantly to encounter examples of his power and of Tibetan hegemony in their journeys through the Himalayas, yet the Dalai Lama like Tibet itself, was almost formless and shapeless. Tibetan hegemony, too, was seldom exerted by armed force. More often it was by unseen connections, through kinship, cultural ties and religious obligations. For example, more typical of the encounter with the Dalai Lama during this period than Manning's were those reported by Moorcroft and Hearsey during their journey to Lake Manasarovar. Whilst complaining about the past troublesome behaviour of the 'independent *Tartars of Ladak*', Moorcroft observed that their deference to the Dalai Lama had resulted in a moderation of their behaviour.

The sacredness of this personage, who is the head of the religion of the Tartars, caused them to desist from their incursions, and probably, would have the same influence in the event of any alteration in the current of trade.[108]

Later, in an exchange of gifts with an old lama, Moorcroft received 'some slips of gauze', which the Dalai Lama had sent to the old priest. In addition, he was given 'some red comfits made of flour, water, and some red colouring matter: they were insipid, but having been made by the holy hands of the head of the church of this country, were said to possess extraordinary virtues'.[109] In contrast to Manning's direct and intimate encounter with an individual who stood outside any particular social form, Moorcroft's Dalai Lama was an aloof and elusive presence exerting his power through the channels of religious ritual, trade, law and order.

Naturally, the Dalai Lama was also integral to British attempts to understand Tibetan religion. This in itself was complicated by European confusions about Buddhism and the exact relationship of Tibetan religion to it. Early in the century, the term 'Buddhism' was not even in common usage. Francis Buchanan Hamilton writes only of 'the followers of Buddh' or 'the sect of Bouddh': 'The Lamas are the priests of the sect of Bouddh, in Thibet and the adjacent territories ...' .[110] He drew a distinction between a *Guatama* who lived in the sixth century BC and a *Sakya* who lived in the first century AD, and continued by pointing out that the Tibetans 'consider the Buddhs as emanations from a supreme deity, view many of their Lamas as incarnations of a Buddh, and accordingly worship them as living Gods, although they do not consider them equal to Sakya, who is the Lama of Lassa'.[111] Until the sudden availability of Sanskrit texts after 1830, made possible by Brian Hodgson's labours, the full nature of Buddhism, let alone the Tibetan variant, would remain obscure. Nevertheless, it was already becoming clear that Tibetan religion was not an isolated anomaly but part of a spiritual belief embraced by a considerable proportion of the world's population. In many ways it was this sheer scale of Buddhism that drew the attention of many Western observers. It also seemed that the Dalai Lama was a significant figure not only in Tibet but wherever the 'followers of Buddh' were to be found.

The relationship between Tibetan religion and Buddhism was to be a controversial issue throughout the nineteenth century and well into the twentieth, but as we shall see, by mid-century systematic studies of both had been attempted. However, it was easier for the West to produce a rational and coherent 'Buddhism' from *textual* sources than from the seemingly chaotic and cultural-bound *practices* of Tibetan religion. Tibetan Buddhism, unlike other forms, was never to be imagined independent of its land of origin. Travellers, rather than scholars, continued to dominate the shaping of Tibetan Buddhism in the Western imagination throughout the century. Their direct encounters with the religion's practitioners produced complex and contradictory impressions: attitudes towards monasticism were generally mixed and somewhat reserved; recluses and hermits were treated carefully and with some respect; the ordinary Tibetans, despite being the object of scorn for their superstitions and gullibility, evoked consistent respect for their all-pervading sincerity and faith.[112] At this stage, only a passing interest was shown in Tibetan metaphysics and ritual. The tireless labours of Csoma de Koros, for example, were as much inspired by linguistics and Hungarian nationalism as by religious curiosity.

Whenever the Tibetan religion was compared with Islam, no matter what was thought of its internal contradictions, it was always viewed most favourably. Moorcroft, for example, wrote that whilst Islam has encouraged temperance, 'it has introduced much more dissoluteness, dishonesty and disregard for truth, than prevails in those places where Lamaism still predominates'.[113] Yet, he continued, Lamaism itself is 'a strange mixture of metaphysics, mysticism, morality, fortune-telling, juggling and idolatory. The doctrine of the metampsychosis is curiously blended with tenets and precepts very similar to those of Christianity and with the worship of grotesque divinities.'[114] Here were all the contradictions that Tibetan religion aroused in the contemporary Western mind.

As the myriad images of Tibet and its religion slowly began to present themselves to the Western imagination – although not yet to assemble themselves into any coherent shape – they always seemed paradoxical, enticing yet distasteful. Moorcroft's comment that the monks at a monastery he visited 'seem a happy, good humoured set of people, dirty, greasy and in good ease', was typical.[115] Yet this strange religious culture seemed to cast its net across the entire Himalayas – was a unifying influence in the region that could not be ignored. It is understandable that intense efforts were later to be made to unravel it, to understand and evaluate it systematically.

No less prominent than the Dalai Lama, and just as elusive in the emerging fantasy of Tibet, was the city of Lhasa. Again, not until much later in the century would Lhasa appear as a fully evolved and coherent object of Western longing. Yet, as with the Dalai Lama, fragmentary images were slowly being deposited throughout the first half of the nineteenth century, images upon which the fabled city of the Western imagination would eventually arise. At this stage, however. Lhasa was viewed merely as either an important but provincial outpost of the Chinese Empire, or as a centre of influence among the small Himalayan hill states.[116] Only when British policy shifted and the Himalayas came to be regarded as important in their own right did Lhasa become imaginally emancipated from its subservience to Peking. Once again, despite his eccentricity, Manning's attitude towards Lhasa echoed that of many of his fellow-travellers. His impression in 1811 was of a dirty and desolate place of exile for out-of-favour Chinese bureaucrats. Whilst Lhasa was an important place for Tibetans and other people of the mountains and Central Asia, it was hardly a great centre of civilization. Manning's entry into the city is worth recording in detail, so sharp is its contrast with the golden fantasies of the future Victorian era.

When he arrived, he was reminded of Rome. Such an association would continually recur in the fantasies of later travellers, but would be based then upon its wide-ranging influence rather than any physical resemblance, for indeed no other nineteenth-century Briton would actually see the city. Ostensibly, Manning's association had nothing to do with the regional influence of Lhasa; it was also only marginally related to the city's architectural appearance. True to his whimsical imagination, Manning was impressed solely by the proximity of marshland to both capitals. But perhaps he was less naive than he appears, and his association of Lhasa with Rome was stimulated by the many earlier comparisons of Tibetan religion with Catholicism. Moorcroft echoes such sentiments: 'of the *Paraphernalia* of the temple, the resemblance with those of the *Romish* church was very striking.'[117] Any comparison with Roman Catholicism generally had a double edge, given the suspicion directed at that religion by most nineteenth-century British travellers. Manning, for example, comments: 'We are apt to think the Muhammadan religion eminently intolerable: but if it be fairly examined, it will be found much less so than the Roman Catholic, both in practice and in principle'.[118]

Manning was certainly impressed by the Potala palace. He commented that it produced a 'striking and grand effect' and continued: 'The road here, as it winds past the palace, is royally broad; it is level and free from stones ... '.[119] But his admiration stopped there and his subsequent impressions reinforced the growing belief that the Tibetan landscape was disturbingly paradoxical. 'If the palace had exceeded my expectations', he wrote,

> the town as far fell short of them. There is nothing striking, nothing pleasing in its appearance. The habitations are begrimed with smut and dirt. The avenues are full of dogs, some growling and gnawing bits of hide which lie around in profusion, and emit a charnel-house smell; others limping and looking livid; others ulcerated; others starved and dying, and pecked at by the ravens; some dead and preyed upon. In short everything seems mean and gloomy, and excites the idea of something unreal. Even the mirth and laughter of the inhabitants I thought dreamy and ghostly.[120]

One can only wonder how such a place would ever excite the desperate longings of generations of Europeans later in the century, especially when Manning's eye-witness description was readily available.

In these travel accounts, different levels of fantasy and association constantly slide across one another: the Dalai Lama and his Potala place, whilst obviously belonging to Lhasa and to Tibetan religion, were also somehow different; the monasticism, the religion, the people, their culture, even the landscape did not yet add up to a coherent whole. The Dalai Lama was respected, yet the monasticism was suspected; the Tibetans were liked, but their dirt and their customs – such as polyandry – evoked distaste; the austerity of the landscape was considered inspirational, but its barrenness was abhorred. Such contradictions and seemingly irrevocable dissociations were not easily resolved, and not until the very end of the nineteenth century would the West evolve a fantasy-place of sufficient complexity to embrace them all.

As British people's confidence in their imperial presence in the Himalayas increased and became a 'natural' part of their global identity, their curiosity became augmented by arrogance; the Classical era's sense of a common human brotherhood was replaced by a belief in racial and cultural differences. Manning, for example, enthusiastically embraced Asian habits in clothing and was even willing to give due respect to Asian religious formalities: 'Any form and ceremony that is required I shall go through and nothing further.'[121] However, despite his ecstatic encounter with the Dalai Lama, he never desired to embrace Tibetan religion. Such aspirations among Westerners would have to wait until the very end of the century. Manning mused:

> All religions as they are established have a mixture in them of good and evil, and upon the whole they all perhaps tend to civilize and ameliorate mankind: as such I respect them. As for the common idea that the founders of all religions except our own were imposters, I consider it as a vulgar error.[122]

Manning's panhumanism belonged to a passing age: it was soon replaced by a *Weltanschauung* characterized by developing human sciences such as ethnography and sociology, with all their connotations of knowledge and power, assessment and evaluative schemas.[123]

If Manning ('When I entered the temples in Bengal, if there were natives about, I always made a salam') is the last representative of a bygone age, then Lieutenant White stands as a forerunner of the future. At the beginning of this chapter we saw how his 1825 journey into the newly 'acquired' territories of 'Sirmour, Gurwhal and Kumaon' marked the beginnings of an aesthetic appropriation of the Himalayas by the West. These mountains now firmly *belonged* to Britain in a way that lay outside the earlier imaginations of Bogle, Turner, Manning and even Moorcroft. White was visiting territory that had become merely an exciting, unknown extension of Britain. The inhabitants, with their cultures, were now to be administered, controlled and, perhaps, picturesquely admired. How different this world was from Manning's! White strongly advised Westerners to avoid visiting places where their values might be compromised. For example, he wrote that removing one's shoes at a Hindu temple 'is an acknowledgement of the sanctity of the place, which no Christian ought to give'.[124] On the other hand, he suggested, a European should not show 'the haughty superciliousness, arrogance and contemptuous conduct, too characteristic of Anglo-Indians'. He regretted that 'the influx of European travellers' was bringing to the hills these attitudes that were 'so prevalent in the plains'. White was attempting to sort out rules of conduct befitting a race which considered that it possessed, superior knowledge, virtue, wisdom, science, etc. By the middle of the century such an elitist attitude would be fully engaged not only with the people and their cultures, but also with the mountains themselves.

Places and Styles of Travel

The first half of the nineteenth century was a formative period both for the creation of Tibet and the Himalayas as *places*, and also for the establishment of travel writing as a genre. Construction was begun not only on the Himalayan frontier but also on the core-image of Himalayan exploration, on its personae and its dramas. Such an image was never simple and at least seven main themes have been identified in this chapter: Manning exemplified the concern for details, for the intimate, inside stories of the journey, of the traveller and of the place itself, White's concern was with aesthetics; Moorcroft was primarily a commercial adventurer; Gerard prefigured the systematic, scientific explorers soon to be promoted by the Royal Geographical Society; Hamilton's journeys belonged to a tradition of diplomatic, fact-finding missions; Henry and Shipp offered experiences that would be typical of many soldiers who fought in Britain's nineteenth-century Himalayan campaigns; Herbert approached the mountains as a dedicated surveyor.

Notably absent were the expedition leaders and the mountaineers. The former would soon arrive on the scene, whereas the mountains would have to wait much longer for the latter. Finally, with the exception of the Frenchmen Huc and Gabet, the Himalayas and Tibet had not yet witnessed a nineteenth-century missionary, or mystic, assault from the West, and certainly not from Britain. All these styles of engaging with the landscape would add their images to the emerging place of Tibet, struggling to impose their own coherence on its contours. The mid-century would see all these struggles subsumed under the hegemony of systematic, comprehensive and scientific surveys.

A frontier imagination was being born, as critical to the Himalayas as it was to the American West. It would colour every aspect of the mountains, from aesthetics to ethnography. But this was not a colonizing frontier, mobile and expanding, like the American West, but one whose main purpose, *stability and containment*, was quite the opposite.

4

The *Axis Mundi* Appears
(mid-nineteenth century)

Since the sacred mountain is an *axis mundi* connecting earth with heaven, it in a sense touches heaven and hence marks the highest point in the world; consequently the territory that surrounds it ... is held to be the highest among countries.

(M. Eliade [1959. p.38])

Method in the Mountains

In 1869 Nina Mazuchelli, English despite her Italian-sounding name, became the first Western woman to see the famed Mount Everest. 'It was', she exclaimed, 'the dream of my childhood to see this nearest point of Heaven and Earth ... As I stand in these vast solitudes I do so with bent knee and bowed head as becomes one who is in the *felt* presence of the Invisible.'[1] Mount Everest had been declared the highest mountain on the globe some seventeen years previously, during the course of a decade that was a watershed in the British relationship to Tibet.

It began with the publication in English of Huc and Gabet's account of their famous journey to Lhasa in 1846. For the first time a widespread and well-informed public had access to an eye-witness account of this elusive and mysterious city. The first edition immediately sold out.[2] Joseph Hooker's *Himalayan Journals*, which described his extensive botanical journeys through Sikkim and up to the Tibetan border, was similarly an instant success when first published in 1854.[3] Between 1846 and 1847 the western Himalayas were subjected to an exhaustive survey by the three members of the commission established to define Tibet's boundary with the British 'protected' territories of Jammu, Kashmir and Ladakh. Alexander Cunningham, Thomas Thomson and Henry Strachey compiled extensive reports that covered the culture, geology, geography, botany and history of this region. Cunningham's *Ladâk*, published in 1853, is still used as a basic reference.[4]

Between 1854 and 1858 the Schlagintweit brothers journeyed extensively through the Himalayas and Central Asia gathering information that would eventually result in the publication of *Buddhism in Tibet*, the first overview study of its kind[5] A major survey of the Himalayan peaks was undertaken between 1846 and 1855.[6] The Himalayas were hence no longer unknown territory, nor was British understanding of this mountain region fragmented and unsystematized. The tireless Brian Hodgson, from his bases in Kathmandu and Darjeeling, had, since early in the century, produced paper after paper documenting and classifying everything Himalayan: from the geography to the religions, from the racial characteristics of the hill tribes to their languages. His systematization of the Tibetan Buddhist pantheon provided a cornerstone that still supports Western understanding of that religion.[7]

In 1849 Hodgson wrote:

I had been for several years a traveller in the Himalayas, before I could get rid of that tyranny of the senses which so strongly impresses all beholders of this stupendous scenery with the conviction that the mighty maze is quite without a plan.[8]

Tibet and the Himalayas were a part of this search for an imaginative *coherence*, a plan. The great German scholar Max Muller subsequently praised Hodgson for producing a 'rational grammar' of the mountain chaos.[9] Hodgson applied the same energy to classifying what he called the 'babel' of the hill tribes and fitting them into a schema of cultural evolution. The mid-century seemed obsessed with 'blank spots' or 'gaps' on the map[10] People wanted a world in which everything fitted and had its place, but the plan seemed constantly in danger of being overwhelmed by the plenitude of new discoveries.

These comprehensive studies were the culmination of nearly a century of Himalayan and Tibetan exploration by the British and allowed, in their turn, the compilation of several complete regional studies of Tibet. In addition to Schlagintweit's comprehensive work on Tibetan Buddhism, H. Prinsep's *Tibet, Tartary and Mongolia* (Their Social and Political Condition, the Religion of Boodh As There Existing, Compiled from the reports of Ancient and Modern Travellers) was published in 1852. Much shorter, but of a similar intention, was Dr C.H. Gutzlaff's 'Tibet and Sefan', published in the *Journal of the Royal Geographical Society* in 1851.[11] These works were of a totally different order to the summary statements about Tibet compiled by Warren Hastings or by others earlier in the century.

The publication in 1859 of R. Latham's massive two-volume *Descriptive Ethnology* shows just how successful Britain had been in gathering and classifying an astonishing amount of ethnographic material from around the entire globe.[12] This was British imperialism at its most confident. The Great Exhibition of 1851, at the Crystal Palace in London, symbolized the calm assurance of British global identity. Prince Albert opened it with the words:

Nobody who has paid attention to the peculiar features of the present era will doubt for a moment that we are living at a period of most wonderful transition, which tends rapidly to accomplish that great end, to which, indeed, all history points – the realization of the unity of mankind.[13]

Nineteenth-century nationalism provided idealized images of coherence, unification and identity which belied intense internal social fragmentation and conflict. Hooker and other global travellers played a crucial part in the creation of the Great Exhibition.[14] It expressed so well all the cultural contradictions, spiritual hopes and imperial assumptions that underlay British global identity. The globe was presented as a supermarket of fascinating images. Travel and exploration gave these global images a cohesion that was both sensual and visual. British travellers, whether journeying for science or sport, increasingly saw themselves as citizens of the globe.

The Imaginal Transformation of Tibet: from Fascination to Expectation

In the mid-nineteenth century, however, Tibet was overshadowed by events elsewhere on the globe, especially in the Arctic and in Africa. The search for Franklin's ill-fated Arctic expedition, and then for the source of the Nile, dominated British interests in exploration, adventure and geographical research.[15] How did it happen, then, that by the last quarter of the century curiosity about Tibet became transformed into a fascination bordering on compulsion; that a sober concern for scientific observation became attenuated into an attitude of intense spiritual expectation? Of course, even in mid-century one can detect signs of this final transformation. Hooker, for example, could scarcely disguise his excitement when actually standing inside Tibet, even if he was there for only four days. Gutzlaff, perhaps, summed up the general mid-century feeling:

Tibet, situated on the highest plateau of Asia, and encompassed by the most stupendous mountains of the globe, is a wonderful country ... It is ... a territory where extremes meet, and where everything is extraordinary. The inhabitants, not satisfied with their strange country, have strongly contributed to enhance the wonderful by their curious mode of life and creed.[16]

Yet his fascination with what he called 'this magic land' was not unequivocal. About its religion he wrote: 'In mockery of common sense, a preposterous superstition has been established.' He complained about 'the maintenance of innumerable priestly drones', of a 'priest-ridden' country. How different was such an evaluation from Turner's, some sixty years earlier, with its appreciation of the mutual reciprocity of sacred and secular activities.[17] Gutzlaff observed, with some frustration, that 'Tibet remains impervious to civilization and progress.' Yet by the end of the century, this archaic timelessness would be precisely the quality that the West would seek to protect.

But we need to step back from the Himalayas and Tibet, to take note of other events of the 1850s. The uprising of 1857 known as the Indian Mutiny resulted in the final demise of the British East India Company. India came firmly under the control of the British government. The rebellion was a turning point in British imperialism on the subcontinent. A fundamental sense of security was destroyed and the British in India, from that moment, always felt vulnerable to foreign 'trouble making'; were always fearful about the loyalty of their Indian subjects. With the resumption of rivalry with imperial Russia in the 1870s after a mid-century lull, such an erosion of confidence was crucial for Britain's relationship with the Himalayas and Tibet. As we shall see in the next chapter, more than anything else the intensification of the 'Great Game' proved critical for the final imaginative transformation of Tibet into a fully formed sacred place.

Even further removed from the Himalayas than the Indian Mutiny was the publication of two books within a few years of each other. So widespread was their influence that the imaginative transformation of Tibet into a deeply meaningful place is incomprehensible without taking them into account. 1859 saw the publication of Darwin's *Origin of Species*. The Himalayas had played a direct and critical part in the development of Darwin's revolutionary ideas through his close collaboration with Joseph Hooker. Indeed, Hooker's *Himalayan Journals* were dedicated to Darwin, and Hooker took Darwin's *Voyage of the Beagle* as a model for his own travel journals.[18] Whilst Hooker's botanizing in the Himalayas contributed to the genesis of evolutionary theory, the rapid acceptance of this theory, especially in the form of social evolution, would in its turn influence the whole shape of Tibetan imaginings.

The other book was no less significant, but easier to overlook. Volume 4 of John Ruskin's *Modern Painters* was published in 1854; it systematized the quintessence of advanced Victorian ideas about mountain landscape aesthetics. This book emerged at the very apex of British enthusiasm for mountains, often called the 'Golden Age' of Alpine exploration. Its impact was therefore decisive; its influence profound.[19] During this time, climbing was described as an activity that was half-spiritual, half-sport. Like Darwin, Ruskin must be considered as a founder of the modern relationship to the natural world, but his theme was the imaginative experience of natural beauty – the *aesthetics* of ecology, not abstract classification. In Volume 4 he tried to establish the rules for an entirely new way of seeing and relating to the landscapes of the world.

Perhaps even more important for the final transformation of Tibet was the sudden collapse of mid-Victorian confidence after 1865. The carefully orchestrated mid-century synthesis, the 'best of all possible worlds', seemed to peak and then, just as quickly, to vanish. An era of spiritual doubt and social anxiety took its place.[20] It is instructive in this regard to compare Gutzlaff's comprehensive study of Tibet, written in 1851, with Andrew Wilson's popular account *The Abode of Snow*, written in 1875 at the very end of this period. For Gutzlaff, as we have seen, Tibet was indeed a 'magical land', yet hardly one that evoked Western inspiration. Wilson, on the other hand, prefaced his otherwise fairly sober account with a remarkable series of associations. The true 'Abode of Snow', he wrote, was not the Himalayas, nor even the Arctic, but the Antarctic. He argued that as the ice accumulates around the South Pole, a point must be reached when:

> the balance of the earth must be suddenly destroyed, and this orb shall almost instantaneously turn traversely to its axis, moving the great oceans, and so producing one of those cyclical catastrophes which ... have before now interfered with the development and the civilization of the human race.[21]

The mid-century global confidence no longer rested on firm ground. Globalism, which had brought the promise of a secure imperial identity only twenty-five years earlier, now seemed to have brought its own anxieties. Wilson continued:

> How near such a catastrophe may be, and whether when it occurs, a few just men (and it is to be hoped, women also) will certainly be left in the upper valleys of the Himalayas, I am unable to say; but it is well to know that there is an elevated and habitable region of the earth which is likely to be left underpopulated ... Whether humanity will lose or gain by having to begin again from the simple starting point of 'Om mani padme haun', is also a subject on which I feel a little uncertain.[22]

This was an extraordinary fantasy; one which prefigured the desperate hopes of many twentieth-century Tibetophiles and their images of Shangri-La. Tibet was linked here not just to a concern about *Western* identity and aspirations but to the very survival and continuance of civilization, even of humanity itself. Like a Himalayan Ararat, Tibet was imagined to rise above the global catastrophe and 'the jewel in the lotus' to seed the civilization of the future. For Wilson, this famous Tibetan mantra seemed to contain the beautiful and mysterious quintessence of 'many hundreds of human generations'.[23].

With Wilson's fantasies in *The Abode of Snow,* we have reached the final limit of imaginative preparation. As the *fin-de-siècle* uncertainty intensified, Tibet would be summoned to play its part in the West's spiritual search. The cosmic sympathy expressed by Nina Mazuchelli for Mount Everest would be displaced on to Lhasa. This city, with the Potala palace at its 'centre', would become an *axis mundi,* an opening to the transcendent at the very centre of the world. Tibet would then echo Eliade's assertion that 'an entire country ... [can] well present an *imago mundi'.*[24]

Imaginative Resonance

There are moments during the process of imaginative creation when seemingly diverse fantasies start to beat in time and then swell into a single resonance. A great chord is struck and held for a while. Both participants and listeners seem overcome with the primordial, archetypal purity of the sound. Everything then becomes a signifier for this great imaginative chord. At this moment the sacred place is truly born; its imaginative history begins. It then has its own coherence and logic. In the case of Tibet such a moment occurred about three-quarters of the way through the nineteenth century. The harmony of the great chord was then inexorably stamped upon Western fantasies about Tibet. Its presence continued to linger and echo well into the twentieth century, long after the conditions for its birth had dissipated and the separate fantasies had moved on.

A complete realignment of fantasies took place. Old images and themes either acquired new meaning or were repositioned and hence became imbued with fresh, and often more potent, significance. These various imaginative themes on Tibet had had nearly a century to attune themselves to each other. The arrival of new, additional ones precipitated the final transformation. If Ruskin's new way of perceiving and experiencing landscape, Darwin's evolutionary theory, Himalayan mountaineering, photography and tourism were the *catalysts,* then the last, intensely competitive, phase of the 'Great Game' provided the necessary *energy* for the alchemical reaction. The process occurred in three stages. First there had to be a build-up of meaningful fantasies, of both intimate associations and compendious facts. These disparate themes then needed to realign themselves, to establish a correspondence with each other. Finally this cohesive set of fantasies had to organize themselves around a common core, condense themselves into a common image which would then become transferred to – and focused upon – Lhasa.

An Empirical Imagination

So often in these travel accounts the moment of entering Tibet reveals, most consistently, the depth-imagination at work. As Wilson laboriously ascended a pass into Tibet, he remarked that it was, at 16,000 feet, 'above the height of Mont Blanc':[25] simple fact, yet pregnant with meaning for the Alpine-loving British travellers. We have also come a long way from the vague Romantic generalizations so common earlier in the century. For example, Wilson enthused about a view 'that was savage and grand beyond description'. Yet describe it he does, and in such a way as to reveal a casual familiarity with sophisticated mountain details:

> A mountain rose ... almost sheer up from the Sutlej, or from 9,000 feet to the height of 22,183 feet, in gigantic walls, towers, and *aiguilles* of cream coloured granite and quartz, which had all the appearance of marble ... In appearance it was something like Milan Cathedral divested of its loftiest spire, and magnified many million times ... Here and there the white rock was streaked with snow, and it was capped by an enormous citadel with small beds of *névé*; but there was very little snow upon the gigantic mass of rock because the furious winds which forever beat and howl around it allow but little snow to find a resting place.[26]

In this passage, Wilson achieves a blend of empirical accuracy and imaginative eloquence that expresses so well the new way of perceiving landscape championed by Ruskin. Ruskin stamped his influence upon the entire Victorian era. Whether he was addressing landscape, morality, painting, sculpture, architecture, economics, politics or science, his method was always the same: sharp analytical eye and a controlled imagination were combined to produce a critical aesthetic appreciation and critique of the environment in which he lived. By 1875, when Wilson was travelling through the Himalayas, Ruskin was already a national institution.[27]

Ruskin was highly critical of both vague reverie and mere geographical accuracy. By the mid-nineteenth century, it was the latter in particular that had the most status. Hooker, for example, wrote:

> I have been precise in my details, because the vagueness with which terms are usually applied to the apparent altitude and steepness of mountains, is apt to give false impressions. It is essential to attend to such points where scenery of real interest and importance is to be described.[28]

These are sentiments with which Ruskin would have been in total agreement, yet at the same time he would consider that they told only half the story. Ruskin insisted that the imagination, too, was both indispensable for a 'true' description and also subject to a rigour and discipline no less demanding than scientific observation. He was concerned with what he called the branches of 'scenic knowledge', in which precision of description was matched by intensity of feeling.[29]

Ruskin was therefore engaged upon two fronts. Certainly the language of Thomson's *Western Himalayas and Tibet* (1852), acclaimed as 'one of the most substantial books on Himalayan exploration of the 19th century', would have been antithetical to his project.[30] The only adjective Thomson seemed to know was 'remarkable' – 'a very remarkable outburst of granite'; 'a very long and remarkable bend of the river': etc.[31] This work exactly fitted the prevailing mid-century mood: scientific exploration and no-nonsense observation. Thomson's friend and fellow-traveller, Hooker, despaired of exploration without science, and his journals have been acclaimed as classics in the field of scientific travel,[32] but the greatness of these volumes lies precisely in his ability to blend empirical observation with moments of reverie. His attention to light and sound, for example yielded passages of lyrical beauty:

As the sun declined, the snow at our feet reflected the most delicate peach-bloom hue; and looking West from the top of the pass, the scenery was gorgeous beyond description, for the sun was just plunging into a sea of mist, in a blaze of the ruddiest coppery hue.[33]

The landscape, he continued, was bathed 'in the most wonderful and indescribable changing tints'. He was reminded of Turner's paintings. In these he had 'recognized similar effects ... such are the fleeting hues over the ice, in his "Whalers", and the ruddy fire in his "Wind, Steam and Rain", which one almost fears to touch. Dissolving views give some idea of the magic creation and dispersion of the colours ...'. It was no coincidence that Ruskin was the great champion of Turner's empirical accuracy and astute observational powers, as well as his ability to interpret the experience of the landscape.

1. *Mountaineering*

Ruskin's new way of looking had been precipitated by the increasing familiarity with mountain-forms: not in terms of distant views, but through a close *engagement* with them. As we have seen, mountaineering was now in its 'Golden Age'. By mid-century, generations had grappled directly with mountains – seeing them, as it were, from the inside; listening to them. Vague, detached descriptions could no longer suffice among lovers of mountain scenery; they were now connoisseurs. Himalayan travel was no exception to this demand for specific details. By this time the imaginative world of mountaineering had made its mark on the Himalayas: there were disputes about altitude records, general competitiveness, and a sharing of experiences.[34]

Whilst Himalayan climbing was still in its infancy, Alpine exploration had come of age and its history had begun to be compiled: it had its own meticulous chronicler in W. Coolidge.[35] Details became extremely important. Vagueness and inaccuracies were simply not tolerated. Alpine precision was often invoked in an attempt to bring rigour to Himalayan experiences. For example, at one point Hooker compares Himalayan and Alpine peaks in much the same manner as a wine taster would assess different vintages:

> The appearance of Mont Cervin, from the Riffelberg, much reminded me of that of Junnoo, from the Choonjerma pass, the former bearing the same relation to Monte Rosa that the latter does to Kinchinjunga. Junnoo, though incomparably the more stupendous mass, is not nearly so remarkable in outline, so sharp, or so peaked as is Mont Cervin: it is a very much grander, but far less picturesque object. The whiteness of the sides of Junnoo adds also greatly to its apparent altitude; while the strong relief in which the black cliffs of Mont Cervin protrude through its snowy mantle greatly diminishes both its apparent height and distance.[36]

One could not be much more specific. Here is a developed art of mountain landscape aesthetics and perception within which the Himalayas were being contextualized.

2. *Photography*

The other catalyst for this new way of viewing, this empirical imagination, was the development of photography. When Wilson arrived at Dankar, the capital of Spiti, in 1875, he exclaimed: 'Its appearance is so extraordinary, that I shall not attempt any description of it until able to present my readers with a copy of its photograph.'[37]

Since the 1840s, British photographers had been touring the Empire in search of the extraordinary and the picturesque. In 1861 Samuel Bourne became the first to take a camera into the high Himalayas. Hampered by an immense quantity of bulky, unwieldy and fragile photographic material, he was constantly frustrated by the sheer scale of the scenery.

> The scenery in some places was grand and impressive. Huge mountains, frequently clothed with forests of pine, towered aloft on every

hand ... And yet, with all its ponderous magnificence and grand-eur,. strange to say this scenery was not well adapted for pictures – at least for photography ... The character of the Himalayan scenery in general is not picturesque. I have not yet seen Switzerland except in some of M. Bisson's and Mr England's photographs; but judging from these ... I should say that is far more pleasing and picturesque than any part I have yet seen of the Himalayas.[38]

The age of photography has truly arrived when Bourne judges the Himalayas by comparing their photogenic qualities with photographs of the Swiss Alps. Himalayan views would continue to elude photographers until Smythe's sensitive work in the early twentieth century, combined with the associated technical breakthrough in portable cameras. In general, photography would be used for recording architectural details, ethnographic objects and people for classification, or for postcard views. As John Berger comments:

All over the world during the nineteenth century, European travellers, soldiers, colonial administrators, adventurers, took photographs of the 'natives', their customs, their architecture, their richness, their poverty, their women's breasts, their head-dresses; and these images, besides provoking amazement, were presented and read as proof of the justice of the imperial division of the world. The division between those who organized and rationalized and surveyed, and those who were surveyed.[39]

The Himalayas were therefore drawn into a global photomontage that was demanded and created by scientists and public alike. A photograph was treated as 'a visual fact, a discrete bit of information within a materialistic, encyclopaedic view of the world'.[40] Photographs gave the illusion of power: scientific, administrative, aesthetic, voyeuristic.

The very power of photographic 'realism' posed the new landscape aesthetics with a puzzle. As early as 1839 the issue of visual accuracy, precision and fidelity was raised:

Travellers may perhaps soon be able to procure M. Daguerre's apparatus, and bring back views of the finest monuments and of the most beautiful scenery of the whole world. They will see how far their pencils and brushes are from the truth.[41]

Ruskin, too, was unsure of the relation between the new, supposed realism of photography and the specific *character* of landscape. For him, photographs seemed to lack 'veracity' and a kind of *imaginative truth*:

Even in the most accurate and finished topography, a slight exaggeration may be permitted; for many of the most important facts in nature are so subtle, that they *must* be slightly exaggerated, in order to be made noticeable when ... removed from the associating circumstances which enhanced their influence, or directed attention to them in nature.[42]

Bourne would have agreed. He observed that panoramic views in the Himalayas were generally unsatisfactory as photographic subjects. An artist, he mused, can foreshorten perspective, exaggerate and emphasize dominant characteristics in order to produce a result that is more aesthetically accurate, if less topographically literal.[43]

Ruskin's attempt to resolve the tension between empirical literalism and imaginative interpretation was crucial for the late-Victorian appreciation of landscape. However at odds the two positions were, or however tenuous was their attempted synthesis, if Tibet was ever to be a vital place in the British imagination both forms of perception were needed. Without empirical accuracy any description would have been discredited, given the prevailing scientific *Weltanschauung*. But without interpretation, any place would be imaginatively irrelevant. Also, for the *axis mundi* to appear in Tibet in the late nineteenth century , that land had to be of sufficient character to attract inexorably both ways of viewing in equal measure. So, for example, even Thomson, that traveller so dedicated to facts, was forced to exclaim from time to time over the wonderful view. The *activity* of photography, perhaps more than the actual photographs themselves, seemed to symbolize this meeting of science and imagination. As Samuel Bourne writes:

It was impossible to gaze on this tumultuous sea of mountains without being deeply affected with their terrible majesty and awful grandeur ... and it must be set down to the credit of photography that it teaches the mind to see the beauty and power of such scenes as these and renders it more susceptible of their sweet and elevating impressions. For my own part, I must say that before I commenced photography I did not see half the beauties in nature that I do now ...[44]

In this passage, science, technology and the cultivation of the natural sublime dovetail delightfully. In the Himalayas it seemed impossible to remain aloof and objective. The immense landscape always stimulated the imagination.

The Need for a Context: Intimate and Global

The resolution between empirical accuracy and imaginative interpretation was only one aspect of the new way of perceiving landscape championed by Ruskin. He also realized that it was essential for any landscape to belong to a social and historical *context*. Landscape needs such associations; without them there is only meaninglessness and placelessness.[45] In 1871 Leslie Stephen wrote:

> The snowy ranges of California or the more than Alpine heights of the Caucasus may doubtless be beautiful, but to my imagination at least, they seem to be unpleasantly bare and dull, because they are deprived of all those intricate associations which somehow warm the bleak ranges of Switzerland.[46]

If the Himalayas – and ultimately Tibet – were to become sacred places for the British, they had to be an intimate part of British identity. Without this connection these wild landscapes could never provide the location for an *axis mundi*. Such a fundamental reference point must *belong*, in the most intimate way, to a culture, to its sense of itself, to its quest for meaning. The sacred has the paradoxical quality of being both remote and yet also close to the heart.

By 1847 the Himalayas had acquired at least one crucial quality: they were felt to *belong* to Britain. Thomson called them '*our* northern Indian mountains'.[47] Over the next quarter of a century, the process of drawing these mountains deeply into the British imagination was undertaken in earnest. It occurred on many levels, but always through the twin processes of *familiarization* and *globalization*. As we have seen, by mid-century Britain had already adopted a global identity. The Himalayas then took their position within a worldwide mosaic of imaginatively significant places. Familiarization moved in the opposite direction. By naming and making intimate comparisons (of fauna, flora, landscape, culture), sentiments could be transferred from Britain to the Himalayas, and vice versa. Gradually the landscape became familiar and known. A network of associations was established between the British Isles and its imperial perimeter. Finally, Himalayan and Tibetan exploration was of sufficient vintage to have acquired its own history. Particular places began to echo with generations of travellers' tales. Names dates and events started to recur. The Himalayas and Tibet therefore became firmly integrated into the stories the British told about themselves.

1. *Familiarization*

Hooker, for example, on his famous journey of 1848 – 9, constantly compared details of Himalayan scenery with their Alpine equivalent.[48] As we have seen, this practice was also common among earlier travellers, but by mid-century it was of a totally different order in terms of exactitude and familiarity. So upon his entry into Tibet, Hooker observed:

> The mean height of Palung Plains is 16,000 feet: they are covered with transported blocks, and I have no doubt their surface has been much modified by glacial action. I was forcibly reminded of them by the slopes of the Wengern Alp, but those of Palung are far more level. The ice-clad cliffs of Kinchinjhow rise before the spectator, just as those of the Jungfrau, Monch and Eigher Alp do from that magnificent point of view.[49]

But the Swiss Alps were not the only point of comparison; even more familiar was the landscape of Britain itself. Hooker brought the plants of the Himalayas and Tibet into close association with the flora of 'our British moors' and 'our English gardens'. Comparisons were made with British insects, caterpillars and butterflies, ferns, sedges and strawberries.[50] Given the mid-Victorian enthusiasm for botanizing and gardens, such associations would have helped to draw these alien regions of Asia closer to the Victorian bosom.[51] The extensive transportation of exotic plants from the colonial outposts back to Britain also enhanced this familiarization process. As one writer commented at the time: 'Many of the plants [rhododendrons] ... to be found in English gardens are due to the seeds gathered by Sir Joseph Hooker.' The *naming* of fauna and flora also played its part in giving the Himalayas an intimate place in British fantasies: 'A beautiful yellow poppy-like plant grew in clefts at 10,000 feet; it has flowered in England, from seeds which I sent home, and bears the name of Cathcartia ...'. In a footnote Hooker tells us: 'The name was given in honour of the memory of my friend, the late J.F. Cathcart, Esq. of the Bengal Civil Service ...'.[52] Such small-scale naming was perhaps more important than the largely unsuccessful attempts to change the names of the major Himalayan peaks. Of these only Everest has proved enduring. As Gaston Bachelard has stressed in his *Poetics of Space*, it is generally the corners and intimate spaces that evoke meaning, soul and a sense of belonging.[53]

Wilder fancy also played its part in moving the Himalayas and Tibet into a circle of familiar associations. Each era seemed to use its own imaginative criteria by which to establish archaic, almost mythic, connections. Turner in 1783, related Tibet and Ancient Egypt through a common lion symbolism. Sir Richard Temple, writing about a hundred years later, made the same imaginative connection between Tibet and Ancient Egypt, but now, appropriately for the industrious Victorian era, through reflections upon a common system of labour. Even the sober Hooker paused *en route* to reflect upon the relationship between these two cultures:

> The similarly proportioned gloomy portals of Egyptian fanes natur-
> ally invite comparison; but the Tibetan temples lack the sublimity of
> those; and the uncomfortable creeping sensation produced by the
> many sleepless eyes of Boodh's numerous incarnations is very differ-
> ent from the awe with which we contemplate the outspread wings of
> the Egyptian symbol, and feel as in the presence of him who says, 'I
> am Osiris the Great: no man hath dared to lift my veil'.[54]

Comparison has continued to be made betweeen Tibet and Egypt right up
to the present. In Hooker's day, Ancient Egypt was considered to be the
exemplary home of archaic mystery, alongside which Tibet was thought
inferior. However, by the time of Madam Blavatsky, some forty years later,
an equality would be imagined between these two places and their religions. In our own era, Tibetan religion has emerged from the shadows of
its Egyptian counterpart and is often considered its superior.[55]

Apart from Ancient Egypt, Tibet has evoked other cultural comparisons. In the twentieth century attempts have been made to relate
Tibetans with Australian Aboriginals, North American Indians, Aztecs,
Gnostics, and so on.[56] In 1875, the word *Tartar* and its possible connection
with *tartan* drew Wilson's fancy. During a series of ingenious associations,
he wrote:

> It struck me forcibly before I left Zanskar that there must be some
> unknown relationship between the people of that province and the
> Scottish Highlanders. The sound of their varieties of language, the
> brooches which fasten their plaids, the varieties of tartan ... even the
> features of the people, strongly reminded me of the Scotch High-
> landers.[57]

Such reflections as these drew the Himalayas and Tibet deep into the
mythological regions of the British psyche.

The Himalayas and the Tibetan borderland also provided the locations
for numerous spiritual experiences. The scientist Hooker, for example,
exclaimed:

> In such scenes ... the mind wanders from the real to the ideal, the
> larger and brighter lamps of heaven lead us to imagine that we have
> risen from the surface of our globe and are floating through the re-
> gions of space ...[58]

Wilson, too, whilst admiring what he called 'the most picturesque, weird,
astounding and perplexing' mountains of Zanskar, experienced a pro-

found spiritual questioning. 'What am I?' he asked. And in reply he quoted the 'Buddhist hymn, "all is transistory, all is misery, all is void, all is without substance"'.[59] Such experiences as these were to recur time and again, imbuing the region with yet another kind of intimacy, that of the spirit. The Himalayas and Tibet would become a veritable repository of singular spiritual experiences for generations of British travellers.

2. *Globalization*

The Himalayas and Tibet were also part of a wider, more global contextualizing. By mid-century the whole surface of the earth had become a market, a playground and a laboratory for the British. Hooker, for example, having already been to the Antarctic, wanted to visit a temperate zone and had to choose between India and the Andes (imperial connections swayed the final choice); Lambert, in his journal of 1877, presents cogent arguments as to why the Himalayas was the best place to visit for a shooting trip, rather than Europe, Africa, America or elsewhere in Asia. Similarly, Markham selected the Himalayas as a change after having previously hunted in Canada.[60] The Himalayas were clearly just one – albeit very attractive – place within Britain's global map.

This global referencing of the Himalayan region extended to its fauna and flora. Hooker commented: 'there were few mosses; but crustaceous lichens were numerous, and nearly all of them of Scotch, Alpine, European, and Arctic kinds ... I recognized many as natives of the wild mountains of Cape Horn, and the rocks of the stormy Antarctic ocean'.[61] Geologically too, the Sikkim Himalayas reminded Hooker of 'the West coasts of Scotland and Norway, of South Chili, and Fuegia, of New Zealand and Tasmania'. Vegetation was described as 'European and North American', or 'dry Asiatic and Siberian', or 'humid Malayan'.[62]

As Himalayan travel accounts took their place within the wider story of global exploration, the martyrs of this tradition were created. Tales of explorers' hardships and deaths were utterly essential for the Victorian British. Burnes, Moorcroft, Hayward, Dr Stolicza, Adolph Schlagintweit and Csoma de Koros were names that would constantly recur as the Himalayan tradition established itself. Stories such as the arrest and ill-treatment of Hooker and Campbell had importance not only for Sikkim and Darjeeling but also for Britain's more global presence and authority. The blood of Europeans was already mingling with the pristine Himalayan snow. An essential heroic darkness was beginning to be drawn into British imaginative associations with the region.

Light and Colour: the Wilderness Redeemed

As the Victorian era progressed, a disenchantment with mountain Romanticism began. Poetry, literature and art began to turn away from the earlier transcendent vision. Instead, more concern was shown towards the urban social problems that accompanied industrialization. The earlier Romantic landscape tradition increasingly came to be considered irrelevant, even indulgent, by the new generation among whom sobriety, reason and morality were more esteemed.[63] Tourism had also played its part in diluting the spontaneity and freshness of the mountain experience.

By the 1870s the Victorian crisis in confidence was reflected in the changed view of wild landscape. A profound ambivalence now characterized attitudes towards such places. For some, wildernesses were barbaric wastelands that should be avoided; for others they were places of sanctuary and healing. Some viewed wildernesses as mere distractions from pressing social reforms; others looked to them as sources of primal energy which alone could shatter rigid social conventions.[64]

The Himalayas played a unique part in the changing attitude to wild landscape. In Britain the sprawling urban centres, with their gross problems, occupied centre-stage, pushing mountains and the natural sublime to the periphery of concern. At the fringe of Empire, however, such concern for social injustice was muted by the prevailing racist and imperialist ideologies. This allowed the Romantic landscape tradition to linger on and indeed never to be really lost in the Himalayas. As we have seen, even in the heyday of scientific travel these vast mountains continued to evoke lyricism and mystery. It was therefore in these and other similar regions that a genuine aesthetics of wilderness was forged late in the century.

The contextualization of the Himalayas within British history and the close attention given to empirical details combined to bring meaning to this mountain wilderness. For example, when Hooker reached the top of the Donkia Pass into Tibet he was confronted by a 'featureless' landscape: without houses, trees or even snow. Yet he still discovered something of interest:

> I found one flowering plant on the summit; the tufted alsinaceous one ... [and] at 18,300 feet I found on one stone only a fine lichen, the *'tripe de roche'* of Arctic Voyagers and the food of the Canadian hunters; it is also abundant on the Scotch Alps.[65]

As anyone who has travelled in apparently featureless landscapes will testify, it is the patient attention to such details that reveals their beauty. Paradoxically, the vast spaces often support minute, retiring life-forms and encourage an appreciation of subtlety. Also, by mid-century a study *comparative* wildernesses was developing. As the passage from Hooker shows, the wild, empty and barren parts of the world could be related through the most minimal of evidence. Connoisseurs of wilderness were emerging; individuals familiar with the lonely spaces of the planet to be found in the Arctic and Antarctic, North and South America, Australia, Asia, Africa, the oceans, and on the mountain summits. Regular *engagement* with wilderness provoked the development of a new aesthetic.

Of course, explorers and travellers continued to refer to such places as 'dreary', 'desolate', 'sterile'.[66] Yet even in these instances a kind of balance point was often reached and evaluation would then topple over into a different world of appreciation. Thomson, for instance, at one point is forced to exclaim:

> I find it extremely difficult to discribe in an adequate manner the extreme desolation of the most barren parts of Tibet, where no luxuriant forest or bright green herbage softens the nakedness of the mountains, but everywhere the same precipices, heaps of rocks, and barren monotonous desert meets the eye. *The prospect before me was certainly most wonderful. I had nowhere before seen a country so utterly waste.*[67]

The 'waste' was so absolute that it had become 'wonderful'. Wilson, also, gives us numerous examples of this decisive shift in aesthetic balance once the extreme edge of the earlier Romantic paradigm had been reached. A revolution was taking place in the 'scenic sciences' of the West.[68] When Wilson wrote: 'I was entering the wildest and sublimest region of the earth', he had reached the limit of one aesthetic paradigm. Subsequently he reported:

> The view over the Spiti ranges ... was very extensive and striking; for though it was a land of desolation on which we gazed, it was under an intensely dark-blue sky; it was beautifully coloured with snow and cloud, and variegated rock ...[69]

He called it 'that beautiful yet awful scene', and then referred to 'the wild sterility of these Tartar plains,' 'the sublime and terrific character of the scenery'.[70] In this passage can be seen a crucial movement in the emergence of a wilderness aesthetic: a subtle appreciation of colours and light, rather than an exclusive reliance on bold, varied physical forms, or on striking panoramas. In another place Wilson recounts.

> The colour of these precipice walls was of the richest and most varied kind. The predominant tints were green, purple, orange, brown, black and whitish yellow ... In certain lights the precipices appeared

almost as if they were of chalcedony and jasper. The dark-brown manganese-like cliffs looked exceedingly beautiful.[71]

Travellers were attracted by two qualities of this light that was to be found in the Himalayas and in the Tibetan wilderness: its clarity and the subtlety of its changing colours. So Hooker writes:

The transparency of the pale blue atmosphere of these lofty regions can hardly be described, nor the clearness and precision with which the most distant objects are projected against the sky.[72]

Such comments had, of course, been made before, but with less frequency and without a context. Far from being incidental features, they were now increasingly sought out by travellers in the Himalayas and Tibet. The light and colour became part of the region's attraction. The colours never seemed fixed:' ... floods of light shot across the misty ocean, bathing the landscape in the most wonderful and indescribably changing tints.'[73] Even the most reserved of travellers could scarcely restrain their enthusiasm for the colours and light. Sir Richard Temple, on a tour through Nepal in 1876, was forced to exclaim:

Emerald, azure, turquoise – all these phases combined can give you no impression of the indescribable beauty of the colour ... To a spectator on the hills themselves, their colour would be of the dullest and most opaque yellow ochre; but the effect of distance in this clear atmosphere is to throw a sort of etherealized pink-purple over the mountains which has the most lovely effect.[74]

In these regions there was, as Hooker wrote, *both* 'desolation *and* grandeur'.[75] Attention to details of light and colour helped to sustain paradox and overcome monotony:

The deep dark blue of the heavens above contrasted with the perfect and dazzling whiteness of the earthly scene around. The uniformity of colour in this exquisite scene excited no sense of monotony.[76]

It is no coincidence that at the moment of Hooker's most intense aesthetic experience he should reach towards Turner's paintings for assistance. It was Turner who, as Ruskin insisted, was most responsible for first capturing both the empirical and imaginative 'truth' of light and colours in landscape.[77]

A Million Pairs of Lungs: Mountain Air and Tourism

As the Europeans climbed the summits, they discovered not only splendid views but also *mountain air*. As we saw in chapter 2, curiosity about the air was a feature of mountain exploration right from the beginning. Speculations about the air are an important guide to the depth-imagination because, like the gods, the purest mountain air is to be found at the summits and, like them, it has an elusive insubstantiality.

By mid-century, mountain air was unequivocally equated with good health. Wilson was only one of the many who took to the higher Himalayas for health reasons. The hill-stations of Darjeeling, Simla and Dharmsala, among others, were testaments to the efficacy of mountain air:

> I believe that children's faces afford as good an index as any to the healthfulness of a climate, and in no part of the world is there a more active, rosy, and bright young community, than at Dorjiling. It is incredible what a few weeks of that mountain air will do for the India-born children of European parents.[78]

Yet at work within such a seemingly innocent equation as that established between mountain air and health is a more complex metaphor. For Ruskin, mountains, air and clouds, formed a marvellous unity. 'The second great use of mountains', he writes, 'is to maintain a constant change in the currents and nature of the *air.*' Elsewhere he insists that 'our whole happiness and power of energetic action depend upon our being able to breathe and live in the cloud.' Above all, he is adamant that the clouds associated with mountains are superior to those found in the lowlands.[79] As Tyndall, the well-known Victorian mountaineer, commented: 'There is assuredly morality in the oxygen of the mountains.'[80] The pollution of such air was therefore more than simply a matter of physical well-being: it struck a moral and psychological chord. For Ruskin the pollution of his beloved mountain air echoed his disenchantment with nature and provided a bitter criticism of capitalist exploitation.

Leslie Stephen wrote in 1871 'The Alps ... are places of refuge where we may escape from ourselves and from our neighbours. There we can breathe air that has not passed through a million pair of lungs'.[81] Clearly, for Stephen, the pure air of the mountains symbolized the antithesis both of the crowded urban centres of the British Isles and of the upsurge in popular tourism that was threatening the exclusiveness of the Alps. In the Himalayas also, the purity of the air acted as a metaphor for escape. Even in those immense mountains, tourism had become familiar by the final quarter of the century. As Wilson complained in 1871:

... go almost where he may, the lover of peace and solitude will soon have reason to complain that the country round him is becoming 'altogether too crowded'. As for the enterprising and exploring traveller ... his case is even worse. Kafiristan, Chinese Tibet, and the very centre of Africa, indeed remain for him, but, wherever he may go, he cannot escape the painful conviction that his task will ere long be trodden ground.[82]

Cook's Tours began in 1841 and was a revolution unwelcomed by the earlier breed of upper-class travellers. Within a generation or two, lamented Wilson, 'it will be only a question of money and choice ... as to having a cruise upon the lakes of Central Africa, or going to reason with the Grand Lama of Tibet upon the subject of polyandry'.[83] Traveller's *Angst* drove explorers deeper into the rapidly shrinking uncharted lands of Central Asia or up ever higher and more inaccessible peaks. Steamships, railways and efficient roads caused a dramatic change in travel throughout the whole world, and the Himalayas were no exception. Already by mid-century a road had been constructed between Simla and the Tibetan border: 'the great Hindusthan and Tibet road', as it was called. Further east, 'a regularly engineered road' led from Darjeeling to the Jeylap-la Pass, 'on the future highroad between India and China via Tibet'.[84] With measured irony, Wilson continued: 'Nowadays, old ladies of seventy, who had scarcely ever left Britain before, are to be met with on the spurs of the Himaliya.'[85]

Wilson, in fact, bowed to the inevitable and the profitable, so before turning his attention to the 'untrod' higher mountain regions he gave detailed advice to prospective Himalayan tourists: preparations, routes, itineraries. But he carefully reserved the higher sense of aesthetics for the educated classes. Mountain splendours, he wrote, 'to the undeveloped mind of Tommy Atkins ... soon become exceedingly tiresome'.[86] It was as if he was reassuring both himself and his readers that the exclusiveness of the mountains was unlikely to be troubled by the curiosity of the masses.

At times, Wilson's book reads like a travel brochure:

> Whether the traveller be in search of health, or sport, or sublime scenery, there is no other place from which he can have such convenient access as Simla to the interior of the Himalayas, and to the dry elevated plains of Central Asia.[87]

The Tibetan border, Kashmir and the capital of Ladakh at Leh were all within easy reach of Simla. 'Indeed,' exclaimed Wilson enthusiastically, 'now that the Russians have established a post-office at Kashgar, it would be quite possible, and tolerably safe, to walk from Simla to St Petersburg, or to the mouth of the Amur on the Pacific coast.'[88] As the Himalayas became increasingly familiar and well trodden, the land to the north, protected by both its terrain and its policy of exclusion, became more attractive. A kind of empathic relationship began to be established between the mountain peaks, with their pure, uncontaminated air, and the exclusive solitudes of the Tibetan plateau. As the century progressed, this relationship would reach a pitch of intensity. By then travel in the lower reaches of the Himalayas had become almost routine. As one aristocratic traveller wrote, rather wearily, in 1889: 'The subject of Himalayan travel and sport is now so old a story that an attempt to create further interest in it is an almost hopeless undertaking.'[89]

A Morality of the Wilderness

The emergence of a genuine wilderness aesthetic and an appreciation of these previously rejected regions was vital to the eventual creation of Tibet as a sacred place in the Western psyche. Without this revolutionary breakthrough in landscape perception, Tibet might still have been fascinating and mysterious, but it would not have become intimate and *essential*, to Europeans and Americans. When Hooker travelled to Palestine in 1860 he used the word 'Tibetan' as the supreme adjective for describing desolate landscape The 'general character of the scenery', he wrote, was 'Tibetan and wretched'.[90]Clearly the aesthetic redemption of wilderness and the imaginative fate of Tibet were inseparable.

Appreciation of wilderness is not a natural phenomenon – indeed, an aesthetic relationship to such places appears to be unique to industrial cultures. It developed under specific historical, social and psychological conditions. This does not lessen its imaginative significance – in fact, quite the reverse. If we understand the subtle complexity of its genesis, the appreciation of wilderness can be seen as a symbol of great power. Within it are condensed layer upon layer of discrete fantasies. Perhaps the most important of these, especially for the Victorian era, was the question of morality.

Ruskin insisted that there was a direct relationship between natural landscape and a natural morality. This was a two-way process: society's appreciation of landscape was a direct indication of its level of civilization. But he also considered landscape to have its own morality, independent of any cultural interpretation or psychological projection. Here was a protoenvironmental – an *anima mundi* – psychology in the making, one that used morality for its base.[91] The Victorian era expressed high regard for certain moral qualities, especially sobriety, steadiness and patience. To be boring or monotonous was definitely viewed by many as a lesser evil that being impatient or unreliable. Such moral characteristics were even attributed to the Tibetan people themselves. So Wilson writes:

I found it impossible to move among these people especially in the more primitive parts of the country, without contracting a great liking for them, and admiration for their honesty, their patience, and their placidity of temper ...[92]

Wilderness regions seemed to embody these moral qualities, so respected by many Victorians, to a high degree.

In one remarkable passage, Ruskin shows clearly just how important the regard for these moral qualities was for the imaginative redemption of landscape that had previously been rejected or overlooked because it was dreary or monotonous. He referred to 'a spot which has all the solemnity with none of the savageness of the Alps ... And there is a deep tenderness pervading that vast monotony ... Patiently, eddy by eddy, the clear green streams wind along their well-known beds.'[93] Ruskin's influential studies of precipices also offered a kind of redemption of the wilderness: 'Forever incapable of comfort or of healing from herb or flower, nourishing no root in their crevices, touched by no hue of life on buttress or ledge, but, to the utmost desolate ...'. Yet he considered that such places were not destitute of significance, nor of sombre dignity. They were, he wrote, 'robed with everlasting mourning'.[94]

Ruskin reserved similar respect for the pine tree, that denizen of 'scenes disordered and desolate'. Like the ocean, it was a signifier of the infinite: 'The pine is trained to need nothing, and to endure everything. It is resolvedly whole, self-contained, desiring nothing but rightness, content with restricted completion. Tall or short, it will be straight.'[95] Wilson, on his journey through the Himalayas, was similarly struck with the character of trees and their relationship to the wild landscape that is their home. For him they were a reminder 'that the struggling and half-developed vegetable world aspires towards heaven, and has not been unworthy of the grand design'.[96]

The Victorian penchant for attributing moral characteristics to landscape has often been the source of ridicule, yet as we have seen, this habit was a precursor to an environmental psychology. It played an important role in initiating a more sympathetic relationship to apparently bleak and barren environments.[97]

Origins, Ancestors and Evolution

The general acceptance of Darwin's theory during the second half of the nineteenth century drew all the landscapes of the world, with their associated races, fauna and flora, into a deep relationship with each other. They suddenly all shared the same immense evolutionary context. The final transformation of Tibet into a sacred landscape was, to a significant extent, a child of evolutionary theory. Tibet and the Himalayas suddenly became positioned on a trajectory that involved fantasies about sources and origins, missing links, evolutionary directions and goals, and about the survival of the fittest. Even the most desolate wilderness or the most primitive life-form could not now be overlooked or rejected, for it too played its part in the global evolutionary and ecological context. In particular, such ideas quickly found their way into ethnography, and sociological and anthropological theory. Whilst there were a number of different forms of Social Darwinism, they all shared the same root-metaphors.[98]

When Wilson stood atop the Kung-ma Pass into Tibet and contemplated the mountain 'Lio Porgyul', he was moved to comment: '[It] might well be regarded as a great fortress between Iran and Turan, between the domains of the Aryan and the Tartar race.'[99] From the mid-nineteenth century onwards, the term *Aryan* suddenly came into common use, not philologically, nor only mythologically, but as a concept of 'scientific' ethnography. Its usage was embedded within broad racial and cultural concerns which involved descriptions, classifications, evaluations and a kind of ethno-ecology, a study of the relationship between culture, race and environment.

By mid-century a vast quantity of basic ethnographic data had been gathered by Himalayan travellers. The attempts to organize this material rationally were usually based upon either comparative linguistics or the measurement of skulls or the use of racial stereotypes.[100] Although the study of cranial characteristics continued throughout the century, it was the use of racial stereotypes that became almost the trademark of travel texts. The principal theme of these stereotypes was the idea of racial *character*. Hooker's comments about the inhabitants of Sikkim were typical:

> A more interesting and attractive companion than the Lepcha I never lived with: cheerful, kind and patient with a master to whom he is attached; rude but not savage, ignorant and yet intelligent … In all my dealings with these people, they proved scrupulously honest. Except for drunkenness and carelessness, I never had to complain …[101]

The interest of travellers in *racial character* was generally orientated towards practical purposes rather than disinterested science. For example, the Himalayan hill tribes were to be administered, controlled and put to use by the British, as well as just studied. By means of such stereotypes the character of different races could be compared and their relative value to the British assessed. A point was subsequently reached where some ethnographic training was considered desirable for any aspiring colonial administrator.[102]

'The Lepcha is timid, peaceful and no brawler; ... the Ghorkas are brave and warlike, the Bhotanese quarrelsome, cowardly and cruel.' A mixture of physical, moral, historical and behavioural observations, these stereotypes were pithy portraits and allowed instant evaluations to be made. They became a kind of traveller's shorthand, yet were embedded within the prevailing ideas of ethnographic science. Such assertions were chacteristically unequivocal and precise:

> The Bhutias may be divided into three classes – those of Tibet, Sikkim, and Bhutan ... Taking the inhabitants of Bhutan ... as the type, they are a dark, powerful, finely made race, Tibetan in feature, language and religion; but of a very unpleasing character, being described as vain, rude, inaccessible, sulky, quarrelsome, turbulent, cowardly and cruel, and grossly immoral and drunken withal. Their brethren of Sikkim and Tibet – especially the latter – share their bad qualities in a lesser degree, are fairer ... and more robust.[103]

As Europe and America shifted their attention to the origin, evolution, success and decay of cultures, these racial stereotypes acquired heightened imaginative power due to the emergence of the Aryan myth.

Whilst the term Aryan had first arisen in the eighteenth century through the discovery of a linguistic relationship between Greek, Latin and Sanskrit, by the 1850s it had outgrown its philological origins. It became associated with the idea of an 'original race' who formed the light-bearing vanguard of true civilization. Darwin's evolutionary theory gave the Aryan fantasy a much-needed scientific framework which also dovetailed beautifully with imperial demands. Races were hierarchically assessed in terms of their cultural achievements, military prowess, intelligence, linguistic complexity, brain size, religion, physical beauty, or whatever theme was deemed important. As Latham wrote in his comprehensive, descriptive ethnology of Asia, Africa and Europe (1859):

> We may look ... upon the divisions and sub-divisions of the numerous groups that have been under notice, with a view of deciding upon their relative importance as material or moral forces in the history of the world.[104]

Not surprisingly, the 'Aryans' always came out on top, thereby justifying the West's right to global dominance. Sir Richard Temple, for example, whilst Lieutenant-Governor of Bengal, journeyed through Sikkim and commented:

> The Lepchas are the aboriginal race and a pleasant people, hardy enough, but weak in character and decreasing in numbers ... The

Bhutias ... are of Tibetan origin and somewhat stolid ... The Paharis from Nepal are of the Aryan race ... They are industrious and enterprising cultivators, greatly superior to other races in this quarter, and destined to do more and more for the settlement and colonization of these hills. They are the men who break up the land with the plough, and show the other races how to give up the barbarous method of tillage without it.[105]

The Aryan myth was above all part of a search by the West for its origins. As a spiritual crisis deepened in Europe, so new beliefs were sought.[106] The Aryan myth combined the compelling root-metaphors of a racial homeland with a racial purity unweakened by urban life and undiluted by intermarriage, added to a heroic science of struggle and survival.

The Aryans were the long-lost 'ancestors': vigorous, dominant, heroic. Brian Hodgson at one point wrote of 'our ancestors when they burst the barriers of the Roman Empire'. Hooker referred to the ancient invasion of India 'by the Indo-Germanic conquerors'.[107] The 'Turanian' Tibetans, by contrast, while brave and ferocious, lacked sensitivity, intelligence and passion. Wilson, for example, argued that the violence of Chinese and Tartar punishment had its basis in physiology: 'it is certain that the Turanian race is remarkably obtuse-nerved and insensitive to pain, which goes some way to account for the cruelty of its punishments.'[108] As for the 'curious and revolting' custom of polyandry, whatever its merits for controlling population, Wilson insisted that:

This could only happen among a race of a peculiarly placid, unpassionate temperament, as the Turanians unquestionably are, except in their fits of demoniacal cruelty. They have no hot blood, in our sense of the phrase ...[109]

The Tibetans were also not considered to be a heroic race:

The Tibetan population is hardly ... of sufficiently strong *morale*, for heroic or chivalric efforts, such as have been made by the ancient Greeks, the Swiss, the Waldenses, the Scotch Highlanders, and the mountaineers of some other parts of Europe, and even of Asia.[110]

In contrast to Aryan vigour and energy, the Tibetans were considered lazy. Similarly, their religion was often thought to be an evolutionary dead end. When referring to the 'Aryan' Sikh conquest of Ladakh, Cunningham wrote that 'the indolent votaries of an almost worn-out faith were no match for the more active and energetic worshippers of Mahadeo and Parbati'.[111] Wilson, too situated Tibetan religion within the framework of Social Darwinism:

This tendency of Budhists to seclude themselves from the world has interfered with Budhism being a great power in the world ... It is forced to give way ... whenever mankind reaches a certain stage of complicated social arrangements, or, as we call it, civilization; but there is a stage before that, though after the period of tribal fighting, when a religion like Budhism naturally flourishes. Now Tibet is still in that position at the present day, and so Budhism (in the shape of Lamaism) is still supreme in it ...[112]

Some British considered the Himalayas a fit place for Anglo-Saxon colonization, almost as if its inhabitants were not of sufficient stature to do justice to this mighty landscape.[113]

A variety of quests for many disparate origins converged, upon these elavated regions. By 1825 Csoma de Koros had already made his way towards the land to the north of Tibet in an attempt to discover the source of the Hungarian people. The mid-century had also witnessed the search to find the sources of the great rivers of India – the Sutlej, Indus, Ganges, Brahmaputra.[114] Most of the major rivers of southern Asia seemed to have their origins somewhere within Tibet. The nineteenth century seemed obsessed with searching for the source of the world's great rivers, of which the Nile was probably the most famous. Rivers are rich symbols – holy, life-giving metaphors for life itself. An imaginative resonance was struck between this symbolism and the quest to find the source of the 'Aryan nation'. Wilson expressed the pregnancy of these underlying fantasies; upon his first sight of the Himalayas he exclaimed excitedly:

These were the Jumnotri and Gangotri peaks, the peaks of Badrinath and of the Hindu Kailas; the source of mighty sacred rivers; the very centre of the Himaliya; the *Himmel* or heaven of the Teuton Aryans as well as of Hindu Mythology. Mount Meru itself may be regarded as rising there its golden front against the sapphire sky; the Kailas, or 'Seat of Happiness', is the *coelum* of the Latins; and there is the fitting, unapproachable abode of Brahma ...[115]

A triple process of imaginative realignment, focusing and condensation can be seen at work in this enthusiastic passage. At the summit of the mountains and on the high-altitude plateau of Central Asia are assembled the Aryan gods, pure air, a pure race, the source of the world's rivers and of European ancestral origins, the source of the world's true civilization. These regions represented – and at the same time *evoked* such qualities as heroism, patience, vigour, ruggedness, freedom, steadiness. Most importantly, this land is *the highest in the world*. As Hooker remarked whilst gazing into Tibet: 'There is no loftier country *on the globe* ... '.[116] If this was the highest region on the globe, then the air must surely be the purest and the racial ancestors the most vigorous. In addition to being the highest, this land was conceived to be '*the centre* of the world'.[117] Wilson quoted the Arabs who, he claimed, called the Himalayas 'The Stony Girdle of the Earth'.[118] Finally, this region was referred to as the 'Roof of the World'. Davies has recently encapsulated the Aryan fantasy in a clear and forceful way: 'This original race "in columns of masterful men" had once marched "down from the roof of the world, founding empires and civilizing the West".'[119]

Admittedly, the precise boundaries of the region were somewhat vague: Everest was obviously the exact highest point in the world; the Pamirs in particular were known as the 'roof of the world'; the 'stony girdle' applied to the whole mountain range; Tibet was specifically called the highest country. Yet concern with such geographical precision quickly began to yield before an imaginative focusing. Eventually the Potala palace at Lhasa would provide the core-image around which these metaphors would cluster.[120] It would then come to signify the *axis mundi* of the globe, providing at one and the same time a connection with *memoria*, with the Ancients, with archaic beginnings, as well as with renewal, hope, aspiration, the gods.

Such fantasies also influenced British expectations about the people who inhabited these regions. So, Hooker mused: 'the Lepcha in one respect entirely contradicts our preconceived notions of a mountaineer, as he is timid, peaceful and no brawler.'[121] The Tibetans, too, hardly measured up to the ideal of the mountaineer, and it was something of a contradiction that these illustrious summits should be inhabited by such an unheroic race.[122]

Highroads and Back Doors: Lhasa and its Lamas

But what circumstances caused these disparate images to be gathered together, condensed and then subsequently displaced and focused so specifically on to the city of Lhasa?[123] As the mid-century travellers mapped, hunted, fought, classified, preached or just enjoyed themselves in the Himalayas, it seemed as if all roads, both real and imagined, led to Lhasa. Yet simultaneously, every entrance was denied.

Four *literal* highroads towards the Tibetan border were available to British travellers in the third quarter of the nineteenth century. In 1870, T. Cooper reported that a regular route existed between Peking and Lhasa. As it became possible for Westerners to travel freely through China, this route had distinct possibilities.[124] The other three roads all began in territory that was either British or within British influence. From Ladakh in the west, there was another well-trod ancient route between Leh and Lhasa. From the south, but still towards the western end of the Himalayas, the British constructed 'the Great Hindusthan–Tibet Road'. Wilson gave a graphic description of what was more like a 'cut bridle-path', and recounted the numerous deaths that had befallen travellers attempting the journey from Simla to the Tibetan border.[125] Finally, the British had high hopes that the road from Darjeeling, at the eastern end of the Himalayas, would soon have its terminus at Lhasa.[126]

By the 1870s, three generations of British travellers had optimistically journeyed along these and other routes in an attempt to enter Tibet. Entry stories had become an inevitable motif of Himalayan travel accounts. Indeed, advice was freely given on how to behave when stopped by Tibetan border guards. A traveller's lore began to develop. For example, when a certain Captain Bennett of the Royal Fusiliers reached the expected turning point at the frontier whilst on a shooting trip, he was prepared:

> I had previously read Dunlop's book, 'Hunting in the Himalayas', and took care not to waste time sitting down and arguing the point with them, but determined to have my own way and proceed accordingly.[127]

Bluff, bluster, persistence, disguise, trickery or courting favour by using Western medicine were the usual methods adopted in an attempt to get across the border. The Tibetans generally resorted to passive resistance. A kind of game, or ritual, seemed to be regularly enacted at the border, with little animosity between the players, either British or Tibetan.[128] Serious and frustrating as such incidents were, they were seldom violent. Often the traveller might gain a few miles or a few days, but eventually always yielded to Tibetan pressure. By thus repeatedly thwarting the representatives of British imperial power, albeit on a small scale, the Tibetans gained a kind of grudging, if somewhat patronizing, respect from British travellers. It seemed absurd that the all-powerful and otherwise irresistible British should be denied by these strange, unwarlike people, with their superstitions, bizarre religion, and disarming good nature. Unlike elsewhere in Asia, here the British were confronting non-Europeans on more or less equal terms. The ritual was territorial, each side making lots of noise and gestures yet preserving the status quo. It was the sort of direct, 'man-to-man' contact that the confident British travellers could respect. These were not shadowy officials, but ordinary people. The sportsman and hunter F. Markham, for example, after being prevented from entering Tibet, referred to the Tibetans as a, 'good humoured, jolly looking race'. Cooper ended up joking with the border guards.[129]

However, away from the personal side of these encounters, many thought that such exclusion was detrimental to British status in the region. Wilson, for example, complained:

> It hurt our position in India for the people there to know that there

is a country adjoining our own territory into which Englishmen are systematically refused entrance, while the nations of British India and of its tributary states are allowed to enter freely, and even to settle in large numbers at the capital, Lassa.[130]

Here was the painful twist. While the all-conquering British were excluded from Tibet, the people they had conquered could move with relative ease across the border. Elsewhere, for example in the Arctic, exploration was, by mid-century already a matter of national pride and British manhood.[131] Like Tibet, the Arctic was a closed land, but unlike Tibet it was closed only physically. It presented a simple struggle between British heroism and its technology on the one hand, and the raw, untamed powers of nature on the other. Tibet, however, was a closed land through a mixture of both physical and political impediments. On the face of it neither barrier seemed insurmountable, but together they were strangely effective. As the quest for the North Pole lost its grip on the popular imagination, Tibet would replace it as the next mysterious, but far more complex, *closed land.*

Even the position of Tibet, 'on high', made it seem as if the people living up there entertained presumptuous and aristocratic airs of superiority over the British, who had to toil upwards just to meet them, only then to be unceremoniously turned down. For example, the influential Captain Montgomerie, who organized the use of Indian pundits to survey Tibet secretly, was outraged that every year, before allowing traders to enter, the Tibetans would enquire about the 'political and sanatory condition of Hindustan'. He continued: 'The inquiry seems to be carried out with all that assumption of lofty superiority for which Chinese officials are famous. Looking down from their elevated plateaux, they decide as to whether Hindustan is a fit country to have intercourse with.'[132] One can understand his chagrin. Here was Britain – 'the most powerful government in the East', as Hooker wrote – being regularly humiliated and forced to scramble around looking for back doors.[133] To add insult to injury, the British never seemed able to find any Tibetan officials with whom to open normal diplomatic relations.

Nevertheless, exclusion heightened the pleasure and excitement when travellers did eventually manage to gain even a brief glimpse of the forbidden land. Expectation, too, was intensified. Captain Bennett's remarks were typical: 'I was curious to see a place which was so studiously shut out from European eyes.'[134] As the Himalayas became more familiar, so the attraction of the mysterious, unknown land over the border increased.

Not only did all roads seem to lead to Lhasa in a literal sense, but also in terms of the routes of power. Over the course of nearly a hundred years the British had become increasingly aware of the influence of Lhasa throughout the Himalayan region, but by the middle of the nineteenth century their accumulated evidence and experiences had crystallized into a more fundamental appreciation of the city's hegemonic position. In Hooker's journal of 1855, he made repeated reference to Lhasa: it was the focus of pilgrimage; the centre of craft, art and culture; the seat of religious, judicial, political and military decision-making; its soldiers were feared by the hill peoples and even the British in Darjeeling were nervous about an attack from over the border.[135] When Wilson travelled close to the Tibetan border in 1875, he was prey to fantasies about being poisoned by 'agents of the Lassa Government, whose business is to prevent Europeans passing the border'.[136]

Gutzlaff, in his 1849 report to the Royal Geographical Society, shows how far British fantasies about Lhasa had developed by mid-century:

> The soil throughout the L'hasa district is fertile ... the inhabitants of the less favoured parts ... therefore look upon L'hasa (the seat of the Dalai-Lama) as a paradise ... So many sacred objects are here accumulated that it surpasses in wealth Mecca and Medina, and is visited by pilgrims from all the steppes of Central Asia, with occasionally a devotee from China ... [137]

The Dalai Lama and the Potala palace began to provide an even sharper focus for these fantasies: they somehow seemed to embody the fantastic essence of Tibet. Tibet therefore regularly came to be referred to as the 'domains of the Grand Lama', who, as we have seen, was frequently compared with the Pope. Western travellers were repeatedly confronted with evidence of the Dalai Lama's prestige.[138] The Potala palace was a similar object of Western fascination, and Gutzlaff drew a vivid image of it:

> The palace of the Dalai-Lama ... is 367 feet in height, and has above 10,000 apartments, being the largest cloister in the world. Its cupolas are gilded in the best style; the interior swarms with friars, is full of idols and pagodas, and may be looked upon as the greatest stronghold of paganism ... There is, perhaps, no spot on the wide globe where so much gold is accumulated for superstitious purposes. The offerings are enormous ... and the Dalai-Lama is said to be the most opulent individual in existence.[139]

No wonder the first task assigned to the Indian pundits was to investigate Lhasa. Nain Singh, trained in survey work, set out in 1864 with a compass fixed to the top of his walking staff and notes hidden inside his prayer wheel, he used rosary beads to measure the vast distances by counting his regulated paces. He fixed Lhasa's exact position and altitude and brought an eye-witness description of the city back to the British in India.[140]

The degree of attention beginning to be given to Tibet and Lhasa necessarily brought its all-important religion into the spotlight. Certainly Buddhism in general had long been recognized as a major world religion. As Hooker remarked, it was:

> ... a religion which perhaps numbers more votaries than any other on the face of the globe. Boodhism in some form is the predominating creed, from Siberia and Kamschatka to Ceylon, from the Caspian steppes to Japan, throughout China, Burmah, Asia and a part of the Malayan Archipelago. Its associations enter into every book of travels over these vast regions ... [141]

In addition to being of global significance, Buddhism was generally respected *philosophically*, but by 1875, the Tibetan variant was already being considered as a degeneration from 'the highly philosophical faith of the older books, with which ... Mr Edwin Arnold has made the British reader familiar'.[142]

Western distaste with Tibetan Buddhism during this period revolved around four issues: the gross superstition of its practitioners, the irrationality of its practices, its Tantric philosophy and the autocratic power of its lamas. Wilson wrote, with some degree of exasperation:

> In a certain formal sense the Tibetans are undoubtedly a praying people, and the most pre-eminently praying people on the face of the earth. They have praying stones, praying pyramids, praying flags ..., praying wheels, praying mills, and the universal prayer. 'Om mani pad me haun', is never out of their mouths.[143]

To the British upper-class travellers, deeply embedded within the Victorian industrial culture with its ethics of efficiency, material progress, practicality and thrift of time as well as money, such an excess of prayful zeal was almost a sin. Wilson commented on the proliferation of mani-walls, sometimes miles long, consisting of stones carved with religious prayers: 'These stones are usually prepared and deposited for some special reason ... [but] the prodigious number of them in so thinly peopled a country indicates an extraordinary waste of human energy.'[144]

Tantra was especially singled out for vitriolic abuse by British travellers at this time. Temple, for example, was scathing, calling it the 'evil teaching of the Tantrik philosophy' and 'the filthy esoteric doctrines of the Tantrik philosophers'.[145] The explicit, often violent, sexual and occult symbolism of Tantric Buddhism was unacceptable even by the moral standards of secular art in mid-Victorian Britain, let alone within a religious system. To these well-read travellers it was simply inconceivable that such doctrines bore but the barest relationship to the noble philosophy of self-denial that was believed to constitute original, pure Buddhism. Tantra was blamed for much of the supposed corruption in Tibetan Buddhism.

Whilst such ideas could be found in earlier British travel accounts, they had achieved a new coherence by the 1870s. Buddhism, like so much else about the Himalayas, had been definitively mapped, systematized, evaluated and located within a framework of global evolution. At the same time, Britain had consolidated its own identity – global, imperial, progressive – a new Roman Empire bringing peace, prosperity and civilization to the world. Previously isolated ruminations about Tibet suddenly became congealed into facts, and these in their turn reinforced British certainty and confidence.

During the middle years of the century a new element emerged in Britain's estimation of Tibetan Buddhism, which was eventually to have far-reaching consequences. It was a direct outcome of the feeling of certainty about Britain's imperial identity and shows clearly how fantasies about Tibet were a part of this. While travellers seemed to have mixed feelings about individual lamas – fat and jolly, pious and compassionate, lazy and indolent – opinions about the *system* of power they exercised over the populace were uniformly negative. Lamas as a group were invariably described as crafty and devious in their ability to manipulate the ordinary people of Tibet and the Himalayan region. It was even reasoned that the Chinese Emperor paid homage to the Dalai Lama and his religion only in order to exploit the Lama's capacity to manipulate and control the previously aggressive Mongolian tribes.[146] The ambivalence towards the Tibetan system shown by earlier travellers such as Bogle and Turner was beginning to harden into an unequivocal antipathy.

The high lamas of Lhasa were blamed for the policy of excluding Europeans from Tibet. It was reasoned that they were jealous of their privileges, afraid of losing their power. Tibet was described as 'priest-ridden'. Much was made of the terrible punishments meted out by the autocratic lamas of Lhasa. It even seemed as if the ordinary Tibetans would welcome Europeans, were it not for their deep fear of the lamas' social, spiritual and physical power. As Wilson commented after being denied entry:

> no wonder that the people of that country are extremely afraid of disobeying the orders of the Government ... crucifying, ripping open the body, pressing and cutting out the eyes, are by no means the worst of these punishments.[147]

A fantasy was beginning to take shape in which Britain would eventually see itself as a possible liberator of Tibet from the unpopular, oppressive and cruel dictatorship of the high lamas in Lhasa. The country's theocratic bureaucracy gradually seemed to function as the *shadow* of Britain's autocratic bureaucracy in India. As the latter became increasingly viewed as an exemplary form of benign paternalism, so the system in Lhasa would be envisaged as exploitative and dictatorial. Paradoxically, the Dalai Lama would never be tainted by the supposedly evil system of which he was the undisputed ruler. Like the individual lamas, he was always imagined at a remove from the excesses of the system.

A strange division was made in the European – and particularly the British – fantasy between individuals and a shadowy, Kafkaesque bureaucracy populated by invisible, ruthless officials. Such a belief dovetailed nicely with prevailing mid-century reasoning about British superiority in Europe: this superiority was based not so much on racial characteristics as upon minimal government interference, free enterprise, true competition and trust, as well as freedom from tariffs, bureaucracies and the secret police that plagued continental Europe.[148] The lamaistic government of Tibet seemed to combine some of the worst features of the European police states with the excesses of oriental totalitarianism. In addition, its resemblance to Papism confirmed the worst fears of the British travellers.

As knowledge about Tibet increased, so did the paradoxes and con-tradictions, which could no longer be regarded as anomalies. Somehow they had to be integrated into the 'place' of Tibet, and it was always to the land itself that British fantasies returned in order to give focus and coher-ence to the paradoxes. As Hooker mused from the top of the Donkia Pass:

> I took one more long took at the boundless prospect … There is no loftier country on the globe than that embraced by this view, and no more howling wilderness … Were it buried in everlasting snows, or burnt by a tropical sun, it might still be as utterly sterile; but with such sterility I had long been familiar. Here the colourings are those of the fiery desert or volcanic island, while the climate is that of the poles.[149]

Even as a wilderness Tibet seemed to combine the most extreme of paradoxes, and it was the British *experience* of this wilderness that was to be so important in the last part of the nineteenth century.

In Search of the Grand Design: Tibet and the Wilderness Experience

At about the same time that Hooker was grappling with the contradictions of the Tibetan landscape, the British public were attempting to come to terms with another wilderness, the Arctic. The loss of the Franklin exped-ition and the report that its ill-fated members had resorted to cannibalism administered a profound shock to British sensibilities.[150] The Arctic quest symbolized the struggle between human confidence, courage and intelligence and the awesome, immense power of nature. Many were simply unwilling to accept that the wilderness would win out and crush the finest, heroic aspirations Britain could produce. A few years later, the deaths of Britain's most experienced and respected climbers on the Matterhorn also provoked deep soul-searching about the wisdom and sanity of such activities.

During this period a crucial shift was taking place in the British relationship to natural wilderness. A new 'wilderness experience' was taking shape alongside the earlier appreciation of the natural sublime. This previous experiential paradigm relied upon a sense of danger, fear, immensity and awe to evoke uplifting emotions. Hooker, for example, recorded one night in the mountains:

> In such scenes ... the mind wanders from the real to the ideal, the larger and brighter lamps of heaven lead us to imagine that we have risen from the surface of our globe and are floating through the regions of space, and that the ceaseless murmur of the waters is the Music of the Spheres.[151]

Even when such reveries threatened to overwhelm the traveller and the immensity seemed to reduce the individual to insignificance, a kind of spiritual confidence remained to give hope and cohesion. As the pioneering British photographer Samuel Bourne recounted in 1886:

> What a puny thing I felt standing on that crest of snow! – a mere atom, and scarcely that in so stupendous a world! To gaze upon a scene like this till a feeling of awe and insignificance steals over you, and then reflect that in the midst of this vast assemblage of sublime creation *you* are not uncared for nor forgotten, cannot fail to deepen the veneration ... for that Almighty, but Beneficent Power, who upreared the mountains ...[152]

But the calamities in the Arctic and in the Alps combined with a growing loss of confidence both in orthodox religion and in material progress. Whereas in mid-century the crushing of individual human significance by the awesome scale of nature was viewed as an unthinkable catastrophe, two decades later this very same experience was the basis of a new landscape sensibility.[153] In 1875, Wilson beautifully expressed this experiential shift:

> At night, amid these vast mountains, surrounded by icy peaks, shining starlike and innumerable as the hosts of heaven, and looking up to the great orbs flaming in the unfathomable abysses of space, one

realizes the immensity of physical existence in an overpowering and almost painful manner. What am I? What are all these Tibetans and Paharries compared with the long line of gigantic mountains? And what the mountains and the whole solar system as compared with any group of great fixed stars?[154]

On and on goes Wilson in this reverie, into vaster and vaster imaginings. It is sobering to compare his anguished vision with those of Bourne or Hooker only a few years earlier. We have clearly entered a different cosmology, one in which the old faith seems lost and bewildered by the new discoveries of science and by the new awareness of wilderness landscape. Wilson painfully reflected on the seeming futility of life: 'Our civilizations reach a certain point, and then die corruptly, leaving half-savage races, inspired by coarse illusions, to reoccupy the ground and react the same terrible drama.'[155] He mused on the 'enormous waste and the useless, endless cruelty of Nature'. This is the shadowside of a global identity, a kind of supreme overview that ends with Wilson gloomily intoning: 'All is transitory, all is misery, all is void, all is without substance.'[156]

The experience of wilderness did not *fill* him with confidence, but rather *emptied* everything of significance. Yet precisely at this moment of desperation, Wilson found some comfort, some meaning: 'How wonderful the order and perfection of the inorganic universe as compared with the misery and confusion of the organic!' He then continued: 'There is some refuge ... for the spirit in the order and beauty of this unfeeling inorganic nature.'[157] He called this order and beauty 'the grand design', and in it we can detect a profound shift into a kind of ecological faith. The years of meticulously observing, collecting, classifying and systematizing every conceivable kind of data from around the globe, while destroying long-established beliefs, slowly produced in their stead a new order of faith, a new ground of being.[158]

The combination of empirical observation and controlled imagination, as championed earlier by Ruskin, gave a steadiness to the centre of this new wilderness experience. As Wilson averred, 'Logical thought becomes impossible when we rise into these 18,000 feet regions of speculations; and it may be safer to trust our instincts, such as they are.'[159] It was precisely in these isolated regions that these new wilderness experiences were taking shape – in fact, were being welcomed, however terrifying they may have seemed at first. And it was in these wilderness regions that the *axis mundi* would arise, bringing renewed hope of a connection between humanity, nature and the Divine.

Tibet and the Alchemical Gold

As we have seen, the ideas of Ruskin and Darwin prepared the ground for the final transformation of Tibet into a sacred landscape for the British and other Europeans. By evolving a new way of perceiving and experiencing the natural world, they helped to redeem the bleak and awesome wildernesses. In addition, they drew Britain, Europe, the Himalayas and Tibet into an evolutionary kinship, a shared social, historical and natural context. New activities such as Himalayan mountaineering, photography and tourism brought to a climax nearly a century of travel and exploration in these regions. As the Himalayas became increasingly familiarized, Tibet, by virtue of its exclusion policy, grew in fascination. But although it was unexplored by the British, it was by no means unknown. Fantasies about Tibet had acquired density and coherence; Tibet's boundaries were well defined. By mid-century it had become a paradoxical land in the imagination of British travellers. With growing spiritual and social uncertainty in Britain and Europe, eyes were already turning towards the Himalayas and Tibet in some kind of expectation. As an ancestral source of the Aryan race, these lofty regions were quietly beginning to evoke deep longings.

In addition to these new themes, old ones were being reworked and imbued with fresh significance. We have already seen how the established fantasies about mountain air and Ancient Egypt were revitalized and brought into line within a new imaginative context, but one such theme in particular, which had constantly been present in Western fantasies about Tibet since earliest times, came to symbolize many of the new aspirations. The association of gold and Tibet had first been made by Pliny, Megasthenes, Herodotus and Ctesias. As we saw in chapter 2, ancient rumours told of gold-digging ants in the mountains to the north of India. Gold was consistently mentioned in Western accounts about Tibet, but it was never a major focus of attention.[160] By the middle of the nineteenth century, however, gold had become a small but important symbol in European fantasies. It is a perfect illustration of Freud's theory of *condensation* in the formation of dream symbolism. Whilst Lhasa and the Potala palace would eventually become the prime focus around which disparate fantasies would assemble themselves, before this occurred the same process could be seen at work, albeit on a smaller scale, around the core-image of gold. It was a precursor to the final, massive *condensation* and *displacement* of fantasies on to Lhasa.[161]

The key issue for mid-century British travellers was obviously the rigid policy of exclusion that kept them out of Tibet. 'Why is it', asked Wilson, 'that the Lassa authorities are so extremely anxious to keep all Europeans out of their country?'[162] He was not alone in asking this question, and many answers had been proposed. Wilson eliminated the reasons usually given: 'It has by no means such an amount of fertile land as to make it a desirable object of conquest ... '. Moreover, the lamas had shown considerable tolerance towards Christians, so it could hardly be religious jealousy which kept the doors so firmly shut. Quietly but confidently, Wilson asked: 'Is it possible that gold ... deposits in Tibet may have something to do with the extreme anxiety of the Chinese to keep us out of that country?' Psychologically, this is a classic example of reversal. Instead of asking why British travellers went to such extremes in their attempts to enter Tibet, Wilson shifted the focus entirely on to the Tibetans and tried to puzzle out why *they* went to such lengths to keep the British out. As in all such cases, the accusation reveals more about the fantasies of the accuser than it does about the accused. Why, therefore, were the British so anxious about Tibetan gold, and what connection did it have with their fantasies about Tibet as a closed land?

The British were certainly curious. The Panchen Lama had sent gold dust and ingots to Warren Hastings in 1775, first stimulating British interest. Mid-century reports consistently mentioned the great quantities of gold rumoured to be found in Tibet. Then in 1867 the experienced Pundit Nain Singh was clandestinely sent to investigate the largest of the gold fields. He produced a detailed account of the community and the mines at Thok Jalung in western Tibet.[163]

The reports of gold kept coming in. In 1870 Cooper, fording a river on his journey from China into eastern Tibet, was amazed to see an abundance of gold dust stirred up by the hoofs of his cattle: 'But gold, like all else of a yellow colour in Tibet is sacred to the Grand Lama ... and I was forbidden even to take up a handful of the golden sand.'[164] Tibet never exploited its apparently rich gold and mineral resources. According to Cunningham, this was due to a belief that it disturbed the spirits of the land.

In these reports, a number of themes were beginning to overlap: the restriction on Westerners entering Tibet paralleled the restriction on the mining of gold within Tibet itself; the sacred colour yellow related gold to the power and prestige of the lamas through the distinctive colour of their robes and their ceremonial hats; the relationship between gold and the religion was mirrored by the connection between gold and the *genius loci*. Gold therefore drew land and religion into a direct conjunction. But it was the mid-century gold rushes in California and Australia that most profoundly affected the aristocratic sensibilities of Himalayan travellers. In 1853 Cunningham wrote: 'The crowds that have flocked to the recent "diggings" in California and Australia have fully justified the fears of the Gyalpo.'[165] But this was sheer speculation. Cunningham had absolutely no idea what the high lamas were concerned about. Once again, the traveller's own fears are being assigned to the Tibetans. Over twenty years later Wilson repeated the same fears, but in much stronger terms:

> ... the Mandarins have quite enough information to be well aware that if it were known in Europe and America that large gold-fields existed in Tibet, and that the *auri sacra fames* might there, for a time at least, be fully appeased, no supplications, or prayers either, would suffice to prevent a rush into it of occidental rowdies ... [166]

Here is another projection of the traveller's own anxieties. Quite clearly, the extensive gold deposits in Tibet were no secret. Nain Singh's report of 1869 had given the West a detailed eye-witness account of what it had already suspected. Wilson was really afraid of the desecration of Tibet's untrod purity by the masses, the 'occidental rowdies'. Such fears have already been encountered in the fantasies about polluted mountain air and in the nervous self-assurance that uneducated Westerners would quickly be bored with mountain scenery.

Gold therefore embodied the paradoxical position in which Wilson and other travellers found themselves as regards Tibet's rigid exclusion policy. Without such a policy, Tibet would quickly lose much of its mystery and inevitably yield to global tourism. It therefore began to symbolize an uncontaminated place, outside the social problems of industrialization and urbanization. For the disgruntled elite and disenchanted social reformers alike, Tibet held out hope of escape. The continued closure of this land was therefore *essential* and Wilson, whilst protesting against it, was unconsciously defending this policy: if the *real* 'secret' about the 'wealth' of Tibet ever leaked out, the place would surely be overrun and hence made worthless.

Gold is, of course, a major symbol for the goal of psychic transformation. For the alchemist it represented both the aspiration and the completion of the *opus*, the spiritual journey. As Jung writes, gold is a symbol of eternity, of paradise, and hence of the psychological centre. In relation to gold, he quotes an alchemical text: 'Visit the centre of the earth. There you will find the global fire.'[167] Wilson echoed these sentiments when he wrote:

> It is no wonder, then, that a Chinese proverb speaks of Tibet as being at once *the most elevated and the richest country in the world* ... If the richest mineral treasures in the world lie there ... there is abundant reason why strangers should be kept out of it and why it should be kept sacred for the Yellow religion ... The great cluster of mountains called the Thibetan Kailas ... well deserves to be called *the centre of the world*. It is, at least the greatest centre of elevation.[168]

What better symbol than gold to embrace the aspirations and fears, the hopes and resentments, being slowly conjured up by Tibet in the imaginations of Western travellers? Even within this fantasy we can feel the inexorable pull of the Potala palace, drawing the imagination like a magnet: 'Its cupolas are gilded in the best style ... There is perhaps no spot on the wide globe where so much gold is accumulated for superstitious purposes.'[169] The Potala palace was not just a receptacle for pagan gold and Tibetan superstition; it would also soon become that place on the whole globe where the greatest accumulation of *imaginative* gold, the aspirations of Western travellers, could be found.

Gold speaks of salvation, paradise, boundless wealth, the centre of the world, the meeting point of earth and heaven. It also has other, darker associations: greed, jealousy, intrigue, lust and power. In the mid-nineteenth century the gold was still mainly in the ground, unworked, but even then the gold-capped spires of Lhasa were glinting on the horizon, and British aspirations would soon shift dramatically towards the *complexio oppositorum*, the towering mass of contradictions contained within the Potala palace.

5

Outside Time and Space
(1875–1914)

In 1904 *The Times's* special correspondent, Perceval Landon, accompanying the British expedition fighting its way to Lhasa, paused to visit the
Nyen-de-kyi-buk monastery. After tea with the abbot, Landon asked permission to see one of the immured monks for which the monastery was
famous. These monks had taken a vow to live in darkness, each walled up
and entombed within a small cell just large enough for him to sit in meditation. Some monks entered this rock-hewn home for six months, others
for three years and ninety-three days, and many for life. Landon followed
the abbot into a small courtyard and watched, 'with cold apprehension',
whilst three sharp taps were administered to a stone slab that covered the
entrance to one of these cells. 'It was,' he wrote, 'the most uncanny thing
I saw in all Tibet. What on earth was going to appear when that stone slab,
which even then was beginning to quiver, was pushed aside, the wildest
conjecture could not suggest.'[1] At first the stone seemed to be stuck, or
else the anchorite behind was too weak to move it.

> Then very slowly and uncertainly it was pushed back and a black
> chasm revealed. There was a pause of thirty seconds; during which
> imagination ran riot, but I do not think that any other thing could
> have been as intensely pathetic as that which we actually saw. A
> hand, muffled in a tightly-wound piece of dirty cloth, for all the
> world like the stump of an arm, was painfully thrust up, and very
> weakly it felt along the slab. After a fruitless fumbling the hand
> slowly quivered back again into the darkness. A few moments later
> there was again one ineffectual effort, and then the stone slab moved
> noiselessly again across the opening.

Normally this happened just once a day, to provide the recluse with unleavened
bread and water. Now Landon bitterly regretted his selfish curiosity:

> ... a physical chill struck through me to the marrow. The awful
> pathos of that painful movement struggled in me with an intense
> shame that we had intruded ourselves upon a private misery ...

Finding the 'Tibetan mind' incomprehensible, Landon eagerly welcomed his return to the warm sunlight. He believed that such a life was one of 'painfully useless selfishness', a 'hideous and useless form of self-sacrifice'. These recluses seemed to embody, albeit in an extreme form, the more general malaise of Buddhism in Tibet. Travellers constantly referred to the ignorant, monk-led people and to the idleness of its monks. It seemed as if the lamas had an omnipotent grip over the Tibetan imagination.[2] The event impressed itself deep in Landon's memory. 'Even now,' he reflected, on his return,

> the silver and the flowers and the white linen and the crimson-shaded lights of a dinner table are sometimes dimmed by a picture of the same hand that one shook so warmly as one left the monastery, now weakly fumbling with swathed fingers for food along the slab of the prison in which the abbot now is sealed up for life: for he was going into the darkness very soon.

This incident highlights the encounter betweeen two utterly opposite cultures. Explorers represented the extreme vanguard of an extroverted, aggressive, expansionist culture which valued above all else involvement in the world, individuality, earnestness and will. To this cultural idea of 'manliness', the extreme introversion and world-denial of hermits and recluses was a form of madness. The idea of someone voluntarily walling himself, or herself, up in a cave for life defeated the muscular imagination of Victorian travellers. The absolute immobility of these 'buried anchorites' seemed to mock the exertions of Western explorers, their agonizing journeys across the vast open spaces of Tibet.

Not only did these anchorites seem indifferent, even hostile, to geographical space, they also denied historical, social, time. For the West in the nineteenth century, such action was almost blasphemous. Landon was not merely viewing an alien ritual, he was confronting the annihilation of Victorian ontology. Here was Otherness in its darkest, most absolute form. Yet strangely enough, his reaction was not one of anger, nor of crusading, missionary zeal, but of shame and melancholy, clearly he felt that he was clumsily intruding not just upon an individual's meditation, but into the innermost soul of Tibet. Tibet was not a land of ignorant savages but, for the West at the close of the nineteenth century, a place that quietly demanded respect. Despite its excesses, Tibet offered something unique and indispensable to many. The disgust and frustration of travellers was always tempered by fascination, the urgent calls for modernization and progress always deflected by a longing, by a hope and a promise of something that only Tibet seemed able to provide.

An International Community of Tibetophiles

The classic age of Tibetan exploration began in 1872 when Colonel Nikolai Prejevalsky of the Imperial Russian army set off on the first of his four great expeditions. Attempts to enter Tibet and to reach Lhasa increased at a staggering rate as the century neared its close. The exploits by the Indian pundits, especially those of Sarat Chandra Das in 1879 and 1881, seemed to sting Europeans and Americans into action.[3] From Russia came not only Prejavalsky but also his protégé Kozlov, who actually met the Dalai Lama in 1905; [4] Captain Grombtchevsky explored the extreme west of Tibet between 1888 and 1890; Pievtsoff covered similar terrain at about the same time.

France, like Russia and Britain, also had its own well-established tradition of Tibetan and Central Asian exploration, beginning with Huc and Gabet, Fathers Fage, Desgodins, Thomine, Renou and Brieux. In addition to these men of religion, Gabriel Bonvalot and Prince Henry of Orléans travelled across northern Tibet between 1889 and 1890. Grenard and Dutreuil de Rhins (who was murdered) also struggled painfully across the vast northern Tibetan landscape between 1891 and 1894. From America came the well-respected Tibetan scholar and ethnographer William Rockhill, who visited Tibet from China between 1888 and 1889. From Holland and Canada came the missionaries Susie and Petrus Rijnhart on their tragic journey of 1898, during which both their young child and Petrus died.

British explorers were relatively reticent until Captain Hamilton Bower, a 'sort of damn them all man', traversed northern Tibet in 1891.[5] The British, however, had long been active in Central Asia with explorers such as Forsyth, Johnson, Shaw, Younghusband and Bell.[6] Then in 1892 Annie Taylor, fired by missionary zeal, set off, with just four Tibetan and Chinese companions, to make the immense journey from China to Lhasa. She was the first known Western woman to enter Tibet.[7] Mr and Mrs St George Littledale, accompanied by their nephew, 'a rowing Blue from Oxford', and their fox terrier, struggled towards Lhasa between 1894 and 1895. Henry Savage Landor tried to bully his way across Tibet in 1897, only to be captured and tortured by the Tibetan authorities. A.D. Carey, Ney Elias, Dalgleish (also murdered), Captains Malcolm and Wellby, made up the long list of British explorers in Tibet. Then of course there was the Swede Sven Hedin, one of the most famous Central Asian and Tibetan explorers of his time.[8] In addition to those who set their sights on Lhasa, there were dozens of travellers along the border with Tibet in Ladakh, the Himalayas and western China.

By the 1880s, a whole generation had been raised on the stories of Tibetan travel. Tibetan travel writing was a well-established genre by the close of the century, even though most of the books were published only in the final two decades. Himalayan travel literature had already found its way into the second-hand bookshops.[9]

In 1895 one British journalist exclaimed, 'Tibet may be said to be at present in a state of siege'.[10] Indeed, since 1888 not only had Tibet to contend with scores of hopeful explorers, it had also been involved in sporadic and quite bloody border clashes with British troops.[11] But it was Lhasa, far from the frontier, that was the greatest lure, the long-sought-for goal. As Landon commented in 1904:

> 'In the whole history of exploration, there is no more curious map than that which shows the tangled lines of travellers' routes towards this city, coming in from all sides, north, south, east and west, crossing, interlocking, retracing, all with one goal, and all baffled ...'.[12]

By the close of the century much of Tibet was known. Only the region around Lhasa completely resisted Western penetration; hence its special status, already high, became enhanced. Travellers competed with each other – if not in actually reaching Lhasa itself, then in coming the closest to it: in 1895 the Littledales came within seventy miles; Rockhill in 1889 was thwarted only 110 miles from Lhasa; Bonvalot was turned back in 1890 just ninety-five miles from that impossible city. Annie Taylor was arrested in 1892 barely three days' ride away. But such claims did not pass without dispute. For example, Waddell, no doubt out of hurt British pride, insisted that the party led by the Frenchman Bonvalot had been stopped a full week from Lhasa, and not the single day that they claimed.[13]

Landon was quite correct about the weaving of explorers' tracks around Lhasa. Grenard reported crossing the routes previously taken by Bower, Prejevalsky and Rockhill. Bonvalot intersected Prejevalsky's route, as also did Younghusband on several occasions.[14] Rockhill followed Huc's old route for a considerable distance. Macauley's path in 1884 constantly coincided with the one taken by Hooker over thirty years before.[15] Knight kept company with Bower and Durand in Ladakh just before their famous journey into Tibet. Carey joined company for a while with Ney Elias, also heading for Turkestan. Whilst crossing the Akka-tagh Mountains in 1896, Hedin observed that he made camp just ten minutes from the place where the Littledales had stopped ten years earlier. On the same jouney he also intersected the route taken by Bonvalot seven years before. In China he met the Rijnharts shortly before they left on their tragic journey into Tibet.[16]

All these explorers were conscious of forming a community. They read each other's journals, disputed each other's claims, met or just missed each other *en route*. In response, the peoples of the Himalayas, Tibet and Central Asia began to absorb the Western travellers into their own stories.

Prejevalsky, for example, quickly became a legend.[17] Grenard reported a lively discussion among a group of Tibetans about the West, its inventions and its explorers – 'of Bonvalot, of the French Prince, of the "Captain" (Captain Bower), of Mr Rockhill ...'. The Tibetans even incorporated the rival imperialist leaders into their frame of reference. So, the Russian czar was deemed to be the reincarnation of the great fourteenth century Tibetan monk and religious reformer Tsong-ka-pa. Queen Victoria was likewise thought to be the reincarnation of the goddess Palden-Llamo. Appropriately, in Lhasa, where anti-British feeling was prevalent, the form of Palden-Llamo was imagined as wrathful and war-like, whereas in Tashi Lumpo, which was more sympathetic to Britain, the goddess was envisaged in her more peaceful, benign manifestation.[18]

In addition, travellers frequently used locals who had accompanied previous expeditions. Parpi Bai, a Turkestani, employed by Hedin, had travelled across Tibet several times with many different explorers, including Carey and Dalgleish, Bonvalot and Prince Henry, Dutreuil de Rhins and Grenard, as well as several minor Russian expeditions. Grenard called him a 'veteran of exploration'.[19] On his journey Grenard also met a Chinese political agent who was proud to have travelled with Rockhill. Bonvalot used the services of an interpreter named Abdullah who had once accompanied the famed Prejevalsky. The Littledales employed a Ladakhi who had travelled for a while with Dutreuil de Rhins. Younghusband was accompanied by Liu-San, who subsequently went to Tibet with Rockhill. In Ladakh in 1904, the solitary Scottish traveller Jane Duncan used the services of Aziz Khan, who had also been Younghusband's servant.[20] Lhasa was not only encircled by the crisscrossing routes of travellers, it was also at the centre of a web of fantasies and people's lives.

The intensity of Western exploration in Tibet reached a crescendo by the turn of the century, not just in terms of the numbers of travellers, but also in terms of the country's cohesion and its status as a special world of its own. No wonder Millington called his account *To Lhassa at Last*! One can almost hear the sigh of relief.[21]

The Crisis of Time and Space

This flurry of Tibetan exploration took place during a period when Western culture was experiencing a profound crisis in its basic values. Study after study has called attention to the suddenness of the transformation in these values between 1870s and the onset of World War I.[22] Modernism had upset the equilibrium and confidence of mid-Victorian culture: the promise of harmony between religion and science, capital and labour, city and country, art and nature, aristocracy and democracy. Shannon writes: 'Crucial to the sense of crisis in the later nineteenth century was an awareness of the sheer unprecedentedness of the predicament of a civilization confronted with the cultural consquences of fully developed industrialization.'[23]

Indeed, the changes were overwhelming, both in Europe itself and in its overseas possessions. Imperial expansion and rivalry were intense. It has been estimated, for example that the British Empire expanded by one-third in the final years of the nineteenth century, the age of the 'New Imperialism'. By 1900 Britain ruled over one-fifth of the globe, and it was not alone in this rapid expansion: Russia, Germany and France were also partners in the imperial scramble.[24] Yet this expansion was not accompanied by unequivocal support and confidence at home. The 'New Imperialism' had many critics.[25]

Social, technical, artistic and intellectual changes were also causing anxiety. Kern puts it succinctly:

> From around 1880 to the outbreak of World War I a series of sweeping changes in technology and culture created distinctive new modes of thinking about and experiencing time and space. Technological innovations including the telephone, wireless telegraph, X-ray, cinema, bicycle, automobile, and airplane established the material foundation for this reorientation; independent cultural developments such as the stream-of-consciousness novel, psychoanalysis, Cubism, and the theory of relativity, shaped consciousness directly.[26]

Intense debates ensued about *time*. Was the past a source of freedom or of inertia? Did the historicism of the nineteenth-century sciences and philosophies cramp the myriad perspectives of which human imagination was capable? The present seemed dominated by a new simultaneity as communication systems spread around the globe. Was the future a source of hopeful expectancy, or did it promise only cultural degeneracy? As Western culture embraced the globe, limitless space disappeared. The globe appeared to be shrinking under the dual demands of imperialism and internationalism.[27] In contemporary literature, according to Kern, there was an increasing feeling of claustrophobia at home, yet also a sense of overpowering emptiness overseas. Reactions to these vast spaces, so newly discovered and claimed by imperialism, ranged from intoxication to depression, from inspiration to horror.[28]

The world seemed to become increasingly homogenized, placeless.[29] Geopolitics emerged to dominate global thinking. Friedrich Ratzel had first proposed this perspective in 1882. Geography, for him, was a science of distances, whilst modern politics was a 'school of space'. He taught that 'among nations the struggle for existence is a struggle for space. In the great new empires that sprawl over ever greater distances, spatial extension is a source of spiritual rejuvenation and national hope.'[30] Britain had its own spokesperson and theorist for geopolitics in Mackinder. For him, the end of unlimited space, the development of global electronic communications and the extension of worldwide transportation systems were creating a new globalism. He believed that the world was moving towards a single dominant global empire, and that whoever controlled what he called the 'Asian heartland' would control the world.[31] Such ideas were popularized through journals such as the *National Geographical Magazine* (1889), *Annales de Géographie* (1891), *The Geographical Journal* (1893) and the *Geographische Zeitschrift* (1895).[32] Lord Rosebery, British Foreign Minister in 1893, insisted:

It is said that our Empire is already large enough, and does not need extension. That would be true enough if the world were elastic, but unfortunately it is not elastic ... We have to consider not what we want now, but what we shall want in the future.[33]

The sense of space and time was changing. The concept of empty space became important when it was discovered that virtually none was left. Measures were taken to protect the rapidly vanishing wilderness regions.[34] Reflection began on the importance of 'the frontier' to the cultures of both America and Britain.

Each nation appeared to have its own unique attitude towards time and space. Austria-Hungary seemed convinced that its time was running out, whilst Russia felt it had time to spare. Germany believed it needed more space. 'Austria-Hungary thought its space was excessively heterogeneous and disintegrating. Russia was universally viewed (and feared) as the country with boundless space.'[35] Fears about the Russian capacity to control and utilize their vast spaces were symbolized by the completion of the trans-Siberian railway in 1903.[36] The unprecedented Russian expansion in Central Asia was viewed with increasing alarm by the British in India, especially as the subcontinent came to be seen as the heart of the British Empire, crucial both to its coherence and to its very meaning.[37]

In 1886 British India could envisage no threat from another European power that would justify an intervention in Tibet.[38] By 1902, however, such a threat from the Russians was perceived in very real terms and entirely reversed Britain's former Tibetan policy. Tibet had suddenly become the most important site of Anglo – Russian competition. In addition to Russian expansion, there was also a belief that the Chinese Empire was on the verge of collapse. Such an event would release a vast area of the globe into a kind of spatial anarchy.[39] The British also had strong fears about French expansion in South-East Asia. Some considered their annexation of Tibet to be a very real possibility. It was little wonder, then, that so many late-nineteenth-century British travellers in and around

Tibet had the backing of military intelligence.[40]

Late-nineteenth-century imperialism was concerned with contesting, controlling, reordering and redefining geographical space. It was also concerned with the stories told about such annexation and reorganization, about the identity of nations in the Global Age.

Fin-de-siècle Tibet

Tibet was not just *any* place, not just *one* among many within the Western global imagination. For a few years at the turn of the century it became *the* place. It was for the fin de siècle what Tahiti and China had been for the eighteenth century, what the Arctic was for the early-to-mid-nineteenth century and the source of the Nile for the late nineteenth century. The acclaim given to explorers of Tibet and Central Asia was exceptional; it was as if Tibet touched some fundamental surface of the era's imagination.• Tibet consistently provoked powerful images, beginning in the 1870s with Blavatsky's claims about spiritual masters living in the Himalayas, mahatmas who guided the destiny of the world.[41] The lama in Kipling's story *Kim* also captured the British imagination.[42] As we shall see, references both to Blavatsky's mahatmas and Kipling's lama abounded in Tibetan travel writing at the time.

Two other seminal works of fiction assigned small but critical roles to Tibet. After Sherlock Holmes survived his plunge into the Reichenbach Falls, locked in mortal combat with the arch-criminal Professor Moriarty, he went to Tibet disguised as a Norwegian explorer named Sigerson.[43] It was from Tibet that Arthur Conan Doyle had Holmes reborn; Tibet marked the furthest point of his absence. Holme's historical reality and his presence in London were both so strong that only Tibet, outside such constraints of time and space, could provide him with sanctuary during his missing years. So too, Tibet figured in Riders Haggard's classic tale *She*. After their encounter with this immortal woman somewhere in nineteenth-century Africa, the main protagonists summarily declared that they would go to Central Asia and Tibet, 'where, if anywhere on this earth, wisdom is to be found, and we anticipate that our sojourn there will be a long one. Possibly we shall not return'.[44] Doyle's Tibet was unknown, far away, almost totally Other: a Geographical underworld of unknown landscapes replaced that of industrial society. A detective took time out to become an explorer. Haggard's Tibet lay at the end of an aspiration; it set some exemplary standard in spiritual wisdom. It was where one went when all else failed, or had been attempted – a place not of absence and return, but of promise and transcendence. Kipling's lama was totally unworldy, utterly indifferent to, and ignorant of, historical time and global geography. Blavatsky's mahatmas were formless, disembodied, floating, unfixed by either space or time.

The unconscious of this era could therefore be seen not only in the individual psychopathologies of patients in Vienna and Zurich but also, strongly, in its geographical fantasies. Geographical exploration, in its widest sense, was as crucial to the shaping of ideas about time and space as was the work of Freud, Bergson and Durkheim.[45] I am not implying a simple relationshop here – for example, that explorers read Durkheim or Bergson (although some, like Younghusband and Rockhill, did), or vice versa. However, the radical theorizing in the social and physical sciences was a response to a common milieu and, indeed, contributed to that milieu. Images of Tibet and other places, like those of the personal unconscious, provided the era with both a vessel for the enactment of its fantasies and a means for resolving its identity crisis.[46]

Tibet and Orientalism

Said has pointed out that 'Orientalism ... is not an airy European fantasy about the Orient, but a created body of theory and practice in which ... there has been considerable material investment.'[47] The late nineteenth century witnessed an intensification of Tibetology. In Britain, the Royal Geographical Society continued to fund and direct exploration.[48] Botany, geology, philology, ornithology and surveying were joined by anthropology, archaeology and folklore, as the grid of Western science threw itself over the Himalayas and Central Asia.[49]

This was part of a more general tightening of global imagining, a redefining and reclassifying of geographical places. As Said says, 'there emerged a complex Orient suitable for study in the academy, for display in the museum, for reconstruction in the colonial office, for theoretical illustration in anthropological, biological, linguistical, racial and historical theses about mankind and the universe ...'.[50]

The scattered fragments of knowledge about Tibet were reassembled and given a new coherence under the stimulus of the renewed Cold War with Russia. In addition to volumes such as Sandberg's *The Exploration of Tibet* (1904), most accounts of Tibetan travel began with a detailed summary – a litany, almost – of Western exploration in that country. Such constant retelling served to legitimize Western aspirations. The Royal Geographical Society, in particular, through activities of men such as Clements Markham, did not only bring coherence to disparate texts; it was involved in what Foucault calls the *production* of knowledge.[51] As the well-known explorer Francis Younghusband insisted in 1910, 'I shall ... emphasize ... that there has always been intercourse of some kind between Tibet and India ... Tibet has never been really isolated.'[52] Such claims gained intensity as the British sought to justify their 1904 armed intervention into the country. Not only were the Tibetans seen as intransigent, disruptive and aggressive along the common frontier with India, their policy of exclusion was made to appear more like a rejection of long established customs.[53]

There were, of course, *many* imaginative Tibets produced at the turn of the century: Hedin's heroic landscapes; Younghusband's enthusiastic blend of politics and mysticism; Blavatsky's home of occult masters; Landor's adventure playground; Rockhill's ethnographic paradise. But they all seemed to issue from a common centre, each reflecting a fragment of some shared, overall concern. Said has insisted that 'Orientialism depends for its strategy on this *flexible* positional superiority, which puts the Westerner in a whole series of possible relationships with the Orient without ever losing him the relative upper hand.'[54] But Tibet seemed always to have the ability slightly to elude the total embrace of Western Orientalism. It always sustained an independent Otherness, a sense of superiority, albeit limited.

While the renewal of the 'Great Game' with Russia after 1875 activated Tibet in Western fantasies, this *fin-de-siècle* Tibet can by no means be reduced to the requirements of imperialism. Although ostensibly *outside* the matrix of historical space and time, Tibet was in fact integral to it – indeed, vital to the stability of this matrix in Central Asia. As we shall see, imperialism kept Tibet firmly connected to the struggle over global space and time. Yet its role was as a no-man's-land, a limbo place, a buffer zone, outside history and territorial acquisition.

Tibet promised a different order of time and space outside the strictures of European modernism. Here was a paradox: should this place be penetrated or protected, assimilated or upheld in its autonomy, educated into the twentieth century or preserved as a vital link in the West's connection with the Ancients of its imagination? As we shall see, this dilemma went beyond the needs of imperialism and expressed, in an essential way, the spiritual and psychological unconscious of that era.

Beyond Time and Space: No-man's-land

As we have seen in previous chapters, Tibet was initially conceived to be on the *other* side of the frontier with India, but the threatened collapse of the Chinese Empire in Central Asia and Russian expansion into that region forced the British to reassess the frontier question.[55] The Crimean War frustrated Russian aspirations in the Balkans and caused their efforts in Central Asia to be intensified.[56] Their empire in that region was consolidated in just thirty years: in 1860 Russian troops captured Tashkent and in 1868 a treaty was signed with Bokhara. General Kaufmann entered Khiva at the head of a substantial army in 1873, whilst Khokand was annexed in 1876. The Russian frontiers with Persia and Afghanistan were finally fixed in 1885 and 1895. The construction of the trans-Siberian railway between 1891 and 1903 symbolized this dynamic – and to the British threatening – eastward rush of Russian influence.[57]

After 1894, with the imminent disintegration of the Chinese Empire uppermost in their minds, Anglo-Indian strategists began to create 'buffer zones' along the land frontier of India. Previously, Chinese territory had separated rival European empires; now such a separation had to be a matter of deliberate policy.[58] In the west, an independent Afghanistan had by 1881 become a relatively stable frontier zone. By 1896 the British had established Siam as a buffer against French imperial expansion from the east.[59]

Imperial philosophy at the turn of the century stressed the absolute necessity for empires to avoid common frontiers. These, it was argued, would inevitably promote friction and lead to wars. Neutral zones of mutual non-interference were considered essential between the aggressive boundaries of the Western empires. When the vast spaces of Central Asia offered scant resistance to the Russian momentum eastward, Russophobia reached a new pitch in India. Such fears became an inevitable part of the atmosphere of travel in that region. Every traveller seemed, officially or unofficially, to be part of the 'Great Game'.

While travellers mused on the possibility of making Tibet a British Protectorate, or of annexing that part known as the Chumbi Valley 'as a health resort ...', politicians talked about Tibet as a *buffer zone*. As Lord Curzon, Viceroy of India, insisted in 1901, 'Tibet ... must be a buffer between ourselves and Russia'.[60] The natural strength of the Himalayas was beginning to be thrown in doubt as true mountaineers crossed them with relative ease and as Russian intrigue moved closer to India.[61] Also, from 1880 onwards, there was constant political and social unrest along this long frontier, increasing India's feeling of vulnerability.[62] Above all, however, there was a sense – mentioned again and again by British travellers – of Britain's low prestige on the border with Tibet, due to a vacillating and weak attitude towards the Tibetan question.[63]

The British hesitation over Tibet was a result of their policy of mutual exclusion in that region. As Landon wrote:

> We have no wish to interfere with Tibet so long as Tibet does not imperil our tranquillity in Bengal. While we ourselves seek no exclusive rights in that country, we have at the same time no intention of allowing any other power to secure them.[64]

This was written in 1904 and betrays a certain doubt. Earlier, in 1887, another British traveller was more confident: 'as long as Lhasa remains closed to us, it will remain closed also to Russia'.[65]

With the image of Tibet as a buffer zone, the nothern frontier of India suddenly gained considerable depth. But how secure was it? The strength of Tibet as part of India's frontier depended upon its own internal stability. It also required a reliable British intelligence network to monitor what was going on in that country. Above all, such a defensive buffer role depended upon the natural strength of Tibet's vast wilderness. All three factors gradually came under grave suspicion once the Anglo-Indians began to treat Tibet as a vital part of their northern frontier. In 1883 there were riots in Lhasa against Nepalese merchants. It was generally believed that the city was verging on political chaos, its government in disarray and many of its citizens hostile even to the Dalai Lama.[66] Also, despite Kipling's account in *Kim*, British intelligence was notoriously inept. In 1900 the Buriat Mongol monk Dorjieff, who was resident at Lhasa, adviser to the Dalai Lama and at the very centre of the international political storm rising over Tibet, managed to travel quite freely and totally undetected through the length of India. Dorjieff's easy journey – he was obviously a political agent and not, as the Russians claimed, merely a monastic representative – prompted Lord Curzon to assume personal responsibility for military intelligence on this frontier.[67]

Finally, even the much-vaunted wilderness of Tibet was causing anxiety. The closing years of the century saw an unprecedented increase in British and European exploration of its northern frontier. Grenard called the Akka-tagh Mountains, which mark this boundary, 'the most absolute of frontiers, a frontier for the sky as well as for the earth, for birds as well as for men'. It was, he wrote, a region 'where nothing dies since nothing lives there …'.[68] To the north of these mountains lay the feared Gobi and Takla Makan deserts; to the south was the vast wilderness of Tibet's northern plateau. It seemed a formidable barrier. Bower, too, was certain of its effectiveness against Russian penetration.[69] However, the subsequent discovery that Tibet was not all wasteland weakened its image as an impassable barrier. Landon, for example, warned: 'We have discovered for the first time the true nature of Southern Tibet. It is far from resembling the dreary waterless deserts of the north, so well described by Sven Hedin and others …'.[70] It was feared that these 'fertile fields of southern Tibet' would provide an invading force with a marvellous base for its final assault across the Himalayan frontier of India.

With the removal of Chinese authority and the collapse of internal government, it was possible that Tibet would degenerate from being a buffer zone into a power vacuum, especially one that would be filled by the Russians. Lamb comments that in 1894, 'Tibet did not seem to be a dangerous "power vacuum" because of its geography',[71] but by 1902 it had openly become the site of Anglo – Russian competition. Both sought to influence its politics, yet also to ensure its status as a no-man's-land. Many British travellers in the region speculated freely about this situation.[72]

By the beginning of the twentieth century, Tibet was firmly located as a *strategic absence* from the 'Great Game'. It seemed as if the country's desire for isolation and the preservation of its traditional way of life dovetailed with imperial requirements. But although a Tibet in limbo, unchanging and static, was an ideal, it had its dangers. Tibetan otherworldliness always made it seem vulnerable to the sophistication and aggression of modern politics. It was felt that some cautious communication with Tibet had to be established just to ensure that it remained a no-man's land.

While imperial politics provided the architectural plans which built Tibet into India's northern frontier-wall, Tibet was not just another buffer state. The flamboyant Lord Curzon, who masterminded the expeditionary force into Tibet, gave a lecture in 1906 entitled *Frontiers*. He spoke of the fascination with boundaries, the romance of frontiers, the kind of literature inspired by them, the type of 'manhood' fostered by them – even the effect on national character of being engaged in expansionist frontier struggles. He saw the American West's pivotal place in American culture as a parallel to Britain's frontier struggles, particularly in the north of India.[73]

In addition to being places where something begins, frontiers are essential to a fantasy of *completion*. Empires have boundaries which are well marked, well established, and firmly defended. Curzon warned that the Roman Empire collapsed because it could not maintain its boundaries.[74] He wrote of 'silent men in clubs tracing lines upon unknown areas'. The frontier of an empire marks the boundary between the known and the unknown. Frontiers were 'the razor's edge'. Tibet was entangled in this frontier imagination, imbued with a mixture of both the romance of the unknown and the defence of the known – locked, in the most direct and tangible way, into the heart of both imperial strategy and its mythologizing. It was, as Knight wrote in his popular travel book, a place 'Where Three Empires Meet'.[75]

This brief but special conjunction between imperial India and Tibet, mobilized imaginative themes about that country which had been quietly gathering for over a hundred years. Travellers' attitudes towards Tibet, its landscape, its culture, its peoples, cannot be naively reduced to political exigencies. As we have seen, Tibet had its own story in the British imagination, its own historical momentum. True, this creation of Tibet was always related to the growth of British imperialism, but it was never wholly determined by it. The country's unique qualities transformed a turn-of-the-century imperial political crisis into a *mythological event*, one that somehow expressed the soul-drama of the age. All the imaginative themes surrounding Tibet suddenly came to fruition; all seemed to echo the same concerns about space and time.

Once upon a Time

To understand how it was that Tibet came to glow with aura of other-worldliness, we have to leave imperial strategy behind and listen closely to the travellers' *direct* encounter with that elusive place, their experience of being outside space and time.

1. Outside History

Captain Hamilton Bower, in his famous 1892 journey across northern Tibet, remarked: 'These lamas press with a heavy burden on the necks of the people, and the poor Tibetans, timid and superstitious, bear the yoke quietly.'[76] Bower argued that in order to protect their privileges, the lamas persuaded the people to oppose the entry of Westerners. Such a belief was common among travellers at that time. Louis, in his influential 1894 book *The Gates of Tibet*, wrote: 'The lamas have ... realized that every contact with the outer world meant a narrowing of their power and dominion.'[77] In addition, many believed that the lamas were so backward in worldly affairs that they would not be able to relate to the outside world even if they wanted to.[78] Others argued that the Tibetans, with or without the lamas' prompting, were just basically traditionalists. Landon wryly remarked: 'A thing is so in Tibet because it has always been so; research is not encouraged; progress is a form of heresy.'[79] Grenard, with some humour, wrote: 'the Tibetan, unlicked highlander that he is ... does not want to see anything new; and when, by chance, circumstances make him come out of his hole, he is uncomfortable, bewildered, and thinks only of returning home at the earliest possible moment ...'.[80]

Whilst most travellers were scornful, or condescending, about Tibet's refusal to enter Western history, or to acknowledge its own inclusion on the West's new global map, a few were angry. In 1895, for example, Whitley expostulated: 'It affords a striking illustration of the determination of ignorance and superstition to resist the advance of progress and civilization.'[81] Others were not so sure of the benefits of this 'progress'. In 1899 William Carey exclaimed: 'Round three of its sides, like seas breaking on a rocky coast, rich empires have risen up rolled on, and disappeared ... [Tibet's] peoples have watched from their high station, with listless eyes, all the procession of the past.' Such grandiose, vain struggle, he continued, 'affected little, if at all, the rough race dwelling on the roof of the world ... Through all the centuries Bodland [Tibet] stood still, impassive, looking down like some grim image on a grassy green, while all this many-coloured life bloomed and danced about its feet.'[82]

Clearly, a position outside history was also a possible source of dour wisdom. The Russian mystic Madame Blavatsky, of course, had earlier taken such a belief to its logical conclusion, eternalizing the dimensionless and personifying it in the timeless figures of the mahatmas.[83] They were the voice of wisdom from the *axis mundi*, from outside time and space. When Landon wrote that 'Lhasa never changes', one suspects that he wanted it always to be that way.[84] Imperial politics and Tibetan isolationism coincided in some strange way with a deep inner need of many Westerners.

2. *An Absence on The Map*

Even before they set out, the travellers' attention was drawn to Tibet by its absence on the colourful new global maps. To such a map-conscious era, this lacuna was magnetic. Bower, for example, wrote of 'the true Tibet, a huge white blank on our maps; and that blank', he insisted, 'I determined to visit'. It was, as Landon called it, 'the last country to be discovered by the civilized world'.[85] Hensoldt asked, 'How is it that so vast a portion of our planet's surface should, for centures, have remained *terra incognita* to our Western civilization ...?' The experienced mountaineer, Douglas Freshfield, standing on the Jonsong-la in 1899, looking into Tibet, commented: 'Far as the eye could reach ... the unknown, unnamed mountains of Tibet indented the bright horizon with their spears and horns.' In so many ways, Tibet marked 'the limits of the Unknown'.[86]

3. *Threshold to another World*

'Tibet is the most forbidding country to be found on the globe. It towers above the clouds the largest and loftiest mass of rock in the world.' William Carey went on to call it 'the enchanted land'.[87] Indeed, just to be 'above the clouds' placed Tibet into the 'once upon a time', the 'land far away', of fairy-stories. Like the giant's castle at the top of the beanstalk, or the palace of the gods atop Mount Olympus, Tibet was 'above the clouds', ethereal, not of this world, a land of dreams. Even the border war between Britain and Tibet in 1888 was hardly taken seriously. 'It has one characteristic', commented *The Spectator*, 'which takes it out of the range of common conflicts. It has been waged ... above the clouds ... and not remote from the ... line of eternal snow.'[88] To be above the clouds was to be close to eternity, to the timeless. In 1904 *The Spectator* again could not quite treat the capture of Lhasa by British troops as a serious event: 'It is more like the adventure which children love as "Jack and the Beanstalk" than any ever recorded by grave historians.' One writer playfully described the attitude of some people towards Tibet in terms of Brünnhilde 'asleep in her mountain top', with the viceroy playing 'the part of Siegfried'.[89]

Time and again, on the border with Tibet, travellers, no matter where they came from, felt that they were stepping into another world: 'Before us – all that vast silence of mountains muffled in snow – that is Tibet. Look at it well ... One step more and you have crossed the threshold.'[90] As Louis rested at this evocative boundary, he mused:

> I remained there alone, enjoying the scene of indescribable grandeur, solitude and silence around me ... The earth itself seems absorbed into the infinity of space; a dark blue sky, dazzling white snow, and grey moving mist intermingling with sky and snow, as if snowy slopes and summits and mist *had detached themselves from the earth below to join hands with the eternal vault above* ...

He felt transported 'into regions of peace, unknown, not of this world'.[91] Hensoldt similarly commented: 'The world of Tibet differs so completely from everything south of the Himalayas – and for the matter of that, from every other region on the face of the globe – that we seem as if transferred to another planet.'[92]

Tibet was not always experienced as an *enchanted* otherworld. Landon, for example, wrote: 'The first sight of Tibet ... is not without a sombre interest of its own ... All is bare and dull.' Later he continued:

> Crossing the Tang la into Tibet proper was a terrible experience. The frozen mist, laced with splinters of ice, was blown horizontally into our faces by the wind which never sleeps over this terrible Pass ... We had crossed the frontier ... and we trudged over as forbidding a floor as exists on earth.

He called it 'the accursed, frozen waste'. Earth time seemed to have no relevance in such a place.[93]

4. *An Initiation*

William Carey, wrote with a typical rhetorical flourish, 'One step more, and you have ... passed through the mysterious *portals*; you have entered the Forbidden Land.'[94] Louis also wrote of the '*gates* of the promised land of Thibet'.[95] For many, to enter Tibet seemed like ritually stepping through the well-guarded doorway of a temple – an initiatory experience. Stone, a deputy inspector-general of police, graphically described his entrance whilst on a hunting trip: 'We passed between jagged rocks into Tibet, with a roaring wind at our backs.'[96] The soldier-Buddhologist Waddell, too, captured the uncanniness of the moment as he stood atop a pass leading into Tibet: 'The cold was bitter, but the piercing wind that swept the top was much more trying than the cold itself ... Yet thousands of tiny birds ... annually migrate over such exposed passes to and from Tibet ...'.[97] On another such pass, he commented: 'So cold was the wind that a young eagle fell dead a few yards from my tent ...'.[98] One is reminded of the very first entrance into Tibet in modern times by a Briton, Bogle, in 1774. His first sight was similarly of death – a funeral, and one of Tibet's seemingly macabre burial grounds.

The entry into Tibet claimed its share of victims, its sacrifices, both human and animal. Of 3,500 yaks assembled by the British army in 1904, only 150 survived the crossing into Tibet.[99] Hedin, on one of his Tibetan explorations, grimly referred to the lengthening 'death-register' of animals.[100] Littledale reported that 'not a day passed but several animals had to be shot or abandoned. It is a gruesome subject which I will not pursue further'.[101] Grenard sorrowfully told a similar tale: 'Our road was marked by the carcasses of our horses.' 'In the end,' he continued, 'all our beasts died, with the exception of two camels. The neighbourhood of the camp became a charnel-house infested with crows and even more horrible huge vultures … '.[102]

Frostbite killed several soldiers in 1904 as the British crossed the Jeylap-la. Bonvalot had to bury one of his Muslim companions in the frozen ground. Grenard's leader, Dutreuil de Rhins, was killed by Tibetans in 1891. Even more tragic was Dr Susie Rijnhart, who lost both her small son and her husband whilst trying to reach Lhasa. Grenard, as always, expressed the melancholy of such losses: ' … all these miseries, added and multiplied together, gave me the impression that I was sinking into a dark and silent depth from which there is no returning!'[103]

As well as birds dropping dead from the sky, other uncanny images seemed to be conjured up as travellers entered Tibet. Both Landon, from *The Times*, and Chandler, from the *Daily Mail*, reported seeing a frozen waterfall, 'which might', wrote Chandler, 'be worshipped by the fanciful and superstitious as embodying the genius of the place … '. Landon also saw a white rainbow just before crossing into Tibet.[104]

5. *The Carnival and the Underworld*

The journey into Tibet was often experienced as a *nekyia*, a descent into the Underworld, a topsy-turvy, upside-down place[105] – an entry into a region of extreme cold and heat, of death and yet also of hope. When confronting the landscape, Stone wrote of 'the topsy-turviness with which one gets familiar in the land of the Lamas'.[106] Where else could one get sunburnt on one side of the body whilst being frostbitten on the other? It was a land of simultaneous extremes, like the black-and-white check of a harlequin's jacket. Travellers constantly reached for adjectives such as 'fantastic', 'illogical', 'weird'. Chandler, for example, struggled to describe his experience of the scenery as he entered the country. It had, he wrote, 'an intangible fascination, indescribable because it is illogical'.[107] Macaulay, on his 1884 diplomatic mission to Sikkim, mused playfully: 'the journey of an Englishman to Lhasa … has been considered something about as visionary as a voyage to Laputa or Atlantis would have appeared to a contemporary of Swift or to a disciple of Plato.'[108]

The Tibetans were renowned for misleading Western travellers and giving wrong directions. 'It is almost impossible to get the correct names of places or lakes in Tibet, as every Tibetan lies on every occasion on which he does not see a good valid rason for telling the truth', wrote an exasperated Bower. Elsewhere he exclaimed: 'it is terribly hard work trying to get geographical information out of Tibetans, and when in exceptional cases, as does occasionally happen, a vein of truth runs through their statements, it is so fine as to be almost impossible to discover'.[109] Even the Tibetans' own relationship to their land seemed perverse – locking themselves up in a cell for life; covering the landscape with stone walls and monuments that had no conceivable practical purpose; living in filth amidst natural beauty; refusing to fish despite abundant lakes. Knight summed it up: the Tibetan, he wrote, 'despises the beautiful, [but] has a love for the grotesque in nature'.[110]

The apparent craziness of Tibet, a land outside the normal order of things, had its influence upon the Western imagination. So when the British contemplated invading Tibet, they dreamt up a bizarre range of pack-animals that it was felt would be needed to tackle such a paradoxical place. In addition to the ill-fated yak-corps, there were the zebrules. Like something from a mythological bestiary, zebrules were a cross between a zebra and a Clydesdale mare. They were not a success.[111] Perhaps this sense of the absurd was most succinctly revealed in a story from the 1888 border conflict between Britain and Tibet. It was reported that British troops nervously fired a volley into a patch of giant rhubarb plants, mistaking them for Tibetan soldiers.[112]

This strange world was not always experienced with such humour. At one point on his journey, Grenard described it as a 'monstrous chaos'.[113] The madness of the landscape at times seemed merely to echo the general absurdity of Tibetan religion and culture. For example, the Tibetan's lack of any sense of time was notorious among travellers. Rockhill described their calendar:

> Tibet has preserved its own system of reckoning time ... Days are divided into lucky and unlucky ones. The latter are disposed of by being dropped out; thus, if the thirteenth is unlucky, they skip it and count the fourteenth twice. As at least half the days of the year are unlucky, this must be a most confusing system.[114]

Surely an understatement. Indeed, frequently, when dealing with Tibetan officials, travellers' journals read like *Alice in Wonderland*. When Chandler reported the negotiations between the defeated lamas and the officers from the British army encamped outside Lhasa, he was perplexed:

'Instead of discussing matters vital to the settlement, the Tibetan representatives would arrive with all the formalities and ceremonial of durbar to beg us not to cut grass in a particular field, or to request the return of empty grain bags to the monasteries.'[115] The British government officially acknowledged, somewhat wearily, 'that the utmost patience is necessary in dealing with the Tibetans'. Francis Younghusband, that paragon of patience and determination, called the Tibetan negotiators 'exasperating', 'inept', 'an intangible, illusive, un-get-at-able set of human beings ...'.[116]

When added to the incessant and seemingly meaningless rotation of prayer wheels and the corresponding prohibition against wheels for transportation, the belief that magic charms would stop bullets and that painted symbols on rocks would stop the British army, one can understand Grenard exclaiming: 'thus is Tibet made to spin distractedly, without rest or truce, in religion's mad round'.[117]

6. Backwards in Time

Time just seemed to have stopped in Tibet. For example, Grenard wryly mentioned finding 'a box containing six cakes of scented soap, which were the only specimens of soap that could be discovered within the radius of Lhasa in the month of January 1894 and which their purchaser was delighted to sell to us after having them for forty years in his shop'.[118] Even the landscape seemed absolutely static. Landon described a scene: 'In this broken ground underneath precipitous mountainsides, where the rocks lay as they had fallen for a thousand years'.[119] Nothing ever seemed to have changed or moved.

Not only did time seem to stand still, or to slow down to a standstill, travellers also continually felt transported *back* in time. Chandler called the Tibetans 'obsolete anachronisms, who have been asleep for hundreds of years'.[120] He reflected: 'The Tibetans are not the savages they are depicted. They are civilized, if medieval.'[121] This medieval quality was highlighted in the only attack that took place on British–Indian soldiers occupying Lhasa. Chandler reported that a lama 'ran amuck outside the camp with the coat of mail and huge paladin's sword concealed beneath his cloak, a medieval figure who thrashed the air with his brand like a flail in sheer lust of blood. He was hanged medievally the next day within sight of Lhasa.'[122] The more standard weapons of the Tibetan soldiers were scarcely more advanced than those of this mail-armoured monk: rusty matchlocks, slings, bows and arrows. Indeed, as Waddell pointed out, 'the Tibetan word for "gun" is "fire-arrow" ... and their commanders are still called "Lords of the arrows".'[123] British soldiers advancing on Lhasa heard rumours of soldiers in chain mail waiting up ahead, and at one point were bombarded by large red and gold bullets made from copper.[124]

The Tibetans seemed to inhabit a pre-Copernican world. The flat-earth theory had long been a source of amusement in the West, a sign of medieval ignorance and stubbornness, if not lunacy. Younghusband reported a conversation with the head abbot of the Tashi Lumpo monastery near Shigatse. He was, wrote Younghusband, 'a courteous, kindly man', 'a charming old gentleman'. However, he firmly interjected when Younghusband 'let slip some observation that the earth was round'. Younghusband continued: '[he] assured me that when I had lived longer in Tibet ... I should find that it was not round, but flat, and not circular, but triangular, like the bone of a shoulder of mutton.'[125] It all seemed like medieval scholasticism gone mad.

Yet there was a charming side to this. Freshfield, while just over the border from Tibet, witnessed a Tibetan Buddhist ritual:

> The scene and its setting were most fascinating, a picture primitive and fantastic, real and at the same time almost incredible in its antique air. In the priestly procession and the simple rites, the ancient world seemed to live again, protected from the changes of centuries.[126]

Grenard thought the relationship between people and priests similar to that of 'the Italians of the middle ages'.[127]

But Tibet also drew the Western imagination back even deeper into time, beyond the medieval and into the archaic. For Landon, 'the Golden Roofs of Potala' were an 'image of that ancient and mysterious faith which has found its last and fullest expression beneath the golden canopies of Lhasa'.[128] While a connection between Tibet and Ancient Egypt had been made many times before, only in this period was Tibetan Buddhism fully imagined to be a direct descendant from that revered ancient religion. It was viewed as a late, and perhaps final, flowering of the world's archaic mystery religions. According to Hensoldt in his paper 'Occult Science in Thibet' (1894), whilst Tibet was not the *source* of archaic wisdom, it was 'the very fountain head of esoteric lore'.[129] Such a belief found its most cogent expression in Blavatsky's monumental writings. Her first major book on the 'mahatmas', published in 1877, was titled *Isis Unveiled*, thus establishing the firmest of imaginative connections between Egyptian and Tibetan religions.[130] Naturally Blavatsky claimed that her global travels had taken her to both Egypt and Tibet and included study with 'Adepts' in both places. 'The Brotherhood of Luxor' is mentioned alongside 'the Tibetan Brotherhood', in *The Mahatma Letters*.[131] It was an ironic coincidence that British imperial policy in Egypt decisively influenced their activities in Tibet at the turn of the century. As Landon reported, 'It is an open secret that our policy in Egypt just then demanded that we should be on good terms with Russia ....'[132]

7. Prehistorical

John White, the political agent for Sikkim, Bhutan and Tibetan Affairs between 1887 and 1908, witnessed the first visit to India by a high Tibetan lama. Of the accompanying retinue he wrote: 'They were an extraordinary collection of wild, only partly civilized, creatures, especially those from Tibet ...'.[133] At one point, Dutreuil de Rhins confided to Grenard that 'he had found it easier to get on with the savages of Africa' than with the Tibetans.[134] Deeper than even the *medieval* and the *archaic* lay the *prehistoric* and the *primitive*. For the Victorians these meant the most elementary, primeval, forms of human life. Hensoldt wrote:

> it would be folly to shut our eyes to the fact that the Thibetans occupy a very low position in the scale of human advancement ... Their culture is inferior to that of the most semi-barbarous races, comparing unfavourable even with that of certain Indian tribes of the American continent, such as the Pueblos, Zunis, etc.

Even in their physiognomy they seemed to be 'the most ill-favoured of Turanian races'.[135] Grenard, too, was reminded of 'American Redskins' by some of the Tibetans. Bonvalot remarked that they had an 'animal intelligence'.[136] Tibet was viewed as a unique laboratory or museum, a protected place where social evolution could be observed in the making, in its most elementary form. Landon wrote that in Tibet we can see 'processes and ideas which in other parts of the world are almost pre-historic'.[137] Waddell was of the same opinion:

> For Lamaism is, indeed, a microcosm of the growth of religion and myth among primitive people; and in large degree an object-lesson of their advance from barbarism towards civilization. And it preserves for us much of the old-world lore and petrified beliefs of our Aryan ancestors.[138]

Even the landscape seemed 'primeval'. Sometimes the vast plains, with their prolific numbers of animals, were reminiscent of Africa. It was like a land before the arrival of humans. 'In every direction antelope and yak in incredible numbers were seen ... No trees, no signs of man ... seemingly given over as a happy grazing ground to the wild animals.'[139] In the midst of this primeval landscape, the imagination of Westerners suddenly began to be drawn towards rumours of wild, hairy men.

The first mention of such creatures by a Westerner was made in 1832 by Brian Hodgson, the British Resident in Kathmandu, who simply reported a Nepalese tale,[140] but nothing more was heard about these 'wild men' until the 1880s. In 1889 Waddell was travelling high in the Himalayas:

Some large footprints in the snow led across our track, and away up to the higher peaks. These were alleged to be the trail of the hairy wild men who are believed to live amongst the eternal snows, along with the mythical white lions, whose roars are reputed to be heard during storms ... These so-called hairy wild men are evidently the great yellow snow bear.[141]

Five years earlier, Colin Macaulay, on a diplomatic mission to Sikkim, had also come across similar tracks at an altitude of 15,700 feet. The Tibetan guide drew his attention 'to a pair of huge footprints going due west ... and visible for a long way across the snow'. Macaulay was told that these belonged to the 'wild men who live in the snow'. Most Tibetans readily believed in these creatures, although none had actually seen one. 'The footprints'. continued Macaulay, 'were certainly remarkable, very large and very broad, quite twice the size of a man's. I suppose they were a bear's.'[142]

Another report came from the respected American Tibetologist Rockhill. On his 1886 journey into Tibet he was told a story by an old lama on his way home from Lhasa: 'Several times, he said, his party had met hairy savages, with long, tangled locks falling around them like cloaks, naked, speechless beings, hardly human ...'.[143] Rockhill continued: 'This story of hairy savages I had often heard from Tibetans, while at Peking ...'. Like Waddell and Macaulay, he believed that such stories referred to bears. Rockhill returned to these creatures later in his journal. This time, a Mongolian reported seeing 'innumerable herds of wild yak, wild asses, antelopes and *geresun bamburshe*. This expression means literally "wild men"'.[144] He referred to a similar report in 1871, by Prejevalsky, who called them *kung guressu*, or 'man beast'. Like the good ethnographer he was, Rockhill situated such tales within the folk history of Central Asia. Such legends, he wrote, were common, especially in the Middle Ages. They were derived from an ancient worship of bears. 'This is certainly the primeval savage of eastern Tibet, the unwitting hero of the many tales I had heard of palaeolithic man in that country.'[145] Finally, Rockhill recounted a story about 'men in a primitive state of savagery' living in Tibet. Again they were described as very hairy, but this time they wore primitive garments made of skin and probably lived in caves.[146]

While stories about wild hairy men had long been integral to the folklore of the Tibetans and other Himalayan peoples, they now entered the mainstream of Western imagining and assumed new shapes. The lack of similar stories before the 1880s seems strange: by then the Himalayas had long been 'the happy hunting ground' for experienced British big-game hunters.[147] Were these tracks not seen by them, or were they not considered worthy of mention? Either way it seems peculiar that a flurry of reports should occur within a few years of each other. Western interest in these stories was still only either ethnographic or an amusing illustration of the native's superstition and lack of scientific descrimination. It would be many years before the hairy wild man would become the unprecedented focus of a Western attention far outstripping, for a few years in the 1950s, the importance given to him even in Tibetan and Nepalese cultures.[148] Divested of any palaeolithic characteristics, the yeti would then be imagined as a remnant of a pre-human missing link, or an evolutionary dead end: it would become part of an entirely different imaginative context. But for the late Victorians this creature merely emphasized the primevalness of Tibet, both in its fauna and landscape and in the superstitions and customs of its people.

Although the medieval and archaic metaphors were clearly associated with spiritual connotations, even the apparent primitiveness of Tibet had subtle overtones of wisdom and vitality. Blavatsky had visited Canada, even before going to Tibet, and reported learning occult secrets from the medicine men of the American Indians. In New Orleans it was said that she investigated voodoo rituals.[149] Such activities were in keeping with her close relationship to the shamanic tradition in Russian religion. Hutch has pointed out that such a tradition was integral to the religious revival that occurred in Russia during Blavatsky's formative early years.[150] Neverless, the elevation of shamanism to a level of respect that equalled archaic and modern religions in Western fantasies would have to wait for over fifty years. Tibetan Buddhism would then be linked with the religions of Australia, North and Central America and elsewhere, as part of a primal tradition which emphasized direct, ecstatic religious experiences in harmony with nature. Significantly, both shamanism and the yeti would then simultaneously capture Western fantasies.

In 1879 Prejevalsky, on his Tibetan expedition, discovered the original horse in the remoteness of Mongolian Central Asia. It was a species which had flourished in the Pleistocene period and had survived in a region too remote for humanity to domesticate. He had discovered one of the wild strains from which our modern horse is a degenerate descendant in terms of toughness and fierceness.[151] Here was the answer to the riddle of the famous ponies of Genghis Khan and the Mongol armies. The Mongols obtained their mounts by domesticating half-castes of these wild horses. They were the original, the archetypal source of vigour and life-energy uncorrupted by civilization. Bonvalot even reported that his small Tibetan horses were carnivorous, feeding 'on raw flesh'.[152] What powerful metaphors of primal vitality for the horse-worshipping Victorians!

8. The Dream Land

Landon referred to the Tibetans as 'these turbulent children'. Younghusband described the Tibetan officials as 'sulking' at the negotiations.[153] Such an image was commonly used, particularly by British travellers, in the nineteenth century. Perhaps its use was related to Britain's colonial presence in India, with its patronizing attitude towards the Indians. Here, too, the local people were frequently referred to as children,[154] but in Tibet this labelling was different. Here the children held power; they were in control of the nation's affairs, and the British had to deal directly with them as diplomatic equals.

For the Victorians, childhood was associated with a period of pre-responsibility and a kind of pre-adult sense of space and time. Given the spectrum of imaginative contexts already discussed – topsy-turvy land, fairy stories, myth, madness, medieval, archaic, primitive, primeval – the image of the child is particularly revealing. At the turn of the century many in the West bracketed the mentality of children and primitives with dreams and psychopathological states, viewing them as congruent with fundamental – almost pre-socialized – psychological processes.[155] Such a primary functioning of the mind was also discussed in terms of the primeval and the instinctual. Myth and fairy story commonly began to be used as examples of pre-rational thinking. Similarly, to be archaic or medieval was to be pre-scientific, even pre-rational. Nowhere was this bracketing more pronounced than in psychoanalysis. In his pioneering works of 1900 on sexuality, dream and the unconscious, Freud readily drew upon these areas to construct his psychodynamic models. In doing this he was merely expressing commonly held associations.[156]

In accounts about Tibet, such associations, while stated less explicitly than in psychoanalysis, were nevertheless assumed. The Tibetans' bewildering attitude towards sexuality – permissive, polyandrous, polygamous, monogamous and celebate in equal measure – was attributed to a kind of childlike pre-moral mentality rather than an adult immorality. As Landon put it, 'in the conventional sense of the word, morals are unknown in Tibet'.[157] Their indifference to – even celebration of – their own filth also suggested a pre-responsible mentality. Even rumours of matriarchy, then popularly considered to be one of the earliest forms of human social organization, were touched upon in several travel texts.[158]

Children, primitives and psychotics were imagined to move in a world outside the 'normal' laws of time and space, in a reality separate from society and history. They were believed to be closer to the instinctual unconscious, further from the constraints of the superego, the civilizing imperative. For Freud, the past – whether in an individual's life, in the life of a culture, or in the evolution of the human species – was a source of hope, healing and vitality, as well as of ignorance and irresponsible destruction. This forgotten, repressed past *was* the unconscious. Tibet, as portrayed in these *fin-de-siècle* travel accounts, had all the characteristics that symbolized the Western notion of the unconscious. Even the tyranny of the lamas, when compared with the childlike peasants, was couched in a language that suggested a renegade, unbalanced superego ruled by a wilful child, the Dalai Lama.[159]

No wonder, then, that Tibet should be imagined as a dream world and that Western explorers at the turn of the century should be irresistibly drawn to it in exactly the same way that their introspective colleagues were being drawn to the idea of the individual unconscious. Both were symbols of a *complexio oppositorum*. Both attempted to bring some cohesion to a Western imagination that had been fragmented into a bewildering range of apparently irreconcilable opposites. Landon compared the romantic fantasies conjured up by 'the Golden Roofs of Potala' with those of Rome in 'the opium-sodden imagination of De Quincey'.[160] Even the landscape seemed to echo this impression: 'There was a lack of proportion and perspective that produced a strangely unreal effect. It was like a land in a dream.'[161] As the twentieth century progressed the unconscious would cease to be viewed mainly negatively, as a place of repressed memories, and would gradually under the influence of Jung and the Surrealists, be seen as a source of wisdom, creativity and religious inspiration. As we shall see, Tibet would by then be well prepared to step into the vanguard of this new fantasy of the unconscious.

9. Boundless Space, Boundless Light

As travellers journeyed into Tibet they moved into a world full of light and boundless space. Grenard, a member of the ill-fated scientific expedition sent to Tibet by the French government in 1891, exclaimed: 'Spread throughout the whole of Tibet are great spaces covered with snow and rocks and occupied by rugged slopes on which nothing grows.'[162] The relentless Swedish explorer Sven Hedin wrote of 'the boundless wilds of Tibet'.[163] Bonvalot complained: 'there seems to be no end to these lofty tablelands, and the westwind blows incessantly'.[164] Those coming from the north felt that they were utterly alone, cut off from human life: 'the usual monotony of our horizon ... produced the effect of a country which is uninhabited, or which has been.'[165]

Carey, travelling across northern Tibet during two years' leave from the Bombay Civil Service, groaned: 'For 80 days we had not seen a single human being outside the caravan, and my men were naturally gloomy and dispirited.'[166] Such a reaction to the apparently endless emptiness was common. Bonvalot, traversing a similar region, wrote wearily about 'the solitude being deeper and weighing heavier than ever'.[167] The boundless and windswept spaces consistently evoked their direct opposite, a dense and weighty depression. Grenard, in his usual evocative prose, wrote of 'immense countries where nothing passes but the wind, where nothing happens but geological phenomena ... For sixty days, man attracted our attention only by his absence.' He continued, 'the barrenness was absolute'. The reaction was not surprising: 'Our men, terrified at this endless mountain desert, were seized with an ardent longing to escape from it, to see something different.'[168] Landon referred to one part of Tibet as 'the accursed frozen waste'.[169] Sometimes travellers simply did not know whether to describe Tibet as wretched and barren or sublime and awe-inspiring.[170]

Crossing such vast spaces caused travellers gradually to lose their sense of distance and the passing of time. 'It is difficult', wrote Bonvalot, 'to imagine how hard it is to find one's way among these highlands, where a man loses all sense of perspective, his eye wandering over immense spaces without seeing ... either trees, houses, human beings, animals ... '.[171] The deceptive distances added to the sense of an illusion, to the feeling of being in an entirely alien, dimensionless space.

Time, too, seemed to dissolve into a boundless – sometimes 'sublime' – monotony.[172] As his party approached the northern frontier of Tibet, Grenard described a land that 'was barren, dull, silent as death and infinitely desolate'. Further along, the experience was still the same: 'We heard nothing but the incessant harsh, furious whistle of the west wind ... We saw nothing but a succession of dismal hills ... Nothing grew ... Nothing moved in the sky or on the ground.' Encountering a great lake, he wrote that it was 'motionless ... as if it were sleeping in the absolute silence of surrounding nature ... '.[173]

Whilst most travellers felt crushed beneath the formlessness of this vast silence, space and stillness, a few experienced moments of cosmic reverie. Younghusband, for example, recounted how, after the treaty with Tibet had been signed at the Potala in Lhasa, after all the struggles, fighting, bloodshed, frustrations and diplomacy of the previous months, he

> went off alone to the mountainside ... The scenery was in sympathy with my feelings ... I was insensibly suffused with an almost intoxicating sense of elation and good-will ... Never again could I think evil, or again be at enmity with any man ... Such experiences are only too rare, yet it is these few fleeting moments which are reality ... that single hour on leaving Lhasa was worth all the rest of a lifetime.[174]

Some years earlier, taking seventy days to cross the Gobi desert, the seeds of such an experience were sown: 'Anyone can imagine the fearful monotony of those long dreary marches seated on the back of a slow and silently moving camel ... But though these were very monotonous, yet the nights were often extremely beautiful ...'. He concluded: 'When we have been for months cut off from civilization, when there are none of the distractions of daily life to arrest our attention, then, in the midst of the desert, or deep in the heart of the mountains, these truths approach realities.'[175] The spiritual Younghusband embraced the immense spaces and welded such experiences into a unique – almost ecological – mysticism. Others, too, felt these stirrings.[176] Silence and solitude were sometimes healing to travellers weary of the crowded confusions of urbanized life. So Bonvalot wrote of being 'lost in space', and continued:

> the steppe, the desert, is a very fascinating place of sojourn for one who has lived in large cities, and has been put out of humour by the petty miseries of civilization. Solitude is a true balm, which heals ... its monotony has a calming effect upon nerves made over-sensitive from having vibrated too much; its pure air acts as a douche which dries petty ideas out of the head.[177]

Not only was the space boundless, the light in Tibet also seemed to possess a unique luminosity. It evoked astonishing, almost unreal colours from the landscape and sky. Landon referred to Tibet as a 'land of thin, pure air and blinding light ... '. Grenard similarly wrote of 'the pure light'. High in the Himalayas, Freshfield could not contain his enthusiasm as he experienced 'a marvellous expression of space, light, colour; an example of Nature at once luxurious and sublime ... The atmosphere was transfused with light, and the earth robed in transparent colours.'[178]

Crossing the fertile plains around Lhasa, Landon was overcome with the beauty of the light:

> The colour of Tibet has no parallel in the world. Nowhere, neither in Egypt, nor in South Africa, nor even in places of such local reputation as Sydney or Calcutta or Athens, is there such a constancy of beauty, night and morning alike ...

Indeed, he drew attention to one phenomenon peculiar to Tibet, a five-fingered aurora of rosy light that arches at sunset over the sky from east to west. 'This', he wrote, 'is no ordinary light.' He concluded:

> These sunsets are as unlike the cinnamon, amber, and dun of South Africa as the crimson, gold-flecked curtains of Egypt, or the long contrasting belts of the western sky in mid-ocean. So peculiar are they to this country that they have as much right to rank as one of its characteristic features as Lamaic superstition ...[179]

By the end of the century travellers were already expecting to see, encounter and appreciate these colours. As Chandler stood atop the Jeylap-la Pass and looked into Tibet, he reflected: 'Here then, was Tibet, the forbidden, the mysterious. In the distance all the land was that yellow and brick dust colour I had often seen in pictures and thought exaggerated and unreal.'[180]

Travellers to these regions now no longer referred to early Romantic landscape painters, but to Turner and the Impressionists. After yet another lengthy description of a sunset, equal in quality to the famous word-paintings of Ruskin, Landon wrote: 'J.W.M. Turner, probably as a result of his travels, was the first painter to recognize this atmospheric truth.'[181] On the same expedition, Millington enthused: 'a short sojourn in Tibet, a country freed from the obscurities of a thick atmosphere, and full of great dense mountains and lakes, and of startling crude contrasts of bright colours, quite revolutionizes ... one's ideas of landscape art.' For him, the quiet tones of Impressionism could not do justice to the bold blocks of colour in Tibet: these, he asserted, needed a cruder, more childlike and naive rendition.[182] But Impressionism did capture the momentary nature of landscape and light, and it was this dynamic and transient quality that so impressed *fin-de-siècle* travellers in the Himalayas and Tibet.[183]

This sudden celebration of Tibetan light and colour was both the culmination of a century of travel in the wilderness regions of the planet and, as we have seen, the outcome of a long revolution in landscape aesthetics. The Himalayas and Tibet were crucial to this late flowering of landscape Romanticism. Suddenly the preparatory work of Ruskin and Turner found fertile ground in the imagination of these Central Asian travellers. In addition, the era was ripe for such a revolution. The celebration of uncanny luminosity and unearthly colours reinforced Tibetan Otherness, its place above the demands and stresses of the modern world, outside space and time.

But some travellers were reticent. Waddell, for example, while extoling the 'swift kaleidoscopic play of colours', also felt disturbed. As these bright lights faded, there arose 'a cold steely grey that seemed to carry them far away, spectral-like into another world'.[184] Always threatening the brightness of Tibetan light, its blue skies and bold colours, was Tibetan gloom. Landon moaned: 'Everything under foot or in the distance was grey and colourless.'[185] Whilst contemplating a particularly beautiful scene, Grenard mused about the 'harmony of delicate splendour which defies description and which was rendered yet more perfect by the supreme calm that reigned overall, for the least movement, would have appeared like a discord in this picture'.[186] It was as if the luminous beauty of Tibet was so dreamlike that travellers were afraid a sudden movement, or slight noise, would shatter the illusion. At the turn of the century, the harmonious and appealing otherworldliness of Tibet was still elusive, fragile and delicate. The longings were tentative and mostly subliminal.

10. *The Eternal Sanctuary*

Chandler described Tibet as one of 'the most secret places of the earth'. Landon wrote of its 'mystic and fascinating seclusion', and the 'sacrosanct character of the country'. [187] Lhasa, of course, was the 'Eternal Sanctuary', the 'Sacred City'.[188] But there were other secret places in Tibet. The fertile land along the Tsangpo river came as a surprise to Chandler: 'We looked down on the great river that has been guarded from European eyes for nearly a century. In the heart of Tibet we had found Arcadia ...'.[189] Elsewhere, Landon came upon 'an enchanted valley with a lake, the Yam-dok-tso', whose 'claim to sacred isolation has been respected far more than that of Lhasa itself'. He reflected:

> Nowhere in Tibet has our incursion meant less to the people than here, up at the Yam-dok-tso, and one feels that in years to come the passing and repassing beside the holy waters of the unending line of our quick-stepping, even-loaded mules and tramping, dust-laden men with light-catching rifle barrels will only take its proper place among the myriad other and equally mysterious legends that wrap with sanctity the water of this loveliest of all lakes.[190]

The image of Tibet as an eternal sanctuary outside – or even indifferent to – space and time coincided with Western fascination about the Buddhist Nirvana.[191] Grenard, for example, whilst contemplating 'Samtan Gamcha' Mountain in northern Tibet, was moved to observe:

> This mountain, which, secluded in the mist of this almost dead re-gion, seemed not to deign to see this low world from the height of its cold and impassive serenity and to be trying with its sharp top, to penetrate and to absorb itself in the heavenly void, was indeed the visible emblem of the Buddhist soul, which strives to isolate itself and to collect itself in the contemplation of eternal things ... , which aims ... at becoming one, in the infinity of silence and of space, with Nirvana, the only absolute and perfect life, which does not feel, nor suffer, nor change, nor end.[192]

Louis experienced similar reveries whilst resting on a pass leading into Tibet. He wrote of 'the solemnity of the absolute stillness around! ... a sub-lime nothingness of sound, an all-absorbing silence which seems to trans-port one into regions of peace unknown, not of this world ... '. At that moment, Louis exclaimed, 'I could realize, if not explain, what had given rise in the mind of the contemplative Buddhist, to the idea of the Nirvana, as happy state of absorbing and exclusive contemplation and medita-tion.'[193]

While the fantasy of Tibet as a place of mystic, Nirvana-like seclusion and Otherness beckoned seductively, many travellers struggled against its allure. Even Younghusband, who was so sympathetic to mystical experience and religion, was critical. He felt that the Tibetans had mis-taken the real Buddhist ideal by 'withdrawing from the world into the desert and into the mountain to secure present peace for the individual, instead of ... manfully taking their part in the work of the world, aiming at the eventual unison of the whole'.[194] Others argued that the Tibetan Buddhist image of endless reincarnation was itself a source of oppression – devaluing, as it did, the present, holding it ransom to eternity.[195] The vastness of the Buddhist eternity, like the new sense of time in Western cosmology, seemed to annihilate the meaning of history.

One hundred and twenty-eight years before the expedition to Lhasa, Bogle had begun the modern British involvement with Tibet. At one point on his journey he had paused to reflect on the hermitages perched high on the mountainsides. He looked on the contemplative life with some favour. In 1904 Millington was of the opposite opinion. For him the tiny monasteries standing on hilltops were generally 'stagnant', the monks 'sordid', 'their minds vacant and what remains of their religion stale or even polluted'. He argued that in the larger monasteries, the 'religion is clear and more vital and life less stagnant'.[196] The Victorian travellers definitely preferred social action and involvement to solitary contemplation.

At the turn of the century many Western travellers indeed found healing and wisdom in Tibet. However, these came from the solitude and silence experienced whilst traversing its boundless, luminous spaces far from the confusions and turmoil of modern life. Victorian travellers, no matter how sympathetic to Buddhism they may have been (and many were), found the Tibetan *way* of gaining wisdom, in the world-denying immobility of a cramped, dark and airless cell, repugnant. For the majority of them the theory and practice of Tibetan Buddhism held little attraction.

The Underworld of Tibetan Travel

As we have seen, Tibet offered complexity and paradox, as well as coherence and fascination. Moments of absolute wretchedness seemed to compete with moments of sublime beauty. Travellers felt compelled to invent paradoxical phrases: 'majestic glooom', 'barren but fascinating', 'desolate but grand', 'sublime monotony'.[197] If the land was full of extremes, then so was the culture. Westerners just could not seem to decide how to evaluate Tibetans, whether they were peasants, nomads, aristocrats or lamas. Even the Dalai Lama was frustratingly paradoxical. After one attack by the Tibetans against the British camps at Kangma, Chandler commented:

We have learnt that the Tibetan has courage,. but in other respects he is still an unknown quantity. In motive and action he is as mysterious and unaccountable as his paradoxical associations would lead us to imagine. In dealing with the Tibetans one must expect the unex-

pected. They will try to achieve the impossible, and shut their eyes
to the obvious. They have a genius for doing the wrong thing at the
wrong time.[198]

Tibetans were described as cowards but also as courageous, as gentle
and peaceful yet violent and aggressive, as humorous and gay but also
sullen. Bower, for example, was of the opinion that

> the inhabitants laugh a great deal ... A noisier, cheerier lot I have
> never seen, and one is always inclined to be prepossessed in favour
> of a light-hearted people. But in the case of the Tibetans a very little
> knowledge serves to dispel all prepossessions – lying, avaricious
> and cowardly; kindness or civility is thrown away on them, and
> nothing but bullying, or a pretence of bullying, answers.[199]

Many travellers would have agreed with this estimation. Henry Savage
Landor was disgusted at the Tibetan men's cowardice. They were, he
wrote, ' a miserable lot, though powerfully built, and with plenty of
bounce about them'.[200] The answer for Landor, when dealing with any
trouble, 'was a good pounding with the butt of my Mannlicher [rifle]'.[201]
Yet even Landor acknowledged that 'we had great fun with them, for the
Tibetans are full of humour, and have many comical ways'.[202] Contempt
and affection for the Tibetans seemed to coexist. Bower and Landor were,
of course, the most aggressive of travellers, but even the more sensitive
ones reached similar conclusions.[203] Rockhill reported that many groups
living around the border feared aggression by Tibetans. He was especially
sympathetic towards the Mongolians, who, he wrote, 'are bullied by their
Tibetan neighbours'. On the other hand, he praised the 'extraordinary
kindness' he received from ordinary Tibetans.[204]

The more astute travellers tried to resolve these paradoxes in the Tibetan
character by blaming social circumstances. This was a feature of the late
nineteenth century, with its upsurge in sociological and anthropological
understanding. Earlier travellers would simply have explained them in
terms of climatic or geographical theories, if not racial and biological ones.
This new social understanding turned its critical attention towards the
power and hegemony of the lamas. But instead of providing a simple explanation or an easy resolution of the paradoxes, this shift in focus merely
uncovered a different order of contradictions:

> In general, it may be said that the Tibetan possesses gentleness not
> devoid of hypocrisy; he is weak, timid, obsequious and distrustful, like
> all weak people. This is a consequence of the clerical government that
> is laid upon him, a tyrannical, sectarian, suspicious government,
> trembling lest it should see its authority escape it, mindful to keep

everyone in a state of servile dependence and making a system of mutual spying and informing the basis of the social edifice. *Fear hovers over the whole of Tibet.*[205]

Such a negative evaluation of the lamas' power was consistent among travellers at this time, no matter what their nationality. Even the respected Japanese Buddhist monk Kawaguchi was of a similar opinion after three years in Tibet.[206] While individual lamas evoked a mixed response – ranging from lazy, indolent, ignorant, immoral and parasitic to self-reliant, sagacious and dedicated – the *system* was, almost without exception, viewed negatively.[207] Lamas, in their role as ecclesiastic or political administrators, were disliked. Their position seemed dictatorial, almost totalitarian, in its fusion of blatant power with absolute ideological and spiritual control. The situation was described as 'despotic', as 'spiritual terrorism' and 'unlimited tyranny'.[208] Landon was severe in his criticism.

no priestly caste in the history of religion has ever fostered and preyed upon the terror and ignorance of its flock with the systematic brigandage of the lamas. It may be that, hidden away in some quiet lamasary ... Kim's lama may still be found. Once or twice in the quiet unworldly abbots ... one saw an attractive and almost impressive type of man; but the heads of the hierarchy are very different men, and by them the country is ruled with a rod of iron.[209]

Tibet seemed a country of slavery, severe punishments, torture, political assassinations, mutual distrust. Grenard reported: 'The lower orders, in general, display towards the magistrates and the agents of authority a crawling servility which I have never seen equalled in either Turkestan or China.'[210] Lamaism was believed to be both the agent for this terror and its cause. That scrupulous ethnographer Rockhill, for example, vividly described the action of some police-monks at a market gathering:

Suddenly the crowds scattered to the right and left, the lamas running for places of hiding, with cries of *Gekor lama, Gekor lama!* and we saw striding towards us six or eight lamas with a black stripe painted across their foreheads and another around their right arms – black lamas ... the people call them – armed with heavy whips with which they belaboured any one who came within reach. Behind them walked a stately lama in robes of finest cloth, with head clean-shaved.

He had come to enforce ecclesiastical law by knocking down a Punch and Judy show and other prohibited amusements, the owners of which were whipped.[211]

With some understatement, Grenard mused: 'the Lhasa government is not a tender one'.[212] Indeed, the focal point of this totalitarianism seemed to be Lhasa, and even the Potala itself. Whilst on the one hand Lhasa was the sacred city, the Rome of Asia, it was also seen as the dictatorial centre of a police state. William Carey, as usual, painted a vivid picture: 'The holy city is more than the home of metaphysical mysteries and the mummery of idol-worship; it is a secret chamber of crime; its rocks and its roads, its silken flags and its scented altars, are all stained with blood.'[213]

But Tibet, and especially Lhasa, was so important to the Western spiritual imagination that some explanation, some understanding, had to be reached. How could filth and tyranny coexist with beauty and compassion: how could deep mystic insight have arisen from such savagery? Some travellers blamed the paradoxical influence of the land. William Carey wrote: 'chief of all is the weird majesty of the land ... In any other environment the lama would be merely a dirty and revolting pretender.'[214]

Others were more sophisticated in their understanding of social control. First, it was clear that the two great industries of Tibet – weaving and religious arts – were monopolized by the two great official powers, the government and the monasteries. Also, the system of land ownership made most Tibetans, who were neither nomad nor brigands, into serfs.[215] But in addition to this crushing economic control, the system exerted political and ideological power. 'The clergy of Tibet', wrote Grenard, 'owes its social and political mastery to several causes and, first of all, to its powerfully organized hierarchy and to the inflexible discipline to which all its members are subjected.'[216] Despite having no standing army and a weak police force, this hierarchy, continued Grenard, 'is able to make its orders obeyed even in the most remote districts. This is due to the terror inspired by the severity with which it punishes the least offences against its authority.' Indeed, any crime against the church or against an individual lama was especially severely punished: 'A theft committed on a lama entails a ten times greater penalty than one committed on a layman; to murder a layman is three or four times as cheap as to murder a monk.'[217] But even more than judicial punishments, respect for lamaism was instilled into the Tibetan by

> a state of mind in which are mingled the fear of blows, superstitious terrors and the sense of his own wretchedness and of his weakness in the face of the evils that beset him. The king and his agents ... are considered to partake of the divine nature; consequently, the people have the same opinion of them as of the gods ...[218]

Landon was even more thorough in his analysis and criticized what he called 'a cynical misuse of the theory of reincarnation, the employment of it as a political lever'.[219] Kawaguchi agreed:

> Whatever may have been the practical effect of incarnation in former times, it is, as matters stand at present, an incarnation of all vices and corruptions, instead of the souls of departed Lamas ... the present mode of incarnation was a glaring humbug, and ... was nothing less than an embodiment of bribery ... At best it is a fraud committed by oracle-priests at the instance of aristocrats who are very often their patrons and protectors.[220]

Neither Landon nor Kawaguchi was attacking the spiritual idea of reincarnation, only its political *misuse* in Tibet. For Landon, its was 'a blind horror of the consequences of ... reincarnation upon which the whole fabric of Lamaism is built'.[221]

The impact of the shadow side of Tibetan religious and cultural life was lessened by some travellers, who reasoned that its excesses and paradoxes were no worse that those of Western feudalism. Grenard thought that most lamas were like good country priests, with all their attributes and failings;[222] Rockhill compared the warrior quality of some Tibetan monks with the Knights Templars of medieval Europe.[223] It was argued that blind obedience and cruelty were an inevitable part of feudalism. Grenard thought that the attitude of laypeople towards the monks resembled that of Italian peasants in the Middle Ages – sneering and complaining behind their backs, subservient to their faces. Landon felt that the Lhasa government was probably no worse than the court of Louis XIV of France.[224]

Of course, there were still a few travellers who adopted an extreme position. For some, no good whatsoever could be said about Tibet or the Tibetan religious system. Prejevalsky, for example, considered Lamaism to be 'the curse of Tibet'.[225] At the other extreme were those for whom Tibet was an exemplary society – Hensoldt considered it cultured, peaceful, honest and well governed. Even that tough, seasoned traveller Sven Hedin wrote of 'Tibet; the country whence the light of holiness streams forth upon the world of Lamaism, just as its waters, in the form of mighty rivers, stream forth to give life and nourishment to the countries which surround it'.[226]

The Dalai Lama, surprisingly, escaped the kind of censure one would have expected to be directed at the absolute ruler of this system. The judgements against him were mild. He was occasionally called an autocrat, or headstrong, but was more usually excused as being naive or misled.[227] For example, on one occasion a music-box of Grenard's ended up as a present for the Dalai Lama. 'It was', he noted, 'a pleasure to us to think that this infidelity might for a moment distract the boredom of this young god exiled upon the earth.' Grenard imagined the Dalai Lama as imprisoned both within the Potala and within the role as a god-king, as being deprived of the joys of childhood and adolescence. William Carey described him as being but 'a toy'.[228]

These seemingly unresolvable paradoxes sometimes forced Western travellers to deepen their reflections upon their own society,[229] but this was rare, and most would have agreed with Bonvalot when he exclaimed that there was 'no reading the hearts of these orientals'.[230] The West had, of course, invented 'these orientals', along with 'the orient', so the inscrutable paradoxes were composed largely of their own projections.[231] They tell us more about the Western unconscious than about the oriental heart. One can clearly hear, for instance the mixture of fear and fascination projected on to the Tibetan lama, the magician-priest, by William Carey:

> Standing in that wild theatre, with his trumpet of human thigh-bone at his lips, and a skull in his hands, he is the very embodiment of the spirit that haunts the mountains, and broods over the wide, inhospitable deserts, and makes sport of man. It is the spirit of awe and mystery that smites the heart with panic and congeals the blood.

'And this', he concluded, 'is the enchantment with which the land is enchanted.'[232] Carey was not alone in his use of the theatre metaphor when writing about Tibet. Indeed, Tibet *was* a theatre: the landscape and the people were the backdrop, but the script was written by Westerners as they enacted their own hopes and fears. For example, the British encountered in Tibet an almost Kafkaesque parody of their own formidable imperial bureaucracy. The Tibetan government, with all its negative characteristics, seemed indescribably slow to operate, with an unwillingness to make big decisions at regional level and an obscurity so profound that ignorance and timidity seemed the essential qualifications for office. It incorporated an underworld of vicious punishments for those who disobeyed rigid orders or inadvertently showed individual initiative. Corruption seemed rampant, and there was total ignorance of international diplomacy. Younghusband could not decide if the bureaucrats were evil or just stupid. In the British imagination, the Indian administration was one of the wonders of the world.[233] It had its faults, but by comparison with the sinister machinations of Tibet it was exemplary. Yet it was as if the British were faced with the shadow of their own bureaucratic imagination, a chilling presentiment of the totalitarian states so characteristic of the dawning twentieth century.

In addition to the zebrules and the flesh-eating horses, two other images from the period seem to encapsulate the paradox of Tibet: the imposing Potala, with golden roofs at its summit, the dirty and uninteresting city of Lhasa at its feet, the dungeons below its foundations and in between a labyrinth of dark passageways, countless rooms full of intrigue, of monks like ants swarming from their nests;[234] or else the scene at Phari, the first town the British 1904 expedition encountered in 'mysterious' Tibet. 'Everything in the place is coated and grimed with filth', wrote a sickened Landon. 'In the middle of the street, between the two banks of filth and offal, runs a stinking channel … In it horns and bones and skulls of every beast eaten or not eaten by the Tibetans … The stench is fearful.' He described 'half-decayed corpses of dogs', 'sore-eyed and mouth-ulcerated children', rubbish rising 'to the first-floor windows and a hole in the mess has to be kept open for access to the door'. Landon admitted that Phari was probably the highest as well as the filthiest town of any size on the planet, but he concluded his observations with a marvellous image:

> The disgust of all this is heightened by an ever-present contrast for, at the end of every street, hanging in mid-air above this nest of mephitic filth, the cold and almost saint-like purity of the everlasting snows of Chumolhari – a huge wedge of argent a mile high … [235]

Loss and Nostalgia

Travellers and explorers at the turn of the century were poignantly aware that the globe was shrinking, that a closure of the earth's previously imagined boundless space was imminent. As Hedin put it, the blank spaces were disappearing.[236] 'The exploration of entirely uncharted territory … came to an end', writes Kern.[237] Lhasa, along with the North and South Poles, was one of the last remaining geographical unknowns. After them there were only the highest mountain summits, the ocean depths, and outer space. Landon's salute to Younghusband for his leadership of the 1904 expedition to Lhasa was almost a funeral oration for exploration.[238] He called the expedition 'this rear-guard of exploration'. For many it was the end and the culmination of a long tradition.

Tibetan travel at this time was always accompanied by a lamentation, by a sense of loss and often by a feeling of nostalgia. Explorers were caught in a double bind, for they themselves were in the vanguard of eliminating the last blank spaces on the maps of the globe. Grenard lamented that 'Tibet … is on the verge of losing a notable part of its originality.'[239] For many of those who finally reached Lhasa in 1904, the triumph was tinged with regret. 'Filth and familiarity very soon destroyed the romance of Lhasa', wrote Chandler. Earlier, as he stood on the threshold of the city, Chandler had sensed misgivings: 'Tomorrow when we enter Lhasa, we will have unveiled the last mystery of the East. There are no more forbidden cities which men have not mapped and photographed.'[240]

Travel accounts invariably situated Tibet *globally*: the last place on *earth*, the highest country in the *world*, and so on. Globalism and internationalism were in their heyday as the century drew to its close, bringing hopes of human unity but also fears of cultural homogenization, loss of uniqueness, and the end to geographical mystery. Global communications threatened the anonymity of the individual, his or her solitude and freedom. In the wake of globalism came a feeling of disenchantment with the world. Globalism and imperialism not only annexed its present landscapes, they also mapped out the future.[241]

The regret for a lost era was prevalent. For Chandler, the final closure of geographical mystery meant the end of fairy stories: 'For now that there are no real mysteries, no unknown land of dreams, where there may still be genii and mahatmas and bottle-imps, that kind of literature will be tolerated no longer … '.[242] To enter Lhasa with a map and a camera, bringing the clear light of reason, seemed to sever the last links with childhood, both culturally and individually: it was the inevitable victory of modernism. Freshfield felt similarly whilst in the Himalayas, gazing towards the distant mountains of Tibet. 'Some of them', he mused, 'perhaps were within the horizon of Lhasa itself: the imagination leapt, using them as stepping-stones, to the golden terraces of Potala, the palace of the Dalai Lama.'[243] Clearly, for him, Tibet was still remote, its romance untainted, but he was not free from ennui. Soon after his Tibetan reverie he came upon a 'fantastic' place, 'an enchanted grotto', a 'fairy dell'. 'Once again', he exclaimed, 'I was carried back to the pantomimes of my childhood.' But then he stopped, sorrowfully, in the midst of this enthusiasm: 'There are no such pantomimes now!'[244] No wonder the age produced such writers as Freud and Proust, both of whom tried to rescue childhood from the disenchantment of modernism and rationality. Both men stressed that some connection with the timeless enchantment of childhood, albeit only in memory, was revitalizing, healing, essential.[245]

Again we can turn to Chandler contemplating the Forbidden City: 'If one approached within a league of Lhasa, saw the glittering domes of the Potala, and turned back without entering the precincts, one might still imagine it an enchanted city, shining with turquoise and gold. But having entered the illusion is lost.'[246] The members of the expedition became blasé about the city. As Major Ottley wrote, 'Life at Lhasa … became dull.'[247] Even Younghusband, so full of enthusiasm and so open to mystic reverie, was touched by moments of sadness. Where, he asked, was the 'inner power for which Tibetan Buddhism was famous, especially here, in Lhasa, its holiest places?'[248]

For some, the disenchantment with Tibet had begun even before reaching Lhasa. Chandler wrote that amidst the filth of Phari, he 'forgot the mystery of Tibet'.[249] Again, after the massacre of Tibetan soldiers at Guru, he had a similar feeling: 'For the moment I was tired of Tibet'.[250] Even the longed-for journey across the Tibetan wilderness was tainted by the necessity of travelling with an army. It was not how it should have been, how it was expected to be: 'Often in India I had dreamed of the great inland waters of Tibet ... and here at last I was camping by the Yamdok Tso itself – with an army.'[251] The intensity of loss matched that of the expectations.

The 1904 expedition seemed to threaten the innocence of Tibet in so many small ways – not wilfully but almost inevitably. Chandler, for example, recounted how Tibetans had traditionally smoked a mixture of dried wild rhubarb leaves and tobacco. 'Now hundreds of thousands of cheap American cigarettes are being introduced and a lucrative tobacco-trade has sprung up.' Everyone smoked them, from 'Sahibs' to 'coolies'. Even 'Tibetan children of three appreciate them hugely, and the road from Phari to Rungpo is literally strewn with the empty boxes.' Later he reported the first wheeled transport into Tibet.[252] One can feel the lost innocence in these accounts – not only for the Tibetans, but for the Westerners too. When the Tibetan's magic charms, prayers and spells did not stop the British bullets, one can almost sense Chandler's disappointment. After the battle at Guru, the Tibetan soldiers just walked slowly away; they did not run, even though they were still being shot at. Chandler wrote:

> the most extraordinary procession I have ever seen. My friends have tried to explain the phenomenon as due to obstinacy or ignorance, or Spartan contempt for life. But I think I have the solution. They were bewildered ... Prayers and charms and mantras, and the holiest of their holy men had failed them ... They walked with bowed heads, as if they had been disillusioned with their gods.[253]

Perhaps something very special in Chandler's imagination had also been disillusioned.

Chandler, like many Westerners at the time, hovered between two worlds. 'There will always be people', he wrote, 'who will hanker after the medieval and romantic, who will say, " ... why could we not have been content that there was one mystery not unveiled, one country of an ancient arrested civilization ... "'. But he failed to convince himself and quickly cried out, 'why could we not have left at least one city out of bounds?'[254]

The increasing sense of global unity was accompanied by a realization of global fragility, destruction, loss. Species were dying out, cultures vanishing, environments becoming polluted. The deforestation of the Himalayas was already causing concern and sadness even at this early date.[255] The loss of the Himalayan forests was associated with the demise of their inhabitants – particularly the Lepchas, who were constantly described as the 'Lotus-eaters', the original inhabitants of 'Arcadia', of 'enchanted woods'.[256] They were the spirits of these forests. Waddell wrote: 'the language of the real aborigines, the Lepchas, is fast becoming extinct'.

173

Freshfield told of the probable end of the Lepchas, 'superseded by the more sturdy Tibetan and the more energetic Nepalese'.[257] Elsewhere in these vast mountain regions, Younghusband wrote of the Baltis: 'a patient, docile, good-natured race, whom one hardly respects, but whom one cannot help liking in a compassionate, pitying way. The poor Balti belongs to one of those races which has gone under in the struggle of nations'.[258] The quiet threat of extinction hanging over these retiring mountain peoples symbolized the passing of another way of life, a kind of childhood's end.

But perhaps the deepest sense of loss, as well as source of irritation, was caused by mass tourism and its effects on the wild places of the world. Tibetan travellers and explorers were obviously aristocratic in their beliefs, and desperately wanted to preserve some part of the globe for their own kind. Bonvalot could not resist making snide remarks from time to time: 'I spend a few moments in admiring the scene, and am straightaway lost in ecstasy before a scene which Messrs. Cook can promise to their clients when, in years to come, they have organized trips to Tibet.'[259] Time was felt to be running out for 'Mysterious Tibet'. Waddell, too, made negative asides about the tourists in Darjeeling, especially the new breed of 'globe-trotters'.[260] Grenard amusingly drew attention to 'a very inconvenient dwelling, but one particularly well situated and arranged to attract the attention of future Baedekers'.[261] For the previous generation of mid-century travellers, Tibet had been a secure and permanent – is somewhat elusive – place, but by the end of the century it was touched by impermanence. Although still a self-contained, mysterious 'Lost World', Tibet was also the representative of a *whole world* that was about to be lost. As Western imperialism remorselessly built Tibet into its geographical frontier, it was also irrevocably being built into another kind of frontier: between what was imagined to have been and what was imagined to lie ahead; between the world of fantasy and romance and that of science and so-called reality.[262] The rhythms of mystic ritual were being replaced by those of industrial routine. As yet this sense of poignant nostalgia was only a dark blush on the contours of Tibet, but already the West was laying the ground for a *new Tibet*, one that would remain pure and untainted by its sudden, rude emergence into the cold light of the twentieth century.

So powerful was the need for a sacred place among many Westerners that even the squalor, cruelty, superstition and everydayness of Lhasa could not totally destroy the romance of Tibet. Something in the Western psyche desperately wanted to believe in Tibet. Fortunately, two essential characters on the Tibetan stage escaped both the shadow that was being cast over the Tibetan landscape and also the direct scrutiny of the rational Western mind that spelt death to any lingering Romanticism. Firstly the Potala was excused its association with Lhasa. Chandler put it quite simply: 'The Potala is superbly detached'. He insisted that 'romance still clings to the Potala. It is still remote'.[263] Although Younghusband had his way and the treaty with Tibet was signed in the Potala's throne room, this was but a hurried, temporary intrusion which only served to increase its fascination. Even more important, however, than the aloofness of the Potala was the absence of the Dalai Lama. In the last chapter we saw how all the paradox and fascination of Tibet became condensed into his young form. By vanishing just before the arrival of the British Army he took with him the still-virgin soul of Tibet. His sanctity was still intact, both for believers and for Westerners: 'The man continues a bogie, a riddle, undivinable, impersonal, remote.' But Chandler was relieved:

> imagine him dragged into durbar as a signatory, gazed at by profane eyes, the subject of a few days' gossip and comment, then sunk into commonplace, stripped of his mystery like the city of Lhasa ... To escape this ordeal he has fled, and to us, at least, his flight has deepened the mystery that envelops him, and added to his dignity and remoteness; to thousands of mystical dreamers it has preserved the effulgence of his godhead unsoiled by contact with the profane world.[264]

The Potala and the Dalai Lama were therefore free to join the new Tibet of the twentieth century, untainted by the *fin-de-siècle* malaise.

In addition to the Dalai Lama and the Potala, two other characters were waiting in the wings. One had been around for a long time but still inspired the fascination of Westerners, whilst at the same time eluding their grasp. This was, of course, the summit of Everest, the highest mountain on the globe. The other was a more recent figure, scarcely formed but full of promise and vitality: the yeti. As we shall see, these two would become central as the twentieth-century Tibet took shape.

There were also two events – one local, the other far away from the Himalayas – that would protect Tibet from further profanation – indeed, almost erase the memory of 1904 and simultaneously heighten the need for a sacred land. After their anguished success in reaching Lhasa, the British promptly withdrew and Tibet became even more firmly closed than before. Western travellers were denied permission *by the British* to enter Tibet, and it disappeared once again under increased Chinese control. Ironically, even when the Dalai Lama fled to India in 1910 and appealed to the British for assistance against the Chinese, who were repressing the Tibetan independence movement, and begged for an agent to be installed at Lhasa, he was turned down. The irony was not lost on Younghusband. 'Was there ever a more tragic reversal of an old position?' he asked with disgust. 'When the Tibetans did not want us we fought our way to Lhasa to insist upon them having us; when they did want us, and had come all the way from Lhasa to get us, we turned them the most frigid of shoulders.'[265]

The other event that protected Tibet from prying Western eyes was the outbreak of the First World War, barely ten years after Younghusband's column had entered Lhasa. The Europe and America at the end of this war, in 1918, were very different from those at the turn of the century. A new Tibet was needed, no longer at the centre of global rivalry yet still central to a deep longing among many in the West.

The Eternal Feminine

Soon after Younghusband and the Anglo-Indian troops had entered Lhasa, Lord Curzon wrote apologetically to the explorer Sven Hedin: 'I am almost ashamed of having destroyed the virginity of the bride to whom you aspired, viz. Lhasa.' For Hedin it was sufficient reason to make him lose 'the longing that had possessed [him] to penetrate the Holy City ...' .[266] Millington described going to Lhasa as, 'assisting in drawing aside a purdah'.[267] Elsewhere it was said that the 'veil of Lhasa' had been 'torn down'. Chandler similarly referred to 'The Unveiling of Lhasa'.[268] Indeed, time and again, Tibet and Lhasa were described as being hidden behind a veil.[269] Waddell, in his classic 1895 study of Tibetan Buddhism, claimed responsibility for 'lifting higher than before the veil which still hides its mysteries from European eyes .... '.[270]

In the late nineteenth century, the Orient was popularly imagined as feminine. An article on 'The Capture of Lhasa' in *The Spectator*, reminded its readers that Asia was '"the women's apartment" of the world ... '.[271] For many travellers, as we have seen, Lhasa was the 'most secret place'. For much of this era of Tibetan exploration, Western culture was highly patriarchal. Travel and exploration, despite the significant exploits of a number of women, was a man's world; it emphasized all the characteristics considered desirable in a man. Some, like Prejevalsky, were actively misogynist. He refused to take any man on his expeditions who had either been married, or was even merely involved with a woman.[272] The Royal Geographical Society was one of the last of the great Victorian institutions to grant equal status to women.[273]

However, even these Victorian women travellers partook of similar patriarchal attitudes. Whilst not denying their achievements – travelling as loners and challenging many assumptions about the role of women, about women's clothing, self-assurance and mobility – these women rarely challenged imperialist attitudes, or the cultural superiority of 'manliness'. Jane Duncan, for example, was quick to defend the ability of women as hunters, to insist that they were the equal of men.[274] The accounts by women travellers in this period were statements asserting their right and their ability to participate in a man's world.

Said has suggested a 'narrow correspondence between suppressed

Victorian sexuality at home, its fantasies abroad and the tightening hold on the nineteenth century male imagination of imperialist ideology'.[275] But to treat the feminization of the Orient simply as a compensating projection of repressed Victorian sexuality is far too static: it loses the imaginative quality of both sexuality and the feminine. As Foucault has argued, the myth of repressed Victorian sexuality has long obscured the workings of power and knowledge.[276] No less than the 'Orient' was the category of 'sexuality' created and produced, particularly in the late Victorian era.

Both the 'Orient' and 'sexuality' were signifiers of deep imaginative processes, of a concern for *meaning*. In both cases, Western attention was drawn to these unconscious processes by the desire for 'the feminine'. This desire cannot just be reduced to the 'male imagination', nor to 're-pressed sexuality'. The image of the eternal feminine has long been at the forefront of fantasies about the unknown and the fascinating.[277] Such an image was, for example, vital for both Freud's and Jung's so-called discovery of the unconscious at the turn of the century.[278] It was no less significant in the 'discovery' of the geographical unconscious. But of course, in both cases – the psychoanalytical and the geopsychological – the images of the unconscious were couched in the prevailing patriarchal rhetoric. Nevertheless, to remain at this somewhat static level of criticism blocks our understanding of the subtle shifts that were occuring at that time in the Western imagination. We need to return to the images, and stick closely to them.

The attitude of these travellers was almost voyeuristic; veils, purdahs, and so on. The most commonly expressed aim, for example, was just to get a 'peep' at Tibet, or at Lhasa. So, on a hunting trip near the border, Stone confided: 'I determined to ... have a peep at least into Tibet.' Colonel Tanner of the Indian Staff Corps similarly described a safe point in the mountains where 'the traveller will be rewarded by a peep at Tibet'. Grenard, like many other Tibetan explorers at the time, was frustrated by being denied access to Lhasa. But 'our annoyances would be quite wiped out', he mused, 'by our satisfaction in having opened ... a peep-hole of which our successors would make a window'.[279] Travellers strained with longing to catch a glimpse of Tibet on the distant horizon: they were thrilled merely to touch Tibetan soil, or even just to see a Tibetan.[280]

Hensoldt wrote of 'the secrets of a region which has so long provoked and tormented Western curiosity'.[281] This curiosity was primarily *visual* – a fascination with *appearances*, with the *display* of the landscape, of the art, the architecture, the costumes, the colours and the light.[282] This is a crucial point, for Eros has many forms. In Tibet, colonization, conquest, domination, taming, destruction, rape, violation and arrogant civilizing were virtually absent and only hovered around the edges of Western fantasies. While words of bravado could occasionally be heard – such as Prejevalsky's famous boast: 'It needs only twenty or thirty sharpshooters and I'll guarantee I'll get to Lhasa' – the mystery of Lhasa was always respected.[283] Even the so-called 'rape' of Lhasa occurred only after years of frustrated wooing and in the face of perceived regional threats from the Russian Empire. It was deeply regretted by most of the British expedition's leaders and caused outrage around the world – not merely for political reasons.

Such respect was not only the result of imperial caution about global stategies and alliances, of upsetting the so-called balance of power; it was also due to the imaginative potency of Lhasa itself and the very special place it occupied in Western fantasies. Landon, for example, described the tense anticipation as members of the expedition strained to catch the first glimpse of Lhasa and the Potala. 'Here there was to be seen a gleam of gold in the far distance, and we thought that Lhasa was at last in sight.' But the glimmer was from a building two miles outside the 'Forbidden City'. Officers vied with each other to be the first to see this fabled place. As the expedition entered the plains on which Lhasa is built, the city was still hidden: ' ... even from that point of view not a stone nor a pinnacle of Lhasa is to be seen. We had to possess our souls in patience still.' These were not thugs bearing down upon a defenceless princess, but pilgrims demanding their right to pay homage. Lhasa and the Potala were not sacred only to the Tibetans and Mongolians, they were now *global* shrines.

At last Landon saw the Potala. This was not a tourist event but one that possessed all the numinosity and awe of the first moon landing. He was gazing at last on the face of the goddess. It was a moment to be savoured, and Landon's beautiful prose pays it due homage:

It was about half-past one in the afternoon and a light blue haze was settling down in between the ravines of the far-distant mountains that to the east ringed in the plain, and nearer to hand on either side threw their spurs forward like giant buttresses from north to south. There was a smell of fresh spring earth and the little rustle of a faint wind in the heads of barley; the sun was merciless in a whitened sky wherein from horizon to horizon there was never a flush of blue ... The hour teemed with a fierce interest of a kind no man will perhaps ever feel again ...

Then as we rode on, it came. In the far, far distance, across and beyond those flat fields of barley, marked here and there by the darker line of low-wooded plantations, a grey pyramid painfully disengaged itself from behind the outer point of the grey concealing spur – Lhasa. There at last, it was, the never-reached goal of so many weary wanderers, the home of all the occult mysticism that still remains on the earth. The light waves of mirage dissolving impalpably just shook the far outlines of the golden roofs ... I do not think anyone of us said much. Life seemed very full.

... We stood a moment on the road just where a sudden flight of dragon-flies pierced the air with lines of quick blue; then we rode.[284]

Even after his mixed experiences whilst living at Lhasa, Landon's respect and fascination remained undiminished. As he rode from the city, he constantly turned to gain his final view: 'When it came to the point, it was no easy thing to see the last of Lhasa ... I had been watching, with concentration and almost sadness, the slowly dwindling palace of the forbidden town. I would have given a good deal then to go back ... '.[285] He crossed over a culvert at which point 'the last vestige of the Potala is hidden from your view forever. The road goes on, but for many miles the warmth had gone out of the sun, the light was missing from the distant slopes ... I went on, something depressed at heart.'

The very vulnerability of Lhasa and Tibet added to their femininity for these Western travellers. When a country had no army to speak of and fought with antique weapons, what glory lay in aggression towards it? Its illogical, unworldly topsy-turviness fitted prevailing fantasies about the feminine, but the feminine was also a source of mystery and, although materially vulnerable, was psychologically and spiritually powerful. William Carey wrote of 'the spell', 'cast' by Lhasa over millions.[286] For Hensoldt it was a place that had 'provoked and tormented Western curiosity'. Aspects of the Dalai Lama encapsulated such fantasies. He was, wrote Hensoldt, who claimed to have reached Lhasa some time in the 1890s and to have spoken with the Dalai Lama, 'no ordinary mortal'. His face was 'of great symmetry and beauty'. Later, Hensoldt recounted how the Dalai Lama's 'beautiful features seemed as if transfigured with a celestial radiance'.[287] This beguiling, irresistibly attractive power is typical of what Jung called the 'anima'.

The anima is not simply the opposite of animus, the psychological compensation for a man's repressed femininity. As Hillman insists, the anima is an archetypal aspect of the psyche. She is a bridge between the world and the unconscious, the mediatrix of the unknown – indeed, of the *unknowable*. Hillman equates definitions of the anima with the

phenomenology of 'unknownness' ... – anima as innocent, empty, vague ... ; the smoke, mist, and opacity; her elusive, engimatic, obscurantist behaviour; her dubious, shady origins or her associations with remote history or alien culture; the images of her turning her back, or veiled, or hidden, or incarcerated in the darkness of primal matter.[288]

We can easily see how Western experiences of Tibet at the turn of the century, even their horror at the monks incarcerated within their rock-hewn caves, echoed such a phenomenology. The experience of anima is also subject to 'sudden unwilled moods and attractions ... '. Certainly these experiences are not always nice, or predictable. They are characterized by contrary emotions: fear and awe, fascination and danger.

It should not surprise us that such a close correspondence exists between Jung's formulation of the anima and the imaginative phenomenology of Tibet at this time: both sprang from the same source. Both Jung's psychological fantasies and, as we have seen, Tibetan travel fantasies, were late developments of European Romanticism, part of its tradition.[289] Both arose from a cultural situation of disenchantment and depersonalization, from an age which felt on the verge of losing its soul.[290] Jung's movement towards an introverted psychology based upon a close psychological reading of philosophical and religious texts and of a close attention to the individual, subjective world of dreams, visions and psychopathology was only one possible solution. Another moved in a more extroverted direction towards travel, landscapes, nature, wilderness and ecology, producing a kind of geo-, or eco-, mysticism.

It is significant, for example, that Jung drew extensively upon Goethe's philosophical and fictional works, but ignored his travel diaries and his scientific studies of nature. Even Jung, however could not fail to arrive at the importance of the *anima mundi*, the soul *in* the world.[291] The *anima mundi*, writes Hillman, is

> that seminal image, which offers itself through each thing in its visible form ... its sensuous presentation as a face bespeaking its interior image ... The world comes with shapes, colours, atmospheres, textures – a display of self-presenting forms. All things show faces ...[292]

Tibet offered the West such faces, and in them Westerners searched for ways to regain their soul. The humorous reference in 1894 to Tibet as 'the modern Brünnhilde asleep on her mountain top', and the viceroy of India as 'Siegfried', whose task was to 'awaken her from the slumber of ages', was therefore more astute than was perhaps realized.[293]

A Treasure House of Wisdom

But the longings evoked by Tibet were complex. As we saw in the previous chapter, gold was the original symbol for the imaginative wealth to be found there. The close of the nineteenth century saw no respite in the fascination with Tibetan gold. Right into the twentieth century it was still thought to be plentiful, and Russian interest in Tibet was, in part, attributed to this precious mineral. The Russo-Chinese Bank was exploiting

Mongolian gold at that time so, as Lamb points out, it was quite logical to assume their interest in Tibetan gold. There were also rumours in London that Rothschild was curious about gold in Tibet and had commissioned a secret surveying expedition, which as it turned out never materialized. The 1904 expedition was instructed to keep a lookout for any signs of gold mining.[294] In 1891 the ethnologist-explorer Dr Leitner reported that the Himalayan glaciers 'cover layers of gold ... [and] there are immense treasures there ... '.[295] William Carey wrote of Tibet's 'inexhaustible wealth of gold ... '. Much of this wealth was thought to be stored up in Lhasa, in the monasteries and in the Potala.[296]

As the previous chapter showed, Tibetan gold had been formed into a highly compact symbol by the condensation of diverse streams of fantasy into a single image, but by the end of the nineteenth century this image was relieved of its complex imaginative load. Lhasa, the Potala and the Dalai Lama were by then quite clearly evocative images in their own right and did not need their symbolic qualities to be displaced on to gold. Nevertheless Tibetan gold continued to represent the unknown fascination and desired wealth of Tibet until more appropriate symbols appeared. But as more and more Westerners crossed over the border and became directly familiar with Tibet, a broader variety of imagery was made available for the imagination. This symbolic enrichment and differentiation facilitated the subtle imaginative transformations that were occuring at that time.

As we have seen, the anima-quality of gold – its seductive, dangerous richness, its promise of power, its astonishing colour – were transferred and released on to the Tibetan landscape, the Potala palace and the Dalai Lama. But in addition, the senex-qualities of gold symbolism, its mixture of wealth, control, order, as well as wisdom and endurance, were beginning to separate out and take shape around Tibetan religiosity. As Jung points out, 'With further differentiations the figure of the (wise) old man becomes detached from the anima and appears as an archetype of the "spirit".'[297] Although this aspect would not become fully mobilized until much later, in the twentieth century, as part of a *new* Tibet, it was already making its appearance. Blavatsky's all-wise, eternal mahatmas were an obvious manifestation of this archetypal quality, but the fantasies of theosophy reached a far wider audience than its followers. Time and again travellers *looked* for the mahatmas, or commented upon their absence. Blavatsky's fantasies struck a chord in the Western psyche that continues to echo to this day.

Rockhill, for example, raised the issue with some Tibetan lamas: 'When told of our esoteric Buddhists, the Mahatmas, and of the wonderful doctrines they claimed to have obtained from Tibet, they were immensely amused.'[298] Landon, too, took Blavatsky's claims fairly seriously and investigated at some length the numerous types of Tibetan magicians and occult practitioners, but he concluded: 'The word Mahatma is not known in Tibet, and ... I do not think, on the whole, that any particular occult knowledge will come to us from Tibet.' Even so, the atmosphere of the Potala, in its oasis 'among ... the highest mountain ranges of the world', almost convinced him.[299] Others, too, took issue with Blavatsky's claims but for different reasons. Hensoldt, for example, while disputing that 'occult science' originated in Tibet, agreed that it reached its culmination there. It was, he wrote, 'the very fountain head of esoteric lore'. Like Blavatsky, Hensoldt argued that Buddhism, especially its Tibetan version, was rational and scientific; that it was totally compatible with Darwin's ideas on evolution.[300] It must surely have been no coincidence that both he and Blavatsky also used the metaphor of a veil, but for them it was the Tibetans, especially the Dalai Lama, who had lifted it. They were of course referring to that other veil, the mystical veil of Isis.[301]

This archetypal quality was also echoed in the many references to Lhasa as the 'Mecca' or 'Rome' of Central Asia, or in Landon's reference to the great fourteenth-century reformer Tsong-kapa as the 'Luther of Central Asia'.[302] It is also significant that at this very moment, a document telling of Jesus's wanderings in the Himalayas and Tibet should suddenly be found in western Tibet, at Hemis monastery in Ladakh.[303] Many Westerners at the end of the century would have sympathized with Hensoldt's claim that Tibet was a storehouse of ancient wisdom: even Landon wrote that it was the last home of occult mysticism.[304] This image was to be carried on and developed by yet another of those intrepid women explorers in Tibet who combined adventure, scholarship and mysticism. In 1912, whilst in India, Alexandra David-Neel became the first Western woman to be granted a private audience with the Dalai Lama. She combined a theosophical background with intensive studies in Orientalism and eventually became an ardent practising Buddhist. In 1914 she entered Tibet to study their esoteric religion and in 1916 set out for Lhasa. But her story, while rounding off one era, really belongs to the next, to post-war Tibet.[305] The anima-fascination with Tibet would then still continue unabated, but the demand for an exemplary image of wisdom, guidance and order would have become desperate after the shock and conflagration of World War I.

Stepping Stones to the Potala

A third imaginative quality of gold was also separating from the compact density of the original, undifferentiated image and beginning its own autonomous development. Gold has evoked distant longings, and has also provided the finance to satisfy them. The youthful puer gazes out over far, unknown horizons, anxious to begin the wandering search of always-elusive goals and aspiring to new frontiers.[306] Kipling's famous protagonist Kim prefigured this quality in its late-Victorian guise. Torn between duty and the excitement of the 'Great Game', Kim was always earnest, always an enthusiastic companion to the spiritual quest, but never allowed himself to be burdened by its heavy dogmas.[307] Like Blavatsky's mahatmas, both Kim and his delightful companion, the old Tibetan lama – earthy but spiritual: wise, but not in the ways of the world; kindly but firm – found a home in the British imagination. It was often with a profound sadness that travellers reported the absence of such qualities among the Tibetan monks they encountered. Landon, for example, thought that 'Kim's lama may exist ... But ... these men are rare ... '. Chandler was of a similar opinion.[308]

Younghusband, born among the Himalayas – always popular, always sensitive to the demands of both imperial duty and mysticism, at ease with British aristocracy, with the ordinary soldier and with the tribespeople of the hills; always restless, always longing – possessed many of Kim's qualities.[309] It was therefore singularly appropriate that he should lead the expedition to Lhasa, and understandable that he should keep one eye open for any signs of 'Kim's lama'. Never one to be discouraged, Younghusband was finally rewarded. The 'Ti Rimpoche', nominally in charge during the Dalai Lama's absence, visited him on the eve of his departure from Lhasa and gave him a small statue of the Buddha. 'He was full of kindness.' wrote Younghusband, 'and at that moment more nearly approached Kipling's lama in "Kim" than any other Tibetan I met.'[310] The whole experience in Tibet was a profound one for Younghusband, and when he died in 1942, an old man, he had a relief of Lhasa carved on his tombstone, beneath which were the words: 'Blessed are the pure in heart, for they shall see God'. Younghusband treasured the Buddha statue above all other things, and his daughter placed it upon the lid of his coffin.[311]

This puer quality had, of course, been manifest in Himalayan travel long before the end of the nineteenth century – one need only remember Bogle's youthful, idealistic earnestness. But Tibet was still somewhat vague in the early years of the century, and gold had helped to give direction, coherence and intensity to those otherwise hazy yearnings. Such a displacement and condensation was, however, no longer required once other, more appropriate images became available. Indeed, once the goal of Lhasa had been reached, the puer imagination focused itself on to the Himalayan mountains. Younghusband, for example, left the army soon after the 1904 expedition and turned his attention to religion, to the stars and to the mountains.[312] As we shall see, he was to become the inspiration behind the British Everest expeditions of the post-war years. But even as the century drew to its close, the Himalayan summits were attracting many a longing gaze. Mountaineering was on the threshold of a new 'golden age', as the giants of the Himalayas and Karakorams began to be challenged by Western climbers. As the earth's empty spaces vanished, it was to these virgin summits that the puer imagination turned. The purity and danger of the everlasting snows superseded the need for gold.

W.W. Graham's controversial claim to have climbed to the 24,076-foot-high summit of Kabru in 1883 was, if true, a new altitude record. It was followed in 1892 by Martin Conway's expedition, which included Charles Bruce and the Swiss guide Matthias Zurbriggen. They climbed to a height of 22,600 feet. In 1895 Mummery, Collie and Hastings attempted Nanga Parbat (26,660 feet) but had to turn back without reaching the summit. Meanwhile the American feminist Fannie Bullock-Workman and her husband were also regularly climbing summits above 20,000 feet in the Karakorams. Disputes, claims and counter-claims were rife. Longstaff, Bruce and Mumm climbed to the summit of Trisul (23,360 feet) in 1907, thereby establishing a new altitude record. The years just before the outbreak of World War I saw a rush of expeditions to these mountains, including the famous one led by the Duke of Abruzzi in 1909 which explored the approaches to K-2,[313]

Douglas Freshfield's expedition of 1899 to circumnavigate Kanchenjunga was one of the most famous of these pioneering attempts. He was already fifty-four years old and one of the most respected figures in climbing. His expedition was almost a pilgrimage:

> There is a ... motive, which is driving not a few of the surviving pioneers of the Alps to extend their wanderings. We long to compare the familiar snows we have known and loved so well with those of still mightier ranges. We, connoisseurs in mountain scenery, as we think of ourselves ... desire, before either our limbs or our eyes fail us, to make acquaintance with the greater ranges of the globe ...[314]

Indeed, the art of Alpine comparisons, already much in evidence in the preceding decades, reached its fullest development in Freshfield's text. His prose, an exquisite tribute to the mountains he loved, was matched in its time only by the photographs of Vittorio Sella who, after Freshfield's expedition, later accompanied the Duke of the Abruzzi's expedition. In his book Freshfield delicately sips each view, sliding the palate of his gaze over every nuance, comparing buttress, névé and slope with those sampled before, in the Alps. His admiration for the peaks overflowed: 'almost incredibly perfect grace of form'; 'the most superb triumph of mountain architecture'; 'possibly the most beautiful snow mountain in the world'.[315] As he gazed in wonder at Siniolchum (22,570 feet) he admitted that it was inaccessible to climbers of his generation, 'but others will come, and, standing on our shoulders will boast, as men did in Homer's day, that they are much better than their fathers'. His vision then turned towards the horizon: 'Far away to the east behind the crags that separate

Lachen and Lachung, the eyes are caught by the distant cliff of Chumalhari rising beyond the Tibetan frontier.'[316]

But Tibet hovered over even these mighty summits. For Freshfield, these mountains were 'stepping-stones to the golden terraces of Potala, the palace of the Dalai Lama'.[317] At the beginning of this study we saw that initially, when the first flush of mountain enthusiasm gripped the British imagination, Tibet was associated with the Himalayas. It partook of the fresh glory of the mountain summits, and thereby had its own mystery enhanced. Over a hundred years later, Tibet was a place of aspiration, fascination and mystery in its own right – the Himalayas marked only one of its frontiers. Now the situation was reversed: the sanctity and fascination of Tibet – and in particular of Lhasa – enhanced the numinosity of the Himalayan summits. The Himalayas were now associated with Tibet. Speculation that summits higher than Everest existed there – indeed, had even been seen in the distance – were an unconscious way of symbolizing Tibet's supreme imaginative power.[318]

Freshfield's book was dedicated to Joseph Hooker, just as Hooker's own famous *Himalayan Journals* had earlier been dedicated to Charles Darwin. Time and again Freshfield referred to Hooker's formative journey, as a young man of thirty-two in the eastern Himalayas. Freshfield visited the same splendid views, experienced similar emotions. When Hooker, by now an old man of eighty-six, received Freshfield's book, he wrote that it was 'with pleasure that I cannot express in words ... You have brought to me visions of my happiest early days that I never hoped to see ... '.[319] An era was coming full circle, closing and passing on.

Only Connect! Communication with the Axis Mundi

Chandler perceptively observed that he was 'part of more than a material invasion'.[320] Westerners were seeking a way not just into the geographical Tibet, but into the fantasy it represented. The paradox they faced was how to establish communication with this unique space – time zone, without simultaneously being the agent of its irrevocable demise or even destruction. By the end of the century Tibet had become a fully formed sacred space for the West, with the *axis mundi* firmly established at the Potala in Lhasa and embodied in the person of the Dalai Lama. The frontiers of this *temenos* were well established and highly charged with symbolic significance. It was a true *complexio oppositorum*, embracing the widest possible range of contradictions; hence it was an invaluable vessel for Western projections at a time of acute social fragmentation. The era was as complex as its fantasies about Tibet.

The range of travelling styles was no less extreme. Some – like Hedin, who prepared by plunging naked into snowdrifts – were desperate in their determination to reach Lhasa. Others, such as Colman Macaulay, were content to travel around the perimeter of Tibet. The contrast was extreme. As explorers struggled grimly across Tibetan wastes, Macaulay was complaining: 'Nothing in luncheon basket but some tinned oatcakes, a pâté de foie, a couple of glasses of whisky and a bottle of green chartreuse'.[321]

Whether being put out by only having green chartreuse to drink or stoically enduring barley-meal day after day, all the travellers had their own, very specific reason for trying to connect with Tibet. For some free access to the country was a God-given right:

> The Pass open and free to all,
> By God's own will
> For ALL the world
> Unto ALL men in heritage

wrote Louis in his poem 'A Legend of the Jeylap-La'.[322] For others, such as Chandler and Landon, eventual Western access to Tibet and Lhasa was inevitable, not because of God's will but due to the unstoppable law of progress. The humorous signpost erected by the British soldiers atop Jeylap-la with one arm pointing 'To Lhasa' and the other back 'To London', was probably the most apt monument to this sense of the inevitable.[323]

Many British travellers at the end of the century felt that it was their duty to reach Lhasa and free the ordinary Tibetans from the oppression of the lamas. Bower, for example, disgusted at the wealth and power of the monks as compared with the poverty and servility of the peasants, decided that 'the only chance of redemption for Tibet lies in foreign intercourse'.[324] Grenard, Macaulay, Louis, Younghusband and Landon, among others, all insisted that the ordinary Tibetan would welcome the British and other Westerners.[325] It was as if the British were creating, in their imagination, an unlikely allegiance with ordinary Tibetans. This allegiance gave British and other Western travellers, frustrated by the lack of communication with the Tibetan government and aristocracy, a sense of a possible connection. The old relationship with the 'Tashi Lama' (Panchen Lama), which dated back to Bogle's time, was also frequently proposed as a possible alternative to the impossible one with the Dalai Lama.[326]

For some travellers the establishment of communication with Tibet was a spiritual necessity and obligation. It was almost inevitable that spiritual guidance should be imagined to come from Tibet. The spiritually inclined Blavatsky, Hensoldt and David-Neel seemed to articulate the voice from the *axis mundi*, the voice from outside conditioned time and space. The form of communication varied from direct oral religious instruction inside

Tibetan monasteries to more long-range psychic transmission, telepathy or astral communiqués.

More conventional means of communication had also been attempted, particularly using letters. In 1889 the Archbishop of Canterbury sent a letter to the Dalai Lama, but Dr Lansdell, his emissary, was prevented from crossing the border on orders from the Anglo-Indian government, which was sensitive to Chinese territorial concerns.[327] Lord Curzon also tried to send letters to the Dalai Lama by means of a rather doubtful character named Ugyen Kazi. As Lamb ironically points out, 'Curzon's survey of the Indian Empire disclosed but three persons who could conceivably be used as intermediaries with the Dalai Lama; a minor Bhutanese official, a fat Chinese and a bibulous Ladaki.'[328] The choice fell upon the first, who was eventually suspected of lying about handing over the letter to the Dalai Lama and even of being a Tibetan spy. The Russians seemed to have more luck, and gifts were exchanged between the czar and the Dalai Lama.[329] This success was understandably a sore point with the British, who probably exaggerated its importance and repeatability, fantasizing a regular correspondence between St Petersburg and Lhasa.

Others preferred more tangible styles of communication – railways, roads and telegraph lines. While an allegiance with the peasants, or a solitary dash on horseback, or an armed expedition with or without the permission of God, or gifts and letters – even monastic instruction, occult transmission or psychic conversations – were all well and good, they were judged to be less reliable than the new communications technology. Telegraph wires, not telepathy, were wanted. By 1870–1 international telegraph lines had brought the East nearer both to the European governments and to their general population. Explanations and rationalizations for overseas actions were increasingly being demanded by a public kept well informed by the new mass-circulation newspapers.

In 1879 Kabul was connected to India by telegraph.[330] British overseas representatives no longer had the flexibility of decision-making that had been allowed by the several months it took a letter to make the round trip to and from London. By the time Waddell journeyed through the Himalayas in 1898, the telegraph line from India extended to Gantok, the capital of Sikkim, only a few miles from the Tibetan border.[331] In 1904 Younghusband soon discovered the pains of being a field agent within easy reach of London. Orders and counter-orders flowed readily from London to the Gantok telegraph stations and then over the Tibetan border, as the thin wires followed closely behind the slowly advancing British troops.[332] News reached the expedition barely three hours after it had been published in London. Waddell dreamt of a railway line extending over the border and into the Chumbi valley; Louis was of a similar mind, and proposed a railway tunnel under the Jeylap-la.[333] When the British left Lhasa, they left behind, despite Tibetan protests, a telegraph terminal at Gyantse, the second city of Tibet.[334] It seemed as if a permanent, reliable and modern line of communication had finally been established.

Relph, in his study *Place and Placelessness*, makes a distinction between being an insider and an outsider: 'From the outside you look upon a place as a traveller might look upon a town from a distance; from the inside you experience a place, are surrounded by it and part of it.'[335] He further subdivides these categories of experience:

> *Existential Outsideness*, in which there is an 'awareness of meaning withheld and of the inability to participate in those meanings'.

> *Objective Outsideness*, 'A dispassionate attitude towards places ... '.

> *Incidental Outsideness* 'describes a largely unselfconscious attitude in which places are experienced as little more than a background or setting for activities ... '.

> *Vicarious Insideness*, a second-hand but 'deeply felt involvement'.

> *Behavioural Insideness* 'involves deliberately attending to the appearance of that place'.

> *Empathetic Insideness* implies 'a willingness to be open to significances of a place, to feel it, to know and respect its symbols'.

> *Existential Insideness* is a complete belonging, the 'complete identity with a place that is the very foundation of the place concept'.

In the case of Tibet and Western travellers at the turn of the century, there were few, if any, *incidental outsiders*: Tibet was rarely a mere background place for travellers in the region. Nor were there many purely *objective outsiders*. Most certainly there was a mix between a *behavioural insideness* (deliberately attending to the appearance of Tibet) and an *empathetic insideness* (a willingness to be open to the significance of Tibet). However both existential attitudes were paramount.

While the experience of *existential insideness* may have occasionally been sustained by travellers such as Blavatsky, David-Neel or Hensoldt, usually it came as a brief moment of attunement. Landon, for example, when surrounded by Lhasa and the Potala, almost became convinced of the veracity of Tibetan religion. Younghusband too, as we have seen, had several profoundly intimate experiences in Tibet. Even Henry Savage Landor, the most aggressively ethnocentric and bullish of Victorian travellers, had flashes of existential rapport with the place.

On the other hand, the experience of *existential outsideness* was almost universal among Western travellers at that time. The belief that Tibet contained meanings, and the urgent desire to participate in these meanings, was a constant background. Every travel account described an attempt to articulate these meanings, to locate them, to journey towards them and embrace them. Every journey into Tibet, or around its perimeter, contained a kind of *nekyia*, a descent into the Underworld, into a landscape of symbols and hidden meanings – a descent into the unconscious not only of the individual, but of the era itself. Grenard's wonderful text presents this descent in its most exemplary form:

> I have now to describe the journey which we performed across a region which man had never penetrated ... The things which we saw in the course of this long march were things great and magnificent, no doubt, but always the same ... barren and dreary things.[336]

As Tibet became an intimate part of the Western psyche, the separation from it was felt as an *exile*. The journey to Lhasa was experienced on a depth level less as a *going* than as a *returning*.

To a reading public in Europe and North America thirsty for global images, these accounts offered a *vicarious insideness*. With the invention of photographic dry-plates in the 1880s, numerous photographic illustrations joined the written text.[337] The formation of the photographic record societies in Britain, Europe and America after 1890 testified to the archival fantasy that surrounded photography.[338] Photographs helped to *fix* Tibet, to capture it, to establish a kind of one-way communication.[339]

Photographs were also being used extensively for mountaineering reconnaissance. Freshfield in particular constantly discussed this.[340] In 1886 photography was placed on the Royal Geographical Society's curriculum for prospective explorers. However, in addition to this practical use of photographs, they also enhanced a sense of vicarious participation. Already a tradition of sensitive mountain photography had been established. It was significant that out of six Europeans in Freshfield's party that left Marseilles in 1899, three were connected with photography – Signor Vittorio Sella, 'one of the first of mountain photographers'; his brother, 'to keep him company'; and a photographic assistant.[341] Freshfield's expectations had previously been stimulated by photographs: 'The picture, so long dreamt of, so often studied in black and white, is at last before ... [my] eyes in all its glory of colour and aerial perspective.'[342]

But photographs also gave Westerners a vicarious sense of power over Tibet. Even if they could not go to the country at will, nor occupy it, nor control it, at least they had possession of its image. This was less the rape of the anima than her photo-exposure. In a kind of primitive sense, to own the image was to gain power over the subject, or at least to possess something of its soul. For example, in Kipling's famous tale, Kim takes the old Tibetan lama to the Lahore museum. The curator, a 'white-bearded Englishman', speaks to the trembling Tibetan: 'Welcome then, O lama from Tibet. Here be the images, and I am here ... to gather knowledge.' The lama then tells of his monastery, where he was the abbot. In reply, the 'curator brought out a huge book of photos and showed him that very place, perched on its crag, overlooking the gigantic valley of many-hued strata'. The lama is suitably impressed, even awed – 'And thou – the English know of these things?' – but he is not totally convinced. He says that there are still things that Western scholars do not know, nor even look for: things to do with spiritual wisdom.[343] The attitude of curator and lama expresses so well the tension and polarity within Western travellers and their attitude towards Tibet: science, technology and power versus spiritual wisdom and mystery.

When Landon returned from Lhasa on horseback he proudly announced that the Forbidden City was only eleven days and three hours from British territory: Ghoom Station, just outside Darjeeling. The elusive had been made tangible: a connection seemed finally to be established. Even the solitary thread of the telegraph wire looping its precarious way over the windswept Jeylap-la Pass and into Tibet seemed evidence, albeit fragile, of communication with this place outside space and time – a permanent Ariadne's thread.

6

Lost Horizons: From Sacred Place to Utopia
(1904–59)

Shortly after the end of World War II the famous Italian Tibetologist Giuseppe Tucci, and his party were invited to dinner by the Maharajah of Sikkim. At the reception, Maraini, the expedition's photographer, became fascinated by the Maharajah:

> I could not take my eyes off him as he tackled his peas; it was an exquisite, microscopic struggle; something between a game of chess and the infinite pains of the miniaturist; something between a secret rite, and a piece of court ceremonial. But now the struggle was over. The last pea, defeated and impaled on the fork, was raised to the royal lips, which opened delicately to receive it, as if about to give, or receive a kiss.[1]

Without a doubt we are standing on the edge of a very different Tibet to the earlier ones of desperate landscapes, sweeping vistas or heroic struggles. Maraini was concerned with the small, intimate details, the poetic glance into corners of everyday life in Tibet. Not since Manning's mid-nineteenth-century account had so much careful attention been given to seemingly irrelevant details of Tibetan and Himalayan life. How the Maharajah of Sikkim ate his peas would have been of no interest whatsoever to Victorian travellers, concerned as they were with science, politics and adventure. Like Manning's obsession with Tibetan hats, Maraini's peas would have been deemed irrelevant and facile to an age thirsty for facts and overviews. But whereas Manning's perspective on Tibet was an exception in its time, Maraini's was typical of the new Tibet taking shape in the imagination of twentieth-century Westerners.

The Tibet that emerged from the trauma of the 1904 expedition was indeed radically different to any that had existed previously. In 1918, with Britain victorious in the world war, the Dalai Lama *telegraphed* his congratulations to the king in London. Earlier in 1914, the Dalai Lama had offered a thousand soldiers to fight on the side of the Allies. He also ordered special religious services to be held for Britain's success in the war. These services continued throughout the conflict that raged thousands of miles away from Tibet.[2] The telegraph line to Gyantse that had been established in 1904 against the wishes of the Tibetan government was extended to Lhasa in 1921 in accordance with their demands.[3] By the 1940s the Dalai Lama had his own telephone and received regular news reports from the British Resident in Sikkim;[4] most of the wealthier people in Lhasa had their own radio sets; electricity was produced for the city by a diesel generator which was supervised in its turn by a young Tibetan engineer who had trained in England.

Many of the young Tibetan officials had been educated in Darjeeling and were fluent in English. British and American books were to be found in their libraries, whilst Western magazines and newspapers were popular among the wealthy Tibetans in Lhasa. There was even a Tibetan-language newspaper printed in Kalimpong and subscribed to by most of the leading Lhasa families.[5] Some of the older Tibetans complained that wireless and electricity made winter in Lhasa stuffy! They need not have worried, for although the changes in Lhasa were startling they were extremely limited, scarcely touching the great mass of the population and their traditional way of life.

These things were, however, harbingers of new attitudes, hopes and fears, among Tibet's leaders. They also revealed the diverse contact being established between the West and Tibet. Western goods began to fill the markets of Lhasa – American corned beef, Australian butter, British whisky. As Heinrich Harrer reported in 1946:

> There is nothing one cannot buy, or at least order. One even finds the Elizabeth Arden specialities, and there is a keen demand for them. American overshoes, dating from the last war, are displayed between joints of Yak's meat and chunks of butter. You can order, too, sewing-machines, radio sets and gramophones and hunt up Bing Crosby's latest records for your next party.[6]

The British assistant engineer responsible for extending the telegraph line from Gyantse to Lhasa in 1921 was impressed with the new, British-trained Tibetan army, complete with fife and drum band, bagpipes and bugles:

> It is quite inspiring to see the battalions fix bayonets, present arms to His Holiness to the tune of 'God Save the King', which the Tibetans had adopted as their national anthem, and march away with gorgeous yellow satin banners flying to the tune of 'The Girl I Left Behind Me'.[7]

In 1921 the 13th Dalai Lama wrote: 'the British and Tibetans have become one family'. This remarkable leader also had his own garage to house a Baby Austin, – numberplate *Tibet 1* – and an American Dodge.[8] He also agreed with the suggestions from Sir Charles Bell, the British Represent-ative in Tibet and his personal friend, to send four Tibetan youths to school at Rugby in England and to open an English school at Lhasa.[9] In 1931 Robert Byron could reflect:

> Tibet, for us now, is no longer the 'land of mystery', a piece of dark brown on physical maps, gripped by an unholy hierarchy, and pos-sessing no amenities of life beyond devil-dances and butter statues; but a physical, aesthetic, and human definition as implied by the words France or Germany. Henceforth it exists on the map of our intelligence as well as of our atlas. If, say the newspapers, this or that is happening in Tibet, this or that means something. In Terra del Fuego it does not.[10]

Indeed, in 1936 Spencer Chapman could lie in bed at Lhasa and listen on his radio to the news from London and the chimes of Big Ben.[11]

A Patchwork of Western Travellers

Despite the renewed travel restrictions after 1904, the next fifty years wit-nessed the richest and widest possible range of travellers ever to enter the 'Forbidden Land'. Despite Byron's disclaimer to the contrary, Western fas-cination with *occult* Tibet increased both in popularity and intensity. At the same time as British officers were making several routine journeys a year from India to Gyantse and even on to Lhasa, other travellers were studying the profundities of Tibetan mysticism from lamas in Himalayan retreats.[12] The West was coming into intimate contact with a broad spec-trum of Tibetan society. Westerners made friends with Tibetans ranging from the Dalai Lama, high-ranking officials, aristocrats and lamas to recluses and peasants.

Nevertheless, it must be stressed that Western contact with the poorer reaches of Tibetan society were extremely limited and mainly confined to the exploits of travellers such as the French mystic-scholar Alexandra David-Neel who, disguised as a beggar woman, gained rare insight into this lowly aspect of Tibetan life. Similarly, refugees such as the Austrian Heinrich Harrer – who, during the Second World War, escaped from a British internment camp in India – were forced by necessity to contact ordinary Tibetans in order to survive in remote regions. One British global traveller, however, complained that it was impossible to get to know the ordinary Tibetans:

> In Greenland one could wander off and be perfectly happy with the Eskimos as long as one could speak the language. There one passed

as an equal and lived, ate, hunted, and travelled just as they did ...
Here it is fundamentally different. In this feudal country one is a
Sahib.[13]

Not only were Western travellers connecting with a bewildering range
of Tibetan lifestyles, they were also finally emancipating themselves from
the conventions of late-Victorian travel writing. As the quotation from
Maraini at the beginning of this chapter shows, strict demands for 'facts'
– political, ethnographic, geographic – were being complemented by
other perspectives. Nowhere is this more clearly demonstrated than in the
accounts of Robert Byron and Peter Fleming – and also, of course, Fosco
Maraini. At long last, humour found its way into Tibetan travel writing –
not humour at the Tibetans' expense, but a wry self-mocking of the travellers themselves. Byron showed his mastery of this style as he struggled to
learn the language:

> G., to whom linguistic obstacles are unknown, insisted on our tak-
> ing Tibetan lessons from a Sikhimese ... His long pigtail and twink-
> ling elfin face, the spit of an autumn leaf, endeared him to us; while
> his sense of humour bore with equanimity G.'s suggestion that the
> whole language was an invention of his own, composed solely to
> annoy us. The inflection defeated us entirely. It seemed humanly
> impossible, when listening to him, to distinguish '*nga*' (meaning 'I')
> from '*nga*' (meaning 'drum'), or to distinguish either of these from '*nga*'
> (meaning 'five'). 'Not "*nga*", he would instruct, 'but "*nga*" '; while we
> strained our ears in vain to catch the remotest difference between the
> two utterances. All we could do was to repeat the accursed syllable in
> bass, baritone, and alto, evoking in reward a pitying grin.[14]

In addition to humour, accounts of personal experiences, whether of
adventures or of the occult, were also in demand. David-Neel, for example, was to the Tibet of magic and mystery what Byron was to that of
whimsy. Her encounter with the lung-gom-pa, one of the legendary
lamas who by means of psychic training could move swiftly, running
nonstop across vast distances of rugged landscape, has become famous
and is a typical example of her heroic-occult prose:

> Towards the end of the afternoon, Yongden, our servants and I were
> riding leisurely across a wide tableland, when I noticed, far away in
> front of us, a moving black spot which my field-glasses showed to be
> a man. I felt astonished. Meetings are not frequent in that region, for
> the last ten days we had not seen a human being. Moreover, men on
> foot and alone do not, as a rule, wander in these immense solitudes.
> Who could the strange traveller be?

She was warned not to stop the rapidly approaching lama, nor speak to him, for this would break his meditation and kill him.

> By that time he had nearly reached us; I could clearly see his perfectly calm impassive face and wide-open eyes with their gaze fixed on some invisible far-distant object situated somewhere high up in space. The man did not run. He seemed to lift himself from the ground, proceeding by leaps. It looked as if he had been endowed with the elasticity of a ball and rebounded each time his feet touched the ground. His steps had the regularity of a pendulum. He wore the usual monastic robe and toga, both rather ragged. His left hand gripped a fold of the toga and was half hidden under the cloth. The right held a *phurba* (magic dagger). His right arm moved slightly at each step as if leaning on a stick, just as though the *phurba*, whose pointed extremity was far above the ground, had touched it and were actually a support. My servants dismounted and bowed their heads to the ground as the lama passed before us, but he went his way apparently unaware of our presence.[15]

During the post-World War I years Tibet also opened its doors to a limited number of tourists, although these were closely restricted to the trade route between India and the town of Gyantse.[16] Nevertheless, the tourist *mentality* could also be found in travellers who had the good fortune to journey deep into the country. In 1949 the Tibetan government, fearful of the rise of Chinese communism on its borders, invited two Americans, Lowell Thomas and his son Lowell Thomas Jnr, to visit Lhasa in order to bring the plight of Tibet to the notice of the American people. Thomas Jnr wrote what has been called 'a slick, journalistic best-seller'.[17] Certainly his book bounces along from one cliché to the next: for example, when given a rare opportunity to photograph the Dalai Lama, he could only exclaim: 'Now we are off for a real photographic spree!'.[18]

Nevertheless, despite the great divergence of interests among Western travellers during the forty years from the end of World War I to the exile of the Dalai Lama in 1959, they were still woven into a fairly cohesive community. The British grip on access to Tibet funnelled most expectant travellers along the same administrative routes. The lineage of British officers responsible for Tibetan affairs – Bell, MacDonald, Richardson, Bailey, Weir, Williamson, Gould – provided the backbone around which British contact with Tibet was organized. The French, too, had their own close network of Tibetophiles, especially at work in the eastern and southeastern corner of the country. Bacot, Guibaut, Migot and David-Neel jealously upheld the memory of previous French travellers and missionaries.[19]

There was a certain amount of international rivalry among travellers in these regions. The British, for example, wanted to keep Mount Everest for themselves alone to climb, and did so successfully until 1952.[20] David-Neel was continually angry with them, holding them responsible for the closure of Tibet to legitimate travellers.[21] Guibaut was more subtle and, whilst eating a particularly tasteless meal, wryly remarked: 'French people have over-sensitive palates. On expeditions Anglo-Saxons have the advantage over them, because with them the need for nourishment comes before the desire to eat something which tastes pleasant.'[22]

The Italians, too, were proud of their long tradition of Tibetan exploration. The medieval travellers Oderic of Pordenone and Marco Polo gave the first Western accounts of Tibet; Capuchins and Jesuits lived in Tibet during the eighteenth century – Ippolito Desideri's account is particularly important. Italian exploration of Tibet and the Himalayas declined in the nineteenth century but resumed with some vigour in the twentieth, which saw journeys by the Duke of Abruzzi, Giuseppe Tucci, Fosco Maraini and others.[23] The Russians, of course, as we have seen, had a long-established tradition of Central Asian and Tibetan exploration. Finally, attention should also be drawn to the emerging line of American travellers in Tibet, beginning in the nineteenth century with Rockhill and including McGovern, Bernard, Tolstoy and Thomas in the twentieth. Other countries, such as Austria, had notable success in climbing the Himalayan peaks.

Tibets

Each of the previous chapters has described a different Tibet – each one complete within itself yet built, like all great edifices, on the foundations of those that went before. All these Tibets also contained within them the seeds of their own demise, for they were not static but in process, constantly undergoing transformation. Earlier chapters have described this process: the genesis of a new Tibet in Western fantasy; the circumstances of its creation; its constituents; its significance for the West; its evolving perfection and its limitations; its decline and abandonment. Above all, these separate Tibets should not be treated as part of a historical evolution towards some ultimate realization about the empirical *truth* of Tibet. So, as the 1904 expedition led by Younghusband set in motion the end of one Tibet, it simultaneously began the production of the next.

Of course, old themes and images continued, but as we shall see they formed new relationships, took on fresh significances: Tibet was still imagined as the northern rampart, the bulwark of India;[24] gold still exerted its fascination and was still invoked to explain possible Russian and Chinese – albeit now communist – interest in Tibet. Also, side by side with gold, uranium, a new mineral precious to the atomic age, began to fulfil a similar function.[25] Tibet still continued to be invoked in the same breath as Ancient Egypt.[26] Its culture, landscape and people were still constantly referred to, throughout the first half of the twentieth century, in terms of 'Alice Through the Looking Glass', 'Knights of the Round Table', 'Fairy Palaces', 'fairy-tale landscapes', or a 'Medieval World'.[27] If anything, such descriptions now became more commonplace, albeit slightly stereotyped and worn. However, Maraini still managed to breathe life into the medieval metaphor, developing it to its fullest expression:

> Tibetan life, viewed as a whole, is typically medieval. It is medieval in its social organization – the predominance of the church and the nobility – and its economic basis is agriculture and stock-breeding. It has the colour and incredible superstition of France and Burgundy, the two most perfect examples of European medievalism; it has a medieval faith; a medieval vision of the universe as a tremendous drama in which terrestrial alternate with celestial events; a medieval hierarchy culminating in one man and then passing into the invisible and the metaphysical ... ; medieval feasts and ceremonies, medieval filth and jewels, medieval professional story-tellers and tortures, tourneys and cavalcades, princesses and pilgrims, brigands and hermits, nobles and lepers; medieval renunciations, divine frenzies, minstrels and prophets[28]

What more could one possibly add? Maraini, consummate artist that he was, took an emaciated metaphor and gave it flesh. In his account Tibet was clearly forged as a link with *memoria*, with the long-lost ancestors of the Western imagination. It was, he wrote, 'perhaps the only civilization of another age to have survived intact into our own time'. He continued:

> Visiting Tibet ... means travelling in time as well as space. It means for a brief while living as a contemporary of Dante or Boccaccio, ... breathing the air of another age, and learning by direct experience how our ancestors of twenty or twenty-five generations ago thought, lived and loved.[29]

There is a richness, if not a freshness, about this new Tibet, in which even the old themes seem to share. What Maraini did for medievalism, Byron did for light and colour. Whilst he was, of course, not the only one to comment on these striking features, Byron said it all with an economy of phrase:

> Vanished for ever was the prussian-blue of Anglo-Himalaya and the Alps, that immanent, formless tint which oppresses half the mountains of the world. A new light was in the air, a liquid radiance ...

here was a land where natural coloration, as we understood it, does not apply.[30]

In Guibaut's account of his journey in South-Eastern Tibet, vivid colours, primitive vitality, archaic tradition and medievalism became synonymous: 'Outside in the courtyard the play of colours, under a brilliant sky, attains an African exuberance. The temple, with its slanting walls, assumes an Egyptian aspect ... The scene recalls the Middle Ages ... '.[31] Two centuries of complex fantasies about Tibet are here condensed into two sentences.

What made all the difference was that this new Tibet was partly *conscious of itself as a production*, as a genre. There was, at least among the better writers, a sense of play, of dreaming the dream along. Byron, for example, wrote: 'This account must now enter upon the stage familiar to all readers of Tibetan travel-books, in which the desolation of the country overwhelms all other impressions.[32]

No other Tibet was so aware of being supported by previous travellers' experiences. Migot, for example, actively sought out the spot where Dutreuil de Rhins was murdered nearly half a century before, and erected a memorial. He did the same for other French travellers in the region, paying them homage.[33] Captain Bailey, journeying through Assam to south-eastern Tibet in order to explore the mysterious course of the Tsangpo river, followed the route taken by Pundit Kintup fifty years earlier. He similarly paid respect to the bravery and skill of his predecessor. Bailey went so far as to seek out the aged Indian explorer himself and ensure his reward and recognition – just in time, for Kintup died shortly afterwards.[34] Again, Byron managed to convey succinctly the experience of this century-and-a-half's preparation when face to face with the actuality of Tibet.

> Turning a corner, I was confronted by a religious procession. It produced a curious feeling, almost fear, this first contact with persons, clothes, and observances of utter strangeness. For many years I had thought about Tibet, read about it, and gazed longingly at photographs of huge landscape and fantastic uniforms. None the less, the reality came as a shock.[35]

But he quickly recovered his poise and skilfully avoided any temptation to inflate the significance of the event. He continued: 'In the rear, borne in a palanquin, came a golden image preceded by a scowling fat monk. One might have been the Virgin, and the other a priest, in an Italian village.'

The self-consciousness of this 'new' Tibet also revealed itself in a clash of stereotypes. Various authors would, from a supposedly superior position, gaze out and encapsulate the prevailing fantasies about Tibet, only then to dismiss them contemptuously as unreal. Creating and deflating all-encapsulating visions of Tibet was a common pastime among contemporary writers:

> For many Westerners Tibet is wrapped in an atmosphere of mystery. The 'Land of Snows' is for them the country of the unknown, the fantastic and the impossible. What superhuman powers have not been ascribed to the various kinds of lamas, magicians, sorcerers, necromancers and practitioners of the occult who inhabit those high tablelands, and whom both nature and their own deliberate purpose have so splendidly isolated from the rest of the world? And how readily are the strangest legends about them accepted as indisputable truths! In that country plants, animals and human beings seem to divert to their own purposes the best established laws of physics, chemistry, physiology and even plain common sense.[36]

Such passages show how sophisticated the reflections on Tibet had become. Whilst David-Neel did her best to question and refine visions of the country such as the one above, Maraini wanted to throw them out altogether. 'In Europe,' he wrote mockingly, 'Tibet is always thought of as a strange country exclusively populated by mysterious sages, who pass their time performing incredible miracles in endless rocky wildernesses inhabited by rare blue poppies.'[37] Instead, Maraini wanted to emphasize the complexity of Tibet: its landscapes, culture and religion. He wanted to show a side of Tibetan life that 'was neither sublime, nor thaumaturgic, nor hieratic, but simply gay, pagan and innocent'.[38]

The problem was that this newly acquired self-consciousness produced an arrogant struggle to establish the *truth* about Tibet, rather than encouraging a de-literalizing playfulness. Nevertheless, writer-travellers such as Maraini, Fleming and Byron used humour to its best advantage in their attempt to keep the imagination mobile within these grand, all-encompassing visions. Maraini, well aware of the leaden seriousness of occult fantasies about Tibet, brilliantly juxtaposed the profound with the trivial. For instance, Lobsang, a Tibetan friend, was telling him about various occult happenings: 'There are certain things that one must not know. Would you like some more tea? Even you strangers ought to have great respect for the gods, you can never tell what will happen.' Lobsang then went on to recount the story of Williamson, the British political officer who died at Lhasa in 1936, supposedly of a heart attack. According to the Tibetans, however, he died because he had photographed, without permission, some images of the wrathful gods:

> You may not believe it, but it's a fact known to everybody in Lhasa and Tibet ... Please help yourself to another biscuit, they're fresh.

Sonam baked them; he's a good lad ... A few hours before Williamson died a perfectly black figure entered his room and snatched his
soul ... Won't you have some more tea?[39]

Byron adopted a slightly different approach. He took for granted the
presence and pressure of Western expectations about fantastic, magical
happenings in Tibet. On the way to Gyantse, he met a British officer. 'Personally, I like Tibet', the officer casually remarked. Having just followed
Byron and his companions through a depressing and gruelling winter
landscape into Tibet, we, the readers, are naturally expecting some profound insight from this man who actually *likes* the place. What attracts
him so much that he alone can shrug off the primitive conditions, the
harsh evironment? Is it the sublime landscapes, the occult mysteries, or
perhaps just adventure? It is in fact none of these: 'The Indian troops at
Gyantse are frightfully keen on hockey. I really get all the games I want.
It's a bit lonely sometimes. But as I say, I get all the games I want.'[40] The
demystification is complete; a fresh space has been created: the imagination is liberated from stereotyped structures.

This is where the centre of gravity of the new Tibet is to be found: in
these flashes of self-consciousness. It was a time when grand visions of
Tibet were being both created and debunked. Sometimes this was all in
terms of the search for the *real* Tibet; sometimes just for its own sake, for
moments of imaginative play. Unlike the previous, nineteenth-century
Tibet, neither a sustained desperate exploration of the landscape nor the
urgent demands of imperial strategy dominated or brought coherence to
this new creation.[41] Of course these two themes, so familiar to the West's
relationship with Tibet, were still apparent, but they were now pushed –
literally geographically – to the fringes.

The two main, peripheral, regions where heroic feats of exploration
occurred during this time were the south-east corner of Tibet and to the
south-west of Lhasa, around Mount Everest. Danger was present in both:
in the south-east corner from the local tribes, the Ngolos and the Mishmis;
in the other region from the wild mountain landscape of Everest. In both,
too, death was common. In the south-east corner, the French explorer
Liotard and the French missionary Père Nussbaum were murdered within
ten days of each other in 1940.[42] The British also suffered in this region:
Williamson, Gregorson, and thirty-seven others were massacred by the
Abors on the border with Tibet in 1911.[43]

The British made several desperate attempts to reach the summit of
Mount Everest. Official expeditions, backed by an uneasy partnership between the Royal Geographical Society and the Alpine Club (also, later, the
Himalayan Club), set out in 1921, 1922, 1924, 1933, 1936, 1938 and finally,
successfully, in 1953. Three British, eight Nepalese and four other Asians
died in these attempts. In 1934 Maurice Wilson, an eccentric yet courage-

ous and determined Briton, died 21,000 feet up Everest after a solo struggle between the power of religious faith and that of the mountain. The unsolved deaths of Mallory and Irvin in 1924, last seen only 800 feet below the summit, became legend. This event was to the history of Himalayan climbing what the deaths of four men on the Matterhorn in 1865 had been to the Alpine tradition. In Mallory, Everest found its true hero and martyr.[44]

A third dangerous region was Tibet's northern frontier. After the collapse of the Chinese Empire. Sinkiang province was in a state of civil war for most of this period. The same applied to Tibet's eastern frontier, although here the danger came more from bandits than from combatants in a civil war. Even the well-respected but aged Sven Hedin had considerable difficulty trying to pass through Sinkiang in 1926. Peter Fleming and the Swiss woman Ella Maillart, on their famous journey from China to India in 1935, gave graphic descriptions of the dangers along this northern route.[45] Leonard Clark's account is vivid in its portrayal of the violent anarchy along Tibet's eastern border, especially immediately after the Second World War.[46]

In these accounts we still read of blanks on the map, of regions unseen by Europeans, of unsolved mysteries such as the Tsangpo Gorge, or the mountain in eastern Tibet that perhaps rivalled Everest.[47] But now it was not a whole country that was unknown, merely its high peaks, its odd corners – 'This whole north-east quarter ... has been almost invariably circumvented by the old-time explorers';[48]

> From now on every stride of our horses adds to our still very meagre balance-sheet of discoveries. From the earliest ages of mankind no traveller along these tracks has thought of marking out the land. We are going to submit this country to the discipline of geography.[49]

Desperate attempts were still made, in disguise, to reach Lhasa – Alexandra David-Neel in 1927, William McGovern in 1923.[50] Both succeeded. In 1913 Major John Noel also used disguise whilst making a clandestine and unofficial solo exploration of the routes to Everest.[51]

There were also old-style, large-scale expeditions such as the one led by Nicolas Roerich, artist and mystic. Crossing immense tracts of Central Asia between 1924 and 1925, he nearly perished of cold and starvation when his journey across Tibet was halted by government officials.[52] In 1925 Edwin Schary, an American, struggled desperately across Tibet in search of the famed mahatmas. MacDonald, the British trade agent at Gyantse, described his arrival: 'One evening at dusk, a begrimed and filthily clad figure covered with festering sores crawled up to the main gate of the Gyantse Fort ... He was really in a terrible condition, verminous, ill-nourished, and really very ill.'[53] Fugitives, such as Harrer, Aufschnaiter,

Kopp and Ossendowski, produced remarkable stories of endurance across bleak uncharted regions of Tibet.[54] There was also the story of the American airmen who accidentally crash-landed in Tibet during the war while flying supplies to China over the notorious 'hump'.[55]

As usual Byron, certainly no hero, managed to play with even *this* stereotypical aspect of Tibetan travel. His journey was by no means dangerous and followed a well-used trading route, stopping each night in government rest-houses. Nevertheless, his suffering was graphic:

> The morning, which came at last, was the crisis of the expedition. My own face, for which I had constructed a mask out of two handker-chiefs, had ceased to drip, and was now covered with yellow scabs, which adhered unpleasantly to the surface of the beard. But those of M. and G. had liquefied in the night, and they arrived in my room to breakfast, speechless with despondency. The cold was intense; the room was filled with the odour of yak-dung and lamp-smoke; my head was pounding; and I had whispered to myself, during the despair of dressing, that if – if either of the others were to suggest an about-turn, I should not oppose him. To endure this pain for three more weeks would be merely the weak-mindedness of the strong. M., his face dripping, unshaven, and crinkling with nausea as it opened to receive a piece of tinned sausage, spoke the first reproach that I had ever known of him: '*Why* have you brought us to this hor-rible place?' And then people say, but the Tibetans are so dirty, aren't they? They may be. But at least they preserve their faces. There can have been no one in the whole country so filthy, so utterly repulsive to look at, as ourselves by the time we arrived at Gyantse.[56]

But these desperate moments, and the few heroic journeys, were almost leftovers from the *fin de siècle*, the golden age of Tibetan exploration. True, the public liked them, but after 1904 they no longer supplied the *place* of Tibet with its basic imaginative coherence.

How Much Time is Left?

'There is little room to turn; one ill-judged movement may cause a fall to the bottom. This is Tibet's danger', wrote Marco Pallis in 1933.[57] Unlike the previous Tibets, which had a timeless permanence about them, in the twentieth century an all-pervading sense of loss was the leitmotiv of West-ern imagining. While the *fin-de-siècle* Tibet was *edged* with imperman-ence, now such fears were *central*. Marco Pallis was one of the most sophisticated and persistent critics of the changes taking place in Tibet and the Himalayan regions.[58] As the above quotation shows, he considered the situation urgent. For these Western travellers Tibet's imaginative status seemed threatened from four directions: tourism, globalism, the influx of Western ideas, and communism. The first three, as we have seen, were not new; but the fourth was most assuredly a child of the times.

Amaury de Riencourt, who journeyed to Lhasa in 1947, wrote of 'almost the last independent civilization left in this shrinking world'.[59] There were fewer and fewer unmapped, unknown, untouched regions on the planet. Following in the wake of the explorers came the tourists. This, as we have seen, was an old fear, but whereas earlier it was thought they might contaminate Tibet, now it was feared tourism would eventually *destroy* it. 'The time is obviously near', wrote Guibaut whilst exploring the dangerous south-eastern corner in 1940, 'when it will be possible to penetrate into Tibet by car or plane. Then Lama civilization will dissolve into tourism.'[60] In 1939 the American explorer Bernard wrote: 'Far-reaching changes, little short of cataclysmic, threaten the land of Tibet and Lhasa its capital.'[61] 'Would it any longer be possible', mused Thomas in 1949, 'for any nation, no matter how remote no matter how isolated by high mountains, to shut itself off from the problems of the world, especially in this age of high speed, high-flying planes, radio short wave, and atomic energy.'?[62] It was this sense of *time running out* that characterized Western imagining.

No sooner had the West found a place outside time and space than, like the freshly opened tombs at Mycenae, all began to crumble and turn to dust before their eyes. 'How much longer will it be able to endure?' cried Maraini.[63] 'A very ancient civilization, now condemned, is about to disappear', lamented Guibaut.[64] Was Tibetan civilization really so fragile, so lacking in resilience? Was the danger from Western ideas and tourism so great? Pallis apart, it did not seem as if any of those bemoaning the certainty of Tibet's fate had made anything but the most cursory study of the problem. What were these Westerners afraid of losing?

As we have seen, previous generations had generally complained about Tibet's refusal to embrace technical ideas. Now this was reversed. While numerous ruling Tibetans were now cautiously enthusiastic about Western ideas, many Westerners were disillusioned with their own civilization. For example, in 1932 Robert Byron discussed the situation with Mary, a Tibetan friend:

And then said Mary: 'I love Tibet. If only it had trains or motors, I think it would be the nicest country in the world'.

'But', I answered, 'the monks don't like that sort of thing.'

'No', she sighed. 'Some people don't seem to want to be civilized.'

I tried to sympathize with that sigh. The hardships of travel in Tibet can hardly be expected to appeal to those whose lifelong fate they are. But I could not. For once train or motors have been introduced, the Tibet that Mary loves will be Tibet no longer.[65]

Here is the answer: it was not Byron's fate to have to live in Tibet. For him, as for many other Westerners, it was a symbol, and it was this symbol that was under threat. Those Westerners who actually lived in Tibet, like Heinrich Harrer, could not sweepingly dismiss *all* Western technology out of hand. 'I could not understand why the people of Tibet were so opposed to any form of progress', he wrote. 'The policy of the Government towards medicine is a dark chapter in the history of modern Tibet ... The whole power was in the hands of the monks, who criticized even government officials when they called in the English doctor.'[66]

Tibet, of course, had never really been isolated – had never been in deep freeze, or immune to outside influences. Indian and Chinese culture had thoroughly revolutionized the country in the past, and continued to influence it profoundly in modern times. In the nineteenth century, the idea of a static, unchanging Tibet had exactly dovetailed with British imperialism's role for it as a no-man's-land in the 'Great Game' with Russia. Now, in the first half of the twentieth, Tibet symbolized everything the West imagined it had itself lost. It was the last living link with its own past. As Pallis wrote, 'It is the last of the Great Traditions ... '.[67] Amaury de Riencourt spelt out the myth in full: 'In this most forbidden city on earth, the last representatives of doomed civilizations meet as they met a thousand years ago ... Here is still a living past.'[68]

Tibet seemed to symbolize, too, a lost innocence. As the unknown regions of the planet succumbed to mapping, as the whole globe threatened to become culturally homogenized and as the West staggered, disillusioned, through two world wars into the dawning of the 'atomic age', it was perhaps not surprising that Tibet should be looked to as a place of sanctuary. No wonder many in the West wanted to freeze Tibet in time. It is also no surprise that the 1953 Everest expedition should have been called 'the last innocent adventure'.[69] Even the ironic Byron succumbed to the dream: 'I think once more of the blue sky and clear air of the plateau, of the wind and sun, of the sweeping ranges, and the chant of ploughman and thresher. Once more I see Tibet immune from Western ideas, and once more I wonder how long that immunity will last.'[70]

Maraini, watching yet another colourful 'medieval' procession as a Tibetan noble journeyed across the countryside, sadly reflected: 'within a few decades these same people would be passing this way in motorcars, in horrible clothes not designed for them, and ... all I was seeing and admiring would be nothing but a memory'.[71] While one can readily sympathize with such sentiments, the desire to keep Tibet 'pure' and free from Western technology was simply the reverse side of the unquestioned nineteenth-century confidence in Western ideas of progress. Where were the beggars, the outcasts, the poor, in these modern accounts? Where was the chronic sickness, the harsh punishments, the corruption? Where the paradox? Thomas, for example, wrote:

> The lamas ... are convinced that they alone of all peoples are not slaves to the gadgets and whirring wheels of the industrial age. They want no part of it. To them the devices, doodads and super-yoyos – the symbols of our western civilization – are toys, of no real value.[72]

Yet the Tibetans themselves were torn by contradictions. Smoking, playing mahjong and football, were banned in Lhasa. Wearing spectacles was disapproved of as un-Tibetan; no European clothes could be worn in the Summer Garden of the Dalai Lama; modern dances like the samba were frowned upon. Yet telephones, radios and cinema shows were welcomed, even encouraged.[73] It seemed as if Westerners wanted to simplify the actual, complex, contradictory situation in Tibet.

The confusion of the Tibetans themselves was understandable. They were confronted by serious threats to their fragile independence. Could Tibet best survive by conservatively clinging to every detail of its tradition, or by selectively modernizing?[74] As the century progressed, it was gradually dawning on even the conservative Tibetan National Assembly 'that isolationism spelt a grave danger for the country'.[75] Even more than the disruptive influence of Western ideas, the spectre of communism threw its shadow across this Tibet. 'The peril is imminent', cried Lowell Thomas Jnr in 1949. He had been specifically brought to Lhasa by the Tibetan government to let America know of what he called, the 'serious problem of defense against Asiatic Communism'.[76] Western travellers wrote of 'the Red Hurricane', 'the Marxist bulldozer', the 'fanatical Communist hordes'.[77] Whilst some were more circumspect and philosophical about communism, the underlying sentiment was generally the same. De Riencourt pleaded:

> Can the Western powers understand the terrifying implications of selfishly abandoning, of delivering, almost, this fabulous country to the most ruthless and destructive tyranny that has ever existed ... If Lhasa is finally conquered by the Reds, the loss will not be merely a local one. It will be a ghastly loss for the whole of Asia and also for every human being, the death of the most spiritual and inspiring country on this globe.[78]

For some, Tibet had clearly moved to the centre of Western *global* mythologizing:

> What is happening in Tibet is symbolical for the fate of humanity. As

on a gigantically raised stage we witness the struggle between two
worlds, which may be interpreted ... either as the struggle between
the past and the future, between backwardness and progress, belief
and science, superstition and knowledge, – or as the struggle between the wisdom of the heart and the knowledge of the brain, between the dignity of the human individual and the herd-instinct of
the mass, between the faith in the higher destiny of man through
inner development and the belief in material prosperity ... [79]

Never before had Tibet functioned so clearly as a vessel for the projection
of Western global fears and hopes. How did this unprecedented
mythologizing come about?

When Lowell Thomas wrote: 'Two World Wars have brought startling
changes to most of the globe, but so far not to Tibet', he was reporting not
historical circumstances but Western fantasies. Tibet had indeed changed
dramatically between 1914 and 1949, but many in the West assiduously
refused to acknowledge it. These Westerners lived in a split world. Quite
clearly they knew about the turmoil of Tibetan history in the twentieth
century, yet at the same time they disavowed it. The West seemed to need at
least one place to have remained stable, untouched, an unchanging centre in
a world being ripped apart. Many hoped that Tibet would be that 'still
centre':[80] 'The Tibetans watched the whirlwind transformation of Asia,
chaos and revolutions all around, the religious riots of India, the gradual disintegration of Nationalist China, the spreading anarchy of South-East Asia,
and the Red tides from the north, with growing apprehension.'[81]

Between 1904 and 1950, the political context within which the Tibetan
drama unfolded had radically changed. Each of the three great empires
upon which the destiny of Tibet had rested over the past 150 years had
undergone upheaval. The old order had gone, the old rules of the game
no longer applied. Two disastrous world wars had returned British attention to its own backyard. It slowly disengaged from its empire, and in 1947
India became independent. Britain was no longer much concerned about
the political fate of Tibet. Russia too had suffered terribly in two world
wars, had been torn apart by revolution and civil war. Tibet took advantage of this chaos to proclaim its independence and throw out the last vestiges of Chinese power – its administration and its soldiers. For nearly forty
years, between 1912 and 1951, Tibet enjoyed an uneasy autonomy.

Western travellers into Tibet almost inevitably had to pass through this
chaos, this terrible violence and lawlessness. Fleming and Maillart came
from China across the northern boundary, Clark fought his way through
eastern Tibet; Ossendowski escaped from Soviet Russia only to fall into
the madness of Central Asian politics between the wars. In 1933 Fleming
summarized it all: 'the situation ... was complex, lurid and obscure and
seemed likely to remain so indefinitely'.[82] No wonder Tibet should seem

a calm and exemplary home of sanity. In a world where modern ideology combined with modern weapons to bring havoc to the traditional cultures of the world, it was understandable that the excesses of Tibetan feudalism should pale into insignificance by comparison.

In the nineteenth century, Britain had feared the encroachment of czarist imperialism into Tibet. During the years between the two global wars of the twentieth century their fears turned to Japanese militarism, to German and Italian fascism, and to Soviet expansionism.[83] After World War Two, with the empires of Russia and China more intact and coherent than ever before – although now under the control of communism – Tibet seemed an unlikely bastion against the spread of international Marxism.

Nevertheless, the country's internal politics were by no means tranquil, but full of drama and incident. Chinese troops occupied large areas of eastern Tibet between 1907 and 1910, besieging and capturing monasteries, ruthlessly slaughtering monks. Lhasa was in the grip of anxiety and when, in February 1910, an advance guard of the Chinese army entered the capital, the Dalai Lama fled to India. In his absence the Chinese issued a decree, ignored by the Tibetans, that deposed him. But in 1911, following the overthrow of the Manchu Dynasty in Peking, the Chinese troops in Lhasa were forced out of Tibet. The Dalai Lama returned home in June 1912.[84]

Despite the Simla Conference of 1913–14 between representatives of Tibet, China and Britain to establish the boundaries of Tibet, Chinese aggression continued in the eastern region. To the north, in Mongolia, the third great incarnated Lama, Djebtsung Damba Hutuktu Khan, the so-called 'Living Buddha' of Urga, was arrested in 1921 and deprived of his throne by the Soviets. He was temporarily reinstated by the victorious White Russian Army under Baron Unberg von Sternberg, but they were soon defeated and the 'Living Buddha' was once more deposed. He eventually died of syphilis in 1924. The Mongolian People's Republic was established; lamaism was ruthlessly crushed; monks were killed or defrocked; monasteries were destroyed. Mongolia had a closer spiritual relationship to Tibet than any other country. No wonder the 13th Dalai Lama wrote:

> ... the present is the time of the five kinds of degeneration in all countries. In the worst class is the manner of working among the Red people [USSR]. They do not allow search to be made for the new Incarnation of the Grand Lama of Urga. They have seized and taken away all the sacred objects from the monasteries. They have made monks to work as soldiers.[85]

He warned that such things could well happen in the centre of Tibet. Yet at precisely the same time, Sir Frederick O'Connor, despite having lived in and around Tibet for many years as a British political officer, could write that nothing seemed to threaten the 'aloofness', 'glamour' and calm of the country and its culture.[86]

Rivalry between the Tashi (Panchen) Lama and the Dalai Lama resulted in the former fleeing for his life in 1923. He never returned to Tibet, and died in exile in 1937. The Dalai Lama had himself already died in 1933 and for over two years Tibet was without either of its great spiritual leaders – a situation which led to confusion, uncertainty, and sometimes violence.[87] In 1932 war again broke out in eastern Tibet between Chinese warlords and Tibetan troops. In 1934 the famous 'Long March of Mao Tse-tung's communist army resulted in disruption and fighting on the eastern border.[88] As Bell wrote: 'By the beginning of 1936 it became clear that Tibet was in danger, not only from direct armed invasion by China, but also from a Chinese military penetration under the shadow of the Tashi Lama.'[89] In that year the British sent a political mission to Lhasa, under the leadership of Gould, to give the Tibetans political and military advice.

Although the Soviets seemed to have given up any direct designs on Tibet after the failure of a mission to Lhasa in 1927–8, they consolidated their grip on Soviet Mongolia and all traces of Buddhism in that country vanished. Nevertheless, Red Army troops and Soviet technicians dominated the north of Sinkiang province – causing considerable alarm among the British, who were concerned as always about the vulnerability of India's northern frontier and trade routes.[90]

In 1940, whilst the rest of the world was caught up in war, the new, infant Dalai Lama was enthroned. In 1942 an American expedition led by Ilya Tolstoy passed through Lhasa in search of a new supply route from India to China, and was favourably received. Then, soon after the termination of the Second World War in 1945, Lhasa experienced a minor civil war. An assassination attempt was made on the current Regent by his predecessor, Reting Rimpoche, who was arrested and died mysteriously in gaol a few days later. His arrest was the catalyst for a small rebellion. The lamas at one of Sera monastery's four colleges murdered their Mongolian abbot and rose against the government. Troops were despatched and there was fierce fighting between the monks and the Tibetan army. After a few days the Sera monks finally surrendered. While this was a very localized disturbance, it nevertheless illustrates the unease and turbulence in the capital at that time.[91]

In 1948 the Tibetan government sent four high officials on a world tour encompassing India, China, the Philippines, the USA and Europe. They were away for two years and it was hoped that the world had now become aware that Tibet was a stable, civilized and independent country. Nevertheless, it did not apply to join the United Nations. By early 1950, Heinrich Harrer could sadly muse: 'It was inevitable that Red China would invade Tibet'.[92] In October of that year the Chinese Red Army attacked the eastern frontier in six places simultaneously. (Ford, an

English radio operator working for the Tibetan government in Chamdo, was captured.) Tibet appealed to the United Nations for help, but it was rejected.[93] Once again, in December 1950, the 14th Dalai Lama, a boy of fourteen, fled to the Chumbi valley. After a short stay he returned to Lhasa. The story of the next nine years was one of an increasing Chinese encroachment and infiltration, often met by armed Tibetan resistance. In 1959 the Dalai Lama again fled – this time, it seems, for good. The Chinese, caught up in the fervour of the Cultural Revolution, destroyed most of the Tibetan monasteries, killed many of the monks, intimidated the rest and severely incapacitated Buddhism as a dynamic and living religious tradition in Tibet. Armed Tibetan resistance continued for several years.[94]

Of course, until the 1950s most of this political turmoil was scarcely felt by the majority of the Tibetans, with the exception of those in the eastern regions or those in direct contact with the Mongolians and the inhabitants of Sinkiang province. Nevertheless, until the final invasion of the Chinese communists in 1959 many in the West still imagined Tibet to be unchanged and unchanging, a country frozen in time, impervious to the twentieth century, aloof, mysterious. Only when it was threatened by communism did the West seriously consider the final demise of this idealized Tibet. This, of course, was because communism was also feared in Europe and America. Communism was already mythologized, already the Antichrist, the bearer of the West's unadulterated shadow. Tibet was merely drawn into the mythic drama as the other side of the equation: the 'Most peaceful nation on earth' versus 'this soulless regime'.[95] 'Are the forces of evil', asked de Riencourt, 'going to blow out the faint light which shines on the Roof of the World, perhaps the only light which can guide mankind out of the dark ages of our modern world?'[96]

To understand this extraordinary polarization into the extremes of good and evil, Tibet versus communism, we need to understand a previous polarization: that between Tibet and Western materialism.

Shangri-La: the Geography of Hope and Despair

Paralleling many Westerners' fears about the erosion of Tibet's supposedly unchanging 'Tradition' was an unprecedented disillusionment with their own culture. In his study of British writers who travelled abroad between the wars, Fussell shows that an aversion to Britain was common among them. He reminds us that Freud's *Civilization and its Discontents* was also a product of that era, and that the English translation of Spengler's *Decline of the West* appeared between 1926 and 1928.[97] The First World War administered a profound shock to Westerners' confidence in their own civilization. It was a time of doubt and reflection on a scale almost unknown in pre-war times. For example, Ronaldshay, Earl of Zetland, visited the Buddhist Himalayas between 1918 and 1921. Whilst deeply respectful towards Buddhism he was sceptical of the Tibetan variant, and in particular their obsession with the mantra 'Om Mani Padme Hum'. 'The determination to ensure the repetition to infinity of this amazing formula obsesses the minds of an entire people', he remarked. 'And yet', he mused, 'these hill folk are a happy people, always ready to laugh and joke … a fact which should provide material of interest for the psychologist who would investigate the true source of happiness in the human race.'[98] Other travellers were not merely reflective, but totally dismissive of Western values and aspirations.

Alexandra David-Neel hated the thought of leaving her Himalayan retreat and returning to Europe:

> Sadly, almost with terror, I often looked at the thread-like path which I saw, lower down, winding in the valleys and disappearing between the mountains. The day would come when it would lead me back to the sorrowful world that existed beyond the distant hill ranges, and so thinking, an indescribable suffering lay hold of me'.[99]

A few years later, in 1923, at the age of fifty-four, she set out for Lhasa disguised as a Tibetan beggarwoman on a pilgrimage: 'I delightedly forgot Western lands, that I belonged to them, and that they would probably take me again in the clutches of their sorrowful civilization.'[100]

But this negative feeling about Western civilization was not simply a reaction to the Great War, even though the memory of that conflict lingered on. (Byron and Fleming, for example, both paid tribute to the war with brief, passing references.)[101] Certainly Byron considered the West spiritually empty.[102] As the twentieth century progressed, these negative feelings showed no sign of abating. After the end of World War II, for example, Harrer was gloomy about the situation in Europe: 'We did not miss the appliances of Western civilization. Europe with its life of turmoil seemed far-away. Often as we sat and listened to the radio bringing reports from our country we shook our heads at the depressing news. There seemed no inducement to go home.'[103] Migot, exploring in the south-east corner of Tibet in 1947, was scathing about Christian missionaries. 'It would really make more sense', he argued, 'if India or Tibet sent missionaries to Europe, to try and lift her out of the materialistic rut in which she is bogged down, and to re-awaken the capacity for religious feeling which she lost several centuries ago.'[104]

Throughout this whole period many Western travellers were avidly *searching* for something in Tibet. At first this was confined to personal meaning, to a spiritual quest. Occasionally it was a search for ideas that could help the West find its way again. 'I would discover what ideas,' wrote Byron, 'if those of the West be inadequate, can with greater advantage be found to guide the world.'[105] By the close of the Second World War, the searching had become desperate. The disillusionment was all-embracing. Tibet seemed to offer hope, not just for a personal despair but for the malaise of an entire civilization, and perhaps for the whole world.

James Hilton's *Lost Horizon*, first published in 1933, brilliantly encapsulated and popularized this symbolic drama. Hilton's novel was an outstanding best-seller in Britain and America, and was quickly made into a film. It introduced a new word and landscape into the English language – 'Shangri-La'. The leading character, Conway, was one of the lost generation – burnt out by the First World War, disillusioned by the post-war situation, alienated from his own extroverted, materialistic and spiritually shallow culture. But in a remote Tibetan-type monastery, hidden in the wilderness of the Kuen Lun Mountains that formed the northern boundary of Tibet, he found hope: 'The Dark Ages that are to come will cover the whole world in a single pall; there will be neither escape nor sanctuary save such as are too secret to be found or too humble to be noticed. And Shangri-La may hope to be both of these.'[106] It was imagined that Shangri-La would preserve the wisdom and beauty of civilization and be the faint light to guide the world.

Hilton's 1933 vision of Shangri-La joined Blavatsky's mahatmas and Kipling's lama in *Kim* as one of the great mythologizings about Tibet. It was for this twentieth-century Tibet what the other two were for the *fin-de-siècle* Tibet. It gathered the threads of fantasy, shaped them, articulated them. When Thomas journeyed to Lhasa in 1949, he glibly wrote: 'Once we crossed the Himalayas into Tibet we were indeed travellers in the land of the Lost Horizon. And it often seemed as though we were dreaming – acting the parts of characters in James Hilton's novel, on our way to Shangri-La.'[107] But more important than such direct but bland references to Shangri-La were the deeper disenchantments and aspirations that resonated in sympathy with Hilton's vision.

'[My] dreams of Tibet helped to keep me going through the tragic days of collapse and the dark years of the Occupation.' So wrote the French explorer Migot about the fall of France in 1940. 'In Paris, joyless and crushed under the weight of defeat, the magic name had been for me the glimmer of light glimpsed at the end of a sombre tunnel ... '.[108] De Riencourt similarly began his account in the dark years of World War II. Incarcerated in a Spanish concentration camp he asked: 'Who ... could then doubt that Western civilization was doomed?' He then recounted talking to a fellow-prisoner, a Hindu: 'Suddenly he uttered a magic word which caught my attention – Tibet.' De Riencourt stopped listening and instead floated off into a reverie:

I pictured myself riding up to Tibet on a cloud, escaping altogether from this modern inferno of wars and concentration camps, searching for this forbidden land of mystery, the only place on earth where wisdom and happiness seemed to be a reality.[109]

After the violence of the two world wars came the hostility of the Cold War, backed up by the terror of atomic weapons. Again the Tibetans offered hope: 'Isolated as they are in their mountain kingdom, undisturbed in their monasteries by war, unrest and the turmoil of modern civilization, they must have ample opportunity to reflect on the madness of the rest of the world.'[110] Did the Tibetans have any solutions for the global malaise? asked Thomas of the lamas in 1949. De Riencourt, too, mused: 'Was it possible that Tibet could provide an explanation of Asia's enigma, perhaps even an answer to modern man's problems?'[111]

For many of these travellers it was questionable whether Western civilization had anything whatsoever of value to offer Tibet. The West seemed spiritually bankrupt, its ideas and inventions a hindrance – perhaps even antithetical – to human happiness. In 1931 Leslie Weir, the first Englishwoman in Lhasa, addressed the Royal Asiatic and Royal Central Asian Societies: 'We cannot realize how much we have sacrificed during these late years of scientific advance and of accelerated speed.' The Tibetans, she continued, 'have retained poise, dignity, and spiritual repose. All of these we have lost in our hectic striving towards scientific achievement. Can civilizations based on science alone, advance healthily if divorced from the spiritual side of life?'[112] A few years later, Byron posed a similar question, albeit in a more sophisticated manner:

To a country, moreover, where justice is cruel and secret, disease rife, and independent thought impossible, Western ideas might bring some benefits. But could the benefits outweigh the disadvantages? In the present state of Western civilization, whose spiritual emptiness in relation to Asia is masked by a brutal assumption of moral superiority, it seems to me that they could not. I prefer to hope that the life we saw at Gyantse will endure, and to wish Tibet luck in her isolation, until such time as the West itself is reformed and can commend its ideas with greater reason to those who have hitherto escaped them.[113]

In 1940 Guibaut's ponderings covered similar terrain. 'Will that which is to come be an improvement?' he asked.[114]

At no other time had the West created Tibet in such direct opposition to its own culture. While Tibet had always been imagined as the Other, this Otherness had never before been pictured as a simple opposite, whether for better or worse, of Western values. Oppositional thinking is itself highly symbolic and when treated literally, in terms of exclusive categories, blocks paradox and the deepening of the imagination. It has been suggested that such antithetical thinking is a neurotic habit, high-lighting a feeling of powerlessness or, conversely, a desire for control.[115]

In 1929 David-Neel wrote about her journey into Sikkim, where she encountered the summer resorts established in the mountains by the British: 'A few miles away from the hotels where the Western world enjoys dancing and jazz bands, the primeval forest reigns.'[116] Twenty years later, de Riencourt set up the same kind of opposition. At Gyantse he was wel-comed into the British trade agency, listened to 'a dance music', drank cocktails:

> But I had only to step out ... and, under the moonlight ... the sprawl-ing lamasery with its hundreds of lighted windows, the distant and mysterious sound of trumpets and drums, the intense cold which made me shiver, everything brought me back to reality.[117]

For these travellers primal consciousness alone was real, the rest was dec-adence and frippery.

In 1933 Byron directly counterposed

> Russia and Tibet: Russia, where the moral influence of the Industrial Revolution has found its grim apotheosis; Tibet, the only country on earth where that influence is yet unknown, where even the cart is forbidden to traverse plains flatter than Daytona Beach, and the Dalai Lama himself rides in a man-borne palanquin ... In Russia the tradition has succumbed to the machine. In Tibet it has remained as completely immune from it ... Russia is lower and more colourless, Tibet higher and more coloured, than any country on earth.[118]

In 1949 Harrer was still posing the same dichotomy: 'It is a question whether the Tibetan culture and way of life do not more than balance the advantages of modern techniques. Where in the West is there anything to equal the perfect courtesy of these people?'[119] Tucci wrote that among Tibetan recluses one 'finds in contemplation poise which we are seeking in vain'.[120]

Contradictions became simplified, paradoxes easily resolved, under the sway of oppositional thinking. The gross subservience encouraged by Tibetan feudalism was forgotten as perfect courtesy was singled out and reified. The West came to be represented either by bad manners, junk and destructive technology, or by dance music and cocktails. De Riencourt groaned: 'The telephone! Was there no place on earth where one could be protected from the curse?'[121] He conveniently forgot that the Dalai Lama himself had insisted on introducing the telephone to Lhasa, and that such modern communication was deemed essential for Tibetan self-defence. 'How will these Tibetans react when technical civilization reaches them, as it eventually must? Will they then ever regain that happiness and peace of mind which they will, just as surely, lose?'[122] Sociological, political, historical and psychological complexities simply vanished beneath the deceptively facile opposition of technology versus peace of mind.

Oppositional thinking cannot be simply adopted as an explanation of the imaginative creation and structure of this twentieth-century Tibet, which was not just born out of a disillusionment with Western culture after 1918[123], but was also supported by the century-old tradition of Western imagining about that country. We need to go deeper into the dynamics of this Western fantasy-making.

Outside Time and Space

For Western travellers, Tibet was still a land outside time and space, a 'Lost World', a place 'Out of this World'. Giuseppe Tucci wrote: 'To enter Tibet was not only to find oneself in another world. After crossing the gap in space, one had the impression of having trailed many centuries backward in time.'[124] Guibaut, too, insisted: 'Whilst other countries are being drawn closer together, while time and space are losing the permanent value which they have possessed for thousands of years ... Tibet, far removed in time and knowledge from our now crazy civilizations, has not changed.'[125]

Tibet was still seen as a land of 'limitless horizons', deceptive distances, immense empty spaces.[126] To go there was to leave the twentieth century behind, to enter a pre-scientific world.[127] Confronted by such a place, de Riencourt mused: 'Here is a living past, so alive and powerful in fact, that one doubts if time is anything more than a convenient symbol invented by modern man ... '.[128] Life in Tibet seemed indifferent to time. In the Tsaidam marshes at its northern edge, Fleming humorously recounted meeting 'an itinerant lama from Tibet; he lived in a small blue tent with an alarm clock which was either five hours fast or seven hours slow'.[129] Chapman, accompanying a British diplomatic mission to Lhasa in 1936–7, had close dealings with the Tibetans and constantly referred to their crazy timekeeping.[130] There always seemed to be plenty of time in Tibet – an enviable situation for most Westerners.[131]

But this image of Tibet no longer dovetailed with British or Western imperial mythologizing. True, it still coincided with British strategic thinking about India's northern frontier, but unlike the situation at the turn of the century, this all now seemed marginal to the fantasy-making of travellers. The Tibetans might still be just as 'majestically vague' about geography, just as indifferent to exact timetables, as they had been fifty years earlier, but such things no longer infuriated Western travellers.[132] Although it was occasionally frustrating, this vagueness was now always tolerated, excused and, more often than not, made into a virtue. Not only had imperial mythologizing changed, so too had the struggle over the definition of time and space. Such a struggle was no longer at the leading edge of cultural change in the West.

Tibet's status as a no-man's-land had depended upon the stability of its surrounding geographical and historical conditions. This stability no longer existed – indeed, Tibet was itself considered to be under threat, not just probably but inevitably. If it was to preserve its imaginative place outside time and space, it clearly had to be located somewhere other than in reference to literal physical geography and politics.

Utopias, tourist landscapes, everyday life and psychic realms, in addition to sacred places, all seem to have a timeless disregard for history and politics – at least, that is how they have been consistently imagined and constructed in the West. Tourism, for example, can often create pseudo-places: monuments and experiences frozen in time. Already, in the period between the wars, travellers' contempt for mass tourism was being superseded by a kind of tourist *Angst*, a feeling of being trapped within an unreal façade.[133] The turmoils and terrors of history, with its wars and revolutions, were also precipitating a retreat into the closed, safe, timeless and localized world of everyday life, with its manageable and comfortable routines.[134] The popularity of psychoanalysis, psychic research, surrealism and occultism after 1918 also tended to celebrate a timeless, dematerialized world.[135] As we shall see, each of these imaginative domains provided the fantasies of Tibet, seemingly so similar to those of the nineteenth century, with radically new contexts, but before examining these we need to focus attention on yet another new imaginative context for Tibet: that of a utopia.

Utopias and Sacred Places

In 1936 Marco Pallis was camped on Simvu Mountain in the eastern Himalayas, gazing up at the awesome peak of Siniolchu:

> But there was something else which ... drew our gaze even more than that icy spire. To the left of it, through a distant gap in the mountains, we could just make out lines of rolling purple hills, that seemed to belong to another world, a world of austere calm ... It was a corner of Tibet. My eyes rested on it with an intensity of longing.[136]

In the phenomenology of the imagination, utopias and sacred places are different. Sacred places are entrances to paradox: they embody tension and contradiction; utopias resolve these, eliminate them. At the centre of the sacred place is the *axis mundi*, the axis that connects heaven, earth and the Underworld. In a sacred place light and dark meet; it is a place of fear as well as one of awe and worship. But with a utopia, the darkness is always outside, excluded. Paradox is not suffered, but removed. Sacred places help to orientate the world; they are part of the social fabric. Regular journeys can, and must, be made to and from such places so that bearings can be taken, guidance received and communication occur with the gods. Utopias by contrast are separated from social life by a revolutionary abyss. They are places of hope and aspiration. Whilst sacred places are for temporary visits, utopias are for future dwelling. Sacred places usually help to stabilize the world, and provide sites for worship and prayer. Utopias, on the other hand, while often escapist, may also provide imaginary places where an alternative society can be envisaged; places where visions can be brought to life and experiments tried out; vantage points where criticism can be directed back at established society.[137]

As the twentieth century moved towards its midpoint, Tibet virtually ceased to be a true sacred place and instead was transformed into a Utopia. Of course, this was not achieved without a struggle. In the accounts of travellers such as David-Neel, Byron, Maraini, Chapman and Harrer, attempts were made to sustain paradox and contradiction. Nor was utopianizing the only option. The place of Tibet was also becoming psychologized, normalized, and also prepared for tourist fantasies.

Hilton's novel *Lost Horizon*, first published in 1933, was the quintessence of a Tibetan utopia. It had an essential authenticity about it – not in the sense of being empirically feasible, but of conforming to the reality of contemporary fantasies about Tibet. The established images are clearly recognizable: the air in Shangri-La is as 'clean as from another planet'; the 'thin air had a dream-like texture, matching the porcelain-blue of the sky'; it is a totally separate culture 'without contamination from the outside world', especially from 'dance-bands, cinemas, sky-signs'; there is no telegraph; there is a mystery, which, it is suggested, 'lies at the core of all loveliness'; time means less – indeed, there is time to spare; Shangri-La is built around the principles of moderation and good manners; the mountains surround it like 'a hedge of inaccessible purity'.[138] The valley itself is a fertile paradise in the midst of a wilderness. Even gold in abundance is to be found there.[139] Also the leading protagonist, Conway, bore a close resemblance to the idolized English Everest climber Mallory. Like Conway, Mallory was strikingly good-looking, surrounded by a kind of mythical aura. Indeed, he was frequently referred to as Sir Galahad. Like Conway, Mallory was a man of decisive action, yet also vague and unworldly. Both men had sufficient mystical inclination to satisfy the spiritual longings of the British public, but not so much as to arouse their suspicions. When Mallory died in 1924 making his attempt on the summit of Everest, his death became a symbol of human inspiration, of the struggle of the spirit against matter, of idealism over the mundane.[140]

At a time when even Lhasa was on the telephone and modern dance-music could be heard from the numerous radios in wealthy Lhasan households, Shangri-La was even more remote, even more exemplary, than the Forbidden City itself. The fantasy that had for so long been projected on to Lhasa was too precious to risk being anchored on to something so vulnerable as a real city, especially one whose imaginative purity was under threat – one, indeed, whose time seemed to be inevitably running out. *The myth of Tibet could no longer be trusted to Tibet*, to the geographical place; instead it had to be transferred on to what was truly timeless and formless. That place alone could never be threatened.

The utopia (u-topia, or non-place) of Shangri-La was an ideal fantasy world at a time when geographical mystery had not yet totally vanished from the surface of the earth. Located, if not literally anchored, in geography and history, it stood midway between the Victorian quest for the Holy City and the mid-twentieth-century concern with metaphysical and psychological systems. Tourism, metaphysics and psychology allowed the fantasy of Tibet to continue despite the utter demise of the geographical place itself. Shangri-La, along with the yeti and the Dalai Lama, were the main bearers of the Tibetan fantasy throughout the first half of the twentieth century. Elusive, mobile, mysterious, they offered a more secure foundation than the fixed inertia of geography and historical culture.

Hilton's Shangri-La is appropriately located beneath an unknown peak, the height of which rivals Everest.[141] Such a mountain had to be located in the most inaccessible parts of Tibet now that the well-mapped Himalayas offered no sanctuary to such mysteries – excepting, of course, the ever-elusive yeti. We have already encountered the belief in such an unknown mountain. It was thought that Colonel Pereira had seen a mountain that was perhaps higher than Everest during his 1922 journey in eastern Tibet.[142] His observations were followed up in 1949 by a bizarre expedition led by the ex-Office of Strategic Services officer Leonard Clark.[143] Hilton clearly situated his unknown mountain in the even more remote Kuen Lun Mountains that border the northern wilderness of Tibet.

As in all utopias, essential questions have to be dealt with, paradoxes resolved. So naturally, whilst eschewing telephones and dancebands, Shangri-La had central heating, a well-stocked library, and a music room with a grand piano, as well as being self-sufficient in food. Paradox was overcome by moderation, courtesy and an abundance of time. There was a ready supply of labour from the inhabitants of the valley, leaving the benign theocracy in the monastery on high plenty of time for contemplation. There was no sex discrimination but also it seemed, in that tranquil world, little sex. With ample time, prolonged youthfulness and a true post-scarcity situation, there was little cause for struggle and dissension.[144]

Above all, utopias must offer a vision as well as an escape, a critique of prevailing society as well as an ideal lifestyle. When the ever-restless and emotionally immature Mallinson, insists: 'We want to return to civilization as soon as possible', he is blithely asked: 'And are you so very certain that you are away from it?'[145] The slowness and apparent inefficiency of the East are contrasted favourably with the restless, hasty West, constantly in search of change.[146] The stability and tranquility of Shangri-Las are naturally contrasted with the turmoil outside – wars, revolutions, the collapse or stagnation of the world order.[147] Out of this chaos came the vision: Shangri-La was to be the lifeboat of culture in the coming dark ages. It alone would protect and carry the fragile flame of civilization, the very best and highest of its attainments, until the global destruction was complete and the time for a new dawn was at hand. 'I see, at a great distance,' said the aged head lama, 'a new world stirring in the ruins, stirring clumsily but in hopefulness, seeking its lost and legendary treasures. And they will all be here ... hidden behind the mountains ... preserved as by a miracle for a new Renaissance ... '.[148]

As we saw in the last chapter, Landon had lamented that the success of the 1904 expedition to Lhasa would cause fairy stories to die out for lack of secret geographical places. Hilton's *Lost Horizon* was a last salute to the fairy stories of Landon's era, but also presaged the direction of future Tibetan fantasies. It was a time of transition. In Landon's account, the entombed monks were considered only negatively, as examples of a tragic and misplaced self-sacrifice. Within the cell Landon could imagine only darkness and annihilation. But in *Lost Horizon* there was doubt. Was Shangri-La a prison or a paradise? asked Mallinson. Even Conway, normally so balanced in his blend of action and contemplation, scepticism and mysticism, was unsure.[149] But as the planet seemed to be quickly running out of space, it appeared that time alone offered hope. And within the confines of Shangri-La, 'time expanded' as 'space contracted' – a decisive solution for an age which was witnessing the finale of exploration, the end of unknown, unmapped lands.[150]

Myth without Place

True fantasy-making, or mythologizing in its deepest sense, demands that imagination be grounded in its *prima materia*, its basic, raw material. In the case of alchemy this was, of course, literally *matter*, the elements, substances. If this connection is lost, the result is often disastrous from a depth-psychological standpoint. Jung pointed to such a split in eighteenth-century alchemy:

[M]any alchemists deserted their alembics and melting-pots and devoted themselves entirely to [Hermetic] philosophy. It was then that the chemist and the Hermetic philosopher parted company. Chemistry became natural science, whereas Hermetic philosophy lost the empirical ground from under its feet and aspired to bombastic allegories and inane speculations ... .[151]

We can trace such a split in twentieth-century Tibetan travel writing and its associated fantasies. In the past there had been a certain correspondence between mythologizing and the geographical place of Tibet. The nineteenth-century strictures of science and politics demanded that imaginative exuberance be restrained by empirical facts. As we have seen, such a struggle between so-called fact and fantasy, or between the details of the outer world and those of experience, had characterized the Western creation of Tibet since the end of the eighteenth century. It was this close attention to empirical detail that distinguished the Tibet of modern times from the fabled place of medieval legend. We have also seen that fantasies of Tibet were not somehow built on to geographical 'facts' but were integral to them, arose from them. Travellers did not look first at the country and then drift off into reverie. The reverie, the fantasy, was an integral part of the looking.

In the twentieth century, this unity of geographical place and fantasy-making began to undergo a profound change. While the landscape and culture of Tibet were still described as 'astonishing', 'medieval', and so on, one can sense that unlike earlier accounts, these were less spontaneous or genuine responses, and more conditioned expectations often verging on clichés. Landscape and culture seemed to have lost their mystery and fascination; instead they became increasingly constricted into a well-prepared, sometimes slick, imaginative framework. The 'Promised Land', 'Eldorado', 'Shangri-La', began to sound banal. Thomas called Tibet 'the goal of goals', the 'Number one Eldorado for explorers and travellers with a keen appetite for the unknown'.[152]

It all sounded rather hollow. Too often in these accounts we trip over words such as 'fabulous' and 'fascinating'. Lowell Thomas Jnr exclaimed: 'we were indeed in mysterious Tibet'. Later he saw 'a drama almost as old as Tibet itself ...'.[153] Even Byron succumbed, and it has been noted that words like 'strange', 'uncanny', 'outlandish', 'astonishing' and 'unnatural' occur far more in his book on Tibet than in any of his other travel accounts.[154] But he studiously avoided such trite comments as 'Yes, the very atmosphere of the land is permeated with religion'.[155] Some texts read like cheap travelogues:

... the few unpleasant aspects of Tibet's capital are more than offset by its fascinating people in their attractive costumes, the hospitality, the gaiety and strangeness of it all, and the pageantry, which has come down in Tibet like a tapestry brought vividly to life from the Middle Ages.[156]

Sixteen years earlier, the novice English explorer Ronald Kaulback had written an account of his difficult trek into south-eastern Tibet, but, like Thomas's, it is full of weak affectations, tourist clichés and breezy banalities. Often it reads like a ripping yarn. Precarious rope bridges 'are great fun to cross' and Kaulback devoted a whole page to describing his fairground-like crossing. This is situated in a chapter boldly headed 'The Promised Land'. In fact his entry into Tibet occupies only a couple of unenthusiastic sentences. 'The Promised Land' was an empty, stereotypical formula. He was genuinely more excited about crossing the rope bridge than about entering Tibet. One was real, the other was an abstraction: one was spontaneous, the other premeditated.[157]

Imagination and geographical place were also being separated by more sophisticated means than mere travel rhetoric. David-Neel, for example, was generally dismissive of the importance of landscape, culture and politics.[158] She was vague about dates and geography, being more concerned with other realities: '... my researches had led me face to face with a world still more amazing than the landscapes I had beheld from the high passes through which one enters Thibet. I refer to the mystic anchorites ... '.[159] For her, the quintessence of Tibet lay in its mystic doctrines and stories, where 'the very soul of Tibet reveals itself in all its mystic powerful originality, a thirst for occult knowledge and spiritual life'.[160]

Marco Pallis echoed similar sentiments: 'At the outset of my story, I tried to climb peaks in a bodily sense; but in the end I discovered the Lama, who beckoned me towards immaterial heights.'[161] Such immaterial heights were, of course, safe from tourists and even, perhaps, from the changes being wrought in traditional Tibetan culture:

Indeed, this world of the Tibetan mystics is a mystery in the mystery of Thibet, a strange wonder in a wonderland country. Very possibly Thibet will soon cease to be forbidden ground, but one may doubt if the secret of its *Tsam Khang* and *riteus*, the aims of their dwellers and the results they achieve, will ever be disclosed to the many.[162]

The Tibetans' notorious geographical and historical vagueness became a virtue from this perspective. De Riencourt wrote:

The fact that in their everyday life the Tibetans ... have a far less precise notion of time or space than ... Westerners partly explains the greater ease with which they explore psychic phenomena and move round mentally in a universe which is precisely devoid of time or space. Thus, by a different road, the Tibetans have reached some of the metaphysical conclusions which modern science is now discovering.

Another commentator insisted that 'Tibet is more than a land, it is a religion'.[163] With such sentiments the devaluation of geographical place is complete.

David-Neel was cultivatedly unenthusiastic about reaching Lhasa: 'unlike most travellers who have attempted to reach Lhasa and' – she added, somewhat smugly –

> have failed to reach their goal, I never entertained a strong desire to visit the sacred lamaist city. I had … [already] met the Dalai Lama, and as for researches regarding the literature, philosophy, and secret lore of Thibet, those things could be pursued more profitably amongst the *literati* and mystics in the freely accessible and more intellectual parts of the north-eastern Thibet, than in the capital.[164]

David-Neel, with her mixture of elitism and daring, completely loses the sense of Tibet as a sacred place with Lhasa at its centre. As if to make her point further, she deliberately set out to be a tourist in Lhasa. This was surely the most arrogant rejection of the whole structure of Tibet as a sacred place.[165] The geographical basis of place was almost irrelevant for her. Mystic reverie became detached from landscape and slid loosely across geographical particularities: 'From the low valleys buried under the exuberant jungle to the mountain summits covered with eternal snow, the whole country is bathed in occult influence.'[166] Every incident – a dust storm, an old hat found by the roadside – became symbolic and was orientated around her mystical experiences.[167] Whilst of course *occasionally* reacting with spontaneous delight to landscape, all too often she resorted to well-worn clichés: '… is not everything a fairy tale in this extraordinary country?'; 'Were we in Thibet or had we reached fairyland?'; 'I had wandered for years in my fairyland'.[168]

The opposite of such imaginative indifference to the particularities of place was a kind of studied and excessive realism. In Chapman's 1936/7 account, for example, we are provided with endless lists of things without any real comment, as if detailed description can replace imaginative interpretation. The following brief passage is typical:

> We had tea in the private chapel, which is the largest and finest room of the house. Hinged casement windows, with a long window-seat below, take up one wall. Opposite are several half-life-sized golden images in ornate glass cases. The images wear golden diadems studded with precious gems, and round their necks are amber necklaces with stones as large as tangerines. On an altar in

front are displayed holy-water vessels, cloisonné lions, a pair of priceless porcelain vases in a glass case, several silver teapots and jugs, and a gold reliquary. At the end of the altar is an ormolu clock and a large terrestrial globe. Another wall displays a line of magnificent thankas framed in purple and gold brocade. Beneath a gay canopy is the throne of the master of the house padded with silken cushions heavily embroidered with dragons and flowers. At the top of two of the pillars supporting the roof are large diamond-shaped scarlet boards bearing Chinese characters in black ...[169]

When Chapman leaves the aridity of these endless lists, he quickly succumbs to tourist rhetoric about gay, spectacular pageants, or delightful, charming and colourful people.[170] His descriptions of landscape become banal and affected: Drepung monastery lit up at night is described as an 'island of a million twinkling lights in the surrounding blackness of the hills, it had an unearthly aspect, like some fairy city floating in the frosty night'.[171] Never before had Tibetan travel writing resorted so much to the epithet of 'fairy': 'unsubstantial it seems, like some fairy castle conjured up by a magician ... '.[172]

It is salutary to compare Chapman's lack of response to such specific features as Atisha's grave, or to the Yam-dok-tso lake, with the sensitive enthusiasm of Landon thirty years earlier.[173] As if in total contradiction to David-Neel, Chapman could think only of the most mundane questions about Tibetan religious life. When visiting Drepung, the largest monastery in the world, he mused: 'I hoped to find some answer to the questions that had continually occurred to me since entering Tibet: "How on earth do all these thousands of monks spend their time? ... ".'[174] It was surely no coincidence that most of the travellers who were responsive to the apparent realism of everyday life in Tibet were indifferent, if not hostile, to Tibetan monasticism and its mysteries.[175]

Mundane realism, tourist rhetoric and psychic preoccupations all resulted in a decisive split between fantasy and geographical *place*. 'Mysterious Tibet' became a floating signifier. Tibetan stories were thought 'fantastic', believed to be true, and then presented as if placeless and timeless.[176] Ethnographic details became vague. Without a context, they seem nonsensical. Kaulback, for example, suddenly tells us that smoking is not allowed in Lhasa, 'for the fumes irritate the Spirits of the Air, who might easily retaliate by bringing a pestilence on the land'.[177] All one can do is think, how quaint! and add it to our list of meaningless superstitions to be found in the East. Kaulback carelessly interprets both the Tibetan 'Wheel of Life' and the mantra 'Om Mani Padme Hum', despite more than a century of Western scholarship and understanding.[178] It scarcely mattered; for him the whole place was unreal anyway.

Byron put his finger on it when he wrote that in Tibet, 'observation consists in the assimilation of pure novelty'.[179] Instead of the Tibetan land-scape being a living symbol, it frequently became a premeditated and con-structed sign. Nowhere is this process more apparent than with regard to mountains and altitude. The action of climbing mountains began to groan under the weight of spiritual metaphors. Everest became the symbol of the loftiest heights of human imagination, whilst it was imagined that the quest for the summit was animated by an invincible spirit.[180] Such artifice became ridiculous when altitude was emphasized and the metaphor of the 'Roof of the World' was taken literally. Tibet then became a 'colossal natural fortress standing in the heart of Asia … Behind the Cyclopean Himalayas and Kuen Lun mountain ranges, Tibet towers on all sides above the three most populated countries in the world.'[181]

Altitude here becomes directly equated with dominance and impregna-bility: 'Nestled in the stratospheric and hardly-known valleys of the Roof of the World, as inexpugnable as if they were situated on the planet Mars, Communist armies and airforce could forcibly dominate the largest part of Asia.'[182] Thomas insisted that Tibet would be 'an ideal jumping-off spot' for the communist armies, especially as everywhere else would be 'mostly downhill'.[183] These absurdly literal fantasies were appropriately taken up in a 1950s children's book in which Hitler escaped from Germany to Tibet with a band of SS troops and set up a battery of missiles armed with atomic warheads. From these unassailable heights he could literally *rain* terror on to the rest of the world down below.[184] In these accounts we have clearly lost all contact with the actualities of geographical place and entered a naive dream world. Myth has concretized into fact. Like eighteenth-century alchemy, mythologizing has lost connection with its *prima materia*. But this naive imaginative relationship was not confined to these outlandish extremes. Whilst in de Riencourt's account upwards and towering suggested a literal *strategic* advantage, in many others this dis-tinctive geographical feature of Tibet implied instead a *spiritual* superior-ity. As we have seen, such a mythic formula was apparent in earlier accounts, but in the first half of the twentieth century it began to be treated unreflectively, as if it were a fact. Guibaut, for example, exclaimed: 'Where better than here, on these high tablelands towering to the skies, can one recapture the terrors of the early ages of mankind?' He continued: 'man … in such unsheltered conditions … can only resort to prayer.' The hermits of these regions,

far removed from the plains where swarm the ant-heaps of human-ity, cannot be like other men who breathe the heavier air of the lowlands! Nowhere but here, in this atmosphere, could the lofty conception of Buddha unite with the dark, primitive rites of ancient Shamanism, to culminate in the monstrosity of Lamaism.[185]

Elsewhere he wrote about Buddhism: 'That proud, lofty religion and the meditations of its monks are certainly well served by the majesty and cold grandeur of these surroundings.'[186]

Despite his enthusiasm, Guibaut was more ambivalent than many. David-Neel, for example, wrote: 'In such scenery it is fitting that sorcery should hold sway.'[187] Similarly, de Riencourt reflected:

> The awe-inspiring landscape of Tibet, the severity of the climate and remoteness of its valleys, the majestic silence and solemn peace in which the Roof of the World is bathed, were certainly responsible for the existence of a psychic knowledge ...[188]

In 1951 the famous Buddhist scholar Christmas Humphreys wrote:

> The physical conditions of Tibet lend themselves to religious thinking. The great spaces, the height of the mountain ranges which surround them, the rarefied air in a land which is largely over 16,000 feet, these and the silence where men are scarce and wild life is rarer still, all lend themselves to introverted thought ... [189]

Another example comes from Sir Charles Bell, the influential commentator on Tibet in the early years of this century, who was a close friend of the 13th Dalai Lama. He wrote:

> Buddhism, of the type that has been formed in Tibet and Mongolia, flourishes characteristically in their great expanses ... The dry, cold pure air stimulates the intellect but isolation .. deprives the Tibetan of subjects on which to feed his brain. So his mind turns inwards and spends itself on religious contemplation, helped still further by the monotony of the life and the awe-inspiring scale on which Nature works.[190]

We find a specific fantasy of religious experience arising from these geographical imaginings: religion as an introverted, solitary and rarefied activity. Indeed, one commentator insisted that 'Tibet is a land so close to the sky that the natural inclination of her people is to pray.'[191] These beautiful images should not blind us to the relationship between religion and landscape which is being expressed. At first it seems such an obvious connection as to be somehow an empirical fact, but this is not so: it is part of the play of the imagination. To associate prayer, altitude and sky in such a way reveals much about the image of sacred places in the Judaeo-Christian tradition and in the imaginative milieu of the West in the twentieth century.

The loss of connection between creative, disciplined imagination and the particulars of geographical place seemed to polarize Tibetan travel accounts. On the one side were those which grounded themselves in the mundane world of everyday life; on the other were those for which psychic reality and occult systems provided the main focus. Both types of account claimed to be showing the real, the quintessential, Tibet, but in both the sense of sacred place and landscape drifted backstage, and was often completely lost. The way was then left clear for the ungrounded fantasies of utopianism and tourism, both of which are completely disengaged from the paradoxical actuality of place, from the direct experience of sacred landscape.

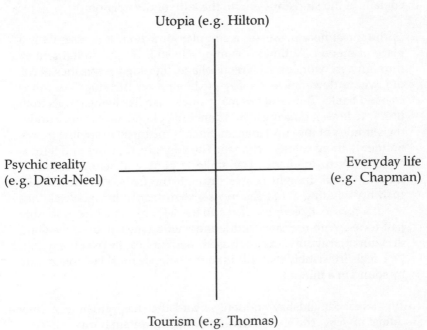

Utopia (e.g. Hilton)

Psychic reality
(e.g. David-Neel)

Everyday life
(e.g. Chapman)

Tourism (e.g. Thomas)

Of course, no travel account can be reduced in its entirety to a single option – there are many moments, for example, when David-Neel's leaves the psychic world but ultimately that is the reality in which her accounts of Tibet are grounded.

Ruskin's mid-nineteenth-century struggle to connect disciplined imagination with detailed empirical observation was discussed in chapter 4. In the *fin-de-siècle* accounts of Freshfield, Landon, Grenard and others, such a finely tuned balance had reached its fullest developments. The twentieth century, too, had its representatives of this art: Ronaldshay from England and Tucci from Italy both continued the tradition, blending careful observation with creative imagination.[192] Neither traveller lost the geographical sense of sacred place, although perhaps Tucci veered more towards psychic reality and Ronaldshay more towards everyday life.

Tucci, one of the great Italian Tibetologists, made several journeys into Tibet in the 1930s and then immediately after the war. 'I felt ensnared in the charm of a country', he wrote, 'where of the outside world there was but a sweetly blurred recollection left, and life was stripped back to its essential meaning of impersonal communication with the cosmic rhythm.'[193] Crossing over the Himalays into Tibet, he exclaimed: 'we are gripped by the ineffable fascination of this land in which the life of the spirit seems almost more intense and profound'.[194] Some thirteen years earlier, in 1920, the Earl of Ronaldshay was particularly sensitive both to the details of the landscape and to the faith of the religion:

> ... the forest here possesses a singular attraction. It is essentially a place of moods. At times it is intensely still. Bright sunlight filters through a fretwork of rich green foliage, lighting up splashes of colour where flowers grow softly cushioned on the slopes of moss-covered banks. Butterflies of many hues flash like living jewels from flower to flower, dancing a mad dance of ephemeral existence under the stimulus of the sun-laden air. Such is the forest in smiling mood. Suddenly there comes a change. The sunlight vanishes and light is swallowed up in shade. The smile is gone and nature seems to frown. A chill draught passes through the trees. Wreaths of mist rush by, winding about the moss-grown trunks like grave-clothes about a corpse. Colour has fled and has left only a picture in sombre half-tones. With the same suddenness with which it arose the wind dies down, leaving a solemn hush brooding heavily over the world. One feels irresistibly that this immense silence must be broken only by sound in a minor key.

In this forest Ronaldshay suddenly heard the deep groan of a Tibetan Buddhist *ra-dong*, the six-to-eight-foot-long mountain horn:

> ... a curious sound which is certainly not musical in the ordinarily accepted meaning of that word, but which is equally certainly harmonious in that it blends so perfectly with the *mise-en-scène*. When listening to it I have realized its relationship to nature. It is the sound which would be produced by the hum of myriads of bees swarming through the forest.

Not only was Ronaldshay sensitive to the many moods of landscape and to the empirical details that created these moods, he was also aware of the crucial role of interpretation:

> It is easy to understand that such works of Nature impel man to wor-

ship. Vast, silent, immovable, they stand for permanence in a world of flux. To the animist they are the embodiment of inexorable power, to the pantheist the incarnation of the sublime. Before we left the pass we were to see them undergo a dramatic transfiguration. From a glorious incarnation of the sublime they became a fierce embodiment of wrath. For up the draughty channel of the Talung valley angry clouds came eddying, transforming the expression of serene repose on the face of the great white world to an angry scowl.[195]

Nothing is fixed; landscape imagination is not frozen.

But it was Maraini's account in particular that seemed to offer a new solution to the dilemma. With a mixture of gentle humour, a concern for details, warm empathy, quiet disrespect and daring imagination, he managed to draw together the human, the geographical and the occult worlds:

How shall one describe the strange excitement induced by the luxuriant vegetation, the monstrous tree-trunks covered with dripping lichen, the caress on one's hand of these huge, string leaves, the feel of the bark, the intoxication of the smells and perfumes? At the same time, how express the revulsion provoked by so much teeming, gliding, creeping, turgid vitality?[196]

He rejected any explanation that deposited a simple correlation between a country's landscape and its inhabitants' character, philosophy, art, religion, or physical appearance. 'The argument', he insisted, 'is perfect, too perfect.'[197] Alongside a deep understanding and sensitivity towards the religion, he maintained a delightful irreverence which protected his account from leaden metaphysics. So he playfully called the famed *Tibetan Book of the Dead* 'a *Baedeker* of the world beyond'; a high, reincarnate lama becomes 'an ambassador of the absolute ... one's own personal representative in the adamantine halls of the cosmos ... '.[198]

When Maraini alighted on the well-worn theme of Tibetan dirt, he neither defended it nor criticized it; instead he poetically acknowledged it: 'The dirt is ancient, stupendous and three-dimensional'.[199] For him, the essence of Tibet lay in its butter, bones and silence. An essay on *chortens*, the Buddhist monuments so typical of Tibet, encapsulates much about his style and reveals his solution to the tension between imagination and observation, between the occult and the mundane, between meaning and landscape. *Chortens* are to the Tibetan landscape what large crucifixes are to Alpine valleys: 'Small and insignificant though they may be in the face of the grandiose nature which surrounds them, they suffice to give form and atmosphere to a whole landscape.' Maraini conveys both the cosmic symbolism of the *chorten* and its place in the sacred landscape of Tibet: 'An old, wind-worn *chorten*, rising against the endless background of ochre,

yellow and red mountains fading away into the blue distances and spark-
ling with snow, is a thing of pure poetry.'[200] In his account, myth-making
and geographical place are inextricably intertwined – indeed, celebrate
each other.

In Search of the Real Tibet

We must return to the humour that entered Tibetan travel accounts at the
beginning of the twentieth century, especially in the works of Maraini,
Fleming and, of course, Byron. This was discussed at the beginning of this
chapter in terms of its de-literalizing power, as an expression of a conscious and playful creation of Tibet. At an aristocratic gathering, Maraini,
in a dinner suit, comments: 'Among all this splendour and delight for the
eye we Europeans looked like penguins.'[201] Byron took this self-
objectification further. On passing through an old monastery, he reports:
'A nondescript crowd gathered on the roof and laughed at us as we rode
by.'[202] The famed Tibetan laughter was no longer a passive background to
delight tourists and travellers; it now came direct from the stage and questioned the audience's role. There was an absurdity about Western travellers in Tibet. Why were they there? Despite David-Neel's protestations
that one should be free to travel anywhere, the old nineteenth-century
imperialistic context was no longer self-evident. Europeans no longer 'belonged' in Central Asia, nor in India, let alone in Tibet, in the same way as
they once had. This humour gives the local inhabitants power, as well as
simultaneously questioning the role of the traveller. On the northern frontier, Fleming remarked how he and Maillart were 'treated … as an obscure
kind of joke … '.[203] Western travellers were beginning to feel out of place
as the old global definitions crumbled.

Unless they were able to laugh at themselves and play with absurdity,
Western travellers had to create new contexts to validate their journeys
into places such as Tibet. If they were out of place as Westerners, objec-
tified, had their roles questioned, then the surest solution was somehow
to *belong* to Tibet. The first half of the twentieth century witnessed an
unprecedented number of travel accounts claiming to have been written
from *inside* Tibetan life; to give the *true* picture.

Migot insisted: '… if in Tibet you do not behave like a tourist in a
museum, if you make an effort to get *inside* the life of the place instead of
only being a spectator, you cannot help undergoing a profound and
unforgettable experience.'[204] He continued:

I had done my utmost, ever since entering Tibet, not to play the
tourist, not to treat Lamaism as so much exotic camera-fodder, not to
study a great religion as an ethnologist might study a quaint tribal

custom. I wanted to immerse myself, as far as a European could, in something which dominates the life of Tibet.[205]

David-Neel, de Riencourt, Harrer, Pallis, Patterson, McGovern and many others all presented their accounts as if from the 'inside': they all insisted that somehow they belonged.[206] Harrer, who had lived in Tibet for many years, had some justification for his claim: 'We were no longer outsiders. We belonged'.[207]

Waddell, the famous British Tibetologist writing around the turn of the century, casually remarked, almost in passing, that some lamas thought he was an incarnation of Amitabha, the Buddha of the Western direction.[208] For him this was merely a convenient fiction that allowed him access to intimate details of Tibetan ritual; certainly he did not use it as a part of his identity. Tibetans, like people from other traditional cultures, use such a device in order to incorporate foreign friends and acquaintances into their social life. Australian Aboriginals and Greek villagers, for example, use honorary kinship designations, whereas the Tibetans use a religious framework. These procedures neutralize alien and potentially disruptive influences; they sustain the coherence of their social world; make sense of and incorporate any intrusions. But as the twentieth century progressed, this polite fiction was used by Westerners, alienated from their own culture, partially to transfer their identity to another.

While many previous Westen travellers had been told they must have been Tibetans in a past life, now such assertions were much sought after. Westerners seemed to want to believe literally in such an apparent acceptance, with its associated sense of belonging. David-Neel, for example, claimed: 'I am one of the Genghis Khan race who, by mistake and perhaps for her sins, was born in the Occident. So I was told by a lama.'[209] Marco Pallis similarly wrote:

> I felt as if I had escaped from an invisible barrier ... I have felt at ease among Tibetans of all ranks as I have not often done elsewhere. I never felt that I was among strangers; rather it was a return to a long lost home. A lama, with whom I was intimate, explained this quite simply by saying that it was no accident, but that I showed unmistakable signs of having been a Tibetan myself in a previous existence ... [210]

Pallis was clearly seduced by this idea.

Paradoxically, whereas such beliefs served to sustain the coherence of Tibetan culture, they were part of a rejection by Westerners of their own milieu. Maraini was critical of what he called a disloyalty to the West.[211] He was intolerant of placeless Westerners, exiled from their cultural roots, searching for a place to which they could belong. For him it was just too easy to reject the dark complexities of one's own culture whilst yearning to be reborn elsewhere.

Each of these travellers, delighting in the intimacy of their contact with Tibetan culture, became convinced of the veracity of their account. Each seemed sure that they alone had contacted the *real* Tibet. De Riencourt, for example, wrote:

> The real Tibet I was searching for was not out in the open. It was not in the magnificent temples and palaces, in the colourful bazaars, in the happy and carefree life of its farmers or in the entrancing charm of Lhasa's social life ... Real Tibet transcends politics and economics; it is invisible, beyond sense perception, beyond intellect. It is the mysterious land of the psyche, of what lies beyond death ... [212]

David-Neel, too, wrote of lifting 'the veil that hides the real Tibet'.[213]

For others, on the contrary, the *real* Tibet did indeed lie in its everyday life rather than in its occult mysteries, and this mundane life was not always pleasant. The ruggedly individualistic and unorthodox Christian missionary George Patterson found his work as a doctor almost overwhelming amid the appalling sickness in the country. For him this was the real Tibet, 'while ten thousand miles away in comfortable chairs beside comfortable fires men and women read of the illusory stupidities of an impossible Shangri-La ... '.[214] Others looked to the landscape. 'Then, after a long slow climb', wrote Ruttledge, leader of the British 1933 Everest expedition, 'we emerged with startling suddenness among the rolling downs of the real Tibet, and were struggling against the blast of the west wind.'[215]

Before the twentieth century there was never any debate about the *real* Tibet. If a traveller's account was authentic, then of course it showed a part of real Tibet. What was *unreal* Tibet? Whilst this doubt reveals a greater sophistication and awareness about the creation of places, it simultaneously betrays an anxiety among these travellers.

Paradox Lost

When Chapman visited Lhasa in 1936 with a British political mission, he took with him extensive cinematographic equipment. The British held frequent cinema parties for the Tibetans at Lhasa – from family gatherings to children's parties, from the Regent to monks. One of the parties was even gatecrashed by a large group of 'boisterous monks' who then had to be forcibly ejected. Their turn to see the films would come later. Easily the favourite film was *The Night Cry*, a Rin-Tin-Tin adventure. Chapman became 'most heartily sick of it' as he showed it again and again whilst the Tibetan audience gasped, cried and shouted encouragement. After Rin-Tin-Tin, Charlie Chaplin movies were the next favourite – *Easy Street, The Waiter, Shanghaied, One O'clock in the Morning, The Crook*. The Tibetans also liked films that Chapman himself had made around Lhasa, especially crowd scenes or Tibetan celebrities. Shows regularly lasted well over four hours, and usually included the Grand National and the Jubilee Procession of King George V.[216] Clearly, at a time when the West was also studying detailed 'inside' accounts of sublime occult rituals, the paradoxes and contradictions of Tibet seemed to be increasing as the century progressed. Yet despite being continually confronted by such extremes, Western travellers continually appeared to want to deny them, to resolve them simplistically.

As confidence in Tibet's future was eroded, the general attitude towards its culture lost its ambivalence. Generalizations about the people abounded. In travel texts there was a surfeit of happy, laughing, serene Tibetans. Pallis called Tibetans 'some of the happiest people on the face of the earth'.[217] De Riencourt wrote of 'merry mule men'; 'cheerful muleteers singing gay songs'; towns 'full of merry people'; 'thousands of gay Tibetans'.[218] Harrer called the Tibetans 'a happy little people full of childish humour'.[219] They were described as essentially courteous and refined; as always polite; as not lying; as having a natural good taste in art; as having only good sense and originality.[220] The Tibetan government also ceased to cast any shadow, and indeed became almost exemplary. Pallis called the nation 'one of the earth's most civilized peoples'.[221] Chapman commented that the government, although corrupt, was efficient.[222] Migot wrote: 'Tibet, where social harmony prevails ... deserves to rank as one of the best-governed countries in the world.'[223] De Riencourt thanked 'the government and people of Tibet, whose hospitality and wisdom are unmatched anywhere else on this earth'.[224]

What an extraordinary turnround from nineteenth-century attitudes towards Tibet! Not only had ambivalence vanished, it had been replaced by unequivocal superlatives. One almost longs for the infamous bandits to come galloping over the horizon – indeed, they still constantly appeared in travel accounts. Guibaut's companion Liotard was killed by Tibetan bandits.[225] Harrer, too, encountered Tibetan robbers:

> Savage punishment is meted out to the evildoers, who normally have their arms hacked off. But this does not cure the Khampas of their lawlessness. Stories were told of the cruelty with which they sometimes put their victims to death. They go so far as to slaughter pilgrims and wandering monks and nuns.[226]

Clark gave vivid descriptions of the bloody fighting in lawless eastern

Tibet. The Tibetans were considered 'the smartest and most dangerous of all Asiatic soldiery including the Japanese'.[227] Robbery seemed endemic to most of Tibet outside the Lhasa region, and lawlessness was the general rule.Guibaut complained that one could not tell the difference between honest people and bandits;[228] Fleming commented on the 'warlike', 'formidable' Tibetans as compared with the 'milder' Mongols.[229] Yet these outrages were ignored, considered atypical, or excused as a kind of over-exuberance. David-Neel, for example, commented patronizingly: 'Thibetans are simple men. Brigandage is for them merely an adventurous sport, in which they do not discover anything fundamentally wicked so long as it does not cause death.'[230]

Travellers went through bizarre contortions to smooth out any paradox or shadow in the Tibetan character. David-Neel wrote: 'insecurity prevails to a large extent in the fairyland of Thibet; but ... though I have had a few disquieting meetings, I have never suffered any loss.' She smugly puts her good fortune down to the right attitude: 'I believe that there exists a mental attitude capable of shaping circumstances more or less according to one's wishes.'[231] Later she met a group who had defended themselves with swords against robbers. 'Encounters with brigands are common enough in Thibet,' she wrote, 'and fail to impress travellers deeply, unless they are extraordinarily bloody.'[232] Even further along her route to Lhasa she came across a group of pilgrims, mostly women, who had been robbed: 'One of them had a gash in her head; another had a terrible wound in the breast; the arm of a third was broken; others were more or less injured.' This happened less than a hundred miles from Lhasa, and on a main highway. It was, she wrote resignedly, 'a common occurence in that lawless country'.[233] One can only wonder how David-Neel squared such incidents with her early patronizing dismissal of Tibetan robbers. It was as if Westerners simply refused to take such things into account.

Intrigue at Lhasa was rife in this period; punishments were harsh; discipline in monasteries could be ferocious. Pallis commented on the tolerance, the open-mindedness of Tibetan religion, and painted an idyllic picture of the life of novice monks; yet further on in his account he wrote about severe beatings given by tutors to their pupils.[234] One young monk even complained to him: 'Tibetan teachers are dirty swine'. Inattention at monastic services would regularly be punished with a beating from the special disciplinary monks who patrolled the congregation.[235] None of this seemed to make the slightest difference to Westerners' one-eyed determination to reify Tibet and its culture. From Pallis to Migot, we are assured that 'there is no rivalry between the various sects of lamas', although a few sentences later Pallis has to admit that occasionally skulls are split and blood is spilt.[236] There was indeed continual monastic intrigue in Lhasa – perhaps not over theology but, ironically, over politics.

Some sense of paradox understandably had to emerge in these travel

accounts. The weight of evidence was simply too great for all trace of contradiction to be erased. David-Neel, from a position of experience and
arrogance, could write that not all lamas were wise. She considered those
of Sikkim to be particularly illiterate and slack. Many lamas in Tibet were
simpletons. Many 'merely vegetate in the monasteries'. She also acknowledged a 'dark side of Tibetan occultism'.[237] But such negative evaluations
were rare, and few travellers were as bold as Maraini: 'Tibet, the land of
exaltation, beauty and horror, the land of open sky and stony wastes ... ,
of lofty peaks ... and of places where dead bodies are hacked to pieces to
provide meals for the vultures; land of simplicity and cruelty, of purity
and orgy'.[238] Whilst most were searching for an unequivocal Tibet,
Maraini was delighting in its contradictions. He wrote of Tibetans as a
people 'who pass with ease from the rigours of asceticism to hearty enjoy-
ment of life, who laugh, play, fight, drink, make love, kill, repent, believe
in miracles and are, in short, full of an inexhaustible vitality'.[239] True,
there was still something larger than life about Maraini's Tibetans, but his
playful humour resisted any temptation to make them superhuman.

Attitude to Tibetan religion was crucial in determining Westerners' overall attitude to Tibet. This was a complete reversal of nineteenth-century
perceptions, in which landscape played such a determining role, providing almost the foundation for any other fantasies. Now, hovering behind
any description of Tibet, was an *expectation* of occult mysteries and power.
As David-Neel wrote, 'the fame which Tibet enjoys in foreign countries is
largely due to the belief that prodigies happen there as plentifully as wild
flowers grow in the fields.' She described 'the fascination exercised by
Tibet as an abode of sages and magicians ... '.[240] Fleming, on first entering
Tibet from China, visited the famous Kambum monastery: 'Several lamas
in dark robes, whose shy, cheerful, earthy faces hardly suggested the tre-
mendous mysteries commonly associated with their calling, came wandering out of various doors and gave us a giggling welcome.'[241]

Was Tibet really a storehouse of spiritual wisdom, the home of occult
mysteries barely dreamt of in the West, or was it all a sham, the naive pre-
tence of a superstitious and credulous people? Everything hinged on this
question. Even the most sceptical were unable to dismiss completely the
possibility that the psychic claims of Tibetan Buddhism were true. Chapman, for example, genuinely disliked the religion. 'I wish I could like
these hostile inscrutable monks,' he wrote, 'but I cannot see what good
they do either to themselves or anybody else.' He described monks as
insolent, sullen, malevolent and parasitic, and found the temples 'repel-
lent and sinister.' For him lamaism was – echoing nineteenth-century
evaluations – a mixture of 'the debased Tantric doctrine that had replaced
the original pure teaching of the Buddha' and the 'pure devil-worship' of
Bon religion.[242] Yet when he discussed levitation, telepathy and other
psychic feats, he paused:

233

To what extent these mysterious powers are really possessed by Tibetans I would hesitate to assert. The power of mind over body is
being more and more demonstrated by the study of *Yogi* ... It must
be borne in mind that to become possessed of these supernatural
powers a course of study lasting for many years is necessary, and
then it is not all who can succeed, even when taught by eastern asce-
tics, who maintain an age-long tradition of psychic research and
experience.[243]

Clearly, when Chapman removed these psychic feats from religion and
imagined them instead within a scientific context they seemed more
plausible.

The period between the wars was one of an intense interest in psychic
research. Whereas Westerners in the nineteenth century were impressed
with Tibetan faith and the archaic originality of the religion, those in the
twentieth century were more drawn to the spiritual masters, to the
esoteric science, its techniques and training. Claims made by Blavatsky
about mahatmas in the Himalayas had evolved a hundred years later into
the kitsch absurdities and occult extravaganzas of Lobsang Rampa.[244]

Late in the nineteenth century, Blavatsky had dismissed the belief that
psychic feats were miracles and insisted instead that they were scientific.
David-Neel was of a similar opinion: 'Tibetans do not recognize any supernatural agent. The so-called wonders, they think, are as natural as common daily events and depend on the clever handling of little-known laws
and forces.'[245] She studied Tibetan religion *as a science*. De Riencourt
quickly became a convert into the occult and insisted upon the scientificity
of Tibetan esotericism. Indeed, he not only claimed that Tibet was far
more advanced in psychic research and practice than the West, but that
the West was only just confirming, through its science, what Tibetans had
known for centuries. While agreeing with Jung that the east is inside all of
us, de Riencourt commented: '... he overlooks the fact that it is only in a
Tibetan monastery that Western man can find the one thing which cannot
be replaced: *thabs*, the Tibetan method, the technique and the example.'[246] Maraini, as alert as ever to the prevailing fantasies about Tibet,
once again brought playful disrespect to the rescue and created imaginative space within the leaden density of systematic occultism. The Tibetans, he wrote, 'study death with the simplicity and detachment of an
industrialist studying a phase of production'.[247] Such de-literalizing was
essential at a time when many Westerners seemed desperate to create an
exemplary spiritual and occult Tibet. 'All Tibetans concentrate on thoughts
of Buddha, Nirvana and their next incarnation', reported Thomas admir-
ingly.[248]

The loss of ambivalence in Western attitudes towards Tibetan culture
throughout the first half of the twentieth century bore a striking

resemblance to the transformation of Western imaginings about the Himalayan mountains. As the Tibetan culture became the home of a happiness and wisdom now lost to the West, so the mountain peaks became unequivocal symbols of spiritual purity. Even Maraini was caught up in this fantasy. He described an episode when he was deep in a cloud-covered valley, then:

> Glory and liberation this morning! For a moment the clouds lifted and after many days we saw the blue sky again, and there at an incredible height ... we saw that divinely pure and unsubstantial thing, consisting only of shape and light, the sparkling pyramid of Kanchenjunga.[249]

We may well ask: What has happened to the ambivalence, to the interplay between the forces of light and darkness which characterized so many traditional imaginings on mountains? Where is the darkness of the sacred landscape? It is all too white, too silent, too pure, too rarefied on the mountain peaks. There is too much light. Often in these accounts such darkness is left down below, in the valleys. Maraini wrote:

> The valleys down below were hot and wet, full of a voracious, imperious or cunning, aggressive or insinuating vitality. Up here we are in a realm of ice and clarity, of ultimate and primordial purity ... Down below night is even more alive than day ... You seem to be surrounded by strange secretions; you feel the touch of strange breath upon you; invisible desires and terrors entwine themselves into the dense tissue of branches, leaves and soil. But up here the night is nothing but light and space ... Time and matter seem no longer to exist. Hence here death immediately suggests eternity. Down below death is decomposition, a minor, unimportant phase in the cycle of living ... Up here night has the solemn, crystalline dignity of the great truths; it is mind, God.[250]

This contrasting polarization reached such intensity that even the inhabitants of the valleys and plains became contaminated by their environment. As Pallis descended from Tibet, he noted: 'Gone ... were the laughing, self-confident faces of the women of Upper Khunu; their sisters here looked shy and rapidly aging, and the golden rings they wore in their noses made their wizened features look all the more dejected.'[251] Migot contrasted the Tibetans with the Chinese. He wrote that among the uniformly clad, slightly built Chinese, 'your eye cannot help being caught by these handsome, gentle giants ... They move slowly through the crowd, dwarfing it ... '. He described the Tibetan women as 'tall, well-proportioned and graceful', with 'deep, sultry voices'. These he compared with the 'shrill, strident fluting of the sing-song Chinese girls'.[252] De Riencourt commented on Tibetan 'gaiety and humour', after India's 'unsmiling faces'.[253] As he climbed up into the Himalayas, he exclaimed: 'I had the extraordinary impression that I was rising, through layers of cloud, from hell to heaven, leaving behind and below me this scientifically technical world which has done so much to increase man's misery.'[254] 'How good it was', wrote a relieved Chapman, 'to see the smiling oblique-eyed faces of the hillmen again after the impenetrable sly hostility of the Bengali Babu. I felt that one had so much in common with these virile, cheerful folk ... '.[255] Later, in Lhasa, he praised the Tibetan nomads: 'They are swarthy independent folk with easy swinging gait and the open faces of mountaineers.'[256]

In one of the most contemporary accounts – by Peter Matthiesson in *The Snow Leopard* – this unequivocal worship of the highest mountain peaks reaches a new intensity. For him the Himalayas are directly associated with sublime feelings of pure insight. They represent the peak of spiritual wisdom and knowledge. They are almost direct proof that impermanence and death can be transcended. The Victorians use of the Himalayas for character-building has become accentuated into the twentieth-century search for the self:

> Then, four miles above these mud streets of the lowlands, at a point so high as to seem overhead, a luminous whiteness shone – the light of the snows. Glaciers loomed and vanished in the greys, and the sky parted, and the snow cone of Machhapuchare glistened like the spire of a higher kingdom.[257]

He describes the valleys as grim: full of decay, degeneration, corruption, impermanence, ignorance and confusion.[258] He too compares the 'friendly and playful children' of the mountains with the 'grim Hindu children of the towns'. He dreaded the return to what he called 'lowland life'.[259]

The landscape of Tibet has here become a geography of hope and despair. All the sombre threads of Western social, political and religious doubts come together – loss of confidence, alienation and the rejection of Western values. Peaks and lamas converge, as in the title of Pallis's popular book. They mutually confirm each other's purity, mastery and unexcelled wisdom. An imaginative resonance is struck up between them. A recent travel account even insists that the lamas are *higher* than the mountains.[260]

In 1951 Eric Shipton, returning from Mount Everest, took the first photographs of what were claimed to be yeti footprints. Public interest and enthusiasm about this mysterious creature had been mounting throughout the century: Indeed, at least sixteen sightings of one form or another had been made by Europeans since 1900.[261] The effect of the photographs was sensational, and several yeti-hunting expeditions were despatched. The most famous of these was the one in 1954 organized on behalf of the London *Daily Mail*. I think it is significant that although the first report of the yeti, the abominable snowman, by a European was by Hodgson in 1832 and the first sighting of apparent yeti tracks was by Waddell in 1889, it was not until the 1930s that the yeti story began deeply to affect the Western imagination. As I observed in chapter 5, the previous lack of sightings, or even of any real interest, is curious given the popularity of the Himalayas with experienced big-game hunters. Can we suppose that the yeti, the primitive human ape, emerged in the 1930s to step into the shadow left vacant by the Tibetans, who were becoming increasingly spiritualized in Western travel literature?

Order and Authority: the Royal Father

On 12 August 1927 *The Tibetan Book of the Dead* (more correctly called 'The Liberation Through Hearing in the Bardo', *The Bardo Thodol*), was published in the West. It immediately found a responsive audience, quickly establishing itself as a classic. While interest in reincarnation had been central to Western occultism, spiritualism, theosophy and other esoteric religions for well over a hundred years, the 1920s was a decade of heightened *scientific* interest. The Tibetan work seemed to be a textbook for the occult science of death. The fame of the man responsible, W.Y. Evans-Wentz, was assured. Evans-Wentz was an erratic and obscure traveller who spent considerable time in the East, much of it in the Himalayan region. He was also an accomplished scholar, translator and student of religion.[262] Such well-respected men in their field as C.G. Jung and Sir John Woodroffe soon set about interpreting and commenting on this esoteric Tibetan text.[263]

Many adjudged *The Bardo Thodol* to be the quintessence of Tibetan wisdom, superior to any similar texts from other cultures, including *The Egyptian Book of the Dead* and the medieval *Ars Moriendo*. It took its place alongside Shangri-La, the yeti and the Dalai Lama as an essential component in the twentieth-century mythologizing about Tibet. Anais Nin, with her finger delicately positioned on the intellectual pulse of the era, remarked on its impact.[264] In one form or another it was referred to by many travellers to Tibet. David-Neel, for example, considered the Tibetans' reflections on death and reincarnation superior even to those made by other Buddhist traditions.[265] Ronaldshay, Govinda and Maraini extensively discussed the ideas of *The Bardo Thodol*.[266] The pragmatic and orderly instructions in this audacious text seemed to confirm the fantasy: *yes*, Tibet was indeed the last home of an exemplary wisdom; among its lamas and magicians there was indeed knowledge beyond Western dreams, knowledge that was both occult and scientific.

Suddenly Tibet, a land of childlike innocence, was transformed into a land of supreme wisdom.[267] The fantasy of the Father stepped out of the shadows and took its place alongside that of the Child. Few doubted that the West could learn something from Tibet – be it wisdom, happiness or contentment.[268] If *The Bardo Thodol* was the scientific evidence of Tibetan knowledge, experience and wisdom, then the Dalai Lama was considered its supreme embodiment. The one reinforced and confirmed the other. The sophisticated reflections on reincarnation and social power to be found in some travel accounts at the turn of the century suddenly vanished and were replaced by an urgent, desperate, unreflective credulity. It is paradoxical that this occurred when, for the first time, numerous Westerners came into direct contact with the Dalai Lama – indeed, even befriended him.

The transformation of the Dalai Lama from the elusive figure of the nineteenth century into the tangible human of the twentieth was abrupt. In 1910, the 13th Dalai Lama appeared on Indian soil and Sir Charles Bell was assigned to look after his needs. They became long-standing friends. Other British officers had the opportunity to meet the 13th Dalai Lama until his death in 1933. An audience with him became a regular feature of any visit by Westerners to Lhasa. Harrer became one of the young 14th Dalai Lama's closest tutors, but despite this unprecedented exposure to Western scrutiny, the Dalai Lama seemed to elude profanation. Landon's worst fears – that the Dalai Lama would become a mere human under the gaze of Western empiricism and reason – were not realized. Even the most unmystical and pragmatic Westerners were impressed by the presence of both the experienced 13th and the youthful 14th Dalai Lamas.[269] The Dalai Lama was quite clearly the centre of Tibetan cultural identity: Chapman wrote that he was 'the very soul of Tibet'.[270] He seemed aloof from any lingering doubts that Westerners had about Tibetan religion – its spiritual purity, its monastic power and organization.

The Dalai Lama was variously described as, the 'god-king', as both 'Dictator and Pope'; as a 'Living Buddha'; as the 'Pope-King'.[271] Chapman wrote of him: 'Even in these days of dictators one cannot but be amazed at his unrivalled power.'[272] Bell commented: 'Backed as he is by the veneration of a people who regard him as more than Pope, as in fact a Divinity ruling on earth, there can be no direct opposition to His Holiness's orders.'[273] For Westerners the Dalai Lama was the embodiment, not of Tibet in general, but of Tibetan wisdom, knowledge, compassion. Gone seemed to be the old criticisms about his absolute power at the head of a corrupt, intrigue-laden, inefficient theocracy. In the 1920s the French Surrealist Antonin Artaud wrote an open letter to the Dalai Lama which, although extreme, echoed the desperate longings of many Westerners at that time: 'O Grand Lama, give us, grace us with your illuminations in a language our contaminated European minds can understand, and if need be, transform our Mind ...'.[274]

Tibet, as exemplified by the Dalai Lama, by other high lamas and by *The Bardo Thodol*, held out the promise of hope and guidance for many Westerners alienated from their own culture. The passionless beauty and geometric perfection of the mountain which dominated Hilton's Shangri-La was an apt symbol of this benevolent but aloof wisdom.[275] Both Pallis and de Riencourt typified the willingness of some Western travellers to surrender total responsibility into the hands of the lamas, those semi-divine wisdom figures. Pallis, for example, wrote that the reincarnated lama is always right. Even if he seems, for example, to be corrupt, his omniscience cannot be doubted. His actions are incomprehensible to us only because they are directed from a plane of wisdom far beyond our understanding.[276] De Riencourt described his experience of an interview with a high lama: 'The Precious One looked at me or rather through me once more. His gleaming eyes bored into my subsconscious mind which he surely knew far better than I did, weighing my Karma ...'. He concluded: 'The enigmatic serenity of his dark features was overpowering. Never before in my life had I met such convincing sincerity and such authority.'[277] No wonder Maraini described Lhasa as 'a Graaltempel' for many Europeans.[278]

Wisdom, guidance, order and archaic continuity: these were the qualities about Tibet that held out hope for many Westerners, and it was the Dalai Lama who personified them in an exemplary manner. He was one of the final embodiments of the Royal Father, the last of a lineage stretching back to the Pharaohs, to the Inca and Aztec rulers.[279] In 1959 the 14th Dalai Lama fled Tibet, perhaps never to return. The Chinese communists destroyed the monasteries, annihilated the monks. Clustered around the Dalai Lama, accompanying him into exile, were numerous high lamas, the last living essence of Tibetan Buddhism.[280] As the Dalai Lama and his followers descended, finally, from their mountain fastness, there were many Westerners who similarly journeyed into an exile from their fantasy landscape. For many it was the end of a dream.

7
Conclusion: The Empty Vessel

When the Dalai Lama fled he took with him into exile the core of Tibet's religious and governmental hierarchy, as well as thousands of ordinary Tibetans. He left behind a geographical place that suddenly seemed devoid of immediate spiritual significance for the West. While Western nations were not completely indifferent to the fate of either the country or the 'divine' ruler and his government in exile, there was little urgency about coming to the Tibetans' aid. This failure cannot be reduced solely to political expediency, timidity or caution. As we have seen, Tibet had been embroiled in Western geopolitical struggles for over two centuries, yet at the same time it was always representative of something else, something compelling over and above political pragmatics. It was this erotic, imaginative compulsion – or fascination – that suddenly all but disappeared during the late 1950s, when Tibet became dramatically emptied as a symbolic vessel. By comparison with its fullness in the past, Tibet as a place was left vacant of spiritual significance for Westerners – except, that is, for a few devotees.

After 1959 Tibet once again became closed to Western travellers; this time more firmly than ever before. It lay behind what came to be called the 'bamboo curtain'. Accounts of the rampant destruction of traditional Tibetan culture by extremist Red Guards filtered through to a West that, by and large, was unheeding of Tibet's misery. Closed and despoiled, Tibet seemed not only to have been emptied of symbolic significance, not just *physically* emptied both by the exile of its religious hierarchy and the wanton destruction of its ancient monasteries, but to have *vanished*, swallowed up into China. The symbolic vessel, so carefully prepared in Western fantasies for over two centuries, had itself been completely shattered and dissolved.

Initially it is easy to place total responsibility for this event on the Chinese communists, who, having firmly sealed the southern and western boundaries of Tibet against the gaze of outsiders, then demolished not only its monasteries but its national frontiers to the north and east. Tibet's symbolic power became diluted, contaminated and lost as the Chinese invaded and subsequently colonized the country. But on the surface these events, while extreme, were not so entirely different from those of the past. Time and again Tibet had been drawn firmly back into the Chinese Empire, had lost its power, had had its sovereignty diminished, and the Dalai Lama had been forced to flee, yet it had still held its symbolic 'charge' for many Westerners. But when the Chinese invaded Tibet in 1959, that land was already an almost empty vessel. We have seen that it was no longer a *place* of intense sacred power for the West. The transformation of Western fantasies within its boundaries had been completed, and Tibet seemed to be no longer needed. Therefore the fracture of the vessel, with the spillage and spoilation of its imaginal contents, should not be blamed solely upon the Chinese. Such an event was already ripe, already prepared for, from *within* the Western imagination itself.

Imaginal Containment

Alchemists frequently illustrated their works with pictures of a transparent alembic, an alchemical vessel, a sealed jar, its bizarre contents clearly revealed locked together in a process of symbolic transformation. In these illustrations, the alembic is often shown placed incongruously in the middle of a busy street with people going about their everyday business, apparently oblivious to the drama being enacted in their midst.[1] The whole history of Western imaginings on Tibet is encapsulated in this image: in the relationship between symbol-containment and its wider psychosocial context. The phenomenology of sacred place, which has been the meta-image of this study, found expression in many striking images, ranging in size from the whole of the immense country itself down to the city of Lhasa, to the Potala palace, or even to just a solitary meditation cell. Within each of these imaginal vessels there occurred a *concentration* of imaginative significance, intensity and power. Within each vessel a Western sense of the sacred, of both the *mysterium tremendum* and the simply mysterious – as well as anxieties, paradoxes and hopes – were confined, condensed and transformed. But what of the relationship between the contents of these vessels and the world outside? In order to understand Tibet's sudden loss of compelling imaginative significance, its relative abandonment by Western fantasy-making, we need to re-examine this process of symbol-containment, concentration and contextualization.

From Mystery to Museum

In chapter 2 it was claimed that the late eighteenth century saw Europe on the edge of a fundamental shift in its global fantasies, especially as regards nature. The expansive, relatively unbounded surface of the globe seemed full of opportunities for the confident middle and upper classes of Europe. Fascination went hand in hand with power. Such places as Tibet began to represent – and above all to encapsulate – such qualities. Within its vague boundaries were focused and concentrated many European longings and aspirations. At the same time the natural world was starting to feel safe for Europeans – not just politically, but ontologically. Not long before Bogle and Turner's visits to the rugged mountains of Tibet, such places were contemptuously shunned by educated people whilst evoking deep unease, if not fear, in many others. However, neither of these late-eighteenth-century travellers revealed any signs of such attitudes.

We may recall the Himalayan traveller, early in the nineteenth century, who gazed into a mountain torrent:

> Those who have brains and nerves to bear the frightful whirl, which may assail the steadiest head, plant themselves on the bridge that spans the torrent, and from this point survey the wild and awful grandeur of the scene, struck with admiration at its terrific beauty, yet, even while visions of horror float before them, unable to withdraw their gaze.[2]

Or the early Himalayan explorer Gerard, encountering a ravine: 'We could scarcely view [the deep chasms] without shuddering. I never saw such a horrid looking place ... '.[3] Giegrich astutely points out the ontological shift revealed in such episodes.[4] These wild places were no longer a fearful window into an all-encompassing Being, but a relatively safe gaze from the shores of an ontologically secure world into just that *one* thing. Dangerous nature had become surrounded by safety; the unknown by the known. Such views were *islands* of intensity, *patches* of savage sublimity surrounded by a relatively safe and comprehensible world. Similarly Tibet gradually ceased to be a concentrated sign, or representative of the earth's mysterious powers, paradoxes and unlimited imaginal potential. Instead it became set apart from the ordinary world. Its heightened imaginal significance and mystery became counterposed to the comparative known-ness outside its borders.

It has also been shown that the imaginative events taking place within Tibet were themselves located within a much broader, global, context. By the mid-nineteenth century virtually the entire globe had been basically mapped. Instead of islands of geographical knowledge afloat on an immense ocean of ignorance and speculation, there were now only a few blank spaces surrounded by a global network of known co-ordinates and contours. Tibet was one such blank space, one such unknown island, and into these shrinking blank spaces were concentrated the last remaining vestiges of Europe's primal relation to geographical unknown-ness, to wilderness.

As we have seen, this situation was subsequently followed, in the late nineteenth century, by an overwhelming belief in the final and general scientific comprehension of nature. The systematic theories of Darwin, his colleagues and their followers seemed to offer a key to nature's last secrets. Overall mystery was replaced by specific problems awaiting only time, effort and technique for their ultimate solution. The vast open spaces that lay protected within Tibet's boundaries no longer came to exert the ontological power they had held in earlier times. Although somewhat unknown in terms of specific geographical, botanical, zoological and cultural features, they were considered virtually known and mapped in terms of their ultimate comprehensibility.

We have seen that this intellectual event was by no means an imaginally negative one. It catalysed yet another revolution in Western landscape aesthetics: the appreciation of wildernesses as places of complex beauty. But on another level this aesthetic opening was achieved at the expense and loss of a deep sense of mystery and awe towards natural landscape. Indeed, many in the West, prompted by Ruskin and others, set about aesthetically mapping the last unknown and previously ignored or rejected landscapes of the earth. It was precisely at this time that the symbolic power which had previously been spread throughout Tibet became focused and concentrated into the city of Lhasa, and thence on to the Potala palace. This process of imaginative concentration eventually led to the isolated personage of the Dalai Lama becoming the embodiment not only of all Tibet's paradoxical mysteries and forces but of those of the wider world. It was seen how many came to imagine him as one of the last remaining vessels of ancient wisdom and occult power in an otherwise disenchanted world.

What then happened to the rest of Tibet, to the immense spaces within the remainder of the sacred place, now that signification had been focused so substantially on to such a small vessel, a mere human frame? As we saw in the last chapter, the land of Tibet gradually became either substantially demythologized through social realism, political pragmatics and travel rhetoric, or else contact was lost with its geographical actuality and it became a vague location for heightened spiritual, or utopian, reveries. Hilton's image of Shangri-La was a fitting conclusion to this dual process of symbolic concentration and geographical abstraction. In its lost, floating reality were concentrated all the qualities previously dispersed throughout the whole of geographical Tibet. The intense cohesion of *fin-de-siècle* Tibet, as a sacred place, was now fragmented into isolated points of heightened imaginative significance: the Dalai Lama of course, but also the yeti, Mount Everest, and remote mystic recluses. The boundaries of Tibet were no longer straining to contain the intense pressure of imaginative transformation; no longer were the walls of the alchemical alembic almost bursting under the heat and fullness of its contents. Tibet was no longer the 'centre of the earth'; the 'global fire' was not to be found there.[5] While the boundaries of Tibet were still vibrant and special for travellers, they simply located and positioned; they did not alchemically *contain*.

The fantasy of Shangri-La was the final chord in one line of imaginative development. It literally had no-place (utopia) left to go. The 'conquest' of Mount Everest also meant that by 1953 these mountain summits had ceased to be the untouched, mysterious preserve of the gods. The yeti, by its very nature, lingers on in the twilight realm as either a curious oddity or an archetypal mythologem. By 1959 only the Dalai Lama and a handful of high lamas remained with something approaching the sense of mysterious possibility previously contained within *all* of Tibet. Surrounding the Dalai Lama was a land that, while still exciting and curiously different for Westerners, was ontologically similar to the world outside. Any mystery, any sense of being outside time and space that it still possessed had more the quality of a museum or tourist attraction than of a *temenos* or sacred place.

Returning to the image of the alchemical alembic located in the busy market place, it can now be seen that in the case of Tibet the reality *inside* the vessel had become substantially the same as that in the world *outside*. Whilst both inside and outside still contained their share of isolated mysteries, symbols of imaginative power, corners for sacred reverie, nevertheless a sense of everydayness had spread itself throughout both spaces.[6]

Extremely esoteric religious practices and powers, as exemplified by the Dalai Lama, were the only bearer of Tibetan mysteriousness. Previously Tibetan religion, as we have seen, had been embedded in its landscape; consistently imagined as belonging to its *place*. By the middle of the twentieth century this position was almost completely reversed: it was not the landscape that provided Western fantasies of Tibet and its religion with coherence, but its esoteric religion that gave Tibet and its landscape imaginative difference and significance. Even Tibetan religion *as a whole* had ceased to be the object of fascination; now only the spiritual masters and their most advanced techniques excited Western fantasies.[7]

So when the Chinese communist army finally marched in force into Lhasa in 1959, it entered a shell that was already substantially empty of heightened, living, imaginative resonance for most Westerners. Indeed, by expelling the final concentrated *essence* of Tibetan occult mystery and authority in the form of the Dalai Lama and his ecclesiastical elite, China inadvertently seeded Western fantasy-making with what could prove a whole new series of transformations in its imaginings about Tibet. Spiritually and psychologically, many in the West provided fertile ground for these exiled Tibetan fantasies. But Tibet itself was left abandoned; a broken shell significantly empty of imaginative resonance except, perhaps, for a few echoes that grow fainter by the day, or as a *memento mori*, a sad reminder of loss. Western involvement in that country quickly seemed like an old dream, almost forgotten. Very soon it hardly seemed possible that the West had at one point seemed to belong in Tibet, to have had an extraordinary relationship with that country. This sense of loss has found one of its most poignant expressions in Harrer's account of his return to Lhasa in 1985. The former tutor to the Dalai Lama, perhaps one of the most widely read of modern writers on Tibet, paints a tragic and harrowing portrait of fear, loss and cultural destruction.[8]

In chapter 6 it was shown how Tibetan 'travel' writing could be usefully considered in four groups, depending on its orientation: everyday life, tourism, mystical religion, or utopianism. In the years after the Chinese communist occupation each of these styles of approaching Tibet has suffered mixed fortunes. Certainly, the fantasy of Tibet as a utopian society, a possible exemplary model for a West desperate and in decline, is rarer than sightings of the yeti. Concern with everyday life in Tibetan culture has, with the closure to Westerners of Tibet itself, received abundant coverage by anthropologists working among Tibetan and related communities in the Himalayan regions (India, Nepal,, Sikkim and Bhutan).[9] The exile of high-ranking Tibetan lamas and the subsequent establishment throughout the Western world of monastic and quasi-monastic communities, well stocked with teachers, instructors, sacred texts and highly skilled translators, has undermined the traditional need for Westerners to travel to the Himalayas to search for the truths offered by Tibetan Buddhism. Of course such journeys still occur, but with few exceptions the accounts are clichéd, unreflective survivals of a bygone genre.[10]

Since the mid-1960s tourism has boomed in the Himalayan regions of India and Nepal – particularly adventure tourism, usually low-budget and involving trekking. Since 1980 Tibet too has been open, albeit in a tentative and highly restricted way, to Western tourists. It has been estimated that in the centuries up to 1979 fewer than 1,250 Westerners ever reached Lhasa, and 623 of these were with the 1904 Younghusband expedition. The last ten years have seen the influx of many thousands of tourists, with China hoping for an even more dramatic increase in the near future.[11] The literature of the popular, 'mass' adventure tourism has had a profound influence on the shaping of contemporary images of Tibetan landscape and culture.[12]

Tibetan Buddhism has become a tourist attraction. Its monks, rituals, monasteries and artefacts throughout the Himalayan region – from Tibet to Ladakh, Nepal to Darjeeling, Bhutan to Sikkim – have become the delight of photographers, trekkers and bargain-hunters. As we have seen, the genesis of this phenomenon can be traced far back, to the second half of the nineteenth century. However, despite the fears of some early travellers, the region had never before been swamped by Western tourists. This is a complex phenomenon with profound cultural and ecological repercussions: it is far more than simply a question of numbers. Earlier tourists viewed their 'sights' against the background of a coherent, 'other' world.

On the other hand, in the contemporary era, tourist culture (literature, images, etc.) has to an extraordinary extent created these 'places': the expectations about them, their representations. The culture of Tibetan Buddhism is instantaneously appealing, visually dramatic and suitably archaic for packaged travel. Travel to these regions is now located within a global smorgasbord of possible destinations, all of which are suitably exotic.[13]

Places in Process

Nevertheless, as this study has shown, the image of a sacred place standing in direct opposition to profane space, the one sharply delineated from the other, is merely one possible movement, one extreme within a range of less polarized imaginal possibilities. At the other extreme lies totally homogenized space, whether envisaged as entirely profane or as entirely sacred. It seems unlikely that either of these possibilities has ever existed in its pure form.[14] However, in the case of Tibet, these extremes *were* approximated on two occasions. Then the one seemed quickly to follow the other: an intensive polarization between sacred and profane worlds, with the hermetically sealed containment of the sacred, was superseded almost immediately by diffusion and loss of imaginal concentration. This dramatic reversal took place within the first half of the twentieth century. But even in these cases, the polarization was never complete except in the fantasies of a few; the containment was never absolute, the threshold was always porous; also, imaginal concentration was never totally diluted or lost.

To focus exclusively upon such extremes distorts the more complex phenomenology of sacred space – the fluidity of its boundaries; the shifts and realignments of its crucial features; its transformations across time; the often contradictory levels of fantasy-making (political and religious, individual and social) sliding across each other, contradicting or reinforcing each other. This study has also shown that the boundary of such a place can be less of a narrow line drawn across time and space than a complex zone expressing an imaginal gradient. The *axis mundi* is less a fixed reference point than a mobile, often pluralistic, series of symbols which locate themselves according to a complex imaginal ecology that weaves itself between the sacred place and its wider context. We have seen that the region inside a sacred place is not necessarily imaginally separate from the demands of the world outside – indeed, there can be continual dialogue between the two spaces. This can be recognized without collapsing the one into the other, or sacrificing their relative autonomy.[15] The rich and multitextured complexity of Tibet's story has also shown that geographical Otherness is rarely an imaginal unity. Rather, it is a multiplicity which echoes Jung's comment: 'The phenomenology of the psyche is so colourful, so variegated in form and meaning, that we cannot possibly reflect all its riches in *one* mirror.'[16]

Imaginal coherence should not be confused with fantasies of wholeness or unity. This imaginal archaeology of Tibet has revealed a diversity of images of European Otherness. There has been a historical sequence of 'Tibets', each related yet also separate, each corresponding both to historical circumstances and also to a kind of internal mythological necessity, an imaginal momentum. We have also seen that at any one time each of these *big* 'Tibets' was in its turn only a temporary coherence of numerous smaller ones: Tibet as a heroic challenge, as the object of mystical inspiration or anima-fascination, the source of senex guidance or of puer aspiration, and so on. Tibet echoed Boon's observations about the anthropological creation of Bali: a compact profusion of visual-spatial symbolism.[17] However, we have also seen how an approximate consensus of imaginal unity was achieved on two occasions: first under the constraints of imperial politics at the end of the nineteenth century; secondly under the pressure of a collective desperation and disenchantment in the first half of the twentieth. But even on both those occasions, Tibet as a sacred place was always the site of an imaginal struggle. Less socially powerful interpretations, less socially sanctioned imaginal voices were never completely silenced but rather pushed to the perimeter of the more publicized paradigm, often to re-emerge later in a more favourable climate. Tibetan travel has had its high priests and its bards, its mystics and its wanderers, its politicians and its renegades, its patriarchs and its clowns.

While this study has followed the process whereby Tibet became transformed from a geographical rumour into a sacred place, I am not suggesting that such a creation will always follow the Tibetan sequence or pattern: an initial, vague feeling of numinosity; then the discovery and establishment of a boundary-zone; followed by the creation of a centre, or series of centres, as *axis mundi*; then its consecration as a fully formed sacred place or *temenos*; and finally its eventual decay, degeneration and abandonment. Even in Tibet, this creative process was not uniform among travellers, nor was it historically linear. For some early visionaries Tibet leapt into their imaginations almost complete, as a fully formed whole, whilst for others, even over a century later, it still failed to evoke deeper resonances.

Sacred places can rarely be established in a step-by-step fashion, each phase neatly compartmentalized from the next. There must usually be a simultaneous intimation, at least, of *all* its aspects: boundary, centre and consecration. However, some aspects are usually emphasized, or imagined, more clearly and forcefully than others. One could easily envisage – for example, in the case of a miraculous event – that the *axis mundi* would instantly be established as the very *raison d'être* of the place. In such cases the mapping of the boundary-zone would come later. A slow process of geographical, political, economic, religious and mythological reasoning and negotiation, as well as of the indeterminate folkways of common habits. But this study has shown that whatever the sequence, sacred places exist in time; that time is a part of a sacred place.

The Echo of Place

We have seen that for many in the West Tibet offered a kind of imaginal continuity, especially at times of social and individual doubt or uncertainty. Such continuity, it has been suggested, is a crucial aspect of a *place*.[18] The most obvious form of continuity was probably the almost mechanical repetition of various discourses – political, social, religious, scientific, and so on – produced by succeeding generations of travellers. Layer after layer of organized imagery were placed one atop the other until a well-defined, overall image of Tibet was confirmed and concretized. As the climax of this process was reached towards the end of the last century, travellers increasingly encountered Tibet with well-prepared expectations. They involved themselves in that country with such expectations uppermost, even trying to impose such fantasies upon Tibet and its people. This process offered many a kind of static sense of identity and imaginal security. This is the level of continuity alluded to by Said and other writers concerned primarily with the overt political repercussions of travel writing in its broadest sense.

But this study has also drawn attention to other levels and styles of imaginal continuity. There were, for example, vestiges of historical memory which became actualized in Tibet: the lingering images of Tartars, the Celestial Empire, the Silk Route, or more recent ones such as Alpine exploration, colonial wars, gold rushes, and so on. Foucault has called such things 'memory traces' and discusses them in terms of leprosy's powerful influence on the way madness was subsequently viewed, handled and physically placed in post-medieval Europe.[19] In the same way, the memory traces intersecting in Tibet were not only located in the mind of the traveller but were embedded in the practices and rituals they followed. Such practices included the unwritten and written rules for organizing and equipping expeditions, the folk mores of expedition life, the genre of recording, expressing and processing experiences and discoveries. All these things created a kind of expedition ritual and context which defined the travellers' attitude towards Tibet as a geographical Other and at the same time confirmed a kind of historical relationship to the place. Such rituals were integral to the creation of Tibet. Place and ritual were inseparable. Through them, the traces of the past wove their way through to the present.

In addition, there was a kind of spatial memory, rather than a purely historical or temporal one. Frances Yates has shown how memory was viewed spatially in Classical, medieval and Renaissance times.[20] Memory was envisaged not as something in the past but as a quality of discrete interior space. As Corbin writes: 'The past is not behind us but under our feet.'[21] Within such a perspective, memory has to do with the placing and organization of images in relation to each other. The process of remembering then becomes a journey through this 'interior' landscape to reclaim these images; such interiority being located both within the subjectivity of the individual and within the world outside.[22] Memory here becomes a true re-collection. Such a re-collection, in the case of Tibet, occurred both on a mundane level (memories of previous explorers, certain specific discoveries and incidents) and on a deeper level (reminders of existential hopes and fears, of social duties and expectations).[23] Tibet became differentiated, throughout the nineteenth century, into discrete zones, some based on geographical features such as the bleak northern plateau, the Chumbi valley, or the Tsangpo river, whilst others were based upon cultural references such as the area around Lhasa, or Tashi Lumpo. Routes into Tibet also began to take on imaginal differentiation. Deeply mythological fantasies such as Aryan ancestors, archaic mysteries, the yeti, or gold were specifically located within this Tibetan 'memory system'. Also, such spatial re-membering occurred within a fairly well-defined global context of imaginal places. Tibet, as we have seen, was just one space located within a well-organized global structure of other complex imaginal places: the European Alps, the source of the Nile, Egypt, the Arctic, Bali, the Andes, the gold fields of Australia, South Africa, California, and so on.

However, there was yet another way in which Tibet offered a profound imaginal continuity, a way that was perhaps less 'grand' than any of those discussed above. Instead of the metaphors of archaeology, or memory systems, memory traces and so on, we could use that of echoing. *Places echo*. This echoing is one of the defining characteristics of a place's placeness. Without imaginal echo there is only geographical location. As we have seen, Tibet was the site of echoes that reverberated across history and through changing imaginal landscapes. As Berry writes: 'Echo ... is not separate from her surroundings.'[24] These echoes and the place of Tibet were inseparable. Again, Berry reminds us that 'As Echo shapes, she is shaped by what's around her.'[25] Echoes counter the narcissistic desire, held by many Westerners, to see a simple reflection of themselves in the mirror of Tibet. Tibet was never a simple mirror to the West's desires. At the very least it gave these projections its own specific form, colour, tone and texture.

This continuity, through the intangible reflections of apparently marginal images, were no less significant than the grander reorganization of global space and time. Unlike the other forms of imaginal continuity, echoes cannot be abstracted from the geographical place, cannot be somehow universalized, systematized and generalized.

Some echoes reverberated deafeningly – gold, Egypt, archaic mysteries – had sent their sounds around the globe. Some were chased, like Manning's hats, in an attempt to grasp them and transform them into something stable and substantial. Some were very personal and soon faded. Recent Himalayan travel writing continues this tradition. Matthiesson, for example, heard his own deep personal doubts and hopes ricochet off every overhang, evoked by every bend in the path. His 1980 book *The Snow Leopard* also records contemporary echoes of a more collective nature: ecological disregard, the energy crisis, pollution, species extinction, Third World oppression.[26] In both cases, the personal and the collective, small details of landscape trigger off associations for Matthiesson which then plunge into imaginal depths, only then to fade quickly.

The details of the place provide the timing, shape, resonance and momentum of the associations; this is what makes them echo. Through echoing, the *place* almost assumes the role of psycho-analyst.[27] Indeed, we have seen how the marginal, ephemeral echoes of Bogle's, Fleming's and Byron's Tibets were overtly used to deepen critical reflection and understanding of their own culture's fantasy-making. Echoes are not a horizontal mimicry but the soundings of imaginal depth. Through its Tibetan echoes the West was occasionally shown a deeper, less conscious aspect of itself. By listening to its Tibetan echoes, the West could perhaps discover its own questions. This procession of imaginal Tibets represented attempts to complete questions the West was asking about its own identity. Berry writes: 'Echo is not only an echo of something but also a kind of response that completes the word to itself.'[28] Many in the West came closer to hearing their questions by listening to the responses from Tibet.

The metaphor of echo demands that we listen to the place as it sounds through the travel texts. It demands an 'acoustic imagination'; an imaginative listening in terms of tone, rhythm, harmony and discord.[29] Instead of grand vistas, powerful rituals, well-regulated mystic assemblies or geopolitics, echoes reveal a more insubstantial and indirect aspect of place, rather like the incident Maraini recorded of the Maharaja of Sikkim eating peas. 'Echo's aesthetics', writes Berry, 'occur in the empty spaces.'[30] Indeed, when one is relieved from the thaumaturgical Tibet and all the other spaces filled with expectations, openings appear which are so suitable for Echo's persistent yet delicate art.

Berry suggests that echoing is a form of alchemical *iteratio*, an attempt at continuity, at concretizing, materializing, at making something take. 'Repetitions', she writes, 'are longings for self-reflection ... Echo longs for this beauty of self-reflected depth ... an aesthetic self-longing.'[31] Perhaps there was also something in Tibet that wanted to see itself echoed in the travellers' tales.

The fantasy of Shangri-La can be seen, like all utopias, as an abstracted memory system, or as a memory trace, perhaps for example of earlier, idealised, spiritual communities. It can also be seen as the product of ritual repetition by generations of travellers, the final layer of a centuries-old archaeological past. But in a sense, too, Shangri-La was the last great cohesive echo that reverberated from Tibet before it fell into ruins. As an echo should, it began life well defined, clearly shaped by its immediate connection with the place, but as its sound radiated further from its echoing source, the form became more diffuse and vague. It still survives as the faintest of echoes, but for most people it has long since lost any connection with a specific place. Perhaps it was Hilton's genius to have gathered up the rapidly fragmenting and vanishing images of Tibet into one last cohesive echo. As Lowenstein put it: 'Orphean echo impels *mythos*'.[32]

The Return of Soul to the World

This study has been a contribution towards the return of soul to the world, to an *anima mundi* psychology. The world presents itself in its images. Jung wrote that the alchemists considered the greater part of the psyche to lie *outside* the body.[33] And as Hillman warns, 'the more we concentrate on literalizing interiority within my person the more we lose the sense of soul as a psychic reality … within all things.'[34] While there was a long tradition which located psyche, in one form or another, somehow within both the individual *and* the world, to a considerable extent this world connotation has been lost in recent centuries.[35] Jung was a seminal figure in reclaiming this world-centred psyche. The primary texts he used were those of European alchemy, through which he realized the imaginative power of matter, and hence of nature. Travellers' tales are also a form of alchemy. As Hillman insists: 'The same imagination, the same soul, that presented itself in fifteenth and sixteenth century alchemy showed itself in the extroverted psychology of the explorers seeking gold, the journey across the perilous seas … the world as metaphor.'[36]

This study has shown how many of these travellers to Tibet were searching for *the secret* which they believed lay in the mysterious unknown. Like the alchemists, some chose a somewhat extroverted path of physical exploration, whilst others were lured into the place in the search for ideas. But in neither case was the place simply passive, a mere blank sheet on to which the travellers could impose their wildest fantasies. The place of Tibet had a logic and coherence of its own, its *genius loci*. Tibet was not a 'silent Other', it was alive, substantial and compelling. It was part of the world calling attention to itself, deepening our soulful appreciation of mountains, of deserts and rivers, of light and colour, of time and space, of myriad peoples and their cultures, of fauna and flora, of the plurality of imaginative possibilities.

Chapter References

1. *An Imaginative Geography*

1. E. Relph, *Place and Placelessness* (London: Pion, 1976); M. Samuels, 'Existentialism and Human Geography', in *Humanistic Geography*, ed. D. Ley and M. Samuels (London: Croom Helm, 1979); C.G. Jung, 'Mind and Earth', in his *Collected Works Vol.10* (London: Routledge & Kegan Paul, 1974).
2. G. Bachelard, *The Poetics of Space* (Boston: Beacon Press, 1969); Yi-Fu Tuan, 'Topophilia', in *Man, Space and Environment*, ed. P. English and R. Mayfield (New York: Oxford University Press, 1972); Yi-Fu Tuan, 'Sacred Space', in *Dimensions of Human Geography*, ed. K Butzer (Chicago: University of Chicago Press, 1978).
3. M. Eliade, *The Sacred and the Profane* (New York: Harcourt, Brace and World, 1959); See F. Yates, *The Art of Memory* (Harmondsworth: Penguin, 1978) for a discussion of space and memory.
4. J. Sumption, *Pilgrimage* (London: Faber & Faber, 1975).
5. E. Said, *Orientalism* (New York: Vintage Books, 1979); H. Baudet, *Paradise on Earth: Some Thoughts on European Images of Non-European Man* (New Haven: Yale University Press, 1965).
6. See Baudet; and B. Stafford, *Voyage into Substance* (Cambridge, MA: MIT Press, 1984).
7. See P. Dodd (ed.), *The Art of Travel* (London: Frank Cass, 1982) for extensive discussion of travel writing; also E. Swinglehurst, *Cook's Tours* (Poole, Dorset: Blandford Press, 1982).
8. See Relph, pp.79.ff; also Eliade, pp.22 – 4; I. Illich, H_2O and the Waters of Forgetfulness (Dallas: Dallas Institute of Humanities and Culture, 1985)
9. See M. Le Bris, *Romantics and Romanticism* (Geneva: Skira, 1981); C. Loomis, 'The Arctic Sublime', in *Nature and the Victorian Imagination*, ed. U. Knoepflmacher and G. Tennyson (Berkeley: University of California Press, 1977); A. Moorehead: *The Fatal Impact* (Harmondsworth: Penguin, 1968); *The White Nile* (Harmondsworth: Penguin, 1976).
10. Said; also Stafford, *Voyage into Substance*; E. Brown (ed.), *Geography: Yesterday and Tomorrow* (Oxford: Oxford University Press, 1980); L. Brockway, *Science and Colonial Expansion* (New York: Academic Press, 1979); J. Boon, *The Anthropological Romance of Bali* (New York: Cambridge University Press, 1977); R. Nash, *Wilderness and the American Mind* (New Haven: Yale University Press, 1973); A. Miller, '*I see no end to travelling*' (Sydney: Bay Books, 1986); C. Glacken, *Traces on the Rhodian Shore* (Berkeley: University of California Press, 1967).
11. See C. Allen, *A Mountain in Tibet* (London: André Deutsch, 1982); P. Hopkirk, *Trespassers on the Roof of the World* (London: John Murray, 1982); L. Miller, *On Top of the World* (London: Paddington Press, 1976); G. Woodcock, *Into Tibet* (London: Faber & Faber, 1971); S. Camman, *Trade Through the Himalayas* (Connecticut: Greenwood Press, 1970); J. MacGregor, *Tibet: A Chronicle of Exploration* (London: Routledge & Kegan Paul, 1970).
12. See A. Lamb, *Britain and Chinese Central Asia* (London: Routledge & Kegan Paul, 1960).
13. See Dodd, *Art of Travel*; Stafford, *Voyage into Substance*; P. Fussell, *Abroad* (New York: Oxford University Press, 1980); F. Barker *et al.* (eds.), *Europe and Its Others*, 2 vols (Colchester: University of Essex, 1984).
14. Fussell, pp.202 – 15.
15. Ibid. pp.108 – 9, 174 – 7.

16. C. Lévi-Strauss, *The Savage Mind* (Chicago: University of Chicago Press, 1973); also J. Hillman, *Re-Visioning Psychology* (New York: Harper & Row, 1975), p.164 on the idea of *bricoleur*; R. Byron, *First Russia: Then Tibet* (1933; Harmondsworth: Penguin, 1985). See also N. Douglas, *Siren Land* (1911; Harmondsworth: Penguin, 1986) for a brilliant example of this collage style.

17. Byron.

18. Fussell, p.214.

19. Bachelard, *Poetics*. See also R. Funk, *Language, Hermeneutic and Word of God* (New York: Harper & Row, 1966), pp.265 – 73, where the travel section of Paul's letters in the New Testament are read as an integral part of Paul's message.

20. Fussell, p.210.

21. W. Mitchell (ed.), *On Narrative* (Chicago: University of Chicago Press, 1981), p.x.

22. P. Matthiesson, *The Snow Leopard* (London: Picador, 1980); P. Bishop, 'The Geography of Hope and Despair: Peter Matthiesson's *The Snow Leopard*', *Critique* XXVI, no.4 (Summer 1985). See also W. Least Heat-Moon, *Blue Highways* (London: Picador, 1984) for a striking image of route. He structures his narrative around the blue roads on maps of US highways.

23. J. Hillman, 'The Thought of the Heart', *The Eranos Jahrbuch 48-1979* (Frankfurt a/M: Insel Verlag, 1980), pp.151 – 3; M. Foucault, *The History of Sexuality*, vol.1 (New York: Vintage Books, 1980), p.58; see also P. Spacks, *Imagining a Self* (Cambridge, MA: Harvard University Press, 1976). This is an examination of autobiography and novel in the eighteenth century, which was a critical period in the intensification of concern over personal identity and subjectivity.

24. H. White, 'The Value of Narrativity in the Representation of Reality', in Mitchell, p.18.

25. V. Turner: 'Pilgrimages as Social Processes', in his *Dramas, Fields and Metaphors* (Ithaca: Cornell University Press, 1974), 'The Centre Out There: Pilgrim's Goal', *History of Religions*, 13, no.3 (February 1973).

26. See Yi-Fu Tuan, *Space and Place* (London: Edward Arnold, 1977); also Bachelard, *Poetics*.

27. See J. Layard, *A Celtic Quest* (Zurich: Spring Publications, 1975). He examines this triple parallelism between geographical boundaries, those of individual psychology and those of social reality.

28. D. Lowenthal, 'Geography, Experience and Imagination: Towards a Geographical Epistemology', in English and Mayfield.

29. Yi-Fu Tuan, 'Sacred Space', in Butzer, p.92; Barker; J. Fabian, *Time and the Other* (New York: Columbia University Press, 1983).

30. Said, pp.157 – 97.

31. Ibid. pp.167.

32. Ibid. pp.166 – 88.

33. J. Hillman, 'Notes on White Supremacy', *Spring 1986* (Dallas: Spring Publications, 1986), pp.45 – 6. We can trace the appearance of the West's unconscious even closer to home than Africa. For example, in the imaginative constructions and reconstructions of places such as Pompeii (moral warnings about imperial decline and sexual permissiveness);Knossos (a golden age of innocence, power and wisdom destroyed by the overwhelming forces of nature); Capri (a languid, earthy paradise underlain by dark myths); Patmos (the visionary extreme of European consciousness). See, for example, H. Wunderlich, *The Secret of Crete* (Athens: Efstathiadis Group, 1983) for insights into the discovery and archaeological reconstruction of Knossos on Crete early in the twentieth century; or N. Douglas's *Siren Land* (Harmondsworth: Penguin, 1986) for a broody, complex evocation of Capri and the Amalfi coast at the turn of the century. On Patmos's evocative power in the nineteenth century, see Hölderlin's poem 'Bread and Wine'.

34. J. Hillman: 'Notes on White Supremacy', 'An Introductory Note: C.G. Carus – C.G. Jung', in C.G. Carus, *Psyche: Part One* (New York: Spring Publications, 1970). On the 'discov-

ery' of the unconscious, see H. Ellenberger, *The Discovery of the Unconscious* (New York: Basic Books, 1970). There is, of course, no fixed category of *the* Other. From disciplines as diverse as anthropology, psychology, religious philosophy, art aesthetics, and so on comes a bewildering array of images and reflections on Otherness. While most of these perspectives attempt to conceptualize 'their' Other as a coherent, unified object, archetypal psychology insists upon its complexity, diversity and contradictory qualities. However, some moves against unified images of Otherness can be seen in these other disciplines. In anthropology, for example, there is Fabian's *Time and the Other*, or Boon's *Anthropological Romance of Bali*. A wide range of discussions, owing much to the deconstructionalist philosophy of Foucault, can be found in Barker, *Europe and Its Others*. Archetypal psychology's insistence on the transpersonal roots of these images of Otherness is similarly echoed by at least some of these post-modernist theorists; see the discussion in E. Casey, 'Jung and the Post-Modern Condition', *Spring 1987* (Dallas: Spring Publications, 1987).

35. S. Freud, *The Interpretation of Dreams* (London: George Allen & Unwin, 1971); C.G. Jung, *Collected Works, Vol.16* (London: Routledge & Kegan Paul, 1974); J. Hillman: *Re-Visioning Psychology* (New York: Harper & Row, 1975), *The Dream and the Underworld* (New York: Harper & Row, 1979).

36. See J. Anderson, *The Ulysses Factor* (New York: Harcourt, Brace, Jovanovich, 1970); W. Noyce, *The Springs of Adventure* (New York: the World Publishing Company, 1958); J. Lester, 'Wrestling with the Self on Mount Everest', *Journal of Humanistic Psychology*, 23, no. 2 (Spring 1983); M. and J. Fisher, *Shackleton* (London: James Barrie, 1957), is an excellent example of the biographical approach to the psychology of exploration.

37. See Relph; Lowenthal, 'Geography, Experience … '; Tuan, 'Topophilia'; R. Sach, 'Conceptions of Geographical Space', *Progress in Human Geography* 4, no.3 (September 1980); T. Saarinen and J. Sell, 'Environmental Perception', *Progress in Human Geography*, 5, no.4 (1981); J. Allen, 'The Place of the Imagination in the History of Geographical Exploration', in *Geographies of the Mind*, ed. D. Lowenthal and M. Bowden (New York: Oxford University Press, 1976).

38. See M. Bowden, 'The Great American Desert in the American Mind: The Historiography of a Geographical Notion', in Lowenthal and Bowden; R. Barthes, 'The Blue Guide', *Mythologies* (London: Paladin, 1973).

39. F. Grenard, *Tibet* (1903; Delhi: Cosmo Publications, 1974).

40. See C. Norberg-Schulz, *Genius Loci* (New York: Rizzoli, 1980).

41. Eliade; Jung, 'Mind and Earth'; J. Hillman, 'Anima Mundi', *Spring 1982* (Dallas: Spring Publications, 1982); E. Casey, 'Getting Placed', *Spring 1982* (Dallas: Spring Publications, 1982); Layard.

42. Relph; Bachelard, *Poetics*; Tuan, 'Sacred Space'; Lowenthal, 'Geography, Experience … '; M. Heidegger, *Poetry, Language, Thought* (New York: Harper & Row, 1975); E. Gison, 'Understanding the Subjective Meaning of Places', in Ley and Samuels.

43. See M. Eliade, *Australian Religions* (New York: Cornell University Press, 1973).

44. Tuan, 'Topophilia'; Tuan, 'Geopiety'.

45. Heidegger.

46. Casey, 'Getting Placed', p.17.

47. Eliade, *Sacred and Profane*, p.25; see also L. Shiner, 'Sacred Space, Profane Space, Human Space', *Journal of the American Academy of Religion* XL, no.4 (December 1972); J. Saliba, '*Homo Religiousus*' in *Mircea Eliade* (Leiden: E.J. Brill, 1976).

48. Eliade, *Sacred and Profane*; D. Eck, 'India's Tirthas: "Crossings" in Sacred Geography', *History of Religions* 20, no.4 (May 1981).

49. Eliade, *Sacred and Profane*, pp.32 – 40; D. Lowenthal, 'Past Time, Present Place: Landscape and Memory', *The Geographical Review* LXV, no.1 (January 1975). Yates, *Art of Memory*, presents a brilliant discussion of the Classical and Renaissance *art* of using structured places for the purposes of reclaiming both empirical memory and also archetypal memory,

memoria.

50.   See J. Nicholas, *Temenos and Topophilia* (London: The Guild of Pastoral Psychology Monograph: 186, 1977); J. Swan, 'Sacred Places in Nature', *The Journal of Environmental Education* 14 (1983).

51.   See P. Porter and F. Lukerman, 'The Geography of Utopia', in Lowenthal and Bowden.

52.   N. Graburn, 'Tourism: The Sacred Journey', in *Hosts and Guests*, ed. V. Smith (Oxford: Basil Blackwell, 1979); S. Bhardway, *Hindu Places of Pilgrimage in India* (Berkeley: University of California Press, 1973); J. Preston, 'Sacred Centres and Symbolic Networks in South Asia', *The Mankind Quarterly* XX, nos.3,4 (January – April 1980); Sumption.

53.   Turner: 'Pilgrimages as Social Processes', 'The Centre Out There'.

54.   Quoted in M. Philip, 'Disconcerting Discourses', *Australian Society* (February 1985); M. Foucault, *Power/Knowledge* (London: The Harvester Press, 1980).

55.   Said, p.216; also M. Edwardes, *The West in Asia 1850 – 1914* (London: B.T. Batsford Ltd, 1967). Despite his insistence on the primacy of geography as an organizer of disparate discourses, Said pays scant attention to the details of *place* and to the images evoked by *specific* places. Nor does he address his influential study to the problem of imaginative creation and production. The context of his work is also limited, dealing primarily with imperial politics and the organization of scholarship.

56.   See I. Sachs, *The Discovery of the Third World* (Cambridge, MA: MIT Press, 1976) for a discussion of Europocentrism; also Said, p.117.

57.   Said, p.5.

58.   Ibid. p.62.

59.   See M. Sheridan, *Foucault: The Will to Truth* (London: Tavistock Publications, 1981), p.34.

60.   T. Gladwin, *East is a Big Bird* (Cambridge, MA: Harvard University Press, 1971).

61.   See R. Jenkyns, *The Victorians and Ancient Greece* (Cambridge, MA: Harvard University Press, 1980); Moorehead, *The White Nile*; Fussell, *Abroad*.

62.   See P. Newby, 'Literature and the Fashioning of Tourist Taste', in *Humanistic Geography and Literature*, ed. D. Pocock (London: Croom Helm, 1981).

63.   Boon, p.149; there are many overt examples of anthropology as a travel account. These include C. Lévi-Strauss, *Triste Tropique* (London: Cape, 1973); J. Briggs, *Never in Anger* (Cambridge, MA: Harvard University Press, 1970); F. Donner, *Shabono* (New York: Delacorte Press, 1982). What makes these studies fit into the genre of travel accounts is the *presence* of the authors wihin the stories. They are shown as experiencing, involved, reacting subjects. The texts also have a certain essayistic and collage-like quality.

64.   Said, pp.93 – 8.

65.   Ibid. pp.63, 67.

66.   See Brown; D. Middleton, *Victorian Lady Travellers* (Chicago: Academy, 1982) discusses the role of the Royal Geographical Society in the nineteenth century; E. Gilbert, *British Pioneers in Geography* (Newton Abbot, Devon: David & Charles, 1972).

67.   Said, p.14.

68.   Ibid. p.22.

69.   Said, p.6; see also his 'Orientalism Reconsidered', *Race and Class* XXVII, no.2 (Autumn 1985).

70.   J. Hillman, 'On Parapsychology', *Loose Ends* (Dallas: Spring Publications, 1978) p.127; H. Corbin: *Creative Imagination in the Sufism of Ibn 'Arabi* (Princeton: Princeton University Press, 1969), 'Mundus Imaginalis or the Imaginary and the Imaginal', *Spring 1972* (New York: Spring Publications, 1972); G. Durand, 'Exploring the Imaginal', *Spring 1971* (New York: Spring Publications, 1971).

71.   Three archetypes are of particular relevance in this study – the puer, the anima and the senex. See J. Hillman (ed.), *The Puer Papers* (Dallas: Spring Publications, 1979); Hillman: *Anima* (Dallas: Spring Publications, 1985), 'On Senex Consciousness', *Spring 1970* (New

York: Spring Publications, 1970), 'The Negative Senex', *Spring 1975* (New York: Spring Publications, 1975).

72.   J. Hillman, 'The Imagination of Air and the Collapse of Alchemy', *The Eranos Jahrbuch 50-1981* (Frankfurt a/M: Insel Verlag, 1982), pp.283 – 4.

73.   J. Allen, 'Imagination and Exploration', tends to consider individual fantasies as leading to a failure in the creation of accurate geographical ideas.

74.   Hillman, *Anima*, p.25.

75.   C.G. Jung, *Collected Works Vol.16: The Practice of Psychotherapy* (London: Routledge & Kegan Paul, 1974); see also J. Hillman, *Healing Fiction* (Barrytown, NY: Station Hill Press, 1983).

76.   J. Hillman, *Re-Visioning Psychology*, p.62. See also G. Dudley, 'Jung and Eliade', *Psychological Perspectives* 10, no.1 (1979); D. Holt, 'Jung and Marx', *Spring 1973* (Dallas: Spring Publications, 1973).

77.   Saliba.

78.   Said, *Orientalism*.

79.   J. Hilton, *Lost Horizon* (1933; London: Pan, 1947).

80.   See Fussell.

81.   D. Rayfield, *The Dream of Lhasa* (London: Paul Elek, 1976), p.115.

82.   See C. Allen, *A Mountain in Tibet*.

83.   P. Fleming, *Travels in Tartary* (1934/6; London: The Reprint Society, 1941), pp.258, 275 – 9.

84.   C. Markham (ed.), *Narratives of the Mission of George Bogle to Tibet and of the Journey of Thomas Manning to Lhasa* (1879; New Delhi: Mañjuśrī Publishing House, 1971); S. Turner, *An Account of an Embassy to the Court of the Teshoo Lama in Tibet* (1800; New Delhi: Mañjuśrī Publishing House, 1971).

85.   G. Bachelard, *Water and Dreams* (Dallas: Pegasus Foundation, 1983), p.4.

86.   W. Booth, *The Rhetoric of Fiction* (Chicago: University of Chicago Press, 1961).

2. *Tibet Discovered*

1.   See G. Woodcock, *Into Tibet* (London: Faber & Faber, 1971); F. de Filippi, *An Account of Tibet: Travels of Ippolito Desideri of Pistoia S.J. 1712 – 1727* (London: n.p., 1927); J. MacGregor, *Tibet – A Chronicle of Exploration* (London: Routledge & Kegan Paul, 1970); C. Markham, *Narratives of George Bogle to Tibet and of the Journey of Thomas Manning to Lhasa* (1879; Delhi: Mañjuśrī Publishing House, 1971).

2.   See A. Moorehead, *The Fatal Impact* (Harmondsworth: Penguin, 1968); B. Stafford, *Voyage Into Substance* (Cambridge, MA: MIT Press, 1984).

3.   M. Nicolson, *Mountain Gloom and Mountain Glory* (Ithaca: Cornell University Press, 1959); G. de Beer, *Early Travellers in the Alps* (1930; London: Sidgwick & Jackson, 1966); L. Stephen, *The Playground of Europe* (London: Longmans, Green & Co., 1871); Stafford.

4.   C. Hibbert, *The Grand Tour* (London: Weidenfeld & Nicolson, 1969).

5.   S. Turner, *An Account of an Embassy to the Court of the Teshoo Lama in Tibet* (1800; New Delhi: Mañjuśrī Publishing House, 1971) p.343.

6.   Markham, p.19.

7.   Ibid. p.100; Turner, p.215.

8.   Kirkpatrick, *An Account of the Kingdom of Nepaul* (London, 1811; New Delhi: Asian Publishing Services, 1975), p.xii.

9.   See E. Said, *Orientalism* (New York: Vintage Books, 1979); H. Baudet, *Paradise on Earth* (New Haven: Yale University Press, 1965).

10.   See Baudet; Stafford; C. Glacken, *Traces on the Rhodian Shore* (Berkeley: University of California Press, 1967); T. Penniman, *A Hundred Years of Anthropology* (New York: William

Morrow & Co., 1974).

11.   R. Phillimore, *Historical Records of the Survey of India* (Dehra Dun: Survey of India, 1945, vol.1).

12.   In Bogle's and Turner's accounts, reference is made to the 'Teshoo Lama', whose correct title is the 'Panchen Lama'. I will refer to him by his correct title throughout this study. Also in these early texts, the term 'Booteeas', was often used vaguely to denote both Bhutanese and Tibetans.

13.   Turner, p.ix.

14.   S. Camman, *Trade Through the Himalayas* (Connecticut: Greenwood Press, 1970) p.31.

15.   Markham, p.5.

16.   Ibid. p.6.

17.   Ibid. pp.6 – 7.

18.   Ibid. pp.8 – 9.

19.   For example, at about the same time J. Goethe shows in his *Italian Journey 1786 – 1788* (San Francisco: North Point Press, 1982), that he was struggling to combine both an objective descriptive style and one that addressed inner experiential questions. In this text one can trace the leading edge of the European literary and aesthetic exploration of mountain landscape.

20.   See D. Siddle, 'David Livingstone: A Mid-Victorian Field Scientist', *Geographical Journal* 140, no.1 (February 1974), on the nineteenth-century debate about amateur versus professional travellers and explorers.

21.   J. Fabian, *Time and the Other* (New York: Columbia University Press, 1983), pp.111 – 13, 149; *Europe and Its Others*, ed. F. Barker *et al.*, 2 vols (Colchester: University of Essex, 1984).

22.   Markham, p.9.

23.   See Camman, pp.20 – 1.

24.   Markham, p.12.

25.   Turner, pp.206 – 7.

26.   Markham, p.9.

27.   Ibid. p.11.

28.   See H. Seton-Watson, *The Russian Empire 1801 – 1917* (Oxford: Oxford University Press, 1967).

29.   Turner, p.209.

30.   Camman, pp.55 – 6.

31.   Turner, p.288.

32.   Ibid. p.289.

33.   See K. Panikkar, *Asia and Western Dominance* (London: George Allen & Unwin, 1955).

34.   Markham, p.318.

35.   Ibid. p.177.

36.   Ibid. p.118.

37.   Baudet, pp.43 – 4.

38.   Ibid. pp.38 – 9.

39.   Turner, p.xiii.

40.   Phillimore.

41.   Said, *Orientalism*, p.117.

42.   Markham, *Narratives*, p.107.

43.   Markham, p.111.

44.   Ibid. p.99.

45.   Ibid. p.112

46.   Turner, p.293.

47.   Ibid. pp.272 – 3; see also Bogle's expansionist attitudes, in Markham, pp.57 – 60.

48.   Kirkpatrick, pp.vi – vii.

49.   Markham, p.6.

50. Baudet, p.49.
51. See Turner's stereotypical generalizations about Asiatics as lacking innovation, being conservative, and so on: *An Account*, pp.41, 367.
52. See Said, *Orientalism*, p.51.
53. Ibid. p.52.
54. Markham, p.14.
55. Ibid. p.15; Turner, pp.v – vi.
56. Turner, p.9.
57. Markham, p.16.
58. Turner, p.v.
59. M. Eliade, in his classic study of sacred space, does not bring out this idea of the boundary being a place in its own right; that the threshold has imaginal depth: *Sacred and Profane* (New York: Harcourt, Brace and World, 1959).
60. Markham, p.18.
61. Ibid.
62. Markham, p.69.
63. Ibid. p.75.
64. Ibid. pp.67-8.
65. Ibid. p.68.
66. Turner, pp.198, 317 – 18.
67. Ibid. pp.197 – 217; Markham, pp.68 – 72.
68. See K. Bazarov, *Landscape Painting* (London: Octopus Books, 1981), pp.86 – 7.
69. Markham, p.20.
70. Turner, p.387.
71. Ibid. p.45.
72. Ibid. pp.20, 53 – 4, 192 – 3.
73. Markham, p.18; cf. Kirkpatrick, pp.137 – 8.
74. See Stephen, p.39.
75. Turner, pp.137, 213 – 14.
76. Cf. also ibid., p.197, where Turner comments on Tibetan beliefs about mountain spirits.
77. Ibid., p.101. See E. Burke, *A Philosophical Enquiry into the Origins of our Ideas of the Sublime and the Beautiful*, ed. J. Boulton (1757; London: Routledge & Kegan Paul, 1958).
78. Markham, p.113.
79. Turner, p.223.
80. Ibid. p.297.
81. Cf. ibid. pp.190, 353.
82. Ibid. p.63.
83. See the plates in ibid. pp.86, 96, 138; and in Kirkpatrick, p.158.
84. Cf. Bazarov, pp.70 – 1, 84 – 6; de Beer, fig. 34, p.185.
85. Turner, p.216.
86. Markham, p.93.
87. Turner, p.127.
88. Ibid. p.184.
89. See Nicolson; Stephen.
90. de Beer, pp.180 – 4; J. Hillman, 'The Imagination of Air and the Collapse of Alchemy', *The Eranos Jahrbuch 50-1981* (Frankfurt a/M: Insel Verlag, 1982).
91. See Hillman, 'Imagination of Air', pp.290 – 1, for detailed discussion on the place of air in the scientific imagination of the eighteenth century; also I. Illich, *H_2O and the Waters of Forgetfulness* (Dallas: Dallas Institute of Humanities and Culture, 1985).
92. Turner, p.102.
93. Ibid. p.198.
94. Ibid. p.388.

95. Ibid. p.45.

96. Ibid. p.408.

97. See Hillman, 'Imagination of Air', for a discussion of the imagination at work in empirical fantasies about air.

98. Turner, p.192.

99. Ibid. p.16.

100. Ibid. p.21.

101. Ibid. p.vi.

102. Markham, p.12.

103. R. Fields, *How the Swans Came to the Lake* (Boulder, CO: Shambhala, 1981), pp.42–7.

104. Markham, p.11.

105. W. Jones, 'On the Gods of Greece, Italy and India', in *The British Discovery of Hinduism in the Eighteenth Century*, ed. P. Marshall (Cambridge: Cambridge University Press, 1970).

106. The apex of this cult of Classical Greece was surely reached in Victorian England: see R. Jenkyns, *The Victorians and Ancient Greece* (Cambridge, MA: Harvard University Press, 1980).

107. Turner, pp.306–7.

108. Kirkpatrick, p.188.

109. Markham, pp.138, 143, 146, 196; Turner, p.307.

110. Markham, p.88.

111. Ibid. p.102.

112. Turner, pp.308–10.

113. See Baudet, pp.49–50, on the respect shown towards Islamic literature in eighteenth-century Europe.

114. Turner, pp.v, 17.

115. Markham, p.87.

116. Turner, pp.306–7.

117. Ibid. p.362.

118. Ibid. pp.243, 256; Kirkpatrick, p.152.

119. Turner, p.312.

120. Ibid. pp.172, 257.

121. Markham, p.143.

122. Turner, p.257.

123. See Fields, pp.32–3.

124. Markham, p.33.

125. Ibid. p.196; see M. Foucault, *The Order of Things* (London: Tavistock, 1980), for an extensive discussion of the organization of knowledge in the Age of Reason.

126. Turner, p.310

127. Markham, pp.12, 80.

128. Ibid. pp.152–5.

129. Ibid. p.196.

130. Turner, pp.334–7.

131. Ibid. pp.334-5.

132. Markham, pp.84, 95.

133. Ibid. p.196.

134. Turner, pp.202, 257.

135. Markham, p.29.

136. Ibid. pp.48, 62.

137. Ibid. p.103.

138. Ibid. p.104.

139. Ibid. pp.27–30; Turner, pp.256–8.

140. Markham, pp.11, 86.

141. Turner, pp.31, 104, 198, 256, 319.
142. Markham, p.23.
143. Turner, pp.102, 171.
144. Markham, p.144.
145. Turner, p.284.
146. Ibid. p.152.
147. Ibid. pp.331 – 2.
148. Ibid. p.284.
149. See, for example, the delightful anthology of eighteenth-and early-nineteenth-century verse in *The Poetry of Geology*, ed. R. Hazen (London: George Allen & Unwin, 1982).
150. Markham, p.18; Turner, p.404.
151. Turner, p.277.
152. Ibid. p.278; see for example, Penniman, pp.34 – 72. He discusses the importance of travel in laying the basis for modern anthropology; see also Stafford.
153. See F. Jacob, *The Logic of Living Systems* (London: Allen Lane, 1974), p.138. Jacob discusses the emergence of the modern concept of 'environment'.
154. Markham, p.18.
155. Turner, pp.281 – 2.
156. See C. Bell, *The Religion of Tibet* (Oxford: Oxford University Press, 1931); C. Humphreys, *Buddhism* (Harmondsworth: Penguin, 1974), p.189.
157. See the discussions in Said, *Orientialism*, Foucault, *Order*.
158. Baudet, pp.59 – 60.
159. Said, *Orientalism*, p.120.
160. Ibid. p.120.
161. See C.G. Jung's use of the term *'complexio oppositorum'*, in his *Collected Works Vol.9ii: Aion* (London: Routledge & Kegan Paul, 1959).
162. Turner, p.xvi.

3. *Inventing the Threshold*

1. G. White, 'Views in India, chiefly among the Himalaya Mountains, 1825', in *Eternal Himalaya*, ed. H. Ahluwalia (New Delhi: Interprint, 1982), p.94.
2. White, p.95; see also L. Barber, *The Heyday of Natural History* (London: Jonathan Cape, 1980) for a discussion of the enthusiasm for natural history between 1820 and 1870. Similarly, for his comments in 1856 on the suitability of the Himalayas for tea plantations and for general colonization by Europeans, see B. Hodgson, *Essays on the Languages, Literature and Religion of Nepal and Tibet* (ed. P. Denwood: New Delhi: Mañjuśrī Publishing House, 1972). For other early-nineteenth-century approaches to the aesthetics of Indian and Himalayan landscape see W. and T. Daniell, *Oriental Scenery*, 6 vols (London: Longman, Hurst, Rees, Orme & Brown, 1795 – 1815); W. Orme, *Twenty Four Views in Hindustan* (London: Edward Orme, 1905); J. Fraser, *Views in the Himala Mountains* (London: Rodwell & Martin, 1820).
3. A. Lamb, *Britain and Chinese Central Asia* (London: Routledge & Kegan Paul, 1960), p.30.
4. J. Keay, *When Men and Mountains Meet* (London: Century Publishing, 1983), p.163.
5. R. Phillimore, *Historical Records of the Survey of India: Vol.II, 1800 – 1815* (Dehra Dun: Survey of India, 1950), p.86.
6. M. Le Bris, *Romantics and Romanticism* (Geneva: Skira, 1981), p.19.
7. Le Bris.
8. See K. Bazarov, *Landscape Painting* (London: Octopus Books, 1981), pp.44, 53.
9. Le Bris, p.30; see the examples of the picturesque in Daniell; Orme; Fraser.
10. White, p.126.
11. Ibid. p.125.

12.   R. Phillimore, *Historical Records of the Survey of India: Vol.III, 1815 – 1830* (Dehra Dun: Survey of India, 1950), p.42.

13.   A. Gerard, 'Narrative of a Journey from Soobathoo to Shipke, in Chinese Tartary, 1818', *Journal of the Asiatic Society* 11, no.1 (1842), p.371.

14.   Gerard, p.375.

15.   Ibid. p.378.

16.   L. Stephen, *The Playground of Europe* (London: Longmans, Green & Co., 1871), pp.258 – 61.

17.   C. Markham, *Narratives of the Mission of Geoge Bogle to Tibet and of the Journey of Thomas Manning to Lhasa* (1879; New Delhi: Mañjuśrī Publishing House, 1971) p.224.

18.   White, p.135.

19.   Le Bris, p.23.

20.   Ibid. p.24.

21.   Ibid. p.30; M. Nicolson, *Mountain Gloom and Mountain Glory* (Ithaca: Cornell University Press, 1959); P. Fletcher, in *Gardens and Grim Ravines* (Princeton: Princeton University Press, 1983), discusses the shift in Romantic aesthetics that occurred in Victorian poetry.

22.   White, p.135.

23.   In Markham, p.248.

24.   Quoted in White, p.177; see also pp.93, 148, 156; also Manning's observations in Markham, p.251.

25.   Cf. the criticism by J. Goethe, in the late eighteenth century, of an overly subjective attitude towards landscape: *Italian Journey: 1786 – 1788* (San Francisco: North Point Press, 1982).

26.   See S. Kern, *The Culture of Time and Space: 1880 – 1918* (Cambridge, MA: Harvard University Press, 1983), for a discussion about the relationship between travel, European imperial expansion and images of extended time and space.

27.   In Markham; and G. Woodcock, *Into Tibet* (London: Faber & Faber, 1971).

28.   M. Huc and Gabet, *Travels in Tartary, Tibet and China, 1844 – 5 – 6* (1850; London: George Routledge & Sons, 1928).

29.   W. Moorcroft and G. Trebeck, *Travels in the Himalayan Provinces of Hindustan and in the Punjab; in Ladakh and Kashmir; in Peshawar, Kabul, Kunduz, and Bokhara: Vol.1* (London: John Murray, 1838); W. Moorcroft, 'A Journey to Lake Manasarovara in Un-des, a Province of Little Tibet', *Asiatik Researches* 12 (1816); G. Adler, *Beyond Bokhara* (London: Century Publications, 1985).

30.   T. Duka, *Life and Works of Alexander Csoma de Koros* (1885; New Delhi: Mañjuśrī Publishing House, 1972); Hodgson.

31.   See the general accounts by Keay, *Where Men and Mountains Meet*; and C. Allen, *A Mountain in Tibet* (London: André Deutsch, 1982).

32.   White; see also J. Fraser, *Journal of a Tour through Part of the Snowy Range of the Himala* (London: 1820); F. Hamilton, *An Account of the Kingdom of Nepal* (1819; New Delhi: Mañjuśrī Publishing House, 1971); A. Eden, *Political Missions to Bootan* (New Delhi: Mañjuśrī Publishing House, 1972).

33.   J. Shipp, *The Path of Glory* (ed. C. Stranks: London: Chatto & Windus, 1969); W. Henry, *Surgeon Henry's Trifles* (ed. P. Hayward: London: Chatto & Windus, 1970); Phillimore, *Survey Vols.II, III, IV.*

34.   Keay, *Men and Mountains.*

35.   Ibid. *Men and Mountains*, pp.80 ff.

36.   Moorcroft and Trebeck, p.338.

37.   Mutual familiarity of each other's work was quite extensive among Himalayan travellers, even in these early years. See, for example, Hamilton's repeated comments on Kirkpatrick's earlier journey over a similar route: *An Account.*

38.   Manning in Markham, p.283.

39. D. Middleton, 'Guide to the Publications of the Royal Geographical Society, 1830 – 1892', *Geographical Journal* 144, Part 1 (January – December 1978).

40. Keay, *Men and Mountains*.

41. T. Freeman, 'The Royal Geographical Society and the Development of Geography', in *Geography: Yesterday and Tomorrow*, ed. E. Brown (London: Oxford University Press, 1980), p.5.

42. Freeman, p.4.

43. See Markham's complaints about Manning, in Markham.

44. See Huc and Gabet, especially the introduction by P. Pelliot.

45. See Keay, *Men and Mountains*, pp.107 – 8, 122 – 3, 132.

46. Wilson's comments in Moorcroft and Trebeck, p.1ii.

47. Moorcroft and Trebeck, p.xiv.

48. Ibid., p.xxxv.

49. H. Baudet, *Paradise on Earth* (New Haven: Yale University Press, 1965), pp.60 ff.

50. Wilson in Moorcroft and Trebeck, p.1v.

51. A. Burns, *Travels into Bokhara* (London: n.p., 1834); and Keay's comments in *Men and Mountains*, p.134.

52. Keay, *Men and Mountains*, p.34.

53. Wilson in Moorcroft and Trebeck, p.1iv.

54. Markham, p.vi.

55. Ibid. p.lxxx.

56. Ibid. p.283.

57. Ibid. p.284.

58. Ibid.

59. Ibid. p.258.

60. Ibid.

61. L. Sterne, *A Sentimental Journey* (1768; Harmondsworth: Penguin, 1970).

62. In Markham, p.214.

63. Ibid. p.290.

64. Ibid. p.289.

65. F. Maraini, *Secret Tibet* (London: Hutchinson, 1952).

66. P. Millington, *To Lhassa at Last* (London: Smith, Elder & Co., 1905).

67. R. Byron, *First Russia: Then Tibet* (London: Macmillan & Co., 1933).

68. P. Matthiesson, *The Snow Leopard* (London: Picador, 1980).

69. See D. Siddle, 'David Livingstone: A Mid-Victorian Field Scientist', *Geographical Journal* 140, Part 1 (February 1974); also J. Jackson in *The Journal of the Royal Geographical Society* 5 (1835), pp.381 – 7.

70. Markham, p.vi.

71. See the discussion of Bogle's journey in the previous chapter; also E. Kawaguchi, *Three Years in Tibet* (1909; Kathmandu: Ratna Pustak Bhandar, 1979); Moorcroft and Trebeck, *Travels*, is full of sensitive ethnographic observations.

72. In Markham, *Narratives*, pp.275, 271 – 3, 267 ff.

73. Ibid. p.286.

74. Ibid. pp.220 – 2.

75. Ibid.

76. Ibid. pp.228 – 9, 240.

77. Ibid. p.288.

78. Gerard, p.363.

79. Ibid. p.390.

80. Ibid. p.366.

81. Ibid. p.367.

82. Moorcroft, p.407.

83. Ibid. p.408.

84. Gerard, p.366.

85. Ibid. p.370.

86. For other examples of entry in Tibet being denied to Westerners at this time, see Phillimore *Survey Vol.III*, p.43; Lamb, *Britain and Chinese Central Asia*, pp.43, 63, 65.

87. Moorcroft, p.402; Allen, *A Mountain in Tibet*.

88. Gerard, p.372.

89. Heidegger, quoted in E. Casey, 'Getting Placed', *Spring 1982*, (Dallas: Spring Publications, 1982), p.18.

90. See V. Turner, *The Ritual Process* (Ithaca: Cornell University Press, 1979) for the idea of a 'liminal phase' in a rite of passage.

91. See H. Colebrook, 'On the Height of the Himalaya Mountains', *Asiatick Researches* 12 (1816); Phillimore, *Survey Vol.II*, pp.86 – 8; *Survey Vol.III*, p.2; Allen, *A Mountain*, p.59.

92. See Lamb, *Britain and Chinese Central Asia*, pp.20 – 4.

93. Ibid. pp.28 – 9, 37, 46. It seems unlikely that British actions in the Himalayas had any significant influence on Peking's policy towards Britain.

94. Ibid. pp.32, 41 ff.

95. See B. Gordon, 'Sacred Directions, Orientation and the Top of The Map, *History of Religions* 10, no. 3 (February 1971).

96. Moorcroft and Trebeck; M. Edwardes, *Playing the Great Game* (London: Hamish Hamilton, 1975), p.20; Lamb, *Britain and Chinese Central Asia*, p.61.

97. Edwardes, *Playiang the Great Game*, pp.10 – 11, 16 – 19, 24; Phillimore, *Survey Vols II, III, IV*.

98. Quoted in Phillimore, *Survey Vol.III*, p.35 (emphasis added).

99. Hamilton, p.89.

100. Phillimore, *Survey Vol.II*, p.86.

101. Quoted in W. Hunter, *Life of Brian Houghton Hodgson* (London: John Murray, 1896), p.287.

102. Phillimore, *Survey Vol.III*, p.39.

103. See Hodgson; also M. Foucault, *Power/Knowledge* (London: The Harvester Press, 1980).

104. Phillimore, *Survey Vol.II*, p.89.

105. In Markham, p.265.

106. Ibid. p.267.

107. See H.P. Blavatsky: *The Book of Golden Precepts* (London: n.p., 1889), *The Voice of the Silence* (London: n.p., 1889).

108. Moorcroft, p.430.

109. Ibid. p.485.

110. Hamilton, pp.56 – 8; H. de Lubac, *La Rencontre du Bouddhisme et de l'Occident* (Paris: n.p., 1952); G. Welbon, *The Buddhist Nirvana and its Western Interpreters* (Chicago: The University of Chicago Press, 1968).

111. Hamilton, p.57.

112. See the appreciative comments about Tibetan religious ritual made in Gerard, p.382; and in Moorcroft and Trebeck, pp.340 – 5; Moorcroft, pp.432 – 4, 465. These can be compared with the negative comments by Hamilton, pp.56 – 8.

113. Moorcroft and Trebeck, p.346.

114. Ibid.

115. Ibid. p.291.

116. Ibid. p.365.

117. Moorcroft, p.433.

118. In Markham, *Narratives*, p.291.

119. Ibid. p.255.

120.   Ibid. p.256.
121.   Ibid. p.290.
122.   Ibid. p.291.
123.   See E. Said, *Orientalism* (New York: Vintage Books, 1979); Foucault, *Power/Knowledge*; also T. Penniman, *A Hundred Years of Anthropology* (New York: William Morrow & Co., 1974), for comments about the place of travel in the development of anthropology.
124.   White, p.159.

4. *The* Axis Mundi *Appears*

1.   L. Miller, *On Top of the World* (London: Paddington Press, 1976), pp.17, 33.
2.   M. Huc and Gabet, *Travels in Tartary, Tibet and China, 1844 – 5 – 6* (1850; London: George Routledge & Sons, 1928); see also the introduction to H. Prinsep, *Tibet, Tartary and Mongolia* (London: W.H. Allen, 1852).
3.   J. Hooker, *Himalayan Journals*, 2 vols (London: 1855; New Delhi: Today and Tomorrow Publishers, 1980); L. Huxley, *Life and Letters of Sir Joseph Dalton Hooker* (London: John Murray, 1918), vol.1, p.363.
4.   A. Cunningham, *Ladâk* (1853; New Delhi: Sagar Publications, 1977); T. Thomson, *Western Himalayas and Tibet* (1852; Kathmandu: Ratna Pustak Bhandar, 1979); H. Strachey, 'On the Physical Geography of Western Tibet', *Journal of the Royal Geographical Society* 23 (1853).
5.   E. Schlagintweit, *Buddhism in Tibet* (1863; New Delhi: Susil Gupta, 1968).
6.   G. Heaney, 'Rennell and the Surveyors of India', *Geographical Journal* 134, Part 3 (September 1968); R. Clark, *Men, Myths and Mountains* (London: Weidenfeld & Nicolson, 1975), pp.93 ff.
7.   B. Hodgson, *Essays on the Languages, Literature and Religion of Nepal and Tibet* (1874; New Delhi: Mañjuśrī Publishing House, 1972). Especially important was his work on the Dhyani Buddhas.
8.   Hodgson, part II, p.1.
9.   W. Hunter, *The Life of Brian Houghton Hodgson* (London: John Murray, 1896), p.287.
10.   See C. Allen, *A Mountain in Tibet* (London: André Deutsch, 1982) pp.68, 140 – 5, 149, for some examples of the quest to find 'missing links' and 'blank spots'.
11.   C.H. Gutzlaff, 'Tibet and Stefan', *Journal of the Royal Geographical Society* 20 (1851).
12.   See T. Penniman, *A Hundred Years of Anthropology* (New York: William Morrow & Co., 1974).
13.   J. and P. Phillips, *Victorians at Home and Away* (London: Croom Helm, 1978), p.18.
14.   Huxley, *Life and Letters*, vol.1, p.364.
15.   T. Freeman, 'The Royal Geographical Society and the Development of Geography', in *Geography: Yesterday and Tomorrow*, ed. E. Brown (Oxford: Oxford University Press, 1980); C. Loomis, 'The Arctic Sublime', in *Nature and the Victorian Imagination*, eds U. Knoepflmacher and G. Tennyson (Berkeley: University of California Press, 1977).
16.   Gutzlaff, p.191.
17.   See chapter 2.
18.   Huxley, vol.1, pp.363, 486; vol.2, p.412.
19.   J. Ruskin, *Modern Painters Vol.4* (1854; Orpington, Kent: George Allen, 1888); D. Robertson, 'Mid-Victorians Among the Alps', in Knoepflmacher, *Nature and the Victorian Imagination*; K. Clark, *The Victorian Mountaineers* (London: B.T. Batsford, 1953); E. Helsinger, *Ruskin and the Eye of the Beholder* (Cambridge, MA: Harvard University Press, 1982).
20.   See the analysis in R. Shannon, *The Crisis of Imperialism: 1865 – 1915* (St Albans, Herts: Paladin, 1976).
21.   A. Wilson, *The Abode of Snow* (1885; Kathmandu: Ratna Pustak Bhandar, 1979) p.ix.
22.   Ibid. p.x.

23. Ibid.

24. M. Eliade, *The Sacred and the Profane* (New York: Harcourt, Brace and World, 1959), pp.36,42.

25. Wilson, p.128.

26. Ibid. pp.120 – 30.

27. See K. Clark, *Ruskin Today* (Harmondsworth: Penguin, 1982); Robertson, 'Mid-Victorians'; D. Cosgrove, 'John Ruskin and the Geographical Imagination', *The Geographical Review* 69, No.1 (January 1979).

28. Hooker, vol.1, p.324.

29. Ruskin, quoted in K. Clark, p.25.

30. See the introduction to Thomson.

31. Thomson, pp.207, 231. Thomson's strictly empirical approach to clouds (pp.244 – 5) is in contrast with Ruskin's use of *both* empiricism and imagination. See D. Cosgrove and J. Thornes, 'Of Truth of Clouds: John Ruskin and the Moral Order of Things', in *Humanistic Geography and Literature*, ed. D. Pocock (London: Croom Helm, 1981).

32. Huxley, vol.1, pp.363 – 4: vol.2, pp.223, 265; see also H. Smith, 'A Trip to Tibet … ', *Proceedings of the Royal Geographical Society* II (1866/67), for a lively debate between Smith, an amateur, and the famous Himalayan scientist-explorer Thomson, about the accuracy of Strachey's observations at Lake Manasarovar. Thomson sprang to the defence of Strachey, his friend and colleague: 'He did not think that a traveller merely going on a fishing excursion should pass a very decided opinion in contradiction of the observations of travellers who had preceded him': see also D. Siddle, 'David Livingstone: A Mid-Victorian Field Scientist', *Geographical Journal* 140, Part 1 (February 1974) for a discussion about the demise in status of the amateur scientist-traveller.

33. Hooker, vol.1, p.254.

34. See Huxley, vol.1, p.303; Wilson, p.238. Both clearly indicate the concern over Himalayan altitude records which started to appear in the mid-nineteenth century. See also K. Mason, 'Johnson's "Suppressed Account" of E61', *Alpine Journal* 34, no.22 (1921), for a discussion concerning Johnson's much-disputed claim to have climbed to 23,890 feet in 1866. This controversy was a long and famous one in Himalayan mountaineering history. Geology, too, contributed towards this direct engagement with the high mountain peaks. There was, for example, an interconnection between geological drawing and the representation of the sublime. The aesthetics of the sublime – mysterious, awe-inspiring, theatrical and wonderful – were encouraged by close attention to geological features. Early-nineteenth-century paintings such as 'Gordale Scar' (1813) by James Ward, which combined topographical and geological precision with bold imaginative interpretation, were direct precursors of Ruskin's ideas: M. Pointon, 'Geology and Landscape Painting in Nineteenth Century England', in his *Images of the Earth* (Lancaster: British Society for the History of Science Monograph, 1981).

35. See R. Clark.

36. Hooker, vol.1, pp.252 – 3; Wilson, p.239,

37. Wilson, p.182.

38. S. Bourne, 'Narratives of a Photographical Trip to Kashmir and Adjacent Districts', *The British Journal of Photography* (23 November – 28 December 1866) 23 November, pp.559 – 60; C. Lambert, *A Trip to Cashmere and Ladak* (London: H. King, 1877) for another example of early Himalayan photography.

39. J. Berger and J. Mohr, *Another Way of Telling* (London: Writers & Readers, 1982) p.97; F. Barker *et al.* (eds), *Europe and Its Others*, 2 vols (Colchester: University of Essex, 1984), vol.1 pp.10 – 11.

40. R. Herschkowitz, *The British Photographer Abroad* (London: Robert Herschkowitz Ltd, 1980), p.7.

41. Ibid. p.6.

42. Ruskin, *Modern Painters Vol.4*, pp.32 – 3.

43. Bourne, 'Narrative of a Photographic Trip … ' (28 Decvember 1866), p.618.

44. S. Bourne, 'Ten Weeks with a Camera in the Himalayas', *The British Journal of Photography* (15 February 1864), p.69; see also Pointon, 'Geology and Landscape Painting'.

45. See Ruskin, in K. Clark, pp.94 – 5.

46. L. Stephen, *The Playground of Europe* (London: Longmans, Green & Co., 1871) pp.48 –9; Wilson, p.216. Intricate associations with wild landscape were beginning to spring up in the British imagination, from Dartmoor to the Outer Hebrides. By the end of the eighteenth century such places, long abandoned by mainstream culture, had come to be imaginatively repopulated, drawn firmly into a new sense of British identity. As the nineteenth century progressed, this network of intimate associations spread wider to encompass the Alps, and then the Himalayas, the Arctic, and so on.

47. Thomson, p.336 (emphasis added).

48. Hooker, vol.1, pp.112 – 15, 327; vol.2, pp.46, 53, 118.

49. Ibid. vol.2, p.102; Wilson, pp.214 – 16, 340 – 1.

50. Hooker, vol.2, pp.43, 46, 50, 77, 84, 86.

51. R. Temple, *Travels in Nepal and Sikhim: 1881 – 7* (Kathmandu: Ratna Pustak Bhandar, 1977) p.8; L. Barber, *The Heyday of Natural History: 1820 – 1870* (London: Jonathan Cape, 1980); Knoepflmacher, *Nature and the Victorian Imagination*; P. Fletcher, *Gardens and Grim Ravines* (Princeton: Princeton University Press, 1983); L. Brockway, *Science and Colonial Expansion* (New York: Academic Press, 1979).

52. Hooker, vol.2, p.202.

53. G. Bachelard, *The Poetics of Space* (Boston: Beacon Press, 1969).

54. Hooker, vol.1, p.218; see chapter 2 for a discussion of S. Turner's association of Tibet with Ancient Egypt; Temple, p.16.

55. See the comparisons between *The Tibetan Book of the Dead* and *The Egyptian Book of the Dead* in C.G. Jung, *Collected Works Vol.II* (London: Routledge & Kegan Paul, 1974), para. 833; also C. Wilson, *The Occult* (New York: Vintage Books, 1973).

56. See A. Elkin, *Aboriginal Men of High Degree* (St Lucia: Queensland University Press, 1980); P. Matthiesson, *The Snow Leopard* (London: Picador, 1980).

57. A. Wilson, pp.262 – 3.

58. Hooker, Vol.1, p.255.

59. A. Wilson, pp.243 – 50.

60. Hooker, vol.1, p.v; Lambert; F. Markham, *Shooting in the Himalayas* (London: Richard Bentley, 1854),p.1.

61. Hooker, vol.1, pp.234, 329 – 30.

62. Ibid. vol.2, pp.7, 34, 60.

63. Fletcher; Knoepflmacher.

64. See Fletcher, pp.18, 82 – 3, 223; R. Clark, pp.136 – 7; See also Ruskin's subsequent doubts about nature as a moral force,*Modern Painters Vol.4*; and in K. Clark, pp. 88 – 9; see also G. Levine, 'High and Low: Ruskin and the Novelists', in Knoepflmacher, pp.138 – 40.

65. Hooker, vol.2, p.137.

66. See Thomson, pp.92, 133, 135, 160, 233.

67. Ibid. p.376 (emphasis added).

68. Cf. the discussion about revolutions in T. Kuhn, *The Structure of Scientific Revolutions* (Chicago: University of Chicago Press, 1970).

69. A. Wilson, pp.92, 129, 132.

70. Ibid. pp.134, 209, 251.

71. Ibid. pp.251 – 2.

72. Hooker, vol.2, p.174.

73. Ibid. vol.1, p.253.

74. Temple, p.121.

75. Hooker, vol.2, p.131 (emphasis added).

76. A. Wilson, p.273.
77. Hooker, vol.1, pp.253 – 4; Ruskin, *Modern Painters Vol.4*.
78. Hooker, vol.1, p.110.
79. Ruskin in K. Clark, pp.97, 105.
80. Robertson, 'Mid-Victorians', p.128; Ruskin in K. Clark, p.118; Cosgrove and Thornes, p.39.
81. Stephen, p.67.
82. A. Wilson, p.1.
83. A. Wilson, p.2; E. Swinglehurst, *Cook's Tours* (Pool, Dorset: Blandford Press, 1982).
84. A. Wilson, pp.20, 78 ff; Temple, p.10; Lambert, p.5.
85. A. Wilson, p.4.
86. Ibid. pp.8, 17 – 18, 29 – 30, 32, 34, 66 – 73.
87. Ibid. pp.63 – 5.
88. Ibid. pp.63 – 4.
89. D. MacIntyre, *Hindu-Koh* (London: n.p., 1889).
90. Huxley, vol.1, p.529.
91. See the discussion in Cosgrove and Thornes.
92. A. Wilson, p.218; see also W. Houghton, *The Victorian Frame of Mind* (New Haven: Yale University Press, 1970).
93. Ruskin in K. Clark, pp.95 – 6.
94. K. Clark, p.106.
95. Ibid. pp.91 – 3.
96. A. Wilson, p.88.
97. Cosgrove and Thornes.
98. G. Himmelfarb, *Victorian Minds* (London: Weidenfeld & Nicolson, 1968) pp.314 ff; Huxley, vol.2, pp.39 – 45; M. Peckham, *Victorian Revolutionaries* (New York: George Braziller, 1970).
99. A. Wilson, p.130.
100. See Penniman, *A Hundred Years of Anthropology*, pp.53, 64 – 7; Cunningham, *Ladâk*; Hooker, vol.1, pp.58 – 9; see H. Spenser, *The Principles of Sociology Vol.1* (London: Williams & Norgate, 1877), pp.677 ff, for an example of the way in which travel accounts were used to establish anthropological ideas. In this case Spenser refers to Wilson's *Abode of Snow*, as well as to Bogle's and Turner's accounts; see also G. Leitner, *Dardistan: 1866 – 1893* (New Delhi: Mañjuśrī Publishing House, 1978) for a vast compilation of facts and measurements so typical of the mid-to late nineteenth century.
101. Hooker, vol.1, p.165.
102. Penniman, p.142; Peckham, pp.175 – 234; Hooker, vol.1, p.174.
103. Temple, p.13.
104. Hooker, vol.1, p.131; Huxley, vol.1, p.270; R. Latham, *Tribes and Races: Vol.1* (1859; Delhi: Cultural Publishing House, 1983), p.502.
105. Temple, p.46.
106. A. Davies, 'The Aryan Myth: Its Religious Significance', *Studies in Religion* 10, no.3 (1981), pp.290 – 5; Penniman, p.149; see also, E.P. Thompson's comments, about Max Mueller's formative contribution to the Aryan mythologizing, in his 'Folklore, Anthropology and Social History', *Indian Historical Review* II, no.2 (January 1978).
107. Hodgson, Part II, p.32; Hooker, vol.1, p.130.
108. A. Wilson, p.147.
109. Ibid. pp.183 – 93.
110. Ibid. p.217.
111. Cunningham, pp.281 – 3.
112. A. Wilson, pp.164 – 5.
113. Ibid. pp.24 – 5, 302; Hodgson, Part II, pp.83 – 90.

114. Allen, *A Mountain in Tibet*, pp.15, 17, 68, 87, 106 – 7, 129.

115. A. Wilson, pp.31 – 2.

116. Hooker, vol.II, p.138 (emphasis added); A. Wilson, p.151.

117. A.Wilson, p.152 (emphasis added).

118. Ibid. p.219.

119. Ibid. p.63; Davies, p.291.

120. The idea of a core-image which gathers and organizes imagery is a fundamental one in theories of imaginative discourse. See, for example, R. Makkreel, *Dilthey: Philosopher of the Social Sciences* (Princeton: Princeton University Press, 1975), p.102.

121. Hooker, vol.1, p.118.

122. A. Wilson, p.217.

123. See S. Freud, *The Interpretation of Dreams* (London: George Allen & Unwin, 1973) for a discussion of the processes of condensation and displacement in dream work.

124. T. Cooper, 'Travels in Western China and Eastern Thibet', *Proceedings of the Royal Geographical Society* 14 (1869/70); W. Gill, *The River of Golden Sand* (London: John Murray, 1880).

125. A. Wilson, pp.78 – 83.

126. Temple, p.116.

127. A. Bennett, 'Rough Notes of a Visit to Daba, in Thibet, in August 1865'; *Proceedings of the Royal Geographical Society* 10 (1865/66), pp.166 – 7.

128. See Bennett; Cooper, p.340; Hooker, vol.2, pp.71 – 81, 89, 127; Wilson, pp.138 – 9, 142 – 5; Smith; Markham, *Shooting*, p.162; A. and R. Schalgintweit, 'A Short Account', *Journal of the Asiatic Society of Bengal* 25 (1856), p.126; J. Edgar, *Report on a Visit to Sikhim and the Thibetan Frontier* (1873; New Delhi: Mañjuśrī Publishing House, 1969) p.11; T. Montgomerie, 'Journey to Shigatze in Tibet', *Royal Geographical Journal* 45 (1875), p.331.

129. Markham, *Shooting*, p.162; Cooper, 'Travels', p.341.

130. A. Wilson, pp.178 – 9.

131. See Loomis.

132. T. Montgomerie, 'Report on Trans-Himalayan Exploration During 1867', *Journal of the Royal Geographical Society* 39 (1869), p.148.

133. Hooker, vol.2, p.215; A. Wilson, p.47.

134. Bennett, p.165.

135. Hooker, vol.1, pp.112, 118, 126, 274 – 282, 288, 342; vol.2, pp.73, 78 – 80, 219, 232, 246; Cunningham, p.261.

136. A. Wilson, p.98.

137. Gutzlaff, p.215.

138. See A. Wilson, p.177; E. Schlagintweit, pp.152 – 3; Hooker, vol.2, p.177.

139. Gutzlaff, pp.214 – 15.

140. Montgomerie, 'Journey'.

141. Hooker, vol.1, p.138.

142. See Temple, p.19, where he refers to the famous poem by Sir Edwin Arnold about the life of the Buddha: 'The Light of Asia'.

143. A. Wilson, p.255.

144. Ibid.

145. Temple, pp.21, 25.

146. See Gutzlaff, pp.204 – 5, 222.

147. A. Wilson, p.146; Gill, p.268; Hooker, vol.1, pp.340 – 1; Gutzlaff, pp.203 – 4, 207, 225; Cooper, p.340; Cunningham, pp.263 – 7; J. Barton, 'Report of Missionary Work in Thibet', *Church Missionary Intelligence* 14 (1863), p.185.

148. B. Porter, *Britain, Europe and the World, 1850 – 1982: Delusions of Grandeur* (London: George Allen & Unwin, 1983), pp.3 – 17.

149. Hooker, vol.2, p.38.

150. Loomis; L. Neatby, *The Search For Franklin* (London: Arthur Barker, 1970), pp.245 – 6.

151. Hooker, vol.1, pp.222, 255; Robertson, p.126.

152. S. Bourne, 'Narrative of a Photographic Trip ... ', *The British Journal of Photography* (7 December 1866), p.584.

153. See M. Le Bris, *Romantics and Romanticism* (Geneva: Skira, 1981) for discussion about this new mid-century Romanticism.

154. A. Wilson, p.243.

155. Ibid. p.247.

156. Ibid. p.245.

157. Ibid. pp.88, 244 – 8.

158. See P. Bishop, 'The Mysticism of Immensity', *Colloquium* 18, no.2 (October 1986) for a discussion of the later results of this shift of religious belief and its new grounding in the vast horizons opened up by the physical sciences in the late nineteenth century. In particular the religious ideas of the Himalayan and Central Asian explorer Francis Younghusband are examined.

159. A. Wilson, p.249.

160. Cunningham, pp.232 – 4.

161. Freud.

162. A. Wilson, pp.147 ff.

163. Gutzlaff; Montgomerie, 'Report'.

164. Cooper, p.338.

165. Cunningham, p.232.

166. A. Wilson, p.148.

167. C.G. Jung, 'Paracelsus as a Spiritual Phenomenon', *Collected Works Vol.13: Alchemical Studies* (trans R.F.C. Hull: London: Routledge & Kegan Paul, 1974), paras 186, 196.

168. A. Wilson, pp.151 – 2 (emphasis added).

169. Gutzlaff, p.215.

5. *Outside Time and Space*

1. P. Landon, *Lhasa*, 2 vols (London: Hurst & Blackett, 1905), vol.1, pp.222 – 8.

2. See H. Bower, *Diary of a Journey Across Tibet* (1894; Kathmandu: Ratna Pustak Bhandar, 1976) pp.13, 271 – 2; N. Prejevalsky, *Mongolia, The Tangut Country, and the Solitudes of Northern Tibet* (London: Sampson Low, Marston, Serle & Rivington, 1876), vol.1, pp.74, 80; J. White, *Sikhim and Bhutan* (1909; New Delhi: Cultural Publishing House, 1983), p.15.

3. S. Das, *Journey to Lhasa and Central Tibet* (1902; New Delhi: Mañjuśrī Publishing House, 1970); G. Sandberg, *The Exploration of Tibet* (1904; Delhi: Cosmo Publications, 1973); P. Hopkirk, *Trespassers on the Roof of the World* (London: John Murray, 1982); C. Allen, *A Mountain in Tibet* (London: André Deutsch, 1982); P. Hopkirk, *Foreign Devils on the Silk Road* (Newton Abbot, Devon: Readers Union, 1981).

4. D. Rayfield, *the Dream of Lhasa* (London: Paul Elek, 1976), p.209; G. Bonvalot, *Across Thibet*, 2 vols (London: Cassell & Co., 1891, vol.2), pp.195 – 6; S. Hedin, *Through Asia* 2 vols (London: Methuen & Co., 1898), vol. 1. pp.3 – 18.

5. This is the comment by Lord Rosebery, the British Foreign Secretary, quoted in the introduction to Bower, p.vii.

6. See Hopkirk, *Foreign Devils*; J. Keay, *The Gilgit Game* (London: John Murray, 1979).

7. Annie Taylor was also the inspiration for setting up the Tibetan Pioneer Mission and generally stimulating British missionary work in the Himalayan region: see W. Carey, *Travel and Adventure in Tibet* (1900; Delhi: Mittal Publications, 1983) pp.143 – 4 (this work contains Taylor's diary). For other missionary activity see J. Barton, 'Report of Missionary Work in Thibet', *Church Missionary Intelligence* 14 (1863); A. Francke, *History, Folklore and Culture of*

Tibet (1905; New Delhi: Ess Ess Publications, 1979), which shows some of the remarkable scholarly work carried out by the Moravian missionaries in the Western Himalayas.

8.   See Hedin; as well as the recent popular accounts by Hopkirk: *Foreign Devils; Trespassers; Allen, A Mountain*; see also the story of Theo Sorensen, missionary, in P. Kvaerne, *A Norwegian Traveller in Tibet* (New Delhi: Mañjuśrī Publishing House, 1973).

9.   D. Freshfield, *Round Kanchenjunga* (1903; Kathmandu: Ratna Pustak Bhandar, 1979) pp.12 – 13.

10.   D. Whitley, 'The Attack on Tibet', *Littel's Living Age* 206 (1895), p.218.

11.   See A. Lamb, *Britain and Chinese Central Asia* (London: Routledge & Kegan Paul, 1960).

12.   Landon, vol.1, pp.22 – 3.

13.   L. Waddell, *Among the Himalayas* (1899; Kathmandu: Ratna Pustak Bhandar, 1978), p.414.

14.   F. Grenard, *Tibet* (1903; Delhi: Cosmo Publications, 1974) pp.51, 53 – 4, 148; Bonvalot, *Across Thibet*, vol.1, p.90; F. Younghusband, *The Heart of a Continent* (1896; London: John Murray, 1937), pp.37, 48, 60.

15.   W. Rockhill, *The Land of the Lamas* (1891; New Delhi: Asian Publication Services, 1975), pp.43 – 4; C. Macaulay, *Report on a Mission to Sikhim and the Tibetan Frontier – 1884* (1885; Kathmandu: Ratna Pustak Bhandar, 1977).

16.   A. Carey, 'A Journey Round Chinese Turkistan and along the Northern Frontier of Tibet', *Proceedings of the Royal Geographical Society* 9 (1887), pp.731, 735; Hedin, *Through Asia*, vol.1, pp.988, 1027 – 8, 1173 – 6; St George Littledale, 'A Journey Across Tibet, From North to South, and West to Ladak', *The Geographical Journal* VII no.5 (May 1896), p.454.

17.   Rockhill, pp.166, 175.

18.   On the Tibetan mythologizing of Queen Victoria and the czar, see Landon, vol.1, pp.356 – 7; for stories of travellers told by Tibetans, see Grenard, pp.115 – 17; Littledale, p.476.

19.   Grenard, pp.45 – 6.

20.   Hedin, vol.2, p.956; Grenard, p.142; Bonvalot, vol.1, p.6; Littledale, p.460; Younghusband, *Heart of a Continent*, p.216; J. Duncan, *A Summer Ride Through Western Tibet* (1906; London: Collins, 1925), p.112.

21.   P. Millington, *To Lhassa at Last* (London: Smith, Elder & Co., 1905).

22.   See S. Kern, *The Culture of Time and Space* (London: Weidenfeld & Nicolson, 1983); R. Shannon, *The Crisis of Imperialism: 1865 – 1915* (St Albans, Herts: Paladin, 1976).

23.   Shannon, p.270.

24.   M. Edwardes, *The West in Asia: 1850 – 1914* (London: B.T. Batsford Ltd, 1967), pp.8, 25 – 6; R. Faber, *The Vision and the Need* (London: Faber & Faber, 1966).

25.   Faber, p.13.

26.   Kern, pp.1 – 2.

27.   Ibid. pp.61 – 4, 68, 89 – 90, 104 – 6, 230 – 3; J. Fabian, *Time and the Other* (New York: Columbia University Press, 1983), pp.111 – 13, 121 – 2.

28.   Faber, p.166.

29.   E. Relph, *Place and Placelessness* (London: Pion, 1976), pp.59 – 61, 79.

30.   Kern, pp.223 – 6.

31.   Ibid. pp.230 – 3; T. Freeman, 'The Royal Geographical Society and the Development of Geography', in *Geography: Yesterday and Tomorrow*, ed. E. Brown (Oxford: Oxford University Press, 1980), p.25.

32.   Kern, p.228.

33.   Ibid. p.92.

34.   Ibid. pp.164 – 7.

35.   Ibid. p.4.

36.   Edwardes, *The West in Asia*, pp.68, 75 – 6.

37.   Faber, pp.119 – 20.

38. Lamb, *Britain and Chinese Central Asia*, pp.172, 266 – 71.

39. Ibid. p.207.

40. Ibid. pp.230 – 1, 294; Keay, *The Gilgit Game*; Hopkirk, *Foreign Devils*.

41. H. Blavatsky, *Isis Unveiled* (1877; Pasadena: Theosophical University Press, 1972).

42. R. Kipling, *Kim* (1898; London: Macmillan, 1943).

43. A. Conan Doyle, 'The Empty House', in *Sherlock Holmes: The Complete Short Stories* (1928; London: John Murray, 1980), p.569.

44. H. Rider Haggard, *She* (1887; London: Macmillan, 1943).

45. Kern, pp.19 – 20, 24 – 7, 41 – 2; Fabian, pp.111 – 13, 121 – 2, claims that anthropological discourse is part of a long tradition of rhetoric that has been concerned with conceiving outlandish images and moving them in a strange, imaginary space. He connects anthropology with earlier memory systems.

46. See F. Barker *et al.* (eds), *Europe and Its Others*, 2 vols (Colchester: University of Essex, 1984); H. Ridley, *Images of Imperial Rule* (London: Croom Helm, 1983).

47. E. Said, *Orientalism* (New York: Vintage Books, 1979), p.6.

48. See W. Conway, *Climbing and Exploration in the Karakoram-Himalayas* (London: T.Fisher Unwin, 1894), p.ix.

49. See Rockhill, *Land of the Lamas*, pp.67 – 73, 176 – 7; H. Tanner, 'Our Present Knowledge of the Himalayas', *Proceedings of the Royal Geographical Society* 13 (1891), p.411; Hopkirk, *Foreign Devils*; Franke; H. Bates (ed.), *Illustrated Travels, Vol.1* (London: Cassell, Petter & Galpin, 1895), p.30.

50. Said, p.7.

51. M. Foucault, *Power/Knowledge* (London: The Harvester Press, 1980); C. Markham (ed.), *Narratives of the Mission of George Bogle to Tibet and of the Journey of Thomas Manning to Lhasa* (1876; New Delhi: Mañjuśrī Publishing House, 1971).

52. F. Younghusband, *India and Tibet* (London: John Murray, 1910), pp.2 – 3.

53. Younghusband's introduction to Landon, vol.1, pp.ix – x.

54. Said, p.7.

55. Lamb, *Britain and Chinese Central Asia*, p.207.

56. Edwardes, *The West in Asia*, pp. 68 – 76.

57. Ibid. p.127; Lamb, *Britain and Chinese Central Asia*, pp.49, 172.

58. Ibid, pp.47 – 8; D. Woodman, *Himalayan Frontiers* (New York: Frederick A. Praeger, 1969); A. Lamb, *The Sino – Indian Border in Ladakh* (Columbia: University of South Carolina Press, 1975).

59. Edwardes, *The West in Asia*, pp.95 – 7, 102 – 13; Younghusband, *India and Tibet*, pp.76 – 7, 236.

60. Quoted in A. Lamb, 'Some Notes on Russian Intrigue in Tibet', *Journal of the Royal Central Asian Society* 46 (1959), p.52; Freshfield, *Kanchenjunga*, p.62; Waddell, *Himalayas*, pp.vi – viii, 279 – 81.

61. E.g. Waddell, *Himalayas*, pp.147 – 8; Lamb, *Britain and Chinese Central Asia*, p.238; Younghusband, *Heart of a Continent*, p.xiv; Lamb, 'Notes', pp.42, 49; Landon, vol.1, p.28.

62. Lamb, *Central Asia*, p.152, discusses the riots in Sikkim which occurred during this period.

63. E. Chandler, *The Unveiling of Lhasa* (1905; London: Edward Arnold, 1931), pp.6, 19; A. Landor, *In the Forbidden Land* (London: William Heinemann, 1899), pp.41, 91, 452; Landon, vol.1, p.48; Lamb, *Central Asia*, p.170; G. Curzon, *Frontiers* (Oxford: Clarendon Press, 1908), p.6.

64. Landon, vol.1, p.25; see also Curzon's comments quoted in Lamb, *Central Asia*, p.260.

65. Ney Elias quoted in Lamb, 'Notes', p.51.

66. Lamb, *Central Asia*, p.155; Landon, vol.2, pp.8, 14.

67. Lamb, *Central Asia*, pp.235, 256 ff; Lamb, 'Notes', p.57; Edwardes, *The West in Asia*, p.91.

68. Grenard, p.39.
69. See Bower.
70. Landon, vol.2, pp.21, 24.
71. Lamb, *Central Asia*, pp.206, 266 – 71.
72. Freshfield, pp.66 – 8.
73. Curzon, pp.55 – 7.
74. Fantasies comparing the British and Roman Empires were common among British imperial theorists at the close of the nineteenth century; see Faber, p.19; F. Hutchins, *The Illusion of Permanence* (Princeton: Princeton University Press, 1967), pp.143 – 51.
75. E. Knight, *Where Three Empires Meet* (1892; London: Longmans, Green and Co., 1935).
76. Bower, p.242.
77. J. Louis, *The Gates of Thibet* (1894; Delhi: Vivek Publishing House, 1972) p.32; Littledale, 'Journey'.
78. Younghusband, *India and Tibet*, p.115; Bower, p.95.
79. Landon, vol.1, p.116.
80. Grenard, p.285.
81. Whitley, pp.218 – 19.
82. Carey, *Travel and Adventure*, p.20.
83. See C. Ryan, *H.P. Blavatsky and the Theosophical Movement* (Pasadena: Theosophical University Press, 1975).
84. Landon, vol.2, p.224.
85. Bower, p.1; Landon, vol.1, p.xi; Waddell *Himalayas*, p.vii; Hedin, vol.1, pp.3 – 18.
86. Freshfield, p.152; Knight, p.69; Yule, in Prejevalsky, p.ix; H. Hensoldt, 'Occult Science in Thibet', *Arena* 10 (1894), p.184.
87. Carey, *Travel and Adventure*, p.19.
88. *The Spectator* (London), 6 October 1888.
89. *The Spectator* (London), 13 August 1904; quoted in Lamb, *Central Asia* p.203; A. and K. Heber, *Himalayan Tibet and Ladakh* (1903; New Delhi: Ess Ess Publications, 1978), pp.34 – 5, refer to 'Hob-goblin-land' and 'eerie wonderland'.
90. Carey, *Travel and Adventure*, p.25; Rockhill (p.56) also entered Tibet from China.
91. Louis, p.69 (emphasis added); see also Chandler, p.28; Grenard, p.10; Freshfield, p.261.
92. Hensoldt, p.648; Hedin, vol.2, p.1000; Chandler, p.82; I. Bird-Bishop, *Among the Tibetans* (New York: Fleming H. Revell Co., 1894), p.40.
93. Landon, vol.1, pp.84, 137, 139.
94. Carey, *Travel and Adventure*, p.26 (emphasis added).
95. Louis, pp.2 – 3 (emphasis added); Freshfield, pp.16 – 17.
96. S. Stone, *In and Beyond the Himalayas* (London: Edward Arnold, 1896), p.286.
97. Waddell, *Himalayas*, p.189.
98. Ibid. *Himalayas*, p.400.
99. Chandler, pp.86 – 7; Landon, vol.2, p.154.
100. Hedin, vol.2, p.1050.
101. Littledale, p.464.
102. Grenard, pp.5, 80.
103. See Landon; Younghusband, *India and Tibet*; Bonvalot, vol.1, pp.188 – 93; Grenard, p.175.
104. Chandler, p.63; Landon, vol.1, pp.122, 136.
105. See J. Hillman, *The Dream and the Underworld* (New York: Harper & Row, 1979), pp.21, 178.
106. Stone, p.160.
107. Chandler, p.50; Knight, p.45; Carey, *Travel and Adventure*, pp.22 – 3.
108. Macaulay, p.71.
109. Bower, pp.82, 106.

110. Knight, p.44.
111. Landon, vol.2, pp.154 – 5.
112. Freshfield, pp.130 – 1.
113. Grenard, p.28.
114. Rockhill, p.241.
115. Chandler, p.290.
116. Younghusband, *India and Tibet*, pp.56, 268.
117. Ibid. pp.174 – 5; Grenard, p.311.
118. Grenard, p.301.
119. Landon, vol.1, p.176.
120. Chandler, p.124.
121. Ibid. p.246.
122. Ibid. p.265.
123. Waddell, *Himalayas*, p.268.
124. Landon, vol.1, p.156; vol.2, p.54.
125. Younghusband, *India and Tibet*, p.128.
126. Freshfield, p.250.
127. Grenard, pp.336 – 7.
128. Landon, vol.2, p.262.
129. Hensoldt, pp.370 – 3.
130. See Ryan, pp.18 – 21, 23 – 8.
131. Ryan, p.51; R. Hutch, 'Helena Blavatsky Unveiled', *Journal of Religious History* 11, no.2 (December 1980), p.324.
132. Landon, vol.1, p.301.
133. J. White, p.49.
134. Grenard, p.136.
135. Hensoldt, pp.186 – 7.
136. Grenard, p.72; Bonvalot, vol.2, p.142.
137. Landon, vol.2, p.126.
138. L. Waddell, *Tibetan Buddhism* (1895; New York: Dover Publications, 1972), p.4; Hensoldt, p.186; Freshfield, pp.90 – 1.
139. Bower, p.35; Whitely, p.220.
140. See J. Napier, *Bigfoot* (London: Abacus, 1976).
141. Waddell, *Himalayas*, pp.223 – 4.
142. Macaulay, p.36.
143. Rockhill, pp.116 – 17.
144. Ibid. p.150.
145. Ibid. p.151.
146. Ibid. p.256.
147. Stone, *In and Beyond the Himalayas*, p.129; see also Bates, *Illustrated Travels*, vol.3, pp.284 – 7: 'any bachelor, with an income of 500 pounds a year and not tied down by a profession, or any other hindrance, can enjoy a trip to the "glorious East", and four months of first rate shooting, amidst the grandest scenery imaginable and in a delicious climate.'
148. Napier.
149. Ryan, pp.19 – 20.
150. Hutch, pp.324 – 5.
151. Rayfield, p.116.
152. Bonvalot, vol.2, pp.64 – 7.
153. Landon, vol.1, p.36; Younghusband, *India and Tibet*, pp.122 – 4, 268; Chandler, *Unveiling*, p.1.
154. Hutchins, pp.73 ff.
155. See J. Hillman, 'Abandoning the Child', in his *Loose Ends* (Dallas: Spring Publications,

1975); N. Chabani Manganyi, 'Making Strange: Race, Science and Ethnopsychiatric Discourse', in *Europe and Its Others*, vol.1, ed. F. Barker.

156. See H. Ellenberger, *The Discovery of the Unconscious* (New York: Basic Books, 1970).

157. Landon, vol.2, p.45.

158. See Grenard, p.262.

159. Grenard, pp. 88 – 9; 'The Capture of Lhasa', *The Spectator* (London), 13 August 1904, pp.213 – 14.

160. Landon, vol.2, p.262.

161. Knight, p.43; Heber, p.35, writes of 'a fantastic dream'.

162. Grenard, p.273.

163. Hedin, vol.2, p.1018.

164. Bonvalot, vol.1, p.207.

165. Ibid.

166. Carey, 'A Journey', p.742; Littledale, p.465.

167. Bonvalot, vol.1, p.207; see also Waddell, *Himalayas*, p.34.

168. Grenard, pp.37, 43 – 4.

169. Landon, vol.I, p.139; Whitley, pp.219 - 20; Littledale, p.460; Stone, p.286.

170. See Waddell, *Himalayas*, pp.34, 416.

171. Bonvalot, vol.1, p.185; Chandler, p.64.

172. See Landor, pp.298, 300; Hedin, vol.2, p.1000; Freshfield, p.146.

173. Grenard, pp.4, 9 – 10; Louis, p.69; Carey, *Travel and Adventure*, p.25.

174. Younghusband, *India and Tibet*, pp.326 – 7; Grenard, p.18.

175. Younghusband, *Heart of a Continent*, pp.39 – 40, 219 – 21.

176. See Hedin, vol.2, pp.1000 – 1; Freshfield, p.113.

177. Bonvalot, vol.1, p.24.

178. Landon, vol.1, p.381; Grenard, p.48; Freshfield, pp.257 – 8.

179. Landon, vol.1, pp.340 – 1, 346.

180. Chandler, p.28.

181. Landon, vol.2, p.115.

182. Millington, pp.118 – 19.

183. See Kern's discussion of Impressionism in terms of its role within the changes in attitude towards space and time that were occurring at the turn of the century: Kern, p.21.

184. Waddell, *Himalayas*, p.337.

185. Landon, vol.1, p.141.

186. Grenard, p.48.

187. Chandler, p.126; Landon, vol.2, pp.29, 43.

188. See Yule's comments in the introduction to Prejevalsky, p.x; also Landon, vol.1, p.146.

189. Chandler, p.227.

190. Landon, vol.2, pp.92, 97, 98.

191. See G. Welbon, *The Buddhist Nirvana and its Western Interpreters* (Chicago: University of Chicago Press, 1968).

192. Grenard, p.61.

193. Louis, pp.69 – 70.

194. Younghusband, *India and Tibet*, pp.315 ff; Grenard, pp.61 – 2, 326 – 9.

195. Landon, vol.2, pp.40 – 1; see Kern for a discussion of the revolution that was occurring in the western conception of immensity at the turn of the century.

196. In Markam, *Narratives*, pp.23 – 4; Millington, p.140.

197. See Grenard, p.18; Knight, p.39; Stone, p.286; Freshfield, p.146; Bird-Bishop, p.40; Duncan, pp.89 – 90.

198. Chandler, pp.146 – 7.

199. Bower, pp.63, 102, 208.

200. Landor, pp.174, 269, 276, 338.

201. Ibid. pp.217, 293.
202. Ibid. p.436.
203. See Littledale, p.469; Grenard, pp.87 ff.
204. Rockhill, pp. 92, 151, 229; and J. White, p.110.
205. Grenard, p.226 (emphasis added); Bower, p.13.
206. E. Kawaguchi, *Three Years in Tibet* (1909; Kathmandu: Ratna Pustak Bhandar, 1979).
207. For a negative evaluation of Tibetan monks, see Prejevalsky, p.74; Landor, pp.255 – 6. For mixed reactions, see Younghusband, *India and Tibet*, pp.266, 310 – 12; Rockhill, p.91. For a positive evaluation, see Hensoldt.
208. See Littledale, pp.473 – 4; Whitley, p.226; Landon, vol.1, p.355; vol.2, p.44; Waddell, *Tibetan Buddhism*, p.573.
209. Landon, vol.1, p.358.
210. Grenard, p.346; Waddell, *Himalayas*, p.213; Rockhill, pp.87, 205, 286.
211. Rockhill, pp.64 – 5; Kawaguchi.
212. Grenard, p.109.
213. W. Carey, *Travel and Adventure*, p.58.
214. Ibid. p.23.
215. Grenard, p.283.
216. Ibid. p.330.
217. Ibid. p.336.
218. Ibid pp.346 – 7; W. Carey, pp.117 – 20.
219. Landon, vol.1, p.355; W. Carey, p.116.
220. Kawaguchi, pp.422 – 3.
221. Landon, vol.2, pp.40 – 1.
222. Grenard, p.95.
223. Rockhill, p.216; Chandler, p.246.
224. Grenard, p.336; Landon, vol.2, p.270.
225. Prejevalsky, p.80; for extreme attitudes also see Grenard, pp.326 - 9; Landon, vol.2, p.46.
226. Hedin, vol.1, pp.4 - 5. Hensoldt. pp. 184–5.
227. See Landon, vol.2, pp.10 – 18.
228. Grenard, pp.88 – 9; W. Carey *Travel and Adventure*, p.56.
229. See Millington, pp.145 – 8.
230. Bonvalot, vol.1, p.139.
231. See Said, *Orientalism*.
232. W. Carey, p.23.
233. See Bower, p.177.
234. Landon, vol.2, pp.283 – 4.
235. Ibid. vol.1, pp.130 – 3.
236. Hedin, vol.1, pp.3 – 18.
237. Kern, p.166.
238. Landon, vol.1, preface.
239. Grenard, p.iv.
240. Chandler, p.248.
241. See Kern, pp.9, 68, 68, 88 – 90, 128, 211 – 13, 228 – 32.
242. Chandler, p.248.
243. Freshfield, p.152.
244. Ibid.
245. See Kern, pp.47 – 9.
246. Chandler, p.251.
247. W. Ottley, *With Mounted Infantry in Tibet* (London: Smith, Elder & Co., 1906), p.236; Millington, p.165.

248. Younghusband, *India and Tibet*, pp.316 – 17.
249. Chandler, pp.77 – 80.
250. Ibid. pp.116 – 18
251. Ibid. p.225.
252. Ibid. pp.38, 93.
253. Ibid. pp.109 – 10.
254. Ibid. pp.247 – 8.
255. Freshfield, pp.2 – 4, 49; Tanner, 'Our Present Knowledge', p.420; Waddell, *Himalayas*, pp.73, 256, 315.
256. See Freshfield, p.55.
257. Waddell, *Himalayas*, pp.243, 286; Freshfield, pp. 78–9.
258. Younghusband, *Heart of a Continent*, pp.208 – 9.
259. Bonvalot, vol.2, pp.73 – 4.
260. Waddell, *Himalayas*, p.21.
261. Grenard, p.20; Freshfield, p.165.
262. Chandler, p.247; Kern, pp.105 – 6, discusses Spengler's work in the context of this period of disillusionment.
263. Chandler, pp.251, 353.
264. Ibid. pp.256 – 60.
265. Younghusband, *India and Tibet*, pp.395 – 6.
266. Quoted in Allen, *A Mountain*, pp.201 – 2.
267. Millington, p.77.
268. See Chandler; 'The Capture of Lhasa', *The Spectator* (London), 13 August 1904.
269. Landon, vol.2, p.29.
270. Waddell, *Tibetan Buddhism*, pp.3 – 4.
271. 'The Capture of Lhasa', *The Spectator* (London), 13 August 1904.
272. Rayfield, pp.130, 154 – 5.
273. See D. Middleton, *Victorian Lady Travellers* (Chicago: Academy Chicago, 1982); L. Miller, *On Top of the World* (London: Paddington Press, 1976).
274. Duncan, p.118.
275. E. Said, 'Orientalism Reconsidered', *Race and Class* XXVII, No.2 (Autumn 1985), p.12.
276. M. Foucault: *Power/Knowledge* (London: The Harvester Press, 1980), *The History of Sexuality* (New York: Vintage Books, 1980).
277. See J. Hillman, *Anima* (Dallas: Spring Publications, 1985) pp.28, 47, for a discussion of one aspect of the 'eternal feminine'; for another see his *The Myth of Analysis* (New York: Harper & Row, 1978), part III; see also C.G. Jung, *Collected Works Vol.5* (trans. R.F.C. Hull; London: Routledge & Kegan Paul, 1974); E. Whitmont, *Return of the Goddess* (London: Routledge & Kegan Paul, 1983).
278. See Hillman, *Anima*, pp.29 – 31, 41 – 7; Ellenberger, *Discovery of the Unconscious*; Hillman, *The Myth of Analysis*, part III. For a more precise discussion, see A. Carotenuto, 'Sabina Spielrein, and C.G. Jung', *Spring 1980* (Dallas: Spring Publications, 1980).
279. Stone, p.274; Tanner, p.418; Grenard, p.99.
280. See Freshfield, p.127; Louis, p.69; Stone; Bird-Bishop, pp.39, 71.
281. Hensoldt, p.182.
282. See Bird-Bishop, pp.40, 146; Duncan, p.90. Landon, vol.2, pp.215 – 16, discusses the hats and clothing of the Tibetans. These examples could be greatly increased by referring to other travellers.
283. Quoted in Rayfield, p.191.
284. Landon, vol.2, pp.157 – 64.
285. Ibid. pp.319 – 20.
286. W. Carey, p.40.
287. Hensoldt, pp.654 – 9; see also chapter 2 where Bogle's similar reaction to the Panchen

lama over a hundred years earlier is discussed.

288. See Hillman, *Anima*, pp.21, 128 – 33.

289. Ibid. pp.29 – 31, 41 – 7.

290. Ibid. pp.103 – 13, on depersonalization and soul-loss.

291. Ibid. pp.109 – 11. It should be noted that Jung made repeated reference to Rider Haggard's novel *She* when discussing the anima.

292. See J. Hillman, 'Anima Mundi', *Spring 1982* (Dallas: Spring Publications, 1982), p.77.

293. Lamb, *Central Asia*, p.203.

294. Ibid. pp.157, 273 – 4; Ottley, pp.234 – 5; Lamb, 'Notes', p.59; also Macaulay, pp.83 – 4; Littledale, p.475; Rockhill, p.209; Waddell, *Himalayas*, pp.vi, 4.

295. Comments in Tanner, pp.422 – 3.

296. W. Carey, *Travel and Adventure*, pp.21, 65, 114; Bower, p.226; *The Spectator* (London), 13 August 1904.

297. Jung, *Collected Works Vol.5*, para. 678; J. Hillman: *Puer Papers* (Dallas: Spring Publications, 1979); 'The Negative Senex', *Spring 1975* (Dallas: Spring Publications, 1975); see also G. Paris, *Pagan Meditations* (Dallas: Spring Publications, 1986) for reflections on Aphrodite and gold.

298. Rockhill, pp.102, 230; Waddell, *Tibetan Buddhism*, p.3.

299. Landon, vol.2, pp.31 – 5, 190 – 1; Hedin, vol.1.

300. Hensoldt, pp.650 – 1; P. Bishop, *Tibetan Religion: Western Imagination* (London: Athlone Press, forthcoming).

301. Hensoldt, pp.370 – 3, 656; Blavatsky, *Isis Unveiled*.

302. See Waddell, *Himalayas*, p.283; Landon, vol.2, p.30.

303. See, for example, the Himalayan veteran Hooker's opinions about this manuscript in 1894 – 5; L. Huxley, *The Life and Letters of Sir Joseph Dalton Hooker*, 2 vols (London: John Murray, 1918, vol.2), pp.334 – 5.

304. Hensoldt, pp.660 – 1; Landon, vol.2, pp.163 – 7.

305. A. David-Neel, *My Journey to Lhasa* (New York: Harper & Row, 1927); Miller, *On Top of the World*, pp.144 – 5.

306. See Hillman, *Puer Papers*.

307. Kipling; Faber, pp.13, 100 – 1, 122.

308. Landon, vol.2, p.50; Chandler, p.278.

309. See G. Seaver, *Francis Younghusband: Explorer and Mystic* (London: John Murray, 1952); P. Bishop, 'The Mysticism of Immensity', *Colloquium* 18, no.2 (October 1986) for details of Younghusband's mysticism.

310. Younghusband, *India and Tibet*, p.325.

311. Seaver, pp.374 – 5.

312. Ibid; see also Younghusband, *Heart of a Continent*; see Freshfield, p.160, for more reflections on mountains and stars by a Himalayan mountaineer.

313. W. Graham, 'Travel and Ascents in the Himalaya', *Proceedings of the Royal Geographical Society*, 6 (1884); Conway; Miller, *On Top of the World*; F. Keenlyside, *Peaks and Pioneers* (London: Elek, 1975), pp.107 – 9; Waddell, *Himalayas*, pp.377 – 92; K. Mason, *Abode of Snow* (London: Rupert Hart-Davis, 1955).

314. Freshfield, pp.3 – 4.

315. Ibid. pp.71, 124 – 5.

316. Ibid. p.126, 127.

317. Ibid. p.152.

318. See Graham, pp.446 – 7; Waddell, *Himalayas*, pp.vi, 359, 391.

319. Huxley, vol.2, pp.452 – 3.

320. Chandler, p.51.

321. Macaulay, pp.24, 37.

322. Louis, pp.142 – 3.

323. Chandler, p.199; Landon; also Whitley; see Millington, p.30, for details of the signpost at Jeylap-la.
324. Bower, pp.147 – 8
325. Grenard, pp.115 – 17; Macaulay, p.16; Louis, p.48; Younghusband, *India and Tibet*, pp.254, 270; Landon, vol.1, p.246; Lamb, *Central Asia*, pp.296 – 7.
326. See J. White, pp.48 – 9; Younghusband, *India and Tibet*, p.123.
327. Lamb, *Central Asia*, p.232.
328. Ibid. pp.245 – 51.
329. Ibid. p.253; also Lamb, 'Notes', pp.54 – 7; Landon, vol.1, p.33.
330. Edwardes, *The West in Asia*, p.95.
331. Waddell, *Himalayas*, p.242; Freshfield, p.242.
332. Younghusband, *India and Tibet*, pp.197 – 200; Landon, vol.1, pp.309 – 11.
333. Waddell, *Himalayas*, p.282; Louis, p.72.
334. Lamb, *Central Asia*, p.309.
335. Relph, pp.48 – 9.
336. Grenard, pp.36 – 7.
337. Kern, p.187; see Macaulay and Landon for extensive comments on, and use of, photographs that are typical of the era. Fanny Bullock Workman was described as a 'Keen Kodaker': in Middleton, *Victorian Lady Travellers*, pp.86 – 7.
338. Kern, p.39.
339. On the use of photographs for ethnographic purposes, see Waddell, *Tibetan Buddhism*; Rockhill.
340. Freshfield, pp.40, 71, 301; Conway, pp.165 – 6.
341. Freshfield, p.29.
342. Ibid. pp.vii, ix, xix, 29, 40, 159, 195 – 8, 263.
343. Kipling, pp.7 – 13.

6. *Lost Horizons*

1. F. Maraini, *Secret Tibet* (London: Hutchinson, 1952) p.47.
2. C. Bell, *Tibet: Past and Present* (London: Oxford University Press, 1927) pp.160 – 1; C. Bell, *Portrait of the Dalai Lama* (London: Collins, 1946).
3. S. Chapman, *Lhasa: The Holy City* (London: Chatto & Windus, 1940), p.11; W. King, 'The Telegraph to Lhasa', *The Geographical Journal* 63 (1924), pp.527 – 31.
4. R. Byron, *First Russia: Then Tibet* (London: Macmillan and Co., 1933), pp.270, 278 – 9; R. Ford, *Captured in Tibet* (London: Pan Books, 1958).
5. A. de Riencourt, *Lost World: Tibet, Key to Asia* (London: Victor Gollancz, 1951), pp.23, 152 – 3; H. Harrer, *Seven Years in Tibet* (London: Rupert Hart-Davis, 1953), p.119.
6. Harrer, p.126.
7. King, p.530.
8. Chapman, pp.145, 185 – 6.
9. Ibid. pp.51, 70 – 1; Bell, *Tibet*, pp.162 – 3.
10. Byron, p.239.
11. Chapman, p.245.
12. See A. David-Neel: *My Journey to Lhasa* (New York: Harper & Row, 1927): *Magic and Mystery in Tibet* (Paris, 1929; New York: Dover Publications, 1971); A. Govinda, *The Way of the White Clouds* (London: Hutchinson, 1969); K. Winkler, *Pilgrim of the Clear Light* (Berkeley: Dawnfire Books, 1982); de Riencourt.
13. Chapman, p.290.
14. Byron, p.196.
15. David-Neel, *Magic and Mystery*, pp.199 – 204.

16. Chapman, p.17.

17. Harrer, p.196.

18. L. Thomas Jnr, *Out of this World* (New York: The Greystone Press, 1950), pp.208 – 9.

19. A. Migot, *Tibetan Marches* (London: Rupert Hart Davis 1960) pp. 226–9: A Guibaut. *Tibetan Venture* (London John Murray, 1949), pp.7 – 8, 15, 79 – 80.

20. W. Unsworth, *Everest* (Harmondsworth: Penguin, 1982); K. Mason, *Abode of Snow* (London: Rupert Hart-Davis, 1955).

21. David-Neel, *My Journey*, pp.xii, xxi – xxvi, 190.

22. Guibaut, p.84.

23. See G. Tucci, *To Lhasa and Beyond* (Rome: Istituto Poligrafico Dello Stato, 1956), pp.5 – 7.

24. See Bell, *Tibet*, pp.150, 154 – 9, 246; F. Bailey, *No Passport to Tibet* (London: The Travel Book Club, 1957), pp.117 – 18.

25. See Guibaut, pp.64, 74, 174 – 6; Bailey, p.188; Thomas, *Out of this World*, pp.31 – 2, 134 – 6.

26. See Migot, p.167.

27. See David-Neel, *My Journey*, pp.xviii, 22 – 3, 27 – 8, 40, 78 – 9, 130, 277; Harrer, p.166; Ronaldshay, *Himalayan Bhutan, Sikhim and Tibet* (1920; Delhi: Ess Ess Publications, 1977), pp.16, 220 – 1, 228 – 30; H. Ruttledge, *Everest 1933* (London: Hodder & Stoughton, 1938), p.81.

28. Maraini, pp.147 – 8.

29. Ibid. p.111.

30. Byron, pp.223 – 4, 240, 246 – 7; Guibaut, pp.94, 108 – 9; Ronaldshay, p.110; Harrer, pp.39, 166; Unsworth, p.47; Ruttledge, p.209.

31. Guibaut, p.49.

32. Byron, pp.238, 301; Guibaut, p.69. Byron's witty style was also part of the changes taking place in the wider field of travel writing between the two world wars. For details of this see P. Fussell, *Abroad* (New York: Oxford University Press, 1980).

33. Migot, pp.226 – 9.

34. Bailey, pp.19 – 22, 279 – 80.

35. Byron, pp.226 – 7.

36. David-Neel: *Magic and Mystery*, pp.v, 291; *Journey*, pp.172 – 5.

37. Maraini, p.145.

38. Ibid. pp.62, 153.

39. Ibid. pp.56, 96 – 7.

40. Byron, p.244.

41. Bell, in *Tibet*, p.268, describes Tibet as 'The Cinderella of the Indian Foreign Department'. This comment was made in 1922.

42. Guibaut, pp.80, 118, 186 – 8.

43. Bailey, pp.27 ff; C. Allen, *A Mountain in Tibet* (London: André Deutsch, 1982), pp.162 ff.

44. See Unsworth; R. Clark, *The Victorian Mountaineers* (London: B.T. Batsford, 1953).

45. P. Fleming, 'News From Tartary', in his *Travels in Tartary* (London: The Reprint Society, 1941); E. Maillart, *Forbidden Journey* (London: William Heinemann, 1937).

46. L. Clark, *The Marching Wind* (London: Hutchinson, 1955); C. Pereira, 'Peking to Lhasa', *The Royal Geographical Journal* LXIV, no.2 (August 1924), pp.97 – 120.

47. See Guibaut, pp.20, 92 – 3, 115; Bailey, p.131; L. Clark, pp.19, 29 – 30, 129 – 130; de Riencourt, p.46.

48. L. Clark, p.29.

49. Guibaut, pp.140, 60 – 1; M. Pallis, *Peaks and Lamas* (1939; London: Cassell, 1946), p.12.

50. See David-Neel, *My Journey*; W. McGovern, *To Lhasa in Disguise* (London: Thornton Butterworth, 1924).

51. See Unsworth, pp.20 – 1.

52. N. Roerich, *Altai-Himalaya* (London: Jarrolds, 1931); G. Roerich, *Trails to Inmost Asia* (New Haven: Yale University Press, 1931).

53. E. Schary, *In Search of the Mahatmas* (London: Seeley, Service & Co., 1937); see also the review of this book in *The Journal of the Royal Central Asian Society* 25 (1938), pp.130 – 3; D. MacDonald, *Twenty Years in Tibet* (London: Seeley, Service & Co., 1932), pp.159 – 63.

54. H. Kopp, *Himalayan Shuttlecock* (London: Hutchinson, 1957); F. Ossendowski, *Beasts, Men and Gods* (Sydney: Cornstalk Publishing Co., 1926).

55. See Thomas, *Out of this World*; R. Tung, *A Portrait of Lost Tibet* (London: Thames & Hudson, 1980), gives details and photographs of Ilya Tolstoy's mission.

56. Byron, p.253.

57. Pallis, p.422.

58. Ibid. pp.121 ff, 210, 227 – 300, 410 ff, where Pallis discusses the effect of the introduction of chemical dyes into Himalayan painting, and the effect of introducing Western clothes and Western-style education into the Himalayan cultures.

59. de Riencourt, pp.7, 46.

60. Guibaut, p.2; David-Neel, *Journey*, p.273.

61. T. Bernard, 'The Peril of Tibet', *Asia and the Americas* 39 (September 1939), pp.500 – 4.

62. Thomas, *Out of this World*, pp.76 – 7.

63. Maraini, p.145.

64. Guibaut, p.2.

65. Byron, p.327.

66. Harrer, pp.148 – 9.

67. Pallis, pp.xii – xiii, 344.

68. de Riencourt, p.128.

69. Unsworth, pp.314 ff.

70. Byron, p.328.

71. Maraini, p.144.

72. Thomas, *Out of this World*, pp.19 – 20.

73. See Harrer, pp.131, 133, 138, 155, 213, on the conservatism at Lhasa. On the other hand, for details of the enthusiasm in Lhasa for modern ideas, see Chapman; King, 'Telegraph'.

74. Harrer, p.136.

75. Ibid. pp.256 – 7.

76. Thomas, *Out of this World*, p.30.

77. See de Riencourt, p.300; Thomas, *Out of this World*, p.30.

78. de Riencourt, p.301.

79. Govinda, p.xi.

80. As Eliot wrote in 1935: 'At the still point of the turning world ... / at the still point, there the dance is,/But neither arrest nor movement'. T.S. Eliot, 'Four Quartets: Burnt Norton', *The Complete Poems and Plays of T.S. Eliot* (London: Faber & Faber, 1978).

81. de Riencourt, p.224.

82. Fleming, p.473; see also the extraordinary adventures of Eric Bailey, explorer and special agent, in and around Tashkent just after World War I, in A. Swinson, *Beyond the Frontiers* (London: Hutchinson, 1971).

83. See Bernard; de Riencourt, pp.180 – 1.

84. Independence from China was not universally accepted or desired in Tibet. For example, Tengye-ling monastery supported Chinese rule and so was destroyed by the Dalai Lamas pro-independence forces. This is mentioned in Chapman, p.139.

85. de Riencourt, pp.179 – 80.

86. F. O'Connor, 'Tibet in the Modern World', *The Geographical Magazine* 6 (1937/8) pp.93 – 110.

87. Chapman, pp.91 – 2.

88. de Riencourt, pp.196 – 7.
89. Chapman, pp.3 – 4.
90. de Riencourt, pp.199 – 200; Fleming; I. Klein, 'British Imperialism in Decline. Tibet, 1914 – 21', *Historian* 34 (1971), pp.100 – 15, presents a discussion of the complex situation in Central Asia and its effect on British involvement in Tibet.
91. de Riencourt, pp.211 – 13; Harrer, pp.205 – 8.
92. Harrer, pp.219 – 20.
93. Ford: Harrer, p.273.
94. For details see Harrer; Ford; de Riencourt; Thomas, *Out of this World*; L. Thomas Jnr, *Silent War in Tibet* (London: Secker & Warburg, 1960); D. Woodman: *Himalayan Frontiers* (New York: Frederick A. Praeger, 1969), 'Tibet and Imperial China' (Centre of Oriental Studies, Australian National University, Canberra, Occasional Paper No.7, n.d.).
95. Harrer, p.287.
96. de Riencourt, p.301.
97. Fussell, p.18. This era of disenchantment also produced other places apart from Tibet that evoked yearning, or intimations of a theocratically organized utopian society. See, for example, N. Douglas on the Sorrento coast, in *Siren Land* (1911; Harmondsworth: Penguin, 1986) or H. Wunderlich, *The Secret of Crete* (Athens: Efstathiadis Group, 1983).
98. Ronaldshay, pp.79 – 80.
99. David-Neel, *Magic and Mystery*, p.78.
100. David-Neel, *Journey*, p.61.
101. Fussell.
102. Byron, p.294.
103. Harrer, pp.116, 160.
104. Migot, p.127.
105. Byron, p.xiii.
106. J. Hilton, *Lost Horizon* (1933; London: Pan Books, 1947), pp.162 – 3.
107. Thomas, *Out of this World*, p.17.
108. Migot, pp.15 – 16.
109. de Riencourt, p.14.
110. Thomas, *Out of this World*, p.276.
111. de Riencourt, p.15.
112. L. Weir, 'The Impressions of an Englishwoman in Lhasa', *Journal of the Royal Asiatic Society*, January 1932, pp.239 – 41.
113. Byron, pp.293 – 4.
114. Guibaut, p.2.
115. See J. Hillman, *The Dream and the Underworld* (London: Harper & Row, 1979), pp.74 – 85.
116. David-Neel, *My Journey*, p.9.
117. de Riencourt, p.53.
118. Byron, p.xv.
119. Harrer, pp.193 – 4; de Riencourt, p.129.
120. Tucci, *To Lhasa*, p.108.
121. de Riencourt, pp.49 – 50; Chapman, pp.100, 102; Pallis, p.288. Maraini is one of the few exceptions to this one-sided viewpoint: pp.58, 85, 107 – 8, 209 – 10.
122. de Riencourt, p.50.
123. Fussell tends to see the creation of overseas places at this time simply as a compensation for the gloom and despondency felt in Britain after World War I.
124. G. Tucci, *Tibet* (London: Elek Books, 1967), p.13.
125. Guibaut, pp.1 – 2, 7 – 8, 29, 31; Unsworth, p.47; David-Neel, *My Journey*, pp.xviii, xix, 22 – 3; de Riencourt, pp.34 – 5.
126. Ruttledge, p.72; Tucci, *Tibet*, p.16; Byron, p.234; de Riencourt, p.41.

127. Byron, p.156; Fleming, p.397.

128. de Riencourt, p.128.

129. Fleming, p.392.

130. Chapman, pp.73, 109 – 10, 246 – 7, 299.

131. Weir; Harrer, p.137.

132. Maraini, p.86.

133. See Fussell; R. Barthes, 'The Blue Guide', *Mythologies* (London: Paladin, 1973).

134. On the concept of everyday life, see H. Lefebvre, *Everyday Life in the Modern World* (London: Allen Lane, 1974).

135. On psychic research after World War I and its relation to Western interpretations of Buddhism, see P. Bishop, *Tibetan Religion and the Western Imagination* (London: Athlone Press, forthcoming).

136. Pallis, p.138.

137. H. Desroche, *The Sociology of Hope* (London: Routledge & Kegan Paul, 1979), pp.113, 168 – 9; see also F. Manuel (ed.), *Utopias and Utopian Thought* (London: Souvenir Press, 1973); I. Tod and M. Wheeler, *Utopia* (London: Orbis Publishing, 1978).

138. Hilton, pp.51, 57, 60, 84, 91 – 2, 94, 147.

139. Ibid. pp.88, 157 – 9.

140. Unsworth, pp.41 – 4, 63, 70 – 1, 99 – 100, 102, 111, 131 – 41.

141. Hilton, pp.43, 45, 50 – 1.

142. Pereira.

143. L. Clark.

144. Hilton, pp.83, 127, 128.

145. Ibid. p.49.

146. Ibid. p.69.

147. Ibid. pp.103, 124, 129, 146.

148. Ibid. pp.130 – 1, 162 – 3.

149. Ibid. pp.150, 177 – 8.

150. Ibid. p.136.

151. C.G. Jung, 'Religious Ideas in Alchemy', in his *Collected Works Vol.12: Psychology and Alchemy* (trans. R.F.C. Hull: London: Routledge & Kegan Paul, 1974), para. 332.

152. Thomas, *Out of this World*, pp.13 – 17; de Riencourt, p.14.

153. Ibid. pp.68, 248, 310.

154. Fussell, p.92.

155. Thomas, *Out of this World*, p.261.

156. Ibid. p.186.

157. R. Kaulback, *Tibetan Trek* (London: Hodder & Stoughton, 1934), pp.54, 95 – 6, also pp.iv, 11 – 12, 15, 19 – 20.

158. David-Neel, *My Journey*, p.xxii.

159. Ibid. p.xix.

160. David-Neel, *Magic and Mystery*, p.167.

161. Pallis, p.423.

162. David-Neel, *My Journey*, p.198.

163. de Riencourt, pp.251 – 2; Huston-Smith, *Requiem For A Faith* (A Hartley Production Film, 1974).

164. David-Neel, *My Journey*, pp.xix – xx.

165. Ibid. p.259.

166. David-Neel, *Magic and Mystery*, p.9.

167. David-Neel, *My Journey*, p.257.

168. Ibid. pp.28, 40, 130, 277.

169. Chapman, pp.104 – 5, 107.

170. See Ibid. pp.106 – 7, 300.

171. Ibid. p.228.
172. Ibid. p.222.
173. See ibid. pp.61, 68; compare with Landon's remarks as noted in chapter 5.
174. Chapman, p.195.
175. See ibid. pp.44, 155, 158; Harrer; Ford.
176. David-Neel, *My Journey*, p.45; de Riencourt, p.285.
177. Kaulback, p.65.
178. Ibid. pp.65, 70 – 1, 82 – 3.
179. Byron, p.xv.
180. See F. Younghusband's introduction to Ruttledge, *Everest*; and Younghusband, *Everest: The Challenge* (London: Thomas Nelson & Sons, 1949); Pallis, *Peaks and Lamas*, pp.190 – 1.
181. de Riencourt, p.223.
182. de Riencourt, pp.224, 293.
183. Thomas, *Out of this World*, p.31.
184. D. Duff, *On the World's Roof* (London: Abbey Rewards, 1950).
185. Guibaut, pp.42 – 4.
186. Ibid. p.93.
187. David-Neel, *Magic and Mystery*, p.9.
188. de Riencourt, p.259.
189. C. Humphreys, *Buddhism* (Harmondsworth: Penguin, 1974), p.189.
190. C. Bell, *The Religion of Tibet* (Oxford: Oxford University Press, 1931).
191. Huston-Smith.
192. See Ronaldshay; Tucci, *To Lhasa*; Younghusband, *Everest*.
193. Tucci, *To Lhasa*, p.107.
194. G. Tucci and E. Ghersi, *Secrets of Tibet* (London: Blackie, 1935), p.17.
195. Ronaldshay, pp.9, 23 – 6, 65 – 7, 75 – 8, 110, 141 – 2, 170, 177 – 8.
196. Maraini, p.42.
197. Ibid. pp.55 – 6.
198. Ibid. pp.84, 172.
199. Ibid. p.82.
200. Ibid. p.60.
201. Ibid. p.48.
202. Byron, p.248.
203. Fleming, p.373.
204. Migot, p.122.
205. Migot, p.184. This attitude among travellers – of wanting to get 'inside' a culture – paralleled developments in anthropology and sociology. Malinowski revolutionized anthropological field work between the wars, whilst at the same time the Chicago School and ethnomethodology were transforming sociological investigations.
206. See David-Neel, *My Journey*, p.61.
207. Harrer, p.173.
208. L. Waddell, *Tibetan Buddhism* (1895; New York: Dover Publications, 1972), p.ix.
209. David-Neel, *My Journey*, p.61.
210. Pallis, pp.229 – 30.
211. Maraini, p.58.
212. de Riencourt, p.258.
213. David-Neel: *Magic and Mystery*, p.22: *Journey*, p.198.
214. G. Patterson, *Tibetan Journal* (London: Readers Book Club, 1956), p.114.
215. Ruttledge, p.77.
216. Chapman, pp.247 – 55.
217. Pallis, pp.230, 255.

218. de Riencourt, pp.31, 37, 57 – 8.
219. Harrer, pp.142 – 3.
220. See Bell, *Tibet*, p.183; Pallis, pp.33 – 4; Ruttledge, p.214; Migot, p.94; Bacot, quoted in Pallis, p.230.
221. Pallis, p.3.
222. Chapman, pp.92 – 3.
223. Migot, p.104.
224. de Riencourt, p.7.
225. Guibaut.
226. Harrer, p.90; see also Schary's condemnation of Tibetan inhospitality: MacDonald, p.163.
227. L. Clark, pp.45, 54 – 7, 112.
228. Guibaut, p.71.
229. Fleming, p.359.
230. David-Neel, *My Journey*, p.142.
231. Ibid.
232. Ibid. pp.218 – 23.
233. Ibid. p.254.
234. Pallis, pp.194 – 5, 263.
235. Ibid. pp.329 – 30.
236. Ibid. pp.257 – 8; Migot, p.104.
237. David-Neel, *Magic and Mystery*, pp.11, 131, 244, 258.
238. Maraini, pp.50 – 2.
239. Ibid. p.143. For a 'balanced' account of Bhutanese character which weighs the various estimations made by Westerners, see Ronaldshay, pp.205 ff.
240. David-Neel, *Magic and Mystery*, pp.288 – 300.
241. Fleming, p.325.
242. Chapman, pp.44, 73, 124, 155, 158, 214.
243. Ibid. pp.214 – 4.
244. See Lobsang Rampa, *Tibetan Sage* (London: Corgi Books, 1980).
245. David-Neel, *Magic and Mystery*, pp.vi, 291.
246. de Riencourt, pp.247 – 8, 252, 257; see also L. Clark, p.331.
247. Maraini, pp.81 – 2, 172; see also Bishop, *Tibetan Religion*, for a fuller discussion of the relation between Tibetan spiritual 'techniques' and Western fantasy-making.
248. Thomas, *Out of this World*, p.118.
249. Maraini, p.42; see also F. Smythe, *Snow on the Hills* (London: Adam and Charles Black, 1946) as well as his numerous other works; Younghusband, *Everest*.
250. Maraini, p.42.
251. Pallis, p.99.
252. Migot, pp.90 – 2.
253. de Riencourt, p.19.
254. Ibid. p.28.
255. Chapman, p.5.
256. Ibid. p.159.
257. P. Matthiesson, *The Snow Leopard* (London: Picador, 1980), pp.16, 26, 121 – 2; J. Lester, 'Wrestling with the Self on Mount Everest', *Journal of Humanistic Psychology* 23, no.2 (Spring 1983).
258. Matthiesson, pp.16, 21; see also P. Bishop, 'The Geography of Hope and Despair: Peter Matthiesson's *The Snow Leopard*', *Critique*, XXVI, no.4 (Summer 1985).
259. Matthiesson, pp.29, 271.
260. E. Haas, *Himalayan Pilgrimage* (London: Thames & Hudson, 1978), p.10.
261. J. Napier, *Bigfoot* (London: Abacus, 1976).

262. Winkler.

263. See Bishop, *Tibetan Religion*, for a full discussion of the place of *The Tibetan Book of the Dead* in Western fantasy-making.

264. G. Stuhlmann (ed.), *The Diaries of Anaïs Nin, Vol.6* (New York: Harvest Books, 1976), p.332.

265. David-Neel, *Magic and Mystery*, pp.23 – 40.

266. Ronaldshay, pp.130 – 1, 134; Govinda; Maraini.

267. See chapter 2 for Bogle's association of Tibet with a state of primitive innocence.

268. See de Riencourt, p.294; Migot, p.184.

269. See Harrer, pp.145 – 6, 225.

270. Ibid. pp.145 – 6; Chapman, p.174.

271. See David-Neel, *My Journey*, p.xviii; Chapman, p.174; Bell, *Tibet*, p.48. Although these titles were similar to those used before by Westerners to designate the Dalai Lama, now they were used seriously and not as mere curiosities.

272. Chapman, p.192.

273. Bell, *Tibet*, p.49.

274. A. Artaud, *Anthology* (San Francisco: City Lights Books, 1972), p.64.

275. Hilton, pp.43, 45, 50 – 1.

276. Pallis, pp.320 – 4.

277. de Riencourt, pp.274, 281.

278. Maraini, p.12.

279. J. Perry, *Lord of the Four Quarters* (New York: George Braziller, 1966); also Bishop, *Tibetan Religion*, for a fuller discussion of the figure of the Dalai Lama as an archetypal father figure for many Westerners involved with Tibetan spirituality.

280. See N. Barber, *From the Land of Lost Content* (London: Collins, 1969).

7. Conclusion

1. See, for example, the work 'Splendor Solis' by the sixteenth-century alchemist Solomon Trismosin, in C. Burland, *The Arts of the Alchemists* (London: Weidenfeld & Nicolson, 1967); and in J. Read, *Prelude to Chemistry* (London: G. Bell & Sons, 1936).

2. G. White, 'Views in India, chiefly among the Himalaya Mountains: 1825', in *Eternal Himalaya*, ed. H. Ahluwalia (New Delhi: Interprint, 1982), p.135.

3. A. Gerard, 'Narrative of a Journey from Soobathoo to Shipke, in Chinese Tartary, 1818', *Journey of the Asiatic Society* 11, no.1 (1842), p.375.

4. W. Giegerich, 'Saving the Nuclear Bomb', *Facing Apocalypse* (Dallas: Spring Publications, 1986).

5. C.G. Jung, 'Paracelsus as a Spiritual Phenomenon', *Collected Works, Vol.13: Alchemical Studies* (trans. R.F.C. Hull; London: Routledge & Kegan Paul, 1974), paras 186, 196.

6. See L. Shiner, 'Sacred Space, Profane Space, Human Space', *Journal of the American Academy of Religion* XL, no.4 (December 1972). He argues that everyday, or 'lived', space is not homogeneous, nor devoid of sacred qualities.

7. For a full discussion of the highly selective import of Tibetan Buddhism into Western fantasy-making in the mid-twentieth century, see P. Bishop, *Tibetan Religion and the Western Imagination* (London: Athlone Press, forthcoming).

8. H. Harrer, *Return to Tibet* (New York: Schocken, 1985).

9. See, for example, C. Furer-Haimendorf, *The Sherpas of Nepal* (London: John Murray, 1964); J. Hitchcock and R. Jones (eds.), *Spirit Possession in the Nepal Himalayas* (Warminster, Wiltshire: Aris & Phillips, 1976); T. Palakshappa, *Tibetans in India* (New Delhi: Sterling Publishers, 1978).

10. A notable exception is D. Snellgrove's *Himalayan Pilgrimage* (Boulder, Co:Prajana Press,

1981), which recounts the author's journey through remote regions of Nepal in 1956. P. Matthiesson's *The Snow Leopard*, while a classic, does hover at times on the edge of cliché. A. Harvey's *Journey to Ladakh* (London: Jonathan Cape, 1983), while sensitive and at times moving, fails to acknowledge the changes that have taken place since the late nineteenth and early twentieth centuries both in the genre of travel writing and in the neo-imperial relationship between the West and Third World countries. A. Blum's *Annapurna: A Woman's Place* (London: Granada, 1980) succeeds precisely *because* it presents all the seemingly unresolvable contradictions between gender, race, culture, power and personal experience. H. Suyin's *Lhasa: The Open City* (New York: Putnam, 1977) unfortunately has to be classed in the category of Chinese propaganda. Vikram Seth's beautiful account of his journey across Tibet to his home in India skilfully avoids most of the pitfalls that await the travel writer in this well-trod, but still little-known region (*From Heaven Lake*, New York: Random, 1987).

11. See P. Allen, 'Tibet, China and the Western World', *History Today* 30, December 1980, pp.25 – 31.

12. In addition to the abundance of glossy travel brochures, there are the pervasively influential and seemingly indispensable guidebooks which are filled with cultural vignettes, snatches of traditional wisdom and splashes of local colour. Among the best are H. Swift, *The Trekker's Guide to the Himalaya and Karakoram* (London: Hodder & Stoughton, 1982) and M. and R. Schettler, *Kashmir, Ladakh and Zanskar* (Victoria: Lonely Planet Publications, 1981). Such guides are now starting to emerge for Tibet.

13. E. Haas's *Himalayan Pilgrimage* (London: Thames & Hudson, 1978) is a typical glossy coffee-table book, filled with images of extraordinary clarity and vitality but, in the end, with a kind of flat sameness about them. The accompanying text echoes the tone of the illustrations. Such books have been produced on most out-of-the-way exotic places, and their geneses can be seen in texts such as *The Geographical Magazine* of the 1930s (e.g. vol.VI, no.6, December 1937). By comparison, see the two photostudies: B. Coburn, *Nepali Aama* (Santa Barbara, CA: Ross-Erikson Inc., 1982) and H. Downs, *Rhythms of a Himalayan Village* (San Francisco: Harper & Row, 1980). These are both of the popular anthropological variety and attempt to locate their intimate, black-and-white photograph within a community context rather than a more voyeuristic tourist one.

14. Cf. M. Eliade, *The Sacred and the Profane* (New York: Harcourt, Brace and World, 1959) with Shiner's analysis.

15. J. Hillman, in *The Dream and the Underworld* (New York: Harper & Row, 1979) insists upon the relative autonomy of the 'underworld' and 'dayworld' perspectives, of the unconscious and the conscious.

16. C.G. Jung, 'Psychology and Literature', *Collected Works, Vol.15: The Spirit of Man in Art and Literature* (trans. R.F.C. Hull; London: Routledge & Kegan Paul, 1974), p.85.

17. J. Boon, *The Anthropological Romance of Bali* (New York: Cambridge University Press, 1977), pp.134 – 5.

18. Eliade; F. Yates, *The Art of Memory* (Harmondsworth: Penguin, 1978); D. Lowenthal, 'Past Time, Present Place: Landscape and Memory', *The Geographical Review* LXV, no.1 (January 1975). T. Moore, 'Animus Mundi', *Spring 1987* (Dallas: Spring Publications, 1987), argues that the animus can be envisaged as the spirit of a place, like its *genius loci*; also that the animus relates to the source of family and ancestral continuity.

19. M. Foucault, *Madness and Civilization* (New York: Vintage Books, 1973).

20. J. Fabian, in *Time and the Other* (New York: Columbia University Press, 1983), pp.111 – 13, 121 – 2, provocatively argues that anthropology, along with other social sciences, was also part of this 'art of memory' tradition.

21. H. Corbin, *Spiritual Body and Celestial Earth* (Princeton: Princeton University Press, 1977), p.90.

22. J. Hillman, 'Anima Mundi: The Return of Soul to the World', *Spring 1982* (Dallas: Spring Publications, 1982).

23. Traditional memory systems operated in such a multilevelled way. See Yates.

24. P. Berry, 'Echo's Passion', in her *Echo's Subtle Body* (Dallas: Spring Publications, 1982), p.113.

25. Berry, p.120.

26. See P. Bishop, 'The Geography of Hope and Despair: Peter Matthiesson's *The Snow Leopard*', *Critique* XXVI, no.4 (Summer 1985).

27. See J. Loewenstein, *Responsive Readings: Versions of Echo in Pastoral, Epic, and the Jonsonian Masque* (New Haven: Yale University Press, 1984) pp.18, 152 n.24. He suggests that Echo acts as a psychoanalyst and also points out that many famous places of echo in Antiquity also symbolized doorways into the Underworld; see also Berry, p.120. In such circumstances it would perhaps be more appropriate to talk of an *axis imaginalis* rather than an *axis mundi*. This term which more specifically relates to an opening into the intermediary realm, the *metaxy*, the imaginal, and perhaps has less of a monotheistic connotation.

28. Berry, p.120.

29. See T. Moore, 'Musical Therapy', *Spring 1978* (Dallas: Spring Publications, 1978); Loewenstein, p.25.

30. Berry, p.115.

31. Ibid. pp.118–19; Loewenstein, p.151 n.21.

32. Loewenstein, p.22.

33. C.G. Jung, 'Religious Ideas in Alchemy', *Collected Works, Vol.12: Psychology and Alchemy* (trans. R.F.C. Hull; London: Routledge & Kegan Paul, 1974), para. 396.

34. Hillman, 'Anima Mundi', pp.73 ff.

35. See R. Bly, *News of the Universe* (San Francisco: Sierra Club Books, 1980) for a discussion of this loss of imaginal relation to the world in eighteenth-and nineteenth-century poetry; also J. Hillman, 'An Introductory Note: C.G. Carus – C.G. Jung, in *Psyche (Part One)* by C.G. Carus (New York: Spring Publications, 1970).

36. J. Hillman, 'The Imagination of Air and the Collapse of Alchemy', *The Eranos Jahrbuch 50-1981* (Frankfurt a/M: Insel Verlag, 1982), pp.283 – 4.

Bibliography

Adler, G.*Beyond Bokhara: The Life of William Moorcroft* (London: Century Publications, 1985).

Allen, C. *A Mountain in Tibet* (London: André Deutsch, 1982).

Allen, D. *Structure and Creativity in Religion* (The Hague: Mouton Publishers, 1978).

Allen, J. 'The Place of the Imagination in the History of Geographical Exploration', in *Geographies of the Mind*, ed. D. Lowenthal and M. Bowden (New York: Oxford University Press, 1976).

Allen, P. 'Tibet, China and the Western World', *History Today*, 30 December 1980, pp.25 – 31.

Anderson, J. *The Ulysses Factor* (New York: Harcourt, Brace, Jovanovich, 1970).

Aragon, L. *Paris Peasant* (1924/5; London: Picador, 1980).

Artaud, A. *Anthology* (San Francisco: City Lights Books, 1972).

Asad, T. and J. Dixon 'Translating Europe's Others', in *Europe and Its Others*, ed. F. Barker *et al.* (vol.1: Colchester: University of Essex, 1984).

Bachelard, G. *The Poetics of Space* (Boston: Beacon Press, 1969).

— *Water and Dreams* (Dallas: Pegasus Press, 1983).

Bailey, F. *No Passport to Tibet* (London: The Travel Book Club, 1957).

Barber, L. *The Heyday of Natural History: 1820 – 1870* (London: Jonathan Cape, 1980).

Barber, N. *From the Land of Lost Content* (London: Collins, 1969).

Barker, F. *et al.* (eds) *Europe and Its Others*, 2 vols (Colchester: University of Essex, 1984).

Barthes, R. *Mythologies* (London: Paladin, 1973).

Barton, J. 'Report of Missionary Work in Thibet', *Church Missionary Intelligence* 14 (1863).

Bates, H. *Illustrated Travels*, 3 vols (London: Cassell, Petter & Galpin, 1895).

Baudet, H. *Paradise on Earth: Some Thoughts on European Images of Non-European Man* (New Haven: Yale University Press, 1965).

Bazarov, K. *Landscape Painting* (London: Octopus Books, 1981).

de Beer, G. *Early Travellers in the Alps* (1930; London: Sidgwick & Jackson, 1966).

Bell, C. *Tibet: Past and Present* (London: Oxford University Press, 1927).

— *The Religion of Tibet* (Oxford: Oxford University Press, 1931).

— *Portrait of the Dalai Lama* (London: Collins, 1946).

Bennett, A. 'Rough Notes of a Visit to Daba, in Thibet, in August 1865', *Proceedings of the Royal Geographical Society* 10 (1865/1866).

Berger, J. and J. Mohr *Another Way of Telling* (London: Writers & Readers, 1982).

Bernard, T. 'The Peril of Tibet', *Asia and Americas* 39 (September 1939).

Berry, P. 'Echo's Passion', *Echo's Subtle Body* (Dallas: Spring Publications, 1982).

Bhardway, S. *Hindu Places of Pilgrimage in India* (Berkeley: University of California Press, 1973).

Bird-Bishop, I. *Among the Tibetans* (New York: Fleming H. Revell Co., 1894).

Bishop, P. 'The Geography of Hope and Despair: Peter Matthiesson's *The Snow Leopard*', *Critique* XXVI, no.4 (Summer 1985).

— 'The Mysticism of Immensity', *Colloquium* 18, no.2 (October 1986).

— *Tibetan Religion and the Western Imagination* (London: Athlone Press, forthcoming).

Blavatsky, H. *Isis Unveiled* (1877; Pasadena: Theosophical University Press, 1972).

— *The Book of Golden Precepts* (London: n.p., 1889).

— *The Voice of the Silence* (London: n.p., 1889).

Blum, A. *Annapurna: A Woman's Place* (London: Granada, 1980).

Bly, R. *News of the Universe* (San Francisco: Sierra Club Books, 1980).

Bonvalot, G. *Across Thibet*, 2 vols (London: Cassell & Co., 1891).

Boon, J. *The Anthropological Romance of Bali* (New York: Cambridge University Press, 1977).

Booth, W. *The Rhetoric of Fiction* (Chicago: University of Chicago Press, 1961).

Boswell, J. *Journal of a Tour to the Hebrides* (1785; London: William Heinemann, 1936).

Bourne, S. 'Ten Weeks With a Camera in the Himalayas', *The British Journal of Photography*, 15 February 1864.

— 'Narrative of a Photographic Trip to Kashmir and Adjacent Districts', *The British Journal of Photography*, 23 November – 28 December 1866.

Bowden, M. 'The Great American Desert in the American Mind: The Historiography of a Geographical Notion', in *Geographies of the Mind*, ed. D. Lowenthal and M. Bowden (New York: Oxford University Press, 1976).

Bower, H. *Diary of a Journey Across Tibet* (London, 1894; Kathmandu: Ratna Pustak Bhandar, 1976).

Briggs, J. *Never in Anger* (Cambridge, MA: Harvard University Press, 1970).

Brockway, L. *Science and Colonial Expansion: The Role of the British Botanical Gardens* (New York: Academic Press, 1979).

Brown, E. (ed.) *Geography: Yesterday And Tomorrow* (Oxford: Oxford University Press, 1980).

Burke, E. *A Philosophical Enquiry into the Origins of our Ideas of the Sublime and the Beautiful*, ed. J. Boulton (1757; London: Routledge & Kegan Paul, 1958).

Burland, C. *The Arts of the Alchemists* (London: Weidenfeld & Nicolson, 1967).

Burns, A. *Travels into Bokhara* (London: n.p., 1834).

Butzer, K. (ed.) *Dimensions of Human Geography* (Chicago: University of Chicago Press, 1978).

Byron, R. *First Russia: Then Tibet* (London: Macmillan & Co., 1933).

Camman, S. *Trade Through the Himalayas – Early British Attempts to Open Tibet* (Connecticut: Greenwood Press, 1970).

'The Capture of Lhasa', *The Spectator* (London), 13 August 1904.

Carey, A. 'A Journey Round Chinese Turkistan and along the Northern Frontier of Tibet', *Proceedings of the Royal Geographical Society* 9 (1887).

Carey, W. *Travel and Adventure in Tibet* (London, 1900; Delhi: Mittal Publications, 1983).

Carotenuto, A. 'Sabina Spielrein and C.G. Jung', *Spring 1980* (Dallas: Spring Publications, 1980).

Casey, E. 'Getting Placed', *Spring 1982* (Dallas: Spring Publications, 1982).

— 'Jung and the Post-Modern Condition', *Spring 1987* (Dallas: Spring Publications, 1987).

Chandler, E. *The Unveiling of Lhasa* (1905; London: Edward Arnold, 1931).

Chapman, S. *Lhasa: The Holy City* (London: Chatto & Windus, 1940).

Chobani Manganyi, N. 'Making Strange: Race, Science and Ethnopsychiatric Discourse', in *Europe and Its Others*, 2 vols, ed. F. Barker *et al.* (Colchester: University of Essex, 1984).

Clark, K. *The Victorian Mountaineers* (London: B.T. Batsford, 1953).

Clark, K. *Ruskin Today* (Harmondsworth: Penguin, 1982).

Clark, L. *The Marching Wind* (London: Hutchinson, 1955).

Clark, R. *Men, Myths and Mountains* (London: Weidenfeld & Nicolson, 1975).

Colebrook, H. 'On the Height of the Himalaya Mountains', *Asiatick Researches* 12 (1816).

Conan Doyle, A. 'The Empty House', in *Sherlock Holmes: The Complete Short Stories* (1928; London: John Murray, 1980).

Conway, W. *Climbing and Exploration in the Karakoram-Himalayas* (London: T. Fisher Unwin, 1894).

Cooper, T. 'Travels in Western China and Eastern Thibet', *Proceedings of the Royal Geographical Society* 14 (1869/70).

Corbin, H. *Creative Imagination in the Sufism of Ibn 'Arabi* (Princeton: Princeton University

Press, 1969).

— 'Mundus Imaginalis or the Imaginary and the Imaginal', *Spring 1972* (New York: Spring Publications, 1972).

— *Spiritual Body and Celestial Earth* (Princeton: Princeton University Press, 1977).

Cosgrove, D. 'John Ruskin and the Geographical Imagination', *The Geographical Review* 69, no.1 (January 1979).

Cosgrove, D. and J. Thornes 'Of Truth of Clouds: John Ruskin and the Moral Order in Landscape', in *Humanistic Geography and Literature*, ed. D. Pocock (London: Croom Helm, 1981).

Cunningham, A. *Ladâk* (London, 1853; New Delhi: Sagar Publications, 1977).

Curzon, G. *Frontiers* (Romanes Lecture; Oxford: Clarendon Press, 1908).

Daniell, W. and T. *Oriental Scenery*, 6 vols (London: Longman, Hurst, Rees, Orme & Brown, 1795 – 1815).

Das, S. *Journey to Lhasa and Central Tibet* (London, 1902; New Delhi: Mañjuśrī Publishing House, 1970).

David-Neel, A. *My Journey to Lhasa* (New York: Harper & Row, 1927).

— *Magic and Mystery in Tibet* (Paris, 1929; New York: Dover Publications, 1971).

Davies, A. 'The Aryan Myth: Its Religious Significance', *Studies in Religion* 10, no.3 (1981).

Desroche, H. *The Sociology of Hope* (London: Routledge & Kegan Paul, 1979).

Dodd, P. (ed.) *The Art of Travel* (London: Frank Cass, 1982).

Donner, F. *Shabono* (New York: Delacorte Press, 1982).

Douglas, N. *Siren Land* (1911; Harmondsworth: Penguin, 1986).

Downs, H. *Rythms of a Himalayan Village* (San Francisco: Harper & Row, 1980).

Dudley, G. 'Jung and Eliade', *Psychological Perspectives* 10, no.1 (1979).

Duff, D. *On The World's Roof* (London: Abbey Rewards, 1950).

Duka, T. *Life and Works of Alexander Csoma de Koros* (1885; New Delhi: Mañjuśrī Publishing House, 1972).

Duncan, J. *A Summer Ride Through Western Tibet* (1906; London: Collins, 1925).

Durand, G. Exploring the Imaginal', *Spring 1971* (New York: Spring Publications, 1971).

Eck, D. 'India's Tirthas: "Crossings" in Sacred Geography', *History of Religions* 20, no.4 (May 1981).

Eden, A. *Political Missions to Bootan* (London, 1865; New Delhi: Mañjuśrī Publishing House, 1972).

Edgar, J. *Report on a Visit to Sikhim and the Thibetan Frontier* (London, 1873; New Delhi: Mañjuśrī Publishing House, 1969).

Edwardes, M. *The West in Asia, 1850 – 1914* (London: B.T. Batsford Ltd, 1967).

— *Playing the Great Game* (London: Hamish Hamilton, 1975).

Eliade, M. *The Sacred and the Profane* (New York: Harcourt, Brace and World, 1959).

— *Australian Religions* (New York: Cornell University Press, 1973).

Eliot, T.S. 'The Four Quartets', *The Complete Poems and Plays of T.S. Eliot* (London: Faber & Faber, 1978).

Elkin, A. *Aboriginal Men of High Degree* (St Lucia: Queensland University Press, 1980).

Ellenberger, H. *The Discovery of the Unconscious* (New York: Basic Books, 1970).

English, P. and R. Mayfield (eds), *Man, Space and Environment* (New York: Oxford University Press, 1972).

Faber, R. *The Vision and the Need: Late Victorian Imperialist Aims* (London: Faber & Faber, 1966).

Fabian, J. *Time and the Other* (New York: Columbia University Press, 1983).

Fields, R. *How the Swans Came to the Lake: A Narrative History of Buddhism in America* (Boulder, CO: Shambhala, 1981).

de Filippi, F. *An Account of Tibet: Travels of Ippolito Desideri of Pistoia S.J. 1712 – 1727* (London: n.p., 1937).

Fisher, M. and J. *Shackleton* (London: James Barrie, 1957).

Fleming, P. *Travels in Tartary* (1934/6; London: The Reprint Society, 1941).

Fletcher, P. *Gardens and Grim Ravines: The Language of Landscape in Victorian Poetry* (Princeton: Princeton University Press, 1983).

Ford, R. *Captured in Tibet* (London: Pan Books, 1958).

Foucault, M. *Madness and Civilization* (New York: Vintage Books, 1973).

— *The Order of Things* (London: Tavistock, 1980).

— *The Archaeology of Knowledge* (London: Tavistock, 1972).

— *The History of Sexuality, Vol.1* (New York: Vintage Books, 1980).

— *Power/Knowledge* (London: The Harvester Press, 1980).

Francke, A. *History, Folklore and Culture of Tibet* (1905; New Delhi: Ess Ess Publications, 1979).

Fraser, J. *Journal of a Tour Through Part of the Snowy Range of the Himala* (London: n.p., 1820).

— *Views in the Himala Mountains* (London: Rodwell & Martin, 1820).

Freeman, T. 'The Royal Geographical Society and the Development of Geography', in *Geography: Yesterday and Tomorrow*, ed. E. Brown (London: Oxford University Press, 1980).

Freshfield, D. *Round Kanchenjunga* (London: 1903; Kathmandu: Ratna Pustak Bhandar, 1979).

Freud, S. *The Interpretation of Dreams* (London: George Allen & Unwin, 1971).

Funk, R. *Language, Hermeneutic and Word of God* (New York: Harper & Row, 1966).

Furer-Haimendorf, C. *The Sherpas of Nepal* (London: John Murray, 1964).

Fussell, P. *Abroad: British Literary Travellers Between the Wars* (New York: Oxford University Press, 1980).

Galton, F. *The Art of Travel* (London: John Murray, 1867).

Gerard, A. 'Narrative of a Journey from Soobathoo to Shipke, in Chinese Tartary, 1818', *Journal of the Asiatic Society* 11, no.1 (1842).

Giegerich, W. 'Saving the Nuclear Bomb', *Facing Apocalypse* (Dallas: Spring Publications, 1986).

Gilbert, E. *British Pioneers in Geography* (Newton Abbot, Devon: David & Charles, 1972).

Gill, W. *The River of Golden Sand* (London: John Murray, 1880).

Gison, E. 'Understanding the Subjective Meaning of Places', in *Humanistic Geography*, ed. D. Ley and M. Samuels (London: Croom Helm, 1979).

Glacken, C. *Traces on the Rhodian Shore* (Berkeley: University of California Press, 1967).

Gladwin, T. *East is a Big Bird* (Cambridge, MA: Harvard University Press, 1971).

Goethe, J. *Italian Journey: 1786 – 1788* (trans. W.H. Auden and E. Mayer: San Francisco: North Point Press, 1982).

Gordon, B. 'Sacred Directions, Orientation and the Top of the Map', *History of Religions* 10, no.3 (February 1971).

Govinda, A. *The Way of the White Clouds* (London: Hutchinson, 1969).

Graburn, N. 'Tourism: The Sacred Journey', in *Hosts and Guests*, ed. V. Smith (Oxford: Basil Blackwell, 1979).

Graham, W. 'Travel and Ascents in the Himalaya', *Proceedings of the Royal Geographical Society* 6 (1884).

Grenard, F. *Tibet* (Paris, 1903; Delhi: Cosmo Publications, 1974).

Guibaut, A. *Tibetan Venture* (London: John Murray, 1949).

Gutzlaff, C.H. 'Tibet and Stefan', *Journal of the Royal Geographical Society* 20 (1851).

Haas, E. *Himalayan Pilgrimage* (London: Thames & Hudson, 1978).

Hamilton, F. *An Account of the Kingdon of Nepal* (London, 1819; New Delhi: Mañjuśrī Publishing House, 1971).

Harbsmeier, M. 'Early Travels to Europe: Some Remarks on the Magic of Writing', in *Europe and Its Others*, ed. F. Barker *et al.* (Colchester: University of Essex, 1984).

Harrer, H. *Seven Years in Tibet* (London: Rupert Hart-Davis, 1953).

— *Return to Tibet* (New York: Schocken, 1985).

Harvey, A. *A Journey in Ladakh* (London: Jonathan Cape, 1983).

Hazen, R. (ed.) *The Poetry of Geology* (London: George Allen & Unwin, 1982).

Heaney, G. 'Rennell and the Surveyors of India', *Geographical Journal* 134, Part 3 (September 1968).

Heber, A. and K. *Himalayan Tibet and Ladakh* (1903; New Delhi: Ess Ess Publications, 1978).

Hedin, S. *Through Asia*, 2 vols (London: Methuen & Co., 1898).

Heidegger, M. *Poetry, Language, Thought* (New York: Harper & Row, 1975).

Helsinger, E. *Ruskin and the Eye of the Beholder* (Cambridge, MA: Harvard University Press, 1982).

Henry, W. *Surgeon Henry's Trifles: Events of a Military Life* (ed. P. Hayward: London: Chatto & Windus, 1970).

Hensoldt, H. 'Occult Science in Thibet', *Arena* 10 (1894).

Herschkowitz, R. *The British Photographer Abroad: The First Thirty Years* (London: Robert Herschkowitz Ltd, 1980).

Hibbert, C. *The Grand Tour* (London: Weidenfeld & Nicolson, 1969).

Hillman, J. 'An Introductory Note: C.G. Carus – C.G. Jung', in *Psyche (Part One)* by C.G. Carus (New York: Spring Publications, 1970).

— 'On Senex Consciousness', *Spring 1970* (New York: Spring Publications, 1970).

— 'The Negative Senex and a Renaissance Solution', *Spring 1975*, (New York: Spring Publications, 1975).

— *Re-Visioning Psychology* (New York: Harper & Row, 1975).

— *The Myth of Analysis* (New York: Harper Colophon, 1978).

— *Loose Ends* (Dallas: Spring Publications, 1978).

— in *Puer Papers*, ed. J. Hillman (Dallas: Spring Publications, 1979).

— *The Dream and the Underworld* (New York: Harper & Row, 1979).

— 'The Thought of the Heart', *The Eranos Jahrbuch 48-1979* (Frankfurt a/M: Insel Verlag, 1980).

— 'The Imagination of Air and the Collapse of Alchemy', *The Eranos Jahrbuch 50-1981* (Frankfurt a/M: Insel Verlag, 1982).

— 'Anima Mundi: The Return of Soul to the World', *Spring 1982* (Dallas: Spring Publications, 1982).

— *Healing Fiction* (Barrytown, NY: Station Hill Press, 1983).

— *Anima* (Dallas: Spring Publications, 1985).

— 'Notes on White Supremacy', *Spring 1986* (Dallas: Spring Publications, 1986).

Hilton, J. *Lost Horizon* (1933; London: Pan, 1947).

Himmelfarb, G. *Victorian Minds* (London: Weidenfeld & Nicolson, 1968).

Hitchcock, J. and R. Jones, *Spirit Possession in the Nepal Himalayas* (Warminster, Wiltshire: Aris & Phillips, 1976).

Hodgson, B. *Essays on the Languages, Literature and Religion of Nepal and Tibet* (ed. P. Denwood, 1874; New Delhi: Mañjuśrī Publishing House, 1972).

Holt, D. 'Jung and Marx', *Spring, 1973* (Dallas: Spring Publications, 1973).

Hooker, J. *Himalayan Journals*, 2 vols (London, 1855; New Delhi: Today and Tomorrow's Publishers, 1980).

Hopkirk, P. *Foreign Devils on the Silk Road* (Newton Abbot, Devon: Readers Union, 1981).

— *Trespassers on the Roof of the World* (London: John Murray, 1982).

Houghton, W. *The Victorian Frame of Mind* (New Haven: Yale University Press, 1970).

Huc, M. and Gabet *Travels in Tartary, Tibet and China, 1844 – 5 – 6* (1850; London: George Routledge & Sons, 1928).

Humphreys, C. *Buddhism* (Harmondsworth: Penguin, 1974).

Hunter, W. *Life of Brian Houghton Hodgson* (London: John Murray, 1896).

Huston-Smith, *Requiem For a Faith* (A Hartley Production, 1974).

Hutch, R. 'Helena Blavatsky Unveiled', *Journal of Religious History* II, no.2 (December 1980).

Hutchins, F. *The Illusion of Permanence: British Imperialism in India* (Princeton: Princeton University Press, 1967).

Huxley, L. *Life and Letters of Sir Joseph Dalton Hooker*, 2 vols (London: John Murray, 1918).

Illich, I. *H₂O and the Waters of Forgetfulness* (Dallas: Dallas Institute of Humanities and Culture Press, 1985).

'In Search of the Mahatmas', (Review) *Journal of the Royal Central Asian Society* 25 (1938) pp.130 – 3.

'An Invasion of Tibet', *The Spectator* (London), 2 June 1888.

Jackson, J. 'Untitled article', *The Journal of the Royal Geographical Society* 5 (1835), pp.381 – 7.

Jacob, F. *The Logic of Living Systems* (London: Allen Lane, 1974).

Jenkyns, R. *The Victorians and Ancient Greece* (Cambridge, MA: Harvard University Press, 1980).

Jones, W. 'On the Gods of Greece, Italy and India', in *The British Discovery of Hinduism in the Eighteenth Century*, ed. P. Marshall (Cambridge: Cambridge University Press, 1970).

Jung, C.G. *Collected Works Vol.5: Symbols of Transformation* (trans. R.F.C. Hull; London: Routledge & Kegan Paul, 1974).

— *Collected Works Vol.9ii: Aion*.

— 'Mind and Earth' *Collected Works Vol.10: Civilization in Transition*.

— 'Psychological Commentary on the Tibetan Book of the Dead', *Collected Works Vol.11: Psychology and Religion: West and East*.

— 'Religious Ideas in Alchemy, *Collected Works Vol.12: Psychology and Alchemy*.

— 'Paracelsus as a Spiritual Phenomenon', *Collected Works Vol.13: Alchemical Studies*.

— 'Psychology and Literature', *Collected Works Vol.15: The Spirit of Man in Art and Literature*.

— 'The Practical Use of Dream Analysis', *Collected Works Vol.16: The Practice of Psychotherapy*.

Kaulback, R. *Tibetan Trek* (London: Hodder & Stoughton, 1934).

Kawaguchi, E. *Three Years in Tibet* (Benares, 1909; Kathmandu: Ratna Pustak Bhandar, 1979).

Kaye, J. 'Islamic Imperialism and the Creation of Some Ideas of "Europe"', in *Europe and Its Others*, ed. F. Barker *et al.* (vol.1: Colchester: University of Essex, 1984).

Keay, J. *The Gilgit Game: Explorers of the Western Himalayas, 1865 – 95* (London: John Murray, 1979).

— *When Men and Mountains Meet: Explorers of the Western Himalayas, 1820 – 75* (London: Century Publishing, 1983).

Keenlyside, F. *Peaks and Pioneers* (London: Elek, 1975).

Kern, S. *The Culture of Time and Space (1880 – 1918)* (Cambridge, MA: Harvard University Press, 1983).

King, W. 'The Telegraph to Lhasa', *The Geographical Journal* 63 (1924).

Kipling, R. *Kim* (1898; London: Macmillan, 1943).

Kirkpatrick, W. *An Account of the Kingdom of Nepaul* (London, 1811; New Delhi: Asian Publishing Services, 1975).

Klein, I. 'British Imperialism in Decline: Tibet, 1914 – 21', *Historian* 34 (1971).

Knight, E. *Where Three Empires Meet* (1892; London: Longmans, Green & Co., 1935).

Knoepflmacher, U. and G. Tennyson (eds), *Nature and the Victorian Imagination* (Berkeley: University of California Press, 1977).

Kopp, H. *Himalaya Shuttlecock* (London: Hutchinson, 1957).

Kuhn, T. *The Structure of Scientific Revolutions* (Chicago: University of Chicago Press, 1970).

Kvaerne, P. *A Norwegian Traveller in Tibet* (New Delhi: Mañjuśrī Publishing House, 1973).

Lamb, A. *Britain and Chinese Central Asia* (London: Routledge & Kegan Paul, 1960).

— *The Sino – Indian Border in Ladakh* (Columbia: University of South Carolina Press, 1975).

— 'Some Notes on Russian Intrigue in Tibet', *Journal of the Royal Central Asian Society* 46 (1959).

Lambert, C. *A Trip to Cashmere and Ladak* (London: H. King, 1877).

Landon, P. *Lhasa*, 2 vols (London: Hurst & Blackett, 1905).

Landor, A. *In the Forbidden Land* (London: William Heinemann, 1899).

Latham, R. *Tribes and Races: Vol.1* (1859; Delhi: Cultural Publishing House, 1983).

Layard, J. *A Celtic Quest* (Zurich: Spring Publications, 1975).

Least Heat-Moon, W. *Blue Highways* (London: Picador, 1984).

Le Bris, M. *Romantics and Romanticism* (Geneva: Skira, 1981).

Lefebvre, H. *Everyday Life in the Modern World* (London: Allen Lane, 1974).

Leitner, G. *Dardistan: 1866 – 1893* (New Delhi: Mañjuśrī Publishing House, 1978).

Lester, J. 'Wrestling with the Self on Mount Everest', *Journal of Humanistic Psychology* 23, no.2 (Spring 1983).

Ley, D. and M. Samuels (eds) *Humanistic Geography* (London: Croom Helm, 1979).

Levine, G. 'High and Low: Ruskin and the Novelists', in *Nature and the Victorian Imagination*, ed. U. Knoepflmacher and G. Tennyson (Berkeley: University of California Press, 1977).

Lévi-Strauss, C. *The Savage Mind* (Chicago: The University of Chicago Press, 1973).

— *Triste Tropique* (London: Cape, 1973).

Littledale, G. 'A Journey Across Tibet, From North to South and West to Ladak', *The Geographical Journal* VII, no.5 (May 1896).

'The Little War with Tibet', *The Spectator* (London), 6 October 1888.

Lobsang, Rampa *Tibetan Sage* (London: Corgi Books, 1980).

Loomis, C. 'The Arctic Sublime', in *Nature and the Victorian Imagination*, ed. U. Knoepflmacher and G. Tennyson (Berkeley: University of California Press, 1977).

Louis, J. *The Gates of Thibet* (1894; Delhi: Vivek Publishing House, 1972).

Lowenstein, J. *Responsive Readings* (New Haven: Yale University Press, 1984).

Lowenthal, D. 'Past Time, Present Place: Landscape and Memory', *The Geographical Review*, LXV, no.1 (January 1975).

— 'Geography, Experience and Imagination: Towards A Geographical Epistemology', in *Man, Space and Environment*, ed. P. English and R. Mayfield (New York: Oxford University Press, 1972).

Lowenthal, D. and M. Bowden (eds) *Geographies of the Mind* (New York: Oxford University Press, 1976).

de Lubac, H. *La Rencontre du Bouddhisme et de l'Occident* (Paris: n.p., 1952).

Macaulay, C. *Report of a Mission to Sikhim and the Tibetan Frontier – 1884* (Calcutta, 1885; Kathmandu: Ratna Pustak Bhandar, 1977).

MacDonald, D. *Twenty Years in Tibet* (London: Seeley, Service & Co., 1932).

McGovern, W. *To Lhasa in Disguise* (London: Thornton Butterworth, 1924).

MacGregor, J. *Tibet – A Chronicle of Exploration* (London: Routledge & Kegan Paul, 1970).

MacIntyre, D. *Hindu-Koh* (London: n.p., 1889).

Maillart, E. *Forbidden Journey* (London: William Heinemann, 1937).

Makkreel, R. *Dilthey: Philosopher of the Human Sciences* (Princeton: Princeton University Press, 1975).

Manuel, F. (ed.) *Utopias and Utopian Thought* (London: Souvenir Press, 1973).

Maraini, F. *Secret Tibet* (London: Hutchinson, 1952).

Markham, C. (ed.) *Narratives of the Mission of George Bogle to Tibet and of the Journey of Thomas Manning to Lhasa* (London, 1879; New Delhi: Mañjuśrī Publishing House, 1971).

Markham, F. *Shooting in the Himalayas* (London: Richard Bentley, 1854).

Marshall, J. *Britain and Tibet 1765 – 1947*: The Background to the India – China Border Dispute, Annotated Bibliography (Bundoora: La Trobe University Library, 1977).

Mason, K. 'Johnson's "Suppressed Account" of E61', *Alpine Journal* 34, no.22 (1921).

— *Abode of Snow* (London: Rupert Hart-Davis, 1955).

Matthiessen, P. *The Snow Leopard* (London: Picador, 1980).

Middleton, D. 'Guide to the Publications of the Royal Geographical Society, 1830 – 1892', *Geographical Journal* 144, Part 1 (January – December 1978).

— *Victorian Lady Travellers* (Chicago: Academy Chicago, 1982).

Migot, A. *Tibetan Marches* (London: Rupert Hart-Davis, 1960).

Millar, A. *'I see no end to travelling': Diaries of Australian Travellers 1813 – 76* (Sydney: Bay Books, 1986).

Miller, D. *The New Polytheism* (Dallas: Spring Publications, 1981).

Miller, L. *On Top of the World: Five Women Explorers in Tibet* (London: Paddington Press, 1976).

Millington, P. *To Lhassa at Last* (London: Smith, Elder & Co., 1905).

Mitchell, W. (ed.) *On Narrative* (Chicago: University of Chicago Press, 1981).

Montgomerie, T. 'Report on Trans-Himalayan Exploration during 1867', *Journal of the Royal Geographical Society* 39 (1869).

— 'Journey to Shigatze in Tibet … '. *Royal Geographical Society* 45 (1875).

Moorcroft, W. 'A Journey to Lake Manasarovara in Un-des, a Province of Little Tibet', *Asiatik Researches* 12 (1816).

Moorcroft, W. and G. Trebeck, *Travels in the Himalayan Provinces of Hindustan and the Punjab; in Ladakh and Kashmir; in Peshawar, Kabul, Kunduz, and Bokhara: Vol.1* (London: John Murray, 1838).

Moore, T. 'Musical Therapy', *Spring 1978* (Dallas: Spring Publications, 1978).

— 'Animus Mundi', *Spring 1987* (Dallas: Spring Publications, 1987).

Moorehead, A. *The Fatal Impact* (Harmondsworth: Penguin, 1968).

— *The White Nile* (Harmondsworth: Penguin, 1976).

Napier, J. *Bigfoot: The Yeti and Sasquatch in Myth and Reality* (London: Abacus, 1976).

Nash, R. *Wilderness and the American Mind* (New Haven: Yale University Press, 1973).

Neatby, L. *The Search for Franklin* (London: Arthur Barker, 1970).

Newby, P. 'Literature and the Fashioning of Tourist Taste', in *Humanistic Geography and Literature*, ed. D. Pocock (London: Croom Helm, 1981).

Nicholas, J. *Temenos and Topophilia* (London: The Guild of Pastoral Psychology Monograph: 186, 1977).

Nicolson, M. *Mountain Gloom and Mountain Glory* (Ithaca: Cornell University Press, 1959).

Norberg-Schulz, C. *Genius Loci* (New York: Rizzoli, 1980).

Noyce, W. *The Springs of Adventure* (New York: The World Publishing Company, 1958).

O'Connor, F. 'Tibet in the Modern World, *The Geographical Magazine*, 6 (1937 – 8).

Orme, W. *Twenty Four Views in Hindustan* (London: Edward Orme, 1905).

Ossendowski, F. *Beasts, Men and Gods* (Sydney: Cornstalk Publishing Co., 1926).

Ottley, W. *With Mounted Infantry in Tibet* (London: Smith, Elder & Co., 1906).

Palakshappa, T. *Tibetans in India* (New Delhi: Sterling Publishers, 1978).

Pallis, M. *Peaks and Lamas* (4th edn, 1939; London: Cassell, 1946).

Panikkar, K. *Asia and Western Dominance* (London: George Allen & Unwin, 1955).

Paris, G. *Pagan Meditations* (Dallas: Spring Publications, 1985).

Patterson, G. *Tibetan Journey* (London: Readers Book Club, 1956).

Peckham, M. *Victorian Revolutionaries* (New York: George Braziller, 1970).

Penniman, T. *A Hundred Years of Anthropology* (3rd edn; New York: William Morrow & Co., 1974).

Pereira, C. 'Peking to Lhasa', *The Geographical Journal* LXIV, no.2 (August 1924).

Perry, J. *Lord of the Four Quarters* (New York: George Braziller, 1966).

Philip, M. 'Disconcerting Discourses', *Australian Society* (February 1985).

Phillimore, R. *Historical Records of the Survey of India, 5 Vols* (Dehra Dun: Survey of India, 1945).

Phillips, J. and P. *Victorians at Home and Away* (London: Croom Helm, 1978).

Pocock, D. (ed.) *Humanistic Geography and Literature* (London: Croom Helm, 1981).

Pointon, M. 'Geology and Landscape Painting in Nineteenth Century England', in his *Images of Earth* (Lancaster: British Society for the History of Science Monograph, 1981).

Porter, B. *Britain, Europe and the World, 1850 – 1982: Delusions of Grandeur* (London: George

Allen & Unwin, 1983).

Porter, P. and F. Lukermann, 'The Geography of Utopia'' in *Geographies of the Mind*, ed. D. Lowenthal and M. Bowden (New York: Oxford University Press, 1976).

Prejevalsky, N. *Mongolia, The Tangut Country, and the Solitudes of Northern Tibet* (London: Sampson Low, Marston, Searle & Rivington, 1876).

Preston, J. 'Sacred Centres and Symbolic Networks in South Asia', *The Mankind Quarterly*, XX, nos 3, 4 (January – April 1980).

Prinsep, H. *Tibet, Tartary and Mongolia* (London: W.H. Allen, 1852).

Rayfield, D. *The Dream of Lhasa: The Life of Nikolay Przhevalsky* (London: Paul Elek, 1976).

Read, J. *Prelude to Chemistry* (London: G. Bell & Sons, 1936).

Relph, E. *Place and Placelessness* (London: Pion, 1976).

Rider Haggard, H. *She* (1887; London: Hodder, 1971).

Ridley, H. 'Slaves and Mistresses', in his *Images of Imperial Rule* (London: Croom Helm, 1983).

de Riencourt, A. *Lost World: Tibet, Key to Asia* (London: Victor Gollancz, 1951).

Robertson, D. 'Mid-Victorians Amongst the Alps', in *Nature and the Victorian Imagination*, ed. U. Knoepflmacher and G. Tennyson (Berkeley: University of California Press, 1977).

Rockhill, W. *The Land of the Lamas* (London, 1981; New Delhi: Asian Publication Services, 1975).

Roerich, G. *Trails to Inmost Asia* (New Haven: Yale University Press, 1931).

Roerich, N. *Altai-Himalaya* (London: Jarrolds, 1931).

Ronaldshay, *Himalayan Bhutan, Sikhim and Tibet* (London, 1920; Delhi: Ess Ess Publications, 1977).

Ruskin, J. *Modern Painters Vol.4* (1854; Orpington: George Allen, 1888).

Ruttledge, H. *Everest 1933* (London: Hodder & Stoughton, 1938).

Ryan, C. *H.P. Blavatsky and the Theosophical Movement* (Pasadena: Theosophical University Press, 1975).

Saarinen, T. and J. Sell 'Environmental Perception', *Progress in Human Geography* 5, no.4 (1981).

Sachs, I. *The Discovery of the Third World* (Cambridge, MA: MIT Press, 1976).

Sack, R. 'Conceptions of Geographical Space', *Progress in Human Geography* 4, no.3 (September, 1980).

Said, E. *Orientalism* (New York: Vintage Books, 1979).

— 'Orientalism Reconsidered', *Race and Class* XXVII, no.2 (Autumn 1985).

Saliba, J. *'Homo Religiosus in Mircea Eliade* (Leiden: E.J. Brill, 1976).

Samuels, M. 'Existentialism and Human Geography', in *Humanistic Geography*, ed. D. Ley and M. Samuels (London: Croom Helm, 1979).

Sandberg, G. *The Exploration of Tibet* (1904; Delhi: Cosmo Publications, 1973).

Schary, E. *In Search of the Mahatmas* (London: Seeley, Service & Co., 1937).

Schettler, M. and R. *Kashmir, Ladakh and Zanskar* (Victoria: Lonely Planet Press, 1981).

Schlagintweit, A. and R. 'A Short Account … ', *Journal of the Asiatic Society of Bengal* 25 (1856).

Schlagintweit, E. *Buddhism in Tibet* (1863; London: Susil Gupta, 1968).

Seaton-Watson, H. *The Russian Empire: 1801 – 1917* (Oxford: Oxford University Press, 1967).

Seaver, G. *Francis Younghusband: Explorer and Mystic* (London: John Murray, 1952).

Seth, V. *From Heaven Lake* (New York: Random, 1987).

Shannon, R. *The Crisis in Imperialism: 1865 – 1915* (St Albans, Herts: Paladin, 1976).

Sheridan, M. *Foucault: The Will to Truth* (London: Tavistock Publications, 1981).

Shiner, L. 'Sacred Space, Profane Space, Human Space', *Journal of the American Academy of Religion* XL, no.4 (December 1972).

Shipp, J. *The Path to Glory* (ed. C. Stranks: London: Chatto & Windus, 1969).

Siddle, D. 'David Livingstone: A Mid-Victorian Field Scientist', *Geographical Journal* 140, Part

1 (February 1974).

Smith, H. 'A Trip to Thibet ... ', *Proceedings of the Royal Geographical Society* 11 (1866 – 67).

Smythe, F. *Snow on the Hills* (London: Adam and Charles Black, 1946).

Snellgrove, D. *Himalayan Pilgrimage* (Boulder, CO: Prajna Press, 1981).

Spacks, P. *Imagining a Self* (Cambridge, MA: Harvard University Press, 1976).

Spenser, H. *The Principles of Sociology Vol.1* (London: Williams & Norgate, 1877).

Stafford, B. *Voyage into Substance: Art, Science, Nature and the Illustrated Travel Account, 1760 – 1840* (Cambridge, MA: MIT Press, 1984).

Stephen, L. *The Playground of Europe* (London: Longmans, Green & Co., 1871).

Sterne, L. *A Sentimental Journey* (1768; Harmondsworth: Penguin, 1970).

Stone, S. *In and Beyond the Himalayas* (London: Edward Arnold, 1896).

Strachey, H. 'On the Physical Geography of Western Tibet', *Journal of the Royal Geographical Society* 23 (1853).

Stuhlmann, G. (ed.) *The Diaries of Anais Nin, Vol.6* (New York: Harvest Books, 1976).

Sumption, J. *Pilgrimage* (London: Faber & Faber, 1975).

Suyin, H. *Lhasa, The Open City* (New York: G.P. Putnam's Sons, 1977).

Swan, J. 'Sacred Places in Nature', *The Journal of Environmental Education* 14 (1983).

Swift, H. *The Trekker's Guide to the Himalaya and Karakoram* (London: Hodder & Stoughton, 1982).

Swinglehurst, E. *Cook's Tours* (Poole, Dorset: Blandford Press, 1982).

Swinson, A. *Beyond the Frontiers* (London: Hutchinson, 1971).

Tanner, H. 'Our Present Knowledge of the Himalayas', *Proceedings of the Royal Geographical Society* 13 (1891).

Temple, R. *Travels in Nepal and Sikhim, 1881 – 7* (London, 1881/7; Kathmandu: Ratna Pustak Bhandar, 1977).

Thomas, L. Jnr *Out Of This World* (New York: The Greystone Press, 1950).

— *Silent War in Tibet* (London: Secker & Warburg, 1960).

Thompson, E.P. 'Folklore, Anthropology and Social History', *Indian Historical Review* III, no.2 (January 1978).

Thomson, T. *Western Himalayas and Tibet* (1852; Kathmandu: Ratna Pustak Bhandar, 1979).

Tod, I. and M. Wheeler *Utopia* (London: Orbis Publishing, 1978).

Tuan, Yi-Fu 'Topophilia', in *Man, Space and Environment*, ed. P. English and R. Mayfield (New York: Oxford University Press, 1972).

— 'Geopiety', in *Geographies of the Mind*, ed. D. Lowenthal and M. Bowden (New York: Oxford University Press, 1976).

— *Space and Place* (London: Edward Arnold, 1977).

— 'Sacred Space', in *Dimensions of Human Geography*, ed. K. Butzer (Chicago: University of Chicago Press, 1978).

Tucci, G. *To Lhasa and Beyond* (Rome: Istituto Poligrafico Dello Stato, 1956).

— *Tibet* (London: Elek Books, 1967).

Tucci, G. and E. Ghersi *Secrets of Tibet* (London: Blackie, 1935).

Tung, R. *A Portrait of Lost Tibet* (London: Thames & Hudson, 1980).

Turner, S. *An Account of an Embassy to the Court of the Teshoo Lama in Tibet* (London, 1800; New Delhi: Mañjuśrī Publishing House, 1971).

Turner, V. 'The Centre Out There: Pilgrim's Goal', *History of Religions* 13, no.3 (February 1973).

— 'Pilgrimages as Social Processes', in his *Dramas, Fields and Metaphors* (Ithaca: Cornell University Press, 1974).

— *The Ritual Process* (Ithaca: Cornell University Press, 1979).

Unsworth, W. *Everest* (Harmondsworth: Penguin, 1982).

Waddell, L. *Tibetan Buddhism* (London, 1895; New York: Dover Publications, 1972).

— *Among the Himalayas* (London, 1899; Kathmandu: Ratna Pustak Bhandar, 1978).

Weir, L. 'The Impressions of an Englishwoman in Lhasa', *Journal of the Royal Asiatic Society* (January 1932).

Welbon, G. *The Buddhist Nirvana and Its Western Interpreters* (Chicago: University of Chicago Press, 1968).

White, G. 'Views in India, chiefly among the Himalayan Mountains, 1825', in H. Ahluwalia, *Eternal Himalaya* (New Delhi: Interprint, 1982).

White, H. 'The Value of Narrativity in the Representation of Reality', in *On Narrative*, ed. W. Mitchell (Chicago: University of Chicago Press, 1981).

White, J. *Sikkim and Bhutan* (London, 1909; Delhi: Cultural Publishing House, 1983).

Whitley, D. 'The Attack on Tibet', *Littel's Living Age* 206 (1895).

Whitmont, E. *Return of the Goddess* (London: Routledge & Kegan Paul, 1983).

Wilson, A. *The Abode of Snow* (Edinburgh, 1885; Kathmandu: Ratna Pustak Bhandar, 1979).

Wilson, C. *The Occult* (New York: Vintage Books, 1973).

Winkler, K. *Pilgrim of the Clear Light: The Biography of Dr Walter Y. Evans-Wentz* (Berkeley, CA: Dawnfire Books, 1982).

Woodcock, G. *Into Tibet: The Early British Explorers* (London: Faber & Faber, 1971).

Woodman, D. *Himalayan Frontiers* (New York: Frederick A. Praeger, 1969).

— 'Tibet and Imperial China', (Canberra: Centre of Oriental Studies, A.N.U. Occasional Paper, n.d.).

Wordsworth, W. *Guide to the Lakes* (1835, 5th edn: ed. E. de Selincourt: Oxford: Oxford University Press, 1977).

Wunderlich, H. *The Secret of Crete* (Athens: Efstathiadis Group, 1983).

Yates, F. *The Art of Memory* (Harmondsworth: Penguin, 1978).

Younghusband, F. *India and Tibet* (London: John Murray, 1910).

— *The Heart of a Continent* (1896; London: John Murray, 1937).

— *Everest, The Challenge* (London: Thomas Nelson & Sons, 1949).

Index

Proper and Mythological Names

Subjects